ANNUAL EDITIONS

Macroeconomics *05/06*

Fifteenth Edition

EDITOR

Don Cole

Drew University

Don Cole, Professor of Economics at Drew University, received his Ph.D. from Ohio State University. He has served as consultant to a variety of public and private organizations, and is co-founder of the Drew University Semester on the European Union in Brussels, Belgium. An innovator in the use of computer-assisted instruction in economics, Dr. Cole is the author of articles on various subjects, including economic policy, monetary theory, and economic education. He is also the editor of over 30 other McGraw-Hill/Dushkin publications, including *The Encyclopedic Dictionary of Economics* and two other Annual Editions anthologies, *Economics* and *Microeconomics*.

McGraw-Hill/Dushkin
2460 Kerper Blvd., Dubuque, IA 52001

Visit us on the Internet
http://www.dushkin.com

Credits

1. **Introduction to Macroeconomics**
   Unit photo—© Getty Images/PhotoLink/R. Morley
2. **Measuring Economic Performance**
   Unit photo—© Getty Images/Duncan Smith
3. **Fiscal Policy and the Federal Budget**
   Unit photo—© Getty Images/PhotoLink/Kent Knudson
4. **Money, Banking, and Monetary Policy**
   Unit photo—© Getty Images/Keith Brofsky
5. **Employment, Prices, and the Business Cycle**
   Unit photo—© Getty Images/Steve Cole
6. **International Economics**
   Unit photo—© Getty Images/PhotoLink

Copyright

Cataloging in Publication Data
Main entry under title: Annual Editions: Macroeconomics. 2005/2006.
1. Macroeconomics—Periodicals. 2. Economics—Periodicals. 3. United States—Economic Conditions—
Periodicals. I. Cole, Don, *comp.* II. Title: Macroeconomics.
ISBN 0–07–310828–6   339'73'05   75–20753   ISSN 1096–424X

Fifteenth Edition

Cover image © Kent Knudson/PhotoLink/Getty Images and Corbis/Royalty Free
Printed in the United States of America   1234567890QPDQPD987654   Printed on Recycled Paper

Editors/Advisory Board

Members of the Advisory Board are instrumental in the final selection of articles for each edition of ANNUAL EDITIONS. Their review of articles for content, level, currentness, and appropriateness provides critical direction to the editor and staff. We think that you will find their careful consideration well reflected in this volume.

Preface

In publishing ANNUAL EDITIONS we recognize the enormous role played by the magazines, newspapers, and journals of the public press in providing current, first-rate educational information in a broad spectrum of interest areas. Many of these articles are appropriate for students, researchers, and professionals seeking accurate, current material to help bridge the gap between principles and theories and the real world. These articles, however, become more useful for study when those of lasting value are carefully collected, organized, and reproduced in a low-cost format, which provides easy and permanent access when the material is needed. That is the role played by ANNUAL EDITIONS.

Annual Editions: Macroeconomics is an anthology that provides up-to-date readings on contemporary macroeconomic issues. In view of the recent explosion of interest in economics, it is essential that students are given opportunities to observe how economic science can help them to understand major economic events in the real world. Annual Editions: Macroeconomics 05/06 is designed to meet such a need.

This anthology is divided into six sections, which generally correspond to the typical sequence of topics in macroeconomic textbooks:

Introduction to Macroeconomics. Macroeconomics involves the study of the economy "in the large"; it concerns such broad issues as how gross domestic product, economic growth, unemployment, and inflation are determined. As articles in this section indicate, macroeconomic reasoning can be applied to a vast assortment of "real world" problems.

Measuring Macroeconomic Performance. Economists use economic data for the purpose of judging an economy's general health and making informed choices among policy alternatives. This section examines various problems associated with the gathering and interpretation of such data.

Fiscal Policy and the Federal Budget. Articles in this section deal with ways in which the federal government might use its spending and tax programs to achieve various macroeconomic goals. Major emphasis is placed upon issues of tax and budgetary reform.

Money, Banking, and Monetary Policy. Monetary policy involves deliberate changes in the money supply and credit availability for the purpose of achieving macroeconomic goals. This section provides an overview of the U.S. banking system and an assessment of the effectiveness of monetary policy.

Employment, Prices, and the Business Cycle. A major goal in the implementation of macroeconomic policy is the simultaneous achievement of high employment, stable prices, and vigorous economic growth. Articles selected for this section discuss some theoretical and policy issues involved in improving the economy's performance in these areas.

International Economics. In recent years the global economy has experienced a series of dramatic events unforeseen even a decade ago: the aftershocks of the 9/11 terrorist attacks; ambitious market reforms in what were formerly centrally planned economies; an acceleration of the process of economic integration in the Americas, Western Europe, and the Pacific Rim; and increased use of protectionist measures by most major traders. This section examines key aspects of these developments.

In this edition of Annual Editions: Macroeconomics 05/06 there are World Wide Web sites that can be used to further explore the topics. These sites are cross-referenced by number in the topic guide.

Whether you are someone who is currently pursuing studies in macroeconomics, or just a casual reader eager to learn more about some of the major economic issues of the day, you will find Annual Editions: Macroeconomics 05/06 to be one of the most useful and up-to-date anthologies available. Your comments can be very valuable in designing the next edition. Please complete and mail the postpaid rating form at the conclusion of this book and let us know your opinions.

Don Cole
Editor

Contents

Preface   iv

Topic Guide   xii

Selected World Wide Web Sites   xiv

UNIT 1
Introduction to Macroeconomics

Unit Overview   xvi

1. **Economics and the New Economy: The Invisible Hand Meets Creative Destruction,** Leonard I. Nakamura, *Business Review (Federal Reserve Bank of Philadelphia),* July/August 2000
   Some believe that a *"new economy"* has emerged—an economy in which the globalization of world markets and high-tech innovations play a major role. What should the fundamental paradigm of economics be in the twenty-first century: *creative destruction* or the *invisible hand?* Leonard Nakamura considers some possible answers to this question.   2

2. **On Making Economics Realistic,** *Challenge,* November/December 2002
   In 2001, George Akerlof was a recipient of the Nobel Memorial Prize in Economic Science for his work in asymmetric information and behavioral economics. In this interview with Professor Akerlof he offers a *broad criticism of conventional economics.*   12

3. **Beyond a President's Control,** Louis Uchitelle, *The New York Times,* July 11, 2004
   We *endow our presidents with mythical power*, holding them responsible for the health of the economy. However, as Louis Uchitelle shows, a president's influence over the twists and turns of the complicated American economy is inevitably less than is advertised.   18

UNIT 2
Measuring Economic Performance

Unit Overview   20

4. **State of the Union: Black Holes in the Statistics,** Robert Eisner, *Challenge,* January/February 1997
   How reliable are official U.S. government statistics? Robert Eisner believes that they are deeply flawed. This applies to measures of GDP, public deficits and debt, domestic and foreign investment and saving, productivity, real wages, and the distribution of income and wealth.   22

5. **Notes From Underground: Money That People Earn and Spend Outside the Realm of Official Economic Calculations Is Nonetheless Real,** Elia Kacapyr, *American Demographics,* January 1998
   A large share of economic activity occurs in the *underground economy,* where goods and services—some legal, some not—are produced but not reported. Elia Kacapyr considers possible implications of this activity for economic policy.   25

The concepts in bold italics are developed in the article. For further expansion, please refer to the Topic Guide.

6. **Technology, Productivity, and Public Policy,** John Williams and Mary Daly, *FRBSF Economic Letter (Federal Reserve Bank of San Francisco),* March 12, 2004

The study of **productivity growth** cuts across many of the fields and approaches in economics—microeconomics, macroeconomics, and international economics; theoretical and empirical analyses—and it is a subject for students of history as well as current events. **26**

7. **An International Tale of Two Consumers,** David Ingram, *The Dismal Scientist,* July 10, 2000

The **personal rate of time preference (RTP)** captures consumers' attitudes toward current versus future consumption. Individuals with a high RTP strongly value current consumption over future consumption. David Ingram explains why the RTP is high in the United States but low in Japan. **30**

UNIT 3
Fiscal Policy and the Federal Budget

Unit Overview **32**

8. **Taxing Terminology: A Primer,** Albert B. Crenshaw, *The Washington Post,* February 11, 2001

The debate over President Bush's tax proposal has produced a good deal of ill-informed or outright contentious rhetoric from both sides, which serves as a reminder of how confusing tax laws are to ordinary citizens and even to some government leaders. Albert Crenshaw explains how **an understanding of basic tax concepts** can de-mystify the debate over tax cuts. **34**

9. **Surplus Mania: A Reality Check,** L. Randall Wray, *Jerome Levy Economics Institute: Policy Notes,* Volume 3, 1999

A **federal government surplus** has finally been achieved, and it has been met with pronouncements that it is a great gift for the future and with arguments about what to do with it. However, L. Randall Wray argues that the surplus will be short-lived, it will depress economic growth, and, in any case, surpluses cannot be "used" for anything. **37**

10. **The Deficit: America's Credibility Gap,** Shawn Tully, *Fortune,* March 8, 2004

Between 1998 and 2001, the U.S. generated more than half-trillion dollars in budget surpluses, and it was widely assumed that the era of **big deficits** was over. But a year later the U.S. budget fell into deficit again, and it's been spiraling downward ever since. Shawn Tully warns of the corrosive effect that deficits will have on the American economy, unless something is done to reduce them soon. **41**

11. **The Tax Man Cometh: Consumer Spending and Tax Payments,** Peter S. Yoo, *Review (Federal Reserve Bank of St. Louis),* January/February 1996

How do consumers respond to changes in income tax rates? Peter Yoo examines several episodes in U.S. history when tax payments changed noticeably. He finds that the response of households was rather modest. **45**

12. **Go Figure,** Jodie Allen, *The New Republic,* July 31, 2000

If tax breaks aren't simple, neither are they very efficient. It has been documented that **tax preferences mostly subsidize activities that would have occurred anyway** (such as saving money, hiring workers, or having kids), and much of the money does not go toward the intended purpose at all. **52**

13. **Social Spending and Economic Growth,** *Challenge,* July/August 2004

Prevailing opinion holds that big government and high taxes reduce economic growth. But in this interview economist Peter Lindert argues that states that spend a lot on **social problems** grow no more slowly than those that spend little. **54**

The concepts in bold italics are developed in the article. For further expansion, please refer to the Topic Guide.

14. **Social Security Reform Need Not Be Drastic,** Augustine Faucher, *The Dismal Scientist,* April 4, 2001
    Most Americans understand that **Social Security** faces a long-term imbalance between the cost of benefits promised under current law and the program's projected income. Augustine Faucher demonstrates why reforming the system need not be drastic.   **58**

UNIT 4
Money, Banking, and Monetary Policy

Unit Overview   **60**

15. **What Should Central Banks Do?,** Frederic S. Mishkin, *Review (Federal Reserve Bank of St. Louis),* November/December 2000
    In the last 20 years, there has been substantial rethinking about **how central banks should do their job.** Frederic Mishkin discusses seven basic principles that can serve as useful guides for central banks trying to achieve their objectives.   **62**

16. **How Does Monetary Policy Affect the U.S. Economy?,** *FRBSF Economic Letter (Federal Reserve Bank of San Francisco),* January 30, 2004
    This article discusses how **Federal Reserve policy actions** affect real interest rates, which in turn affect aggregate demand and ultimately output, employment, and inflation.   **73**

17. **How Does the Fed Decide the Appropriate Setting for the Policy Instrument?,** *FRBSF Economic Letter (Federal Reserve Bank of San Francisco),* February 6, 2004
    The Fed's job of stabilizing output in the short run and promoting price stability in the long run involves several steps. This article discusses the things which complicate the **process of determining how the economy is doing.**   **76**

18. **How Sluggish Is the Fed?,** Glenn D. Rudebusch, *FRBSF Economic Letter (Federal Reserve Bank of San Francisco),* March 2, 2001
    How quickly does the Fed adjust monetary policy in response to developments in the economy? A common view among economists is that the Fed changes the short-term policy at a very sluggish pace over several quarters. Glenn Rudebusch takes issue with this position.   **79**

19. **The Science (and Art) of Monetary Policy,** Carl E. Walsh, *FRBSF Economic Letter (Federal Reserve Bank of San Francisco),* May 4, 2001
    While economists have identified broad principles to guide monetary policy-makers, making policy is not a science. Good policy-making requires good policy-makers since it requires **combining the science of the economist with the art of the practitioner.**   **82**

20. **The New World of Banking,** Jim Campen, *Dollars and Sense,* May/June 2000
    The Gramm-Leach-Bliley Financial Service Modernization Act of 1999 makes possible a new kind of corporation—called a **financial holding company**—that allows any number of banks, insurance companies, and securities firms to be brought together under the same corporate umbrella. Jim Campen suggests that the result is likely to be another wave of financial megamergers.   **85**

21. **Banking Consolidation,** Simon Kwan, *FRBSF Economic Letter (Federal Reserve Bank of San Francisco),* June 18, 2004
    Profound changes in banking laws occurred in the 1990s. As Simon Kwan indicates, the **ever-growing scale of bank mergers raises** some challenging policy questions which must be addressed.   **89**

The concepts in bold italics are developed in the article. For further expansion, please refer to the Topic Guide.

22. **Why an Old Prohibition Against Linking Loans and Services is Obsolete,** Mara Der Hovanesian, *Business Week,* October 27, 2003
Big banks give loans to big companies in return for a promise to do future business deals. The banks make money by selling a bundle of services, while Corporate America gets cheap loans and a bulk discount for one-stop shopping. However, as Mara Der Hovanesian demonstrates in this article, the whole transaction may be illegal. **93**

23. **The Cycles of Financial Scandal,** Kevin Phillips, *The New York Times,* July 17, 2002
In the last few decades, the U.S. economy has been transformed through what Kevin Phillips calls *"financialization."* Securities management, corporate reorganization, derivatives trading, and other forms of financial packaging are steadily replacing the act of making, growing, and transporting things. He asks: *will an era of reform follow a decade of excess*? **94**

UNIT 5
Employment, Prices, and the Business Cycle

Unit Overview **96**

24. **Macro Policy Lessons from the Recent Recession,** Christian Weller, Josh Bivens, and Max Sawicky, *Challenge,* May/June 2004
In this assessment of *economic policy-making during the recent recession* the authors conclude that more coordinated policy could have resulted in an economy that started to recover quickly, would probably have resulted in more job growth, and would not have left America with high future budget deficits. **98**

25. **The New Growth Economics: How to Boost Living Standards Through Technology, Skills, Innovation, and Compensation,** Robert D. Atkinson, *Blueprint,* Winter 2001
Robert Atkinson argues that while the New Economy continues to displace the Industrial Age economy, U.S. economic policies are still rooted in the past. He says that the new administration should jettison the holdover prescriptions of Keynesian and supply-side economics and *embrace a new growth economics focused on boosting productivity and wage growth.* **113**

26. **The Mystery of Economic Recessions,** Robert J. Shiller, *The New York Times,* February 4, 2001
Economists have yet to be able to pinpoint *what ultimately causes recessions.* Robert Shiller argues that, contrary to what many economists believe, changes in the level of confidence in the economy, not the Federal Reserve, are what basically determine its ups and downs. **117**

27. **The Cost of Living and Hidden Inflation,** James Devine, *Challenge,* March/April 2001
Economists generally argue that *inflation* is overstated by the federal government because it does not sufficiently account for the improved quality of products. James Devine argues that if we account for all pertinent changes in the quality of life, inflation is understated. **119**

28. **A Fight Against Fear As Well As Inflation,** Edmund L. Andrews, *The New York Times,* June 20, 2004
Inflation expectations depend heavily on confidence in the Federal Reserve as a guardian of price stability. And if that confidence is to remain strong, they may be forced to move at more than a "measured pace." **124**

29. **Link Between Taxation, Unemployment Is Absent,** Jonathan Weisman, *The Washington Post,* March 15, 2004
Following federal tax increases in 1993, the U.S. unemployment rate dropped steadily for seven years. When taxes were cut in 2001, the jobless rate rose and in 2003 (when taxes were cut again) unemployment increased again. Jonathan Weisman contends that the *relationship between taxes and unemployment* is far more complicated than many people (including politicians) understand. **126**

The concepts in bold italics are developed in the article. For further expansion, please refer to the Topic Guide.

30. **Does Lower Unemployment Reduce Poverty?,** Robert H. Defina, *Business Review,* 2002

In this article, Robert Defina presents empirical evidence that, given numerous short comings in the estimation of poverty levels, the **link between unemployment and poverty** is not as strong as many people think it is.　　**127**

31. **Employment May Be Even Weaker Than You Think,** Francis X. Markey, *The Dismal Scientist,* April 18, 2001

Surveys of employment trends conducted by the Bureau of Labor Statistics (BLS) are the most timely and most watched economic indicators available. In this article, Francis Markey warns of flaws in BLS methods that may currently be overstating the overall number of jobs.　　**134**

32. **More Jobs, Worse Work,** Stephen S. Roach, *The New York Times,* July 22, 2004

Stephen Roach, chief economist for Morgan Stanley, examines job trends since the trough of the last recession in November 2001. Although available evidence suggests that the U.S. job picture has improved, a troubling aspect is that a large share of the new jobs are at the lower end of the economic spectrum.　　**136**

33. **Lighting Labor's Fire,** Barbara Ehrenreich and Thomas Geoghegan, *The Nation,* December 23, 2002

The **collapse of union membership in America**, from a peak of 38 percent in the mid-1950s to 9 percent of the private work force today, is a major reason for increased income inequality. The authors propose a number of approaches and initiatives to bring the labor movement back.　　**138**

UNIT 6
International Economics

Unit Overview　　**142**

34. **Foreign Economic Policy for the Next President,** C. Fred Bergsten, *Foreign Affairs,* March/April 2004

At a time when U.S. foreign policy is dominated by matters of war and terrorism, economic concerns are often pushed to the back burner. While the United States may be in a position to undertake unilateral initiatives for the sake of national security, C. Fred Bergsten explains why, **in economic policy, unilateralism is simply not an option**.　　**144**

35. **Why Do Certain Countries Prosper?,** Virgina Postrel, *The New York Times,* July 15, 2004

The **American economy has done better**—and Europe and Japan have done worse—than most people predicted in the 1980s. Virginia Postrel draws on information from several recent studies to show it's not what you put into the economy that matters, but what you get out of it. Consumption is the goal of production.　　**150**

36. **Perspectives on Global Outsourcing and the Changing Nature of Work,** Christopher B. Clott, *Business and Society Review,* Summer 2004

While **globalization** has reduced barriers to the movement of goods and capital across national boundaries, it **has also created a series of problems**, including job losses, increasing income inequality, and stagnant or deteriorating real wages. Christopher Clott examines the role which multinational corporations have played in globalization.　　**152**

37. **The Fall and Rise of the Global Economy,** John G. Fernald and Victoria Greenfield, *Chicago Fed Letter (Federal Reserve Bank of Chicago),* April 2001

The **worldwide integration of national economies**—through goods and services trade, capital flows, and operational linkages among firms—has never before been as broad or as deep as it is now. John Fernald and Victoria Greenfield describe developments that have contributed to the globalization process.　　**160**

The concepts in bold italics are developed in the article. For further expansion, please refer to the Topic Guide.

38. The "Globalization" Challenge: The U.S. Role in Shaping World Trade and Investment, Robert E. Litan, *Brookings Review,* Spring 2000

Economic engagement with the rest of the world played a key part in the recent U.S. economic boom. However, as Robert Litan warns, American economic policy must steer a middle course between the extremes of either unilateralism or one-worldism.   **164**

39. Should We Worry About the Large U.S. Current Account Deficit?, Paul Bergin, *FRBSF Economic Letter (Federal Reserve Bank of San Francisco),* December 22, 2000

Over the last year the **U.S. current account deficit has reached unprecedented levels.** This **Economic Letter** explores some recent theories and some data to help the reader understand how the current account deficit could be either an optimal situation or a threatening one.   **167**

40. Global Shell Games: How the Corporations Operate Tax Free, Byron Dorgan, *The Washington Monthly,* July/August 2000

More than two-thirds of foreign-based multinational companies doing business in the United States—and only a slightly smaller fraction of U.S. based multinational firms—pay no federal income tax at all. Byron Dorgan takes a look at **how these corporations manage to operate tax free.**   **170**

41. Free Trade on Trial—Ten Years of NAFTA, *The Economist,* January 3, 2004

From the start, the **North American Free-Trade Agreement (NAFTA)** of 1994 was bitterly controversial in all three of the countries taking part—the United States, Canada, and Mexico. Unsurprisingly, a mere ten years experience has settled few of these quarrels.   **173**

42. Trade in the Americas: All in the Familia, *The Economist,* April 21, 2001

The **Free Trade Area of the Americas (FTAA)** would create the world's largest trade zone, stretching from Alaska to Argentina. The Bush administration is all for it; South America's biggest economy, Brazil, is not so sure.   **176**

43. Latin America's Volatile Financial Markets, Jonathan Lemco and Scott B. MacDonald, *Current History,* February 2001

The **major economies of Latin America** have made remarkable progress since the early 1990s. Strong growth has been accompanied by sharply curtailed inflation rates and impressive debt management. Yet, as the authors note, the greatest challenge facing these nations is their heavy dependence on international capital markets.   **180**

44. Japan Learns the Sun May Not Come Out Tommorow, Howard W. French, *The New York Times,* April 8, 2001

Little more than a decade ago, **Japan** still had the gleaming look of one of history's greatest economic success stories. Now, after 11 years of unrelenting decline, the desire by Japan's neighbors to follow its model has been replaced by dismay over its decay.   **184**

45. The Limits to Consumption, Shawn W. Crispin and Philip Segal, *Far Eastern Economic Review,* January 9, 2003

The authors maintain that, if **Asian governments** think expanded domestic consumption is a recipe for sustained economic growth, they should think again. Easy credit is already fueling personal bankruptcies and threatening the health of the financial system.   **186**

46. East Asia: Recovery and Restructuring, Ramon Moreno, *FRBSF Economic Letter (Federal Reserve Bank of San Francisco),* December 29, 2000

The **rapid recovery of East Asian economies** following major crises in 1997 has caught many observers by surprise. Ramon Moreno maintains that the biggest challenge facing East Asian policy-makers today is to decide how many traditional institutional practices to keep and how many to discard in favor of the systems in place in advanced market economies.   **189**

The concepts in bold italics are developed in the article. For further expansion, please refer to the Topic Guide.

47. **China's Economic Power: Enter the Dragon,** *The Economist,* March
10, 2001
Although still poor by traditional standards, ***the Chinese economy*** could potentially experience extraordinary growth over the next two decades and become the
second-largest economy in the world. In this article, ***The Economist*** considers
possible implications for both China and the world economy.   **192**

48. **Changing Today's Consumption Patterns—for Tomorrow's Human
Development,** *UN Human Development Report,* May 1998
World consumption has expanded at an unprecedented pace over the twentieth
century. As this United Nations report shows, competitive spending and conspicuous consumption have turned the affluence of some into the social exclusion of
many.   **195**

Test Your Knowledge Form   **206**
Article Rating Form   **207**

The concepts in bold italics are developed in the article. For further expansion, please refer to the Topic Guide.

Topic Guide

This topic guide suggests how the selections in this book relate to the subjects covered in your course. You may want to use the topics listed on these pages to search the Web more easily.

On the following pages a number of Web sites have been gathered specifically for this book. They are arranged to reflect the units of this *Annual Edition.* You can link to these sites by going to the DUSHKIN ONLINE support site at *http://www.dushkin.com/online/.*

ALL THE ARTICLES THAT RELATE TO EACH TOPIC ARE LISTED BELOW THE BOLD-FACED TERM.

Asymmetric information
2. On Making Economics Realistic

Banking industry
15. What Should Central Banks Do?
16. How Does Monetary Policy Affect the U.S. Economy?
20. The New World of Banking
21. Banking Consolidation
22. Why an Old Prohibition Against Linking Loans and Services is Obsolete
23. The Cycles of Financial Scandal

Business cycles
15. What Should Central Banks Do?
24. Macro Policy Lessons from the Recent Recession
26. The Mystery of Economic Recessions
31. Employment May Be Even Weaker Than You Think
32. More Jobs, Worse Work

Chinese economy
34. Foreign Economic Policy for the Next President
47. China's Economic Power: Enter the Dragon

Classical economics
2. On Making Economics Realistic

Consumers
48. Changing Today's Consumption Patterns—for Tomorrow's Human Development

Consumption expenditures
4. State of the Union: Black Holes in the Statistics
8. Taxing Terminology: A Primer
11. The Tax Man Cometh: Consumer Spending and Tax Payments
12. Go Figure
24. Macro Policy Lessons from the Recent Recession
45. The Limits to Consumption

East Asian economies
45. The Limits to Consumption
46. East Asia: Recovery and Restructuring

Economic growth
1. Economics and the New Economy: The Invisible Hand Meets Creative Destruction
6. Technology, Productivity, and Public Policy
9. Surplus Mania: A Reality Check
13. Social Spending and Economic Growth
24. Macro Policy Lessons from the Recent Recession
25. The New Growth Economics: How to Boost Living Standards Through Technology, Skills, Innovation, and Compensation

Economic indicators
4. State of the Union: Black Holes in the Statistics
5. Notes From Underground: Money That People Earn and Spend Outside the Realm of Official Economic Calculations Is Nonetheless Real
6. Technology, Productivity, and Public Policy
18. How Sluggish Is the Fed?
27. The Cost of Living and Hidden Inflation
31. Employment May Be Even Weaker Than You Think

Environment
48. Changing Today's Consumption Patterns—for Tomorrow's Human Development

European Union
13. Social Spending and Economic Growth
34. Foreign Economic Policy for the Next President
38. The "Globalization" Challenge: The U.S. Role in Shaping World Trade and Investment

Federal deficit
3. Beyond a President's Control
4. State of the Union: Black Holes in the Statistics
24. Macro Policy Lessons from the Recent Recession
34. Foreign Economic Policy for the Next President

Globalization
34. Foreign Economic Policy for the Next President
36. Perspectives on Global Outsourcing and the Changing Nature of Work
38. The "Globalization" Challenge: The U.S. Role in Shaping World Trade and Investment

High-technology industries
1. Economics and the New Economy: The Invisible Hand Meets Creative Destruction
6. Technology, Productivity, and Public Policy
25. The New Growth Economics: How to Boost Living Standards Through Technology, Skills, Innovation, and Compensation
36. Perspectives on Global Outsourcing and the Changing Nature of Work
37. The Fall and Rise of the Global Economy

Income distribution
48. Changing Today's Consumption Patterns—for Tomorrow's Human Development

Inflation
2. On Making Economics Realistic
3. Beyond a President's Control
15. What Should Central Banks Do?
16. How Does Monetary Policy Affect the U.S. Economy?
17. How Does the Fed Decide the Appropriate Setting for the Policy Instrument?
19. The Science (and Art) of Monetary Policy
27. The Cost of Living and Hidden Inflation
28. A Fight Against Fear As Well As Inflation

Interest rates
15. What Should Central Banks Do?
16. How Does Monetary Policy Affect the U.S. Economy?
17. How Does the Fed Decide the Appropriate Setting for the Policy Instrument?
18. How Sluggish Is the Fed?
19. The Science (and Art) of Monetary Policy
24. Macro Policy Lessons from the Recent Recession
28. A Fight Against Fear As Well As Inflation

International trade and finance
1. Economics and the New Economy: The Invisible Hand Meets Creative Destruction
4. State of the Union: Black Holes in the Statistics

34. Foreign Economic Policy for the Next President
35. Why Do Certain Countries Prosper?
36. Perspectives on Global Outsourcing and the Changing Nature of Work
37. The Fall and Rise of the Global Economy
38. The "Globalization" Challenge: The U.S. Role in Shaping World Trade and Investment
39. Should We Worry About the Large U.S. Current Account Deficit?
40. Global Shell Games: How the Corporations Operate Tax Free
43. Latin America's Volatile Financial Markets
45. The Limits to Consumption
48. Changing Today's Consumption Patterns—for Tomorrow's Human Development

Japanese economy

35. Why Do Certain Countries Prosper?
44. Japan Learns the Sun May Not Come Out Tommorow

Keynesian economics

2. On Making Economics Realistic
25. The New Growth Economics: How to Boost Living Standards Through Technology, Skills, Innovation, and Compensation
37. The Fall and Rise of the Global Economy

Latin American economics

43. Latin America's Volatile Financial Markets

Latin American economies

42. Trade in the Americas: All in the Familia

Less-developed countries (LDCs)

48. Changing Today's Consumption Patterns—for Tomorrow's Human Development

Monetary policy

3. Beyond a President's Control
7. An International Tale of Two Consumers
9. Surplus Mania: A Reality Check
15. What Should Central Banks Do?
16. How Does Monetary Policy Affect the U.S. Economy?
17. How Does the Fed Decide the Appropriate Setting for the Policy Instrument?
18. How Sluggish Is the Fed?
19. The Science (and Art) of Monetary Policy
24. Macro Policy Lessons from the Recent Recession
26. The Mystery of Economic Recessions
28. A Fight Against Fear As Well As Inflation

Multinational business

36. Perspectives on Global Outsourcing and the Changing Nature of Work
40. Global Shell Games: How the Corporations Operate Tax Free

NAIRU

2. On Making Economics Realistic

New economy view

1. Economics and the New Economy: The Invisible Hand Meets Creative Destruction
25. The New Growth Economics: How to Boost Living Standards Through Technology, Skills, Innovation, and Compensation

Outsourcing

36. Perspectives on Global Outsourcing and the Changing Nature of Work

Phillips Curve

2. On Making Economics Realistic

Poverty

48. Changing Today's Consumption Patterns—for Tomorrow's Human Development

Productivity

6. Technology, Productivity, and Public Policy
35. Why Do Certain Countries Prosper?

Protectionism

34. Foreign Economic Policy for the Next President
38. The "Globalization" Challenge: The U.S. Role in Shaping World Trade and Investment
48. Changing Today's Consumption Patterns—for Tomorrow's Human Development

Social Security system

13. Social Spending and Economic Growth
14. Social Security Reform Need Not Be Drastic

Taxation

3. Beyond a President's Control
8. Taxing Terminology: A Primer
9. Surplus Mania: A Reality Check
11. The Tax Man Cometh: Consumer Spending and Tax Payments
12. Go Figure
13. Social Spending and Economic Growth
14. Social Security Reform Need Not Be Drastic
24. Macro Policy Lessons from the Recent Recession
29. Link Between Taxation, Unemployment Is Absent
40. Global Shell Games: How the Corporations Operate Tax Free

Taylor Rule

18. How Sluggish Is the Fed?
19. The Science (and Art) of Monetary Policy

Tobin Tax

2. On Making Economics Realistic

U.S. income distribution

1. Economics and the New Economy: The Invisible Hand Meets Creative Destruction
4. State of the Union: Black Holes in the Statistics
8. Taxing Terminology: A Primer
12. Go Figure
30. Does Lower Unemployment Reduce Poverty?
40. Global Shell Games: How the Corporations Operate Tax Free

U.S. trade deficit

24. Macro Policy Lessons from the Recent Recession
39. Should We Worry About the Large U.S. Current Account Deficit?

Underground economy

4. State of the Union: Black Holes in the Statistics
5. Notes From Underground: Money That People Earn and Spend Outside the Realm of Official Economic Calculations Is Nonetheless Real

Unemployment

2. On Making Economics Realistic
3. Beyond a President's Control
19. The Science (and Art) of Monetary Policy
24. Macro Policy Lessons from the Recent Recession
29. Link Between Taxation, Unemployment Is Absent
30. Does Lower Unemployment Reduce Poverty?
31. Employment May Be Even Weaker Than You Think
32. More Jobs, Worse Work
36. Perspectives on Global Outsourcing and the Changing Nature of Work

World Wide Web Sites

The following World Wide Web sites have been carefully researched and selected to support the articles found in this reader. The easiest way to access these selected sites is to go to our DUSHKIN ONLINE support site at *http://www.dushkin.com/online/*.

AE: Macroeconomics 05/06

The following sites were available at the time of publication. Visit our Web site—we update DUSHKIN ONLINE regularly to reflect any changes.

General Sources

AmosWorld

http://www.amosweb.com

Here is a premier Internet site for instructional economic information. Its features include a glossary of over 500 economic terms and concepts, a reading room, and an interactive question-and-answer resource.

Brookings Institution

http://www.brook.edu

Founded in 1916, the Brookings Institution functions as an independent analyst and critic, whose major focus is on public policy issues at the national level. This site offers access to the *Brookings Review*.

The Cato Institute

http://www.cato.org

For years the Cato Institute has"promoted public policy based on individual liberty, limited government, free markets, and peace."

The Dismal Scientist

http://www.dismal.com

This is an excellent site with many interactive features. It provides access to economic data, briefings on the current state of the economy, and original articles on economic issues.

The Mining Company

http://economics.miningco.com

This frequently updated source "mines the Net" for information on economic subjects. Major features include a very large number of Net links and online articles.

Resources for Economists on the Internet

http://econwpa.wustl.edu/EconFAQ/EconFAQ.html

This resource of the WWW Virtual Library on Economics is an excellent starting place for any research in economics.

UNIT 1: Introduction to Macroeconomics

Fairmodel

http://fairmodel.econ.yale.edu

The power of large-scale macroeconomic analysis is available on this site for anyone with access to the Internet.

MBA Lectures in Macroeconomics

http://www.stern.nyu.edu/~nroubini/LNOTES.HTM

Lectures in macroeconomics prepared by Professors Nouriel Roubini and David Backus of the Stern School of Business at New York University are provided at this site.

UNIT 2: Measuring Economic Performance

Bureau of Economic Analysis (BEA)

http://www.bea.doc.gov

Part of the U.S. Department of Commerce, the BEA is the nation's accountant. It issues the Survey of Current Business and is a good data source.

Bureau of Labor Statistics (BLS)

http://stats.bls.gov

The home page of the BLS, an agency of the U.S. Department of Labor, offers Data, Economy at a Glance, Keyword Searches, Surveys and Programs, other statistical sites, and more.

Dr. Ed Yardeni's Economics Network

http://www.yardeni.com

Prepared by the Chief Economist of Deutsche Bank Securities, this site provides chartbooks and studies on such topics as economic indicators, public policy, and global trade.

Economic Statistics Briefing Room

http://www.whitehouse.gov/fsbr/esbr.html

This site has easy access to current federal economic indicators. It provides links to information from a large number of federal agencies.

Internet Public Library: Business and Economics Reference

http://ipl.org/ref/RR/static/bus0000.html

A comprehensive reference library on matters involving the production, distribution, and consumption of goods and services, this site includes many subtopics, including consumer issues and labor and the work place.

New York Times Business Connections

http://www.nytimes.com/library/cyber/reference/busconn.html

This page of links to business and economics sites on the Web was prepared for use by journalists of the *New York Times* for their own research purposes. It includes links to such categories as markets, companies, business news, banking and finance, and government.

UNIT 3: Fiscal Policy and the Federal Budget

Center on Budget and Policy Priorities

http://www.cbpp.org

The Center on Budget and Policy Priorities is a nonpartisan research organization and policy institute that conducts research and analysis on a range of government policies and programs, with an emphasis on those affecting low- and moderate-income people.

The Public Debt

http://www.publicdebt.treas.gov/opd/opd.htm

Here you will find links to The Public Debt of the United States to the Penny, Historical Debt, Interest Expense and the Public Debt, and Frequently Asked Questions.

Tax Wire

http://www.taxanalysts.com

Created by tax analysts, this site provides forums for discussion of a wide variety of tax ideas. It provides up-to-the-minute news on tax development.

U.S. Treasury

http://www.ustreas.gov

Select Browse at this site to open up the U.S. Treasury, which is divided into accessible areas: Banking & Finance, Money, Taxes, Treasury Services, and other areas.

UNIT 4: Money, Banking, and Monetary Policy

History of Money

http://www.ex.ac.uk/~RDavies/arian/llyfr.html

This site provides a chronology of money from ancient times to the present. It also includes articles on such topics as the Origins of Banking and Third World Debt.

Mark Bernkopf's Central Banks of the World: Central Banking Resources Center

http://patriot.net/~bernkopf

Interesting papers on electronic money and its effect on the banking world are available at this Web site.

UNIT 5: Employment, Prices, and the Business Cycle

U.S. Census Bureau

http://www.census.gov

This is a major source of information on U.S. economic, social, and demographic trends. Features include the Statistical Abstract of the United States.

U.S. Department of Labor

http://www.dol.gov

This searchable Department of Labor Web site includes information about the department and its agencies, labor laws and trends, press releases, and texts of regulations.

WorkIndex

http://workindex.com

This annotated guide to Internet resources in human resources, labor relations, benefits, training, technology, recruiting, leadership, and more is sponsored by the School of Industrial Relations at Cornell University.

UNIT 6: International Economics

European Union in the U.S.

http://www.eurunion.org

Topics at this comprehensive Web site of the European Union include EU policies and legislation, information on member states, and EU-U.S. relations. Access to *Europe Magazine* is also provided.

Institute for International Economics

http://www.iie.com

The site of this nonprofit, nonpartisan research institution is devoted to the study of international economic policy, and contains news, views, reviews, working papers, publications, and press releases, plus links to related sites.

Inter-American Development Bank (IDB)

http://www.iadb.org

The Inter-American Development Bank was established in 1959 to help accelerate economic and social development in Latin America and the Caribbean. This site offers access to IDB reports and information on member countries.

International Monetary Fund (IMF)

http://www.imf.org

The IMF is a cooperative institution involving 182 countries that consult each other "for the purpose of maintaining a stable system of buying and selling their currencies."

Organization for Economic Cooperation and Development (OECD)

http://www.oecd.org

This Web site of OECD provides information on OECD activities, news, documentation, and related links. One interesting feature is a link to the Centre for Cooperation with Nonmembers.

Sustainable Development Organization

http://www.sustainabledevelopment.org

This site provides a resource center for investigating issues of sustainable development. Extensive links lead to such categories as agriculture, energy, environment, finance, health, microenterprise, public policy, and technologies.

UNCTAD

http://www.unctad.org

The main task of the United Nations Conference on Trade and Development (UNCTAD) is to accelerate economic growth and development.

World Policy Institute

http://www.worldpolicy.org

The WPI publishes an online version of the *World Policy Journal*, which focuses on core policy issues, with an emphasis on international economic affairs.

World Trade Organization (WTO)

http://www.wto.org

The WTO facilitates the working of the multilateral trading system and negotiates agreements among trading nations.

We highly recommend that you review our Web site for expanded information and our other product lines. We are continually updating and adding links to our Web site in order to offer you the most usable and useful information that will support and expand the value of your Annual Editions. You can reach us at: *http://www.dushkin.com/annualeditions/*.

UNIT 1

Introduction to Macroeconomics

Unit Selections

1. **Economics and the New Economy: The Invisible Hand Meets Creative Destruction**, Leonard I. Nakamura
2. **On Making Economics Realistic**, Challenge
3. **Beyond a President's Control**, Louis Uchitelle

Key Points to Consider

- How does one account for the recent gains in U.S. productivity?

- What role do U.S. presidents play in the overall health of the economy?

- Do you agree with John Maynard Keynes's forecast of economic life in the year 2030? Why or why not?

 **Links: www.dushkin.com/online/**
These sites are annotated in the World Wide Web pages.

Fairmodel
   http://fairmodel.econ.yale.edu
MBA Lectures in Macroeconomics
   http://www.stern.nyu.edu/~nroubini/LNOTES.HTM

Economics is a science of thinking in terms of models joined to the art of choosing models which are relevant to the contemporary world.

John Maynard Keynes

This reader is about the ways in which economists think about economic problems and the advice they give to those who make economic policy. Its focus is on macroeconomics, the branch of economics that provides an overview of the ways in which an economy's major components—households, businesses, and governments—are related. Topics of investigation include such large, economy-wide variables as national output, the extent of unemployment, the general level of prices, and the rate of economic growth. Also considered are ways in which government policies might be used to promote various national goals, including high levels of employment, price stability, and an adequate expansion of output over time.

If you are a newcomer to the study of economics, you may be confused and dismayed by what you hear economists say about economic problems and policies. Someone once summed this up with the observation that "if all economists were laid end-to-end, they would never reach a conclusion." Outside observers want agreement on economic issues, and they are often discontent when they find that deep divisions exist within the economics profession. "Why can't economists agree?" they ask. The simplest answer is that economists, like other human beings, often have strongly held political and social beliefs. Professional quarrels are not primarily over scientific issues—in fact, most economists use the same scientific language in their debates.

Rather, the disagreements among economists frequently reflect fundamental differences in value systems. This is particularly true where macroeconomics is concerned.

This is an exciting time to begin a study of macroeconomics. The last few decades have witnessed major changes in both the U.S. and the global economy. As they look back on this period of turbulence, today's economists—perhaps reflecting a more pragmatic, less ideological position—are asking: What have we learned from this experience that will guide us in understanding what needs to be done at the dawn of a new century? Like bruised combatants after a lengthy battle, they may be somewhat more tolerant of opposing views.

At the time of this writing, the U.S. economy appears to be emerging from an economic recession, following more than eight years of strong economic growth, little unemployment, and low inflation. This has led many economists to ask: how did this happen, and is the performance of the "boom" years of the 1990s repeatable? A handful of economists trace this development to the emergence of a "New Economy." In such an economy those nations which stay ahead of the wave of technological innovation and remain competitive in the global economy will succeed in the new millennium.

George Akerlof, a recipient of the 2001 Nobel Memorial Prize in Economic Science cautions us to take care to avoid unrealistic assumptions in our macroeconomic reasoning. He suggests that more realistic economic models are more useful ones. Then, in "Beyond a President's Control," Louis Uchitelle asserts that any president's influence over the twists and turns of the complicated American economy is inevitably less than advertised.

Economics and the New Economy: The Invisible Hand Meets Creative Destruction

Leonard I. Nakamura*

As the third millennium begins, the buzzwords "new economy" and "new paradigm" are invoked repeatedly to explain the U.S. economy. In general, these words refer to a view that high-tech innovations and the globalization of world markets have changed our economy enough that we need to think about it and operate within it differently. Perhaps what we notice most is a new Zeitgeist of accelerating change in the worlds of work and knowledge, change that's emphasized in books with titles like *Blur* (Davis and Meyer) and *Faster: The Acceleration of Just About Everything* (Gleick). Unsurprisingly, economists by no means agree that there is a new economy or that there is a need for a new paradigm.

One sign that there has been a fundamental shift is that direct production of goods and services no longer absorbs the preponderance of workers' time. In 1975, production of goods and services ceased being the occupation of the majority of U.S. workers. Never before had a society been so productive that it could afford to assign most of its workers to white-collar tasks such as management, paperwork, sales, and creativity.

As recently as 1900, production workers in goods and services accounted for 82 percent of the U.S. workforce (Figure).[1] Over the course of the century, that number declined by large steps, to 64 percent in 1950, and to 41 percent in 1999. Managers, professionals, and technical workers, who are increasingly involved in creative activities, have risen from 10 percent of the workforce in 1900 to 17 percent in 1950, to 33 percent in 1999.[2]

In 1999 the U.S. economy employed 7.6 million professional creative workers—2.3 million engineers and architects, 2.9 million scientists, and 2.4 million writers, designers, artists, and entertainers. At the start of the 20th century, this group numbered 200,000 workers—less than 1 percent of the 29.3 million workers then employed. By 1950, the count had risen more than

FIGURE
The Decline of Production Work
Major occupational categories as proportions of total employment

Source: 1900-70 *Historical Statistics of the United States*. 1980, *Census of Population*. 1990 and 1999, *Employment and Earnings*, January 1991 and January 2000. Production occupations are defined here to include farming, forestry, and fishing; precision production, craft, and repair; operators, fabricators, and laborers; private household and other service workers. Sales and clerical workers include sales workers and administrative support, including clerical workers. Managers, professionals, and technical workers include executive, administrative, and managerial workers, professional specialty workers, and technical and related support workers.

TABLE Professional Creative Workers		
Year	Millions of professional creative workers	Proportion of all employment
1999	7.6	5.7
1990	5.6	4.7
1980	3.7	3.8
1970	2.6	3.3
1960	1.6	2.3
1950	1.1	1.9
1900	0.2	0.7

Sources: 1900–1980, *Censuses of Population*. 1990 and 1999, *Employment and Earnings*, January 1991 and January 2000.

Professional creative workers consist of architects, engineers, mathematical and computer scientists, natural scientists, social scientists and urban planners, writers, artists, entertainers, and athletes.

Minor multiplicative adjustments have been made to exclude teachers of dance, music, and art from the artists and entertainers category in earlier years; teachers of all types are now separated from artists and entertainers in the occupational statistics.

five times to 1.1 million—almost 2 percent of the total of 59 million workers. There are now more than six times as many creative professionals as in 1950, representing 5.7 percent of the workforce (Table).

These professional creative workers are paid for their efforts primarily through property rights to their creations: they (and the corporations that employ them) are granted copyrights, patents, brand names, or trademarks. These property rights in turn create temporary exclusivity, temporary monopoly power that negates the unfettered access to markets so prized in economic theory.

The clash between creativity and traditional economics runs deep. Perfect competition is the central paradigm economists have relied on to describe capitalist economies. This paradigm, which underlies Adam Smith's "Invisible Hand" theorem, focuses on production processes and abstracts from the informational tasks that managers, professionals, clerks, and sales workers perform. The paradigm of perfect competition was formulated by William S. Jevons, Leon Walras, and Carl Menger in the late 19th century, a time when direct production of goods and services dominated work.[3] Is this paradigm still appropriate in an age in which innovation is such an important economic activity; millions of workers are employed in *creative* activities, such as designing, inventing, and marketing *new products;* and more and more economic activity is devoted to creating technical progress?

In light of the changes summarized above, perhaps the theory set forth by Joseph Schumpeter and often referred to as creative destruction is a better paradigm for the current U.S. economy. Paul Romer (1998), a Stanford professor of economics and one of the new Schumpeterian theorists, uses the metaphor of cooking to describe direct production as *following existing* recipes while creativity is seen as *creating*

new recipes. The new recipes that result from creative endeavors allow a higher standard of living. But creative efforts are risky: while some efforts will fail and yield little, if any, payoff, efforts that yield successful new products are richly rewarded. Firms and workers whose products are outmoded by the new products are harmed. The unevenness of reward implies that an economy that devotes a lot of its resources to creative efforts may have greater inequality, as well as a higher average standard of living, than one that is less creative. And if creativity continues to increase in importance, inequality may continue to rise in the long run, or at least may not decline.

FOLLOWING EXISTING RECIPES: THE WORLD OF THE INVISIBLE HAND

Ever since Adam Smith's *The Wealth of Nations* (1776), most economists have espoused the view that a specific aspect of competition called *perfect competition* is the main spur to economic efficiency. In terms of the metaphor of recipes, this type of competition requires that all firms in an industry have access to the same set of recipes. Let's explore this idea to gain insight into the standard demonstration of the Law of the Invisible Hand.

A recipe for producing a good or a service has a list of ingredients: quantities of inputs, including the services of labor and capital, that go into making the final product. The desire to maximize profits induces each firm to produce the product at the lowest possible cost—that is, to use the recipe that allows the firm to produce the good or service at minimum cost—given the prices of ingredients. If many firms compete, and all of them can use the same recipes, no firm can charge more than the lowest cost at which all competing firms can make the product. If it did, a competitor would offer the product at a lower price and make a profit doing so. If prices of inputs change, firms may adopt a different recipe, but they will still seek to produce at lowest cost, and competition will still force firms to charge no more than the new lowest cost. Thus, a consumer buys from firms that, in their own self-interest, produce products as efficiently as the consumer could wish and charge prices that reflect the lowest possible production cost. Guided by the invisible hand of the marketplace, firms are led by self-interest to behave in a way that maximizes each consumer's well being—so long as there is vigorous competition among firms. This is the Law of the Invisible Hand.

In general, Smith's Law of the Invisible Hand implies that government interference in the perfectly competitive economy is unnecessary except for ensuring that monopoly does not arise. If a firm can exclude other firms from its market, thereby monopolizing a good, it will maximize profits by restricting supply and charging more than the cost of production. When that happens, consumers buy less of the monopolized good than they would at the lower price that competition would force firms to charge. The result is that the economy will operate inefficiently: too little of the monopolized good will be produced and consumers will be worse off than they would be if the good were produced competitively. In this theory, monopoly is a primary threat to the efficiency of a capitalist economy.

In some cases, however, a single producer may yield the lowest cost way of producing a good or service, perhaps because the cost of making an additional unit of the good keeps falling as more units are produced by a producer (economists refer to this as scale economies). In such cases, the government's role is to regulate the monopoly so that it does not artificially restrict supply.

Smith's theory also implies that governments can assist the invisible hand by abolishing artificial barriers to trade. This can force into competition firms that otherwise might have monopolized small markets. At the same time, larger markets encourage individuals to specialize in different parts of the production process and coordinate their labor. In turn, specialization—the division of labor—is the chief engine of increased productivity. Division of labor, according to Smith, owes its power to increase productivity to three sources: "first, to the increase of dexterity in every particular workman; secondly, to the saving of the time which is commonly lost in passing from one species of work to another, and lastly, to the invention of a great number of machines which facilitate and abridge labor, and enable one man to do the work of many" (p. 7). Smith saw the inventive activity that improved production techniques as being a byproduct of the division of labor, since, when a worker concentrated attention on one activity, time-saving inventions often came to mind. Of course, even in the 18th century, when Smith was writing, the activity of inventors and other creative workers was evident in the economy, but the flow of payments to creative work was minuscule compared with those that flowed to the labor, land, and capital that directly produced products.[4]

Smith saw progress in economic activity as flowing naturally, almost magically, from wider markets. The theory of the invisible hand, as it has evolved within modern economic growth theory, treats both economies of scale and creative activity as *exogenous*, that is, outside the scope of economic theory, and therefore "magical."[5] But an alternative perspective is to describe economies of scale and technical progress as *endogenous* to the economy, viewing creativity as an economic activity. This perspective on economics found its foremost advocate in a Harvard professor named Joseph Schumpeter, who wrote in the first half of the 20th century, during the years when formal corporate research and development first emerged on a substantial scale.

CREATING NEW RECIPES: THE NEW ECONOMY OF CREATIVE DESTRUCTION

Schumpeter argued that what really made capitalism powerful was profits derived from creativity.[6] He believed that the force of habit was extremely powerful in work life and that since economic development required implementing creativity, overcoming this inertia was crucial.

In his masterwork, *Capitalism, Socialism, and Democracy* (1942), Schumpeter constructed a paradigm for economic theory in which creativity was the prime mover in a modern economy, and profits were the fuel. He argued that what is most important about a capitalist market system is precisely that it rewards change by allowing those who create new products and processes to capture some of the benefits of their creations in the form of short-term monopoly profits.[7] Competition, if too vigorous, would deny these rewards to creators and instead pass them on to consumers, in which case firms would have scant reason to create new products. These monopoly profits provide entrepreneurs with the means to (1) fund creative activities in response to perceived opportunities; (2) override the natural conservatism of other parties who must cooperate with the new product's launch as well as the opposition of those whose markets may be harmed by the new products; and (3) widen and deepen their sales networks so that new products are quickly made known to a large number of customers.[8]

The drive to temporarily capture monopoly profits promotes, in Schumpeter's memorable phrase, "creative destruction," as old goods and livelihoods are replaced by new ones.[9] Thus, while Adam Smith saw monopoly profits as an indication of economic inefficiency, Joseph Schumpeter saw them as evidence of valuable entrepreneurial activity in a healthy, dynamic economy.

Indeed, Schumpeter's view was that new products and processes are so valuable to consumers that governments of countries should encourage entrepreneurs by granting temporary monopolies over intellectual property and other fruits of creative effort. Thus, in contrast to Adam Smith, Schumpeter argued that government action to prevent or dismantle monopolies might harm growth and the consumer in the long run.[10,11] In practice, temporary intellectual property protection has been adopted by all advanced industrial economies, suggesting that this reward system is indeed valuable in promoting economic growth. To this extent, modern economies have not obeyed the law of the invisible hand. We have made monopoly, albeit temporary, an important instrument of national development policy.[12]

On the other hand, the temporary monopoly protections of intellectual property law are not the only way modern societies reward innovators. For example, much scientific research is generated by grants made by public agencies or private foundations. Development of military products is often done for a fixed payment, which is determined by a bidding process, or on the basis of the incurred and audited costs of the developer. However, these alternative reward systems are employed only where a normal market does not exist for the product. For consumer products, it appears that, in general, the marketplace is the best measure of the value of an invention. The more valuable the product, the greater the reward to its creator should be. And that's exactly what a patent or copyright does—gives the creator a reward that rises with consumer value, because the greater a product's consumer value, the more profit a monopolist can realize from its sales, since the monopolist can charge more for it.[13] At the same time, it remains true that the temporary monopoly itself deprives society of the full value of the creation, since to secure their monopoly profits, firms limit supply.

Thus, the full value of the creation is realized only when the monopoly ends.[14] While Schumpeterian theories tell us some form of intellectual property protection for creators is desirable, they do not yet tell us how much protection to award, for instance, how long patents should last.

There are two important drawbacks to an economy of creative destruction. First, an economy of creative destruction knows only one pace—hectic. There is no way to know who created something except for priority—whoever says or does it first. Once something is discovered, it is easy to copy. Someone who independently creates something, but does so belatedly, does not get credit and does not share in the reward. The rewards of creativity go to the swiftest. It is thus no accident that long hours are a frequent correlate of creative activity.

Second, creative destruction, as its name implies, involves risk and change. Those whose products are outmoded by a new product lose their livelihoods. Even those who create a new product can predict but a small part of its consequences. The forces that oppose creativity are not irrational; they are the natural concerns of economic participants as to how they will be affected by creativity.

WHY ARE THE FORCES OPPOSING CREATIVITY SO STRONG?

Why oppose change and growth in the economy? Because of the riskiness of creating, making, competing against, and buying new products.[15] All activities are at risk in an environment of creative destruction.

Creativity Puts Existing Products At Risk. One aspect of competition within the creative destruction paradigm is what might be called leapfrogging competition, but which economists call a "quality ladder."[16] In this form of competition—which can be observed in video game machines, personal microprocessors, computer software, pharmaceuticals, cell phones, and color televisions—companies try to create new generations of the same product so that the bang for the buck (in economic terms, quality-adjusted value per dollar) rises. A clear example is the personal computer (PC), whose power and speed have been rising at rapid rates for over 20 years.

In the competition to supply components of the PC such as modems or memory, any firm that wants to play the game has to invest in creating new, faster, and smaller versions of the component. To earn profits to justify this investment and its uncertainties, the resulting innovation must leapfrog the competition by creating a new generation. The first firm to market with the new generation can often grab the bulk of the entire market and, with it, almost all the profits to be had. Of course, this typically wipes out the profitability of the previous generation and sets the stage for the next leapfrogger, who will then destroy the profits of the current leader.

Another aspect of creative destruction is competition across different types of products. The creation of a new type of product will, first and foremost, increase the variety of products available to consumers.[17] Beyond that, it will enhance the desirability of some kinds of products and lower that of others, just as the automobile increased the demand for rubber tires and gasoline and reduced the demand for horseshoes and buggy whips.

More generally, new products encompass both aspects—they can be seen both as quality improvements and as different products that widen the market. Consider new drugs like Celebrex and Vioxx, improved versions of aspirin that minimize the gastrointestinal side effects of long-term use of aspirin and aspirin substitutes. These products have modestly reduced the demand for aspirin, but because of their current high price, their main effect has been to expand the market to those who have had adverse reactions to aspirin and other aspirin substitutes.

Being Creative Is Inherently Risky. You don't know what will work until you try it. While successful new products may earn immense returns, others inevitably fail and cause losses to their creators and their supporters. Every new product is a step into the unknown.[18] Recent examples of products that were expected to fare well in the marketplace, but did not, include the antibiotic Trovan and the 1998 remake of the movie *Godzilla.* Trovan was expected to be a multibillion dollar antibiotic. Its launch in 1998 was a tremendous success: two million prescriptions were written in a year. But of these users, 14 suffered severe liver damage as a side effect, and several died.[19] As a result, Trovan's distribution was limited to use in supervised settings (that is, hospitals) in the United States, and the European Union banned it outright. Now Trovan is no longer expected to be a blockbuster drug. Similarly, among movies, the remake of *Godzilla* was expected to be the summer blockbuster of 1998. Instead, its sales were very disappointing.

Careers and Sequels. For individual scientists and artists, past success is no guarantee of future success. If we could pick winners, we would give those who are going to be productive the resources they need, but often we recognize talent only after the fact. After he published his *Principia*, Newton's scientific output essentially disappeared. Computer laser typesetting pioneer Wang Xuan, of Beijing University, was quoted in *Science* magazine as lamenting, "When I was in my prime, doing the most advanced research, I was not recognized. [N]ow that my creative peak has long passed... my fame grows while I'm making fewer and fewer contributions."[20] This riskiness extends to those who work with creators, because their continued employment may depend on the success of the creators. Some kinds of downsizing can be viewed as the natural consequence of failed creativity, of the inability of a group to maintain a stream of innovation. Of course, in a world of creative destruction, those who don't even attempt to innovate also get downsized. Workers whose employment is attached to outmoded methods of production or outmoded goods suffer large penalties if they are unable to adapt to change.

Networks and Risk. Another aspect of the risk of creative destruction is the fact that consumers also invest in a product or system.[21] If the product or system becomes outmoded, consumers suffer along with the producer. Hence, consumers also must try to pick winners. This effect becomes sharper when the number of consumers investing in a given system influences its value for each consumer, for example, the more of your friends who have email, the more useful email is to you.

Phonograph records suddenly became a risky investment in the 1980s when compact discs took the market. Compact discs offered enough advantages to ensure that new consumers would want to switch to the new technology. Older consumers had to bear switching costs, in particular, their existing collections of records and stereo equipment became outmoded and new records ceased to become widely available.

Betamax looked like a technology winner to most experts when videocassette recorders (VCRs) were invented in the late 1970s. Beta was competing with VHS, and insiders knew that Sony had had the opportunity to develop either Beta or VHS and had chosen Beta as the superior technology. But the corporations that developed VHS were able to more rapidly lengthen videocassette playback times. Consumers who did adopt Beta eventually found that they had to switch to VHS, as Sony was forced to abandon the system by the greater availability of prerecorded videocassettes on VHS.

When consumers do choose a system, the system's rivals may suffer irreversible setbacks, as the Beta system did. This underscores the risks of competition—network competition creates big winners and big losers.

In 1961, back in the early days of the computer, when each piece of computer software was written for a specific model of computer, IBM decided to create an operating system that would permit computer users to use the same programs across the entire family of IBM computers. The difficulty of creating such a system proved much greater than expected, and IBM nearly failed waiting for its completion in 1966 (see the book by Thomas Watson). But once the system was together and operating, IBM's rivals in the computer business were helpless — and virtually all of their important customers migrated to this new system that could grow as they did. Here the "consumers" were large corporate users, whose investments in software became much more durable once they could be used unchanged on different models of computers. IBM's U.S. competitors became known as the Seven Dwarfs. IBM dominated the worldwide computer market for 20 years thereafter.

The costs associated with the riskiness of creativity must be balanced against the gains obtained. Unfortunately, measuring the economic gains due to new products is harder than measuring those from more efficiently produced existing products.

CREATIVITY IS HARD TO VALUE

The investments that consumers make in using a product, or that firms make in new complements, make that product more valuable. When VCRs first came on the market, they were mainly used to record television programs for playback at a more convenient time. But as VCRs proliferated and were able to play longer tapes, they became a convenient format for playing movies. Businesses that rented prerecorded tapes to consumers further enhanced the value of the VCR. Similarly, the development of software and of the Internet have further enhanced the value of personal computers.

Because we learn about the true value of new products only with experience, and because consumers invest in new product systems only over time—and in doing so enhance their value—it takes a long time to know how valuable any given piece of creativity is. The enthusiasm of the moment—whether highbrow or lowbrow—may not be what lasts. Samuel Johnson said that a century was long enough to judge that Shakespeare's plays were indeed immortal. Shakespeare himself thought that his sonnets would last, but didn't publish his plays.[22] Yet when Harold Bloom argues that Shakespeare created the modern world, he's citing the plays, not the sonnets. Will *Seinfeld* be an important source of humor for the 22nd century? Will John Cage or John Lennon be seen as the more important composer a century from now?

Not only is measuring the value of creativity inherently difficult, but the task is made harder because many of our measures implicitly assume perfect competition. The U.S. Bureau of Economic Analysis (1998) describes the classification of products in the national income and product accounts as follows: "Goods are products that can be stored or inventoried, services are products that cannot be stored and are consumed at the time of their purchase, and structures are products that are usually constructed at the location where they will be used and that typically have long economic lives." This description appears to leave no room for intangible assets, such as the copyright for Windows98 and the patent for Viagra, that result from creative endeavors. These assets are not material and are thus unlike goods and structures, but they may be long-lived, unlike services. Under the theoretical ideal of the perfectly competitive economy, intangible assets do not exist because the monopoly power they imply is ruled out. Put another way, in a perfectly competitive economy, because all recipes are freely available, no one earns a profit from owning one. A direct consequence of the use of the invisible hand paradigm is that the value of creativity disappears from statistical view.

The result is that creativity is poorly measured in the U.S. economy. Our official statistics generally don't treat creativity as an investment (Nakamura, 1999a). This in turn causes the statistics to understate nominal output, savings, and profits. Retail innovations and the proliferation of new products that result from creative activity have made it more difficult to measure the inflation rate (Nakamura 1995, 1998, 1999b). Indeed, our official statistics almost certainly overstate inflation. The combination means that our measures understate real economic growth (Nakamura, 1997).

One of the anomalous features of the U.S. economy is the slow rate of measured productivity growth since the mid-1970s, during this period of intensive creativity. In large part, the reason for this anomaly is that the perfect competition paradigm describes creativity as unimportant, and therefore, our economic statistics tend to ignore it.

However, measures of U.S. economic growth are in the process of being revised. In the 1999 revision to the national income accounts, the U.S. Bureau of Economic Analysis raised the annual growth rate during the period 1978 to 1998 from 2.6 percent to 3.0 percent. As a result of this change, the Bureau of Labor Statistics has raised its estimates of average growth in output per hour in the nonfarm business economy from 1.1 percent to 1.5 percent per year. This change was made primarily because the BEA recognized software as an investment and also improved the measures of financial sector output to reflect product change—in both cases bringing increased awareness of new products' impact on economic growth into the national accounts.

Until the process of revision of our statistical structure is reasonably far along, it will be hard for the economics profession to judge the empirical validity of the paradigm of creative destruction. If there is to be a scientific paradigm shift, then the creative destruction paradigm must explain data better than the invisible hand paradigm does. This in turn requires that the fundamental measures that the economics profession uses to generate data be reformulated to reasonably reflect the value of creativity, not only for the current period but for the past. If upon doing so, we observe long-term acceleration of productivity, this observation would provide valuable empirical evidence that the creative destruction paradigm is superior (Romer, 1986). Moreover, if these arguments are correct, we should then be able to describe the sources of economic growth more precisely and convincingly.

Another point of difference between the invisible hand and creative destruction is a prediction about the distribution of outcomes. The Law of the Invisible Hand suggests that competition between workers and companies will tend to equalize wages, whereas creative destruction suggests that markets may tend to magnify inequalities.

IN THE NEW ECONOMY, INEQUALITY MAY BE ON THE RISE

Inequality and Productivity Growth in the U.S. Productivity growth in the U.S. has been phenomenal if we look at long periods of time, even using traditional measures of output. Output per hour has doubled every 30 to 40 years for the past 120 years, leading to a standard of living roughly 10 times higher than that just after the Civil War (see the book by Angus Maddison). Even the poorest U.S. citizens are far better off than in the distant past.

But over the past 20 years, inequality has risen distinctly in the U.S., and creative destruction appears to have had an important role in its increase. While very highly paid male workers earned less than 2.5 times the pay of poorly paid male workers (precisely, the worker at the 90th percentile in earnings compared with one at the 10th percentile) in the 1960s and the early 1970s, the multiple has since risen fairly steadily. Since the mid-1990s, very highly paid male workers have earned roughly four times what poorly paid male workers earn.[23] On average, workers at companies that are engaged in creative activities—as measured by research and development expenditures, invest-

ment in computers, and on-the-job training—have earned more and had greater income growth.

The rapid technological change in this period appears to have favored the highly educated—those who are best prepared to create, to assist in creativity, and to learn new ways of working to accommodate the resulting changes.[24] Even though the supply of the highly educated has risen rapidly, demand has outpaced supply, and the value of higher education has risen. Quantitatively, the proportion of the working population over age 25 with at least a bachelor's degree has gone up from 22 percent in 1979 to 31 percent in 1999. The median worker with a college degree earned 68 percent more a week than the median worker with a high school degree in 1999, up from 29 percent in 1979.[25]

There is a clear and close connection between the rising value of college education and the rapid growth of managerial and professional work that is increasingly centered on creativity. A college degree is often required for these occupations, and those who earn college degrees generally enter these occupations. As of March 1997, 62 percent of managers and professionals had bachelor's or advanced degrees. Conversely, 68 percent of all holders of bachelor's or advanced degrees were either managers or professionals. At least some of the value imputed to a college degree is likely to be a return to greater continuing investment in knowledge; holders of college degrees are much more likely than others to engage in formal education while working.

And inequality has risen substantially even after we control for measurable changes in education, demographics, and the growth of trade.[26] If the U.S. economy continues to change as dynamically as it has in the recent past—and the evidence on the proportion of the workforce devoted to creativity suggests that it will—there is scant reason for supposing that inequality will decline. Moreover, increases in inequality are occurring not only within the United States but also between the advanced industrial economies and other countries.

Inequality in the World Economy. The paradigm of perfect competition implies that inequality between rich and poor countries should fall as barriers to trade fall. Opening up trade permits countries to specialize more in the products they produce most efficiently. Allowing the unhindered importing of capital lets poor countries adopt the technology of richer ones. Under fairly general conditions, the wages of workers and the return to capital in rich and poor countries will tend to become more similar. Workers in less-developed countries should benefit more than workers in developed countries as both types of economies become more efficient and relative wages of the workers in the less developed countries rise. As global trade increases, average output per person should become less disparate.[27]

But while global trade has increased, the evidence on whether inequality has diminished is, at best, equivocal. Output per worker among the advanced industrial countries has tended to converge, but over long periods of time, the gap between the advanced countries and the less developed countries has not generally diminished. Output per worker throughout the world has risen dramatically, as it has in the United States, but there remain large pockets of poverty in which households produce little more than the bare minimum necessary for subsistence.

According to The World Bank's *World Development Indicators 2000*, the 3.5 billion inhabitants of the low-income countries had an average gross national product per person of $2,170 in 1998.[28] The middle-income countries, with 1.5 billion inhabitants, averaged $5,990 per person that year, while the high-income countries, with 0.9 billion inhabitants, averaged $23,420 per person. As a group, the richest countries generate 11 times as much gross national product per person as the low-income countries.

By comparison, Lant Pritchett has argued that in 1870, the income gap between the high-income countries and the low-income countries must have been less than nine times. While low-income countries have experienced, on average, a very substantial increase in income, so have the high-income countries. The net result is that worldwide inequality has not diminished over the past 130 years. No doubt much of this inequality is the result of bad governance and bad luck, including the rapacity of local oligarchs, disease, war, colonial policy, and civil disorder. This period of history includes extended periods during which trade barriers between nations were quite high and rising, as well.

If we confine our observations to the period since 1960, during which trade barriers around the world have fallen, we also see relatively little decline in income inequality.[29] According to Robert Summers and Alan Heston, gross domestic product per person in 1960 in the high-income countries was 10 times higher than it was in the low-income countries. Thus, the 1998 ratio of 11 times shows scant convergence even in the recent period of trade liberalization.

Can we expect more rapid convergence in an era in which economic value increasingly depends on creative destruction? Consider the advantages the United States has vis-a-vis a less developed country in the race to create. The U.S. has a well-educated, diverse, and disciplined workforce; access to the most recent research; a deregulated economy relatively unencumbered by bureaucratic restrictions; moderate taxes; a smoothly functioning financial market to finance investment; a long history of rule by law and democracy; a military under firm civilian control; and a host of highly innovative corporations. These absolute advantages count for a great deal in the world of creative destruction, where speed, flexibility, and advanced education all count in developing new products and bringing them rapidly to the marketplace. Indeed, to the extent that creative individuals and firms benefit from geographic proximity, the direct economic benefits of successful creativity will tend to be concentrated in the most advanced countries.

The United States will have these advantages whether or not the less developed countries participate in globalization. Even so, in the long run, less developed countries benefit from the improved ability of the world economy to provide new recipes. But the benefits of globalization should not be oversold. In the short run, rapid obsolescence will tend to deter adoption of new technology in nations where indigenous markets are small. And less developed countries will find it difficult to emulate—and are not allowed by the rules of intellectual property protection to copy—the development of new products. The paradigm of creative destruction implies—in all probability—persistent or even rising inequality between countries.

HOW TO THINK ABOUT A CHANGE IN PARADIGM FOR ECONOMICS

What should the fundamental paradigm of economics be: creative destruction or the invisible hand? This is an empirical matter that depends on the importance of creativity. It is, indeed, hard to measure creativity precisely. But if we fail to recognize it in our economic theory or in our economic measures, we are doomed to be precisely wrong rather than approximately correct. Federal Reserve Chairman Alan Greenspan made this point when he said, "But the essential fact remains that even combinations of very rough approximations can give us a far better judgment of the overall cost of living than would holding to a false precision of accuracy and thereby delimiting the range of goods and services evaluated. We would be far better served following the wise admonition of John Maynard Keynes that 'it is better to be roughly right than precisely wrong.' "[30]

How should economists and noneconomists think about the possibility of a paradigm shift in economics? British Nobel laureate economist John Hicks took up this topic in his 1983 paper on "revolutions" in economics:

> "Our special concern [in economics] is with the fact of the present world; but before we can study the present, it is already past. In order that we should be able to say useful things about what is happening, before it is too late, we must select, even select quite violently. We must concentrate our attention, and hope that we have concentrated it in the right place.
>
> "Our theories, regarded as tools of analysis, are blinkers in this sense. Or it may be politer to say that they are rays of light, which illuminate a part of the target, leaving the rest in the dark. As we use them, we avert our eyes from things that may be relevant. . . . But it is obvious that a theory which is to perform this function satisfactorily must be well chosen; otherwise it will illumine the wrong things. Further, since it is a changing world that we are studying, a theory which illumines the right things now may illumine the wrong things another time. This may happen because of changes in the world (the things neglected may have grown relative to the things considered) or because of changes in our sources of information (the sorts of facts that are readily accessible to us may have changed) or because of changes in ourselves (the things in which we are interested may have changed). There is, there can be, no economic theory which will do for us everything we want all the time."

Put succinctly, Hicks argues that economic science must adapt to the nature of the economy. The growing importance of creative endeavors appears to be what's new in the New Economy. If so, the New Economy represents a significant change in the nature of the U.S. economy, one that is difficult to align with the paradigm of perfect competition. The New Economy is highly competitive, but creative destruction, not production, is the center of the competition. This implies, in line with Hicks's views, that for understanding the New Economy, Joseph Schumpeter's creative destruction paradigm may be superior to Adam Smith's invisible hand.

BIBLIOGRAPHY

Aghion, Philippe, and Peter Howitt. "A Model of Growth Through Creative Destruction," *Econometrica 60* (2), March 1994, pp. 323–51.

Berman, Eli, John Bound, and Zvi Griliches. "Changes in the Demand for Skilled Labor within U.S. Manufacturing: Evidence from the Annual Survey of Manufacturing," *Quarterly Journal of Economics* 109, May 1994, pp. 367–98.

Berman, Eli, John Bound, and Stephen Machin. "Implications of Skill-Biased Technological Change: International Evidence," NBER Working Paper 6166, September 1997.

Bureau of Economic Analysis. *National Income and Product Accounts of the United States, 1929-94, Volume 1.* Washington, DC: U.S. Government Printing Office, 1998.

Cornelli, Francesca, and Mark Schankerman. "Patent Renewals and R&D Incentives," *RAND Journal of Economics* 30 (2), Summer 1999, pp.197–213.

Davis, Stan, and Christopher Meyer. *Blur.* New York: Addison-Wesley, 1998.

Dixit, Avinash, and Joseph E. Stiglitz. "Monopolistic Competition and Optimum Product Diversity," *American Economic Review* 67, 1977, pp. 297–308.

Ethier, Wilfred J. *Modern International Economics*, Third Ed. New York: W.W. Norton, 1997.

Fortin, Nicole M., and Thomas Lemieux. "Institutional Changes and Rising Wage Inequality: Is There a Linkage?" *Journal of Economic Perspectives*, 21 (2) Spring 1997, pp. 75–96.

Frank, Robert H., and Philip J. Cook. *The Winner-Take-All-Society.* New York:Viking Penguin, 1996.

Gleick, James. *Faster: The Acceleration of Just About Everything.* New York: Pantheon,1999.

Gottschalk, Peter. "Inequality, Income Growth and Mobility: The Basic Facts," *Journal of Economic Perspectives*, 11 (2) Spring 1997, pp. 21–40.

Grossman, Gene M., and Elhanan Helpman. *Innovation and Growth in the Global Economy.* Cambridge: MIT Press, 1991.

Hicks, John. " 'Revolutions' in Economics," in John Hicks, *Classics and Moderns, Collected Essays, Vol. III.* Cambridge: Harvard University Press,1983, pp. 3–16.

Hunt, Robert. "Patent Reform: A Mixed Blessing for the United States Economy?" Federal Reserve Bank of Philadelphia *Business Review*, November/December 1999, pp. 15–29.

Johnson, George E . "Changes in Earnings Inequality: The Role of Demand Shifts," *Journal of Economic Perspectives*, 11 (2) Spring 1997, pp. 41–54.

Knight, Frank. *Risk, Uncertainty and Profit.* Boston: Houghton Mifflin, 1921.

Krugman, Paul. *Peddling Prosperity.* New York: Norton, 1994.

Maddison, Angus. *Monitoring the World Economy 1820–1992.* Paris: OECD, 1995.

Mandel, Michael J. *The High-Risk Society: Peril and Promise in the New Economy.* New York: Random House, 1998.

Nakamura, Leonard. "Measuring Inflation in a High-Tech Age," Federal Reserve Bank of Philadelphia *Business Review*, November/December 1995.

Nakamura, Leonard. "Is the U.S. Economy Really Growing Too Slowly? Maybe We're Measuring Growth Wrong," Federal Reserve Bank of Philadelphia *Business Review*, March/ April 1997.

Nakamura, Leonard. "The Retail Revolution and Food-Price Measurement,' Federal Reserve Bank of Philadelphia *Business Review*, May/June 1998.

Nakamura, Leonard. "Intangibles: What Put the *New* in the New Economy?" Federal Reserve Bank of Philadelphia *Business Review*, July/August 1999a.

Nakamura, Leonard. "The Measurement of Retail Output and the Retail Revolution," *Canadian Journal of Economics* 32, 2, April 1999b, pp. 408–25.

Parente, Stephen L., and Edward C. Prescott. "Monopoly Rights: A Barrier to Riches," *American Economic Review* 89, December 1999, pp. 1216–33.

Pritchett, Lant. "Divergence, Big Time," *Journal of Economic Perspectives* 11, 3, Summer 1997, pp. 3–17.

Romer, Paul M. "Increasing Returns and Long-Run Growth," *Journal of Political Economy* 94, 1986, pp. 1002–37.

Romer, Paul M. "Endogenous Technical Change," *Journal of Political Economy* 98, 1990, pp. S71–S102.

Romer, Paul M. "Bank of America Round Table on the Soft Revolution," *Journal of Applied Corporate Finance*, Summer 1998, pp. 9–14.

Rose, Mark. *Authors and Owners: The Invention of Copyright.* Cambridge: Harvard University Press, 1993.

Schumpeter, Joseph. *Capitalism, Socialism, and Democracy.* New York: Harper, 1942.

Scotchmer, Suzanne. "On the Optimality of the Patent Renewal System," *RAND Journal of Economics* 30 (2), Summer 1999, pp.181–96.

Shapiro, Carl, and Hal R. Varian. *Information Rules.* Boston: Harvard Business School Press, 1999.

Smith, Adam. *The Wealth of Nations.* Reprinted Homewood, IL: Irwin, 1963.

Stiglitz, Joseph E. *Whither Socialism?* Cambridge: MIT Press, 1994.

Summers, Robert and Alan Heston. "The World Distribution of Well-being Dissected," in Alan Heston and Robert E. Lipsey, eds., *International and Interarea Comparisons of Income, Output, and Prices.* Chicago: University of Chicago Press, 1999.

Sutton, John. *Sunk Costs and Market Structure.* Cambridge: MIT Press, 1991.

Topel, Robert H. "Factor Proportions and Relative Wages: The Supply-Side Determinants of Wage Inequality," *Journal of Economic Perspectives*, 11 (2) Spring 1997, pp. 55–74.

Watson, Thomas J. Jr. *Father, Son & Co.: My Life at IBM and Beyond.* New York: Bantam, 1990.

Notes

1. The 1998 occupational data used here are from the Current Population Survey of the U.S. Bureau of Labor Statistics, published in *Employment and Earnings*, and the data for years before 1972 are from the decennial U.S. Censuses of Population as recorded in the *Historical Statistics of the United States.* Production occupations are defined here to include farming, forestry, and fishing; precision production, craft, and repair; operators, fabricators, and laborers; and private household and other service workers.

2. Managers, professionals, and technical (MPT) occupations include executive, administrative, and managerial workers; professional specialty positions; and technicians and related support. The residual category of occupations is composed of sales and administrative support, including clerical. This sales and clerical category rose from 8 percent of the workforce in 1900 to 19.5 percent in 1950 and grew more rapidly than MPT during that time. It continued to grow more rapidly than MPT until it reached 25 percent in 1970. Since then, however, the proportion of clerical and sales workers has been relatively stable; it amounted to 26 percent in 1999. Much of the function of these workers involves paperwork, the processing of which has been greatly automated in the past 30 years.

3. American economist Frank Knight is generally credited with formalizing the paradigm of perfect competition in the first years of the 20th century. His book *Risk, Uncertainty, and Profit* dates from his 1916 doctoral thesis.

4. Smith ascribes this inventive activity to workers in industries that make capital equipment.

5. In his book Krugman uses the term magic to describe the exogenous sources of economic growth in a nice exposition of this point of view.

6. Good academic introductions to this point of view are in the articles by Paul Romer (1986, 1990) and the book by Joseph Stiglitz. Romer (1998) is a good business-oriented popular discussion. The book by Gene Grossman and Elhanan Helpman is an advanced text.

7. Schumpeter ignores the theoretical possibility that new recipes can be developed and paid for using perfect contracts, where the inventors are paid for their labor and the recipes are then made available freely to all firms. It appears that new consumer products cannot be readily specified in advance, as such a perfect contract would require. The book by Stiglitz discusses evidence that creative destruction is difficult to assimilate into a perfect contract world.

8. Opposition to new products can arise from consumer and political groups, from workers who make rival products within or outside the firm, or from potential distributors. This opposition may be formal or informal, legal or illegal. Consider the recent worldwide opposition to genetically modified agricultural products or the protests at the Seattle meeting of the World Trade Organization.

9. The monopoly is only temporary; it lasts until a better product comes along that drives out the old or until the patent or copyright expires and others are able to copy the idea or process and compete with the originator. If the grant of monopoly were long-lived, the monopolist would have less incentive to create innovations and might have the power to prevent potential competitors from introducing innovations.

10. Schumpeter's book gloomily prophesied that capitalism itself would succumb to socialism because of the intellectual disrepute into which economic theory had plunged monopoly and monopolists, when these very monopolists were the heroes of capitalism, properly understood.

11. Schumpeter may have gone too far; entrenched monopolies can become the enemy of progress. The theoretical model in the article by Stephen Parente and Edward Prescott shows that it is possible for entrenched existing monopolies, such as state-protected employment in the textile industry in India, to prevent the adoption of new, superior technology when entrants have limited ability to profit from the new technology.

12. Mark Rose's study of the development of English copyright law illustrates the explicit balancing of the property rights of the creator against the desirability of limiting monopoly power.

13. The theoretical basis for this, as well as modern views of the underlying complexities, is laid out in the article by Su-

zanne Scotchmer and the one by Francesca Cornelli and Mark Schankerman. One important limitation to the theoretical result is that it assumes away patent races.

14. Robert Hunt's article is a good summary of theoretical and empirical evidence about the uncertainties of optimal patent protection.

15. Discussions of the impact of increasing risk and inequality in the U.S. are found in the book by Robert Frank and Philip Cook and the book by Michael Mandel.

16. The pioneering article is the one by Philippe Aghion and Peter Howitt. Grossman and Helpman's book is a nice exposition, albeit at an advanced level. The competition being described is not easy to model mathematically because the firms engaged in this competition have to worry about both the past and the future—the qualities of existing products and the future products that will be discovered—in calculating the likely profitability of their investments.

17. The seminal paper is the one by Avinash Dixit and Stiglitz.

18. The first economist to focus on the fundamental uncertainties of creativity was Frank Knight, and in his honor, this aspect of uncertainty is often called Knightian risk. Because we cannot rely on new creativity to be like past creativity, an empirical analysis of Knightian risk will likely always be at least somewhat unsatisfactory. It also implies that the confidence of investors (which Keynes called their animal spirits) may be an important determinant of the rate of investment.

19. In clinical trials, 7000 patients were exposed to Trovan and no cases of acute liver failure were reported. ("Questions and Answers about TROVAN Advisory," FDA *Medwatch*, June 9, 1999.)

20. Quoted in the section "Random Samples," *Science* 285, September 10, 1999, p. 1663.

21. Carl Shapiro and Hal Varian's book gives a readable introduction to consumer network effects that have been the focus of much economic research. John Sutton's book discusses the general issue of consumer investments in a system.

22. In Sonnet 18, Shakespeare promised his now forgotten patron that his verse would be immortal, "So long as men can breathe or eyes can see, So long lives this, and this gives life to thee."

23. See the article by Peter Gottschalk.

24. For the background to this argument, see the Symposium on Wage Inequality in the Spring 1997 *Journal of Economic Perspectives*, where articles by Gottschalk, George Johnson, Robert Topel, and Nicole Fortin and Thomas Lemieux present a variety of views on skill-biased technical change.

25. *Economic Report of the President*, February 2000, U.S. Government Printing Office, pp. 135–36.

26. See the Symposium in the *Journal of Economic Perspectives* cited earlier.

27. That international trade tends to increase both equality of returns and efficiency was put on a firm foundation by a series of economists beginning with David Ricardo and con-

tinuing to the present. See, for example, the text by Wilfred Ethier.

28. Product here is measured in terms of its purchasing power in 1998 U.S. dollars.

29. Trade barriers fell first under the General Agreement on Tariffs and Trade and now under the auspices of the World Trade Organization.

30. Testimony of Chairman Alan Greenspan before the Committee on the Budget, U.S. House of Representatives, March 4, 1997.

Leonard Nakamura is an economic advisor in the Research Department of the Philadelphia Fed.

From *Business Review,* July/August 2000, pp. 15-30. © 2000 by Federal Reserve Bank of Philadelphia. Reprinted by permission.

On Making Economics Realistic

Interview with George Akerlof

George Akerlof has been a pioneer in developing theories that explain important deviations from classical economics. In 2001, he, along with Joseph Stiglitz and Michael Spence, won the Nobel Memorial Prize in economic science. His acceptance speech was a forceful denunciation of many standard claims of economics today. In fact, Akerlof believes a truer view of how the economy works reflects the spirit of Keynes. He is concerned that the nation will try to reduce inflation too far.

Q. You presented in your Nobel Prize acceptance speech a broad criticism of conventional economics based on your own work in asymmetric information and behavioral economics. You started with what has become your famous piece on the used car market. What got you interested in this market in the first place?

A. I became interested because, particularly at the time, automobiles and the variation in automobile sales played an especially large role in the business cycle.

Q. When was this?

A. It was the 1960s. I was looking to see whether the tendency to buy new cars rather than used cars could explain this cyclical variation. It had occurred to me that this variation might be due to asymmetric information. The paper did not show this conclusion, but later work by Rick Mishkin did.

Q. What did you end up explaining with your paper?

A. It shows that the market for used cars—because of asymmetric information—is likely to be quite a small market and that other markets with sufficient asymmetric information will, in fact, collapse and will not be there at all. The leading and most obvious such failure is in health care insurance.

So the paper, in fact, does explain quite a bit. First, it explains why some really important markets that should exist simply are not there. Asymmetric information can cause markets in which trades would be beneficial to collapse.

Q. The basis of this market is that the guy selling the used car knows a heck of a lot more about that car than the person buying it?

A. Yes. The person selling the car knows more, and so the buyer does not want to buy The market may not develop, or it may disappear altogether. Here is how it works. Suppose there is a given price for a used car. Those sellers with cars that are very good are not going to offer them for that price. Those with bad cars will usually be happy to offer them at that price. The buyer, seeing that he is potentially going to get one of these bad cars, will insist on a lower price than he is willing to pay for the best car that is being offered. The seller who is just on the margin and has the best car says that that is not sufficient, and so he withdraws. That makes the pool of available cars worse. Then the price that the buyer is willing to pay drops further, which causes a further reduction in the quality as the people at the top of the market continue to withdraw. It is a vicious circle.

Q. This theory provided you, as you say in your Nobel Prize acceptance speech, with some hope that you could return to what you describe as a Keynesian kind of economics, at least in the spirit of Keynes's classic book, *The General Theory*.

A. The whole endeavor—this was just the beginning of a long-term endeavor—was to construct a macroeconomics that was much more specific regarding market institutions and their operation.

Q Did Keynes in some sense make oversimplified assumptions that were easy to criticize by what you called the new classical economists?

A. That is not clear. There is a scattering of equations in Keynes's model, and any equation almost automatically involves simplifying assumptions, but there is also a great deal of prose. In Keynes's prose, there are few oversimplified assumptions. But if you read the equations, you underestimate what he wrote. Some later economists have taken these equations to be most of what Keynes said and did not pay sufficient attention to the fact that putting his prose comments into a model would be much more difficult. So there is a lot more in *The General Theory* than the simple classical model that people took out of it.

Q. That is an important point. So, there you were, sitting in the 1960s with a sort of beginning of a revival—at the very least a kind of neoclassical synthesis. And then, given some of that oversimplification, there was a further rebellion toward new classical economics, with its headquarters, so to speak, at the University of Chicago.

A. Yes, that is right. So the new classical economics challenged the Keynesian theory. It asked the basic question in Keynesian theory, which is why there was such a thing as unemployment. Since the economics of the time operated almost entirely in terms of perfect competition, the question was: Why in competitive markets would there be such a thing as unemployment? The question arises because in competitive markets it is difficult to have a theory of unemployment. In a competitive market, if you have a bushel of wheat, you can by definition always sell your bushel of wheat at the going price.

Q. Perfect competition assumes, in a nutshell, what?

A. There are many buyers and there are many sellers in a market, and no one of them has any market power. That is perfect competition. So, if I have my bushel of wheat, or if I have my thousands of

bushels of wheat, and I decide to take a slightly lower price than is currently being offered, I will be able to sell all my wheat. We see this every day in the stock market. The stock market is a big competitive market. If you have shares of stock—even fairly big blocks of stock—you can typically sell them with only fairly small shadings in the price.

Q. How is this applied to unemployment?

A. If you thought that there were many different buyers and sellers of labor, and markets for labor were therefore very competitive, you would think that an unemployed worker could get a job if he or she simply lowered her reservation wage slightly. Alternatively, the unemployed worker could also get a job, not at a lower wage, by reducing her demands regarding her conditions of employment.

Q. So the theory says that the only reason I cannot get a job is that I am asking too much money?

A. Too much money, or perhaps that you are too fussy about your conditions of employment.

Q. Or you might not want to move.

A. That is right ... some jobs are harder than others. Jobs contain two things: one is the wage, and, of course, the other is all kinds of things like working conditions, location of the job, the title, etc.

Q. The new classicals would say there is no such thing as involuntary unemployment.

A. I think that is right.

Q. Yet, as you point out, we have seen fairly conclusive evidence of involuntary employment—for example, in the Great Depression of the 1930s.

A. That seems to be a good example. Also we see cycles in unemployment. By that I mean that unemployment varies greatly. That variation over the business cycle seems to be an indication that there is something going on other than just market clearing. If there were market clearing, you would think that the number of people searching for jobs, which is the Labor Department definition of unemployment, would not vary tremendously. Farmers usually sell most of the wheat they grow, although sometimes they are happy and sometimes they are sad about the price they receive for it.

Q. Does asymmetric information or behavioral economics explain involuntary unemployment?

A. The leading explanation for involuntary unemployment now is efficiency wages. The efficiency-wage story says that the labor market does not work like the market for the purchase and sale of bushels of wheat because labor is very different from wheat. Just because people are physically present at their jobs does not mean they are automatically going to work hard. They need to be motivated. So, for a whole variety of reasons, employers often pay labor much more than necessary just to get them to show up in the morning—because of morale. They want the workers to work harder. Workers need incentive. If, in fact, employees could get exactly the same jobs just across the street, as perfect markets suggest, they would not have much incentive to work hard. One of the incentives to work is that your employer is paying you something that is especially valuable, so many employers find that it is useful for them to pay more than the market-clearing wage.

Q. So there is a kind of rationing process?

A. Such wages cause rationing in the labor market. If employers pay above the market-clearing wage, more workers are going to apply for jobs than there are jobs available. Employers will pay such high wages for a variety of reasons. A leading reason comes from asymmetric information—that the employers cannot watch workers all the time and know everything they do. Employers cannot completely monitor them. So employers pay workers a higher wage so that, should they be caught shirking, they would lose something if they had to seek employment elsewhere. That gives an incentive. That is one leading theory.

There are various other theories based upon morale. That is, a lot of employers want to pay high wages to workers so they will have high morale, and then the workers will be committed to the workplace and do good work. There is a lot of evidence that, in fact, this is exactly what occurs. There is actually much more evidence for this theory than for the straight market-clearing, perfect-markets story. In almost any labor market, different employers pay a wide variety of wages for what we think is similar-quality labor. If one employer is paying $10 an hour for a given type of labor and another employer is paying $20 an hour for the same type of labor, then, ipso facto, one of these employers, the one with the higher wage, must be paying above market clearing.

Q. This suggests something in the behavior of workers that may not necessarily be accounted for in neoclassical or classical economics.

A. The evidence is that many, many employers are paying above market-clearing wages, which makes the concept of involuntary unemployment meaningful. It means there can be people out there searching for high-wage jobs that are available, yet these people are not settling for lower wages. Such a person is rational to be searching for a high-paying job—such jobs are available—even if she might need a little luck to get one. The existence of high-wage jobs creates a gap between the demand for labor and the supply of labor. Thus there may be unemployed people who are unwilling to take the worst opportunities available to them, but they are rational to be searching because, with luck, a higher-paying job may come along.

Q. Does this imply that there is always involuntary unemployment?

A. I think probably there is always some involuntary unemployment, yes.

Q. What are the policy implications of this? If there is no involuntary unemployment, as new classical economists would say, then there is not much one can do about creating more jobs without creating inflation, I assume. But if there is involuntary unemployment, what does it mean about policy?

A. I want to return to the policy implications. But let us first talk about another issue you raise. An implication of the neoclassical model of the economy is that monetary policy cannot even stabilize the economy.

Q. Can you explain that further?

A. With neoclassical economics, monetary policy is ineffective in stabilizing output. Indeed, it is totally ineffective. Neoclassical economics makes monetary policy ineffective because prices and wages are totally flexible. In that case, a shift in monetary policy that has been foreseen will just result in changes in prices and wages that exactly mimic the increase in monetary policy. A change in the money supply, which would be a change in monetary policy by, let us say, 5 percent, would be accompanied by an increase in wages and in prices by 5 percent. It would have no effect whatsoever.

But new theories of unemployment give a reason that wages and prices would be sticky. Under the new theories of unemployment, there are firms that are very close to indifferent about paying a higher wage or a lower wage. They have chosen a wage that is just at the optimum, and they are at the margin of indifference between higher or lower wages and also higher or lower prices. With just a small bit of laziness on the part of such firms, when there is a change in the money supply, they will leave their wages or their prices fixed. Such sticky prices (or wages) in the presence of an increase in the money supply then result in increased real demand. The reason is that the money supply has risen relative to the price level. With such a relative increase in the money supply, people find themselves with an excess in their bank accounts; they will therefore buy either more goods or more assets. If they buy more goods, demand increases directly. If they buy more assets, interest rates fall, which will also increase demand.

Q. So Alan Greenspan, or somebody like him, does matter?

A. Definitely, yes. And, of course, that is what everyone believes throughout the Western world. Monetary policy does have an effect on output and employment. We should be a bit careful. What the new classical economists said was that monetary policy insofar as it was foreseen would have no effect on the level of output. My view is that monetary policy tends to be very public—that is, it tends to be seen very quickly—so their view says, in practice, that monetary policy has almost no effect on the economy.

Q. Is that a rational-expectations view of monetary policy?

A. Rational expectations says that the systematic part of monetary policy, that part which could be foreseen, will have no effect.

Q. So, you mean if there is a shock—a sudden change in monetary policy—it could have an effect?

A. Yes. I was careful here—I circumvented that part by saying "monetary policy insofar as it was foreseen." The foreseen part would be the systematic part and have little or no impact.

Q. I would like to get to the NAIRU (nonaccelerating interest rate of unemployment). I guess we should combine it with a little definition of the Phillips curve. But new classical economics—and indeed, it has become standard among many economists—argues that there is a given natural rate of unemployment, and if you try to reduce it, the pace of inflation will accelerate—the

NAIRU. Let us go into your analysis, then, as to whether there is a NAIRU or not. You believe there is not.

A. It might be useful for me to begin with an explanation for such accelerating inflation. According to the standard story, in price setting and in wage bargaining, people try to set a real wage that they want—a wage before inflation. People bargain in these real terms, and then they add on the expected rate of inflation. Suppose the Fed keeps unemployment below the natural rate of unemployment. People see that unemployment is low; they sense that the job market is tight. As a result, they see that they can demand a higher real wage. But because demand is so high at that level, there is going to be more inflation than they were expecting. Then they add that higher inflation onto their real wage demands. So there is a vicious circle, which raises inflation, and therefore expected inflation, yet higher. There is an ever-accelerating inflation if unemployment is below the natural rate.

The big problem with the analysis is that, to be consistent, if the unemployment rate is above the natural rate, you ought to have accelerating deflation. People do not talk much about that.

Q. And there is no evidence of that accelerating deflation?

A. Well, we seem to find that, at high rates of inflation and low rates of unemployment, there is fairly good evidence that we get acceleration in the rate of inflation. But if you look at the opposite case—high rates of unemployment—there is much less evidence that you get accelerating deflation. Now, that means that the basic theory of the NAIRU has a problem. Take a look at the Great Depression. For the first few years, from 1929 to 1932, there was rapid and accelerating deflation. But from 1932 to 1942, there was almost no change in the rate of inflation at all. There was not accelerating deflation. And yet, no one I know would argue that in the Great Depression the unemployment rate was not above the NAIRU, and above the NAIRU by a great deal. There simply should have been accelerating deflation, and there was not. So somewhere, some place, the theory breaks down, and the question is, where does it break down?

Q. Where exactly does it break down?

A. It breaks down when the inflation rate is very low. You find that at low rates of inflation, there is a significant trade-off between inflation and unemployment. There are two reasons the standard logic of the NAIRU no longer works when inflation is low. First, workers do not like cuts in their money wages. And because such cuts have significant effects on morale, firms are loath to make such cuts. This resistance to money-wage cuts creates a trade-off not between the acceleration in inflation and the level of unemployment, but between the level of inflation and the level of unemployment.

There is a second reason for the failure of the logic of NAIRU at low inflation. When inflation is low, it does not matter much to workers whether or not you add expected inflation onto the wages they bargain for in real terms. There is evidence that both firms and workers tend to ignore inflation when it is low. This tendency gives a second reason that, at low inflation, there is a trade-off between the level of inflation and the level of unemployment. Again, the logic of NAIRU fails.

Q. What are the policy implications of this situation?

A. The policy implications are very important. Very low inflation is always a telltale sign that the monetary authority is not doing its job: The economy could permanently have more jobs, at almost no cost. Central banks especially should not pursue inflation targets that are too low. A zero-inflation target for any Western country would result in very high unemployment. Calculations by Bill Dickens, George Perry, and me suggest that going from a 2 percent inflation target to a 0 percent target will result in a shift upward of two percentage points in the long-term unemployment rate.

Q. Are there some empirical examples of this conclusion?

A. A good example may be the Canadian economy for the decade of the 1990s. The Canadian monetary authority for the 199 Os had very low inflation targets and maintained very low inflation throughout the course of the decade. Did it have an effect? Canadian unemployment was very high throughout the 1990s. They should have had a very large deceleration in inflation, given the theory. In fact, they got only something like a 0.1 percent change in the inflation rate. They paid a very high price in terms of having high unemployment for negligible gains. For the United States, on our side of the border, it also is a useful warning: that being overly aggressive about trying to reduce inflation to the absolute minimum is a very bad thing.

Q. Let me go to another interesting subject you raised in your acceptance speech. New classical economists would argue there really could not be bubbles in the stock market. Please explain that.

A. Many people in finance believe that asset prices reflect fundamental values—that asset prices basically reflect the present discounted values of the returns that people are going to get from stocks or bonds. The behavioral finance people, especially Robert Shiller of Yale, believe that asset markets can get out of control and that prices deviate quite a bit from market fundamentals. The problem is that it may be a fairly easy task to evaluate one stock relative to another. But it is very difficult to know what the price of all stocks should be. It is just like when one buys a house: It is easy to tell what the price of one house should be compared to the one next to it, but whether houses are a good value or a poor value as a whole is very hard to judge. So there are times of euphoria when stock prices are extremely high, as there are also times when stock prices are tremendously depressed.

Q. And Shiller has shown that the assumption that the market accurately discounts future earnings does not seem to hold up historically.

A. That seems to be the case.

Q. Let me get right to the policy implication of that. Is there a role for the Federal Reserve to try to ameliorate potential bubbles, or actual bubbles?

A. My own view is that the key central policy goal of the Federal Reserve is to make the proper trade-off between inflation and unemployment. In that regard, the Federal Reserve's concern about asset bubbles, which it definitely should be concerned about, is secondary.

Q. Would it not be secondary only to the extent of its significance, of how inflated the market is?

A. It is quite clear that the Federal Reserve in the late 1990s could have cut asset prices by raising interest rates. They could have foreshortened the bubble. But if they had done so, they would have also raised unemployment. I would not trade the prosperity of the late 1990s for a shorter bubble. That prosperity made a huge number of people much happier.

Q. But you do believe in a Tobin tax—a tax on securities transactions—for example?

A. Yes. I think that a Tobin tax is probably a good idea.

Q. Because it would reduce speculation?

A. It is not clear that a Tobin tax would have dealt with this last bubble, but it might have helped, because huge numbers of people were doing a lot of trading, and they were very naive. It might have reduced the trading.

Q Let me ask you about one last area: what you call identity economics and its implications for social policy. Can you explain that a bit more?

A. One problem that economists have not properly analyzed is minority poverty in the United States, and especially African-American poverty. African Americans are more responsive to good schooling than any other segment of the population. And yet, we are starving our inner city schools of the funds that are necessary to hire the very best teachers and also to have the small class sizes that have been shown to be effective. Behavioral economics has, especially with identity theory, made a special case for extra funds to be devoted to the inner city. There are very high returns in terms of better school performance from increased spending.

Q. So, let me get back to John Maynard Keynes. You began your speech by saying that we can revitalize economics in the spirit of Keynes. One of the first things we think about when Keynes's name comes up is that he argued that government could stimulate the economy in times of higher unemployment and undercapacity. Does your thinking revitalize the case for Keynesian stimulus?

A. Yes, definitely Behavioral economics provides a new way of looking at macroeconomics. It is not just a question of having a handful of simple recipes. You need to analyze economies in terms of their institutions, especially in terms of the motivations of the price setters, the wage earners, the employers, and so on. When you do that, you get a macroeconomics that is not rule-based and that is much more flexible in its thinking. For the United States, one major application is that we want to avoid very, very low levels of inflation. A zero-inflation target especially would be a disaster in the United States and would cause the loss of millions of jobs.

Q. Are there any implications for the ongoing debate between fiscal and monetary policy?

A. With fiscal and monetary policy, I think I am probably on the side of Tobin. Tobin always wanted to have a tight fiscal policy, a loose monetary policy. A loose monetary policy yields low interest rates, and low interest rates provide an incentive to invest. This recommendation does not just come from behavioral economics—it is very classical. Behavioral economics neatly combines classical economics with the deviations from it. We do not need to throw away our classical thinking. We add to it, and we fine-tune it to fit reality.

GEORGE AKERLOF is Koshland Professor of Economics at the University of California at Berkeley.

Beyond a President's Control

By LOUIS UCHITELLE

W E endow our presidents with mythical power, holding them responsible for the health of the economy. But any president's influence over the twists and turns of the complicated American economy is inevitably less than is advertised.

George W. Bush is not to be blamed for the recession that overtook the country two months after his inauguration. Nor is he the author of the upturn that seemed so promising in the spring. Now the economy may be weakening again, which suggests that, if he became president, John F. Kerry would preside over a downturn during his opening months in office, followed, eventually, by an upturn.

Both would be beyond his control, or any president's, although Mr. Kerry would be blamed for the downturn and praised for the rebound. Franklin D. Roosevelt exercised more influence than any modern president over the fluctuations of the economy. He did so through huge public spending, a dismantling of the gold standard and similar drastic measures. Yet even he was taken by surprise when a gradually recovering economy performed a U-turn in 1937 and plunged back into depression.

So why do voters focus so narrowly on the quarter-to-quarter health of the economy, forcing the presidential candidates into a game of musical chairs? If the economy is flourishing in the final weeks of a campaign, when the music stops, the incumbent is likely to be re-elected, assuming that other issues—like the Iraq war, in Mr. Bush's case—don't get in the way. But if the economy is heading south in those final weeks, the challenger—Mr. Kerry—is more likely to be our next president.

"Ordinary people don't have a good sense of what the president can and cannot do about the economy," said Andrew Kohut, director of the Pew Research Center, which surveys public opinion. "Their perception is that he is responsible for how they are faring, and if he does not acknowledge their complaints, they judge him as indifferent and not doing a good job."

The first President Bush was a victim of this perception. The 1992 election came 16 months into a recovery that was still too weak to be distinguished in people's minds from the 1990-1991 recession, and Bill Clinton capitalized on that perception with his endlessly repeated slogan, "It's the economy, stupid." Now, Mr. Bush's son is promising more of the strong economic growth and job creation that was so evident in the spring, while keeping his fingers crossed that the nation is not in for another slide, as recent data about the economy increasingly suggest.

The Federal Reserve, of course, has become the true hero—or culprit—for what happens in the near term. A president can have only limited influence. The Bush tax cuts, for example, put money into the pockets of low- and middle-income people, and that contributed to the recovery, although it would have come sooner and been stronger, many economists say, if the tax cuts had been directed much more than they were at lower-income people likely to spend every dollar of such windfalls. Still, despite the shortcomings, the Bush tax cuts helped.

The Kerry formula seeks to recreate the prosperity of the 1990's largely by moving the country back toward the budget surpluses of the Clinton era. As part of the process, Mr. Kerry would rescind the Bush tax cuts on incomes of more than $200,000 annually. The Clinton surpluses, however, were not just President Clinton's doing. Military spending, for example, declined after the cold war, and there was a contribution from tax increases enacted while Republicans still occupied the White House, in addition to a Clinton tax increase.

The deficit reduction and budget surpluses, however, came during Mr. Clinton's watch, and he got the credit. He, in turn, credited deficit reduction and its favorable impact on the bond market as the defining features of the late 1990's prosperity. The president's good luck came to be known as Clintonomics, which Mr. Kerry promises to bring back, although he is realistic about its causes. Ask him about the 90's boom and he cites contributing factors beyond any president's control.

High on his list are the rapid advances in computer technology and the unanticipated surge in labor productivity. "I believe that you had a combination of circumstances in the 1990's, some of which you don't have today repeatable," Mr. Kerry said in a recent telephone interview. Among them, he said, were the fact that "we were coming out of the banking crisis of the late 1980's, early 90's, and we had gone through a consolidation of banks and a certain re-establishment of confidence in the financial sector."

Booms and busts, in sum, do not come and go in response to finger-snapping by presidents. "Where the economy is going to be six months from now is beyond anyone's knowledge or control," said Peter L. Bernstein, a Wall Street economist who has been tracking business cycles for more than 40 years.

True, the nation's presidents are not helpless spectators, certainly not as helpless as their constituents. But they are not masters of the business cycle, either—although that is what most voters expect them to be, the polls tell us. And that is the role that presidential candidates embrace in their campaign oratory.

WE do not hear as much about the great influence that presidents do exercise in shaping the economy in a different way. Booms and busts are largely beyond their control, but distribution of the national income is not. And here, the Bush and Kerry approaches are radically different.

Through tax cuts and other policies, the Bush administration is channeling more income to the wealthiest Americans—record amounts, in fact. The Kerry camp, in contrast, would redistribute income down the social ladder, through practices like a higher minimum wage, extended unemployment insurance, stepped-up spending for education and, above all, subsidized health insurance for millions of Americans who now have no health insurance at all. Both candidates say that, as a spinoff, their approaches will strengthen the economy, but what stands out is who gets what share of the pie.

Income distribution is what a president can control. The news media report this issue, of course, but not nearly as often as the musical chairs.

UNIT 2
Measuring Economic Performance

Unit Selections

4. **State of the Union: Black Holes in the Statistics**, Robert Eisner
5. **Notes From Underground: Money That People Earn and Spend Outside the Realm of Official Economic Calculations Is Nonetheless Real**, Elia Kacapyr
6. **Technology, Productivity, and Public Policy**, John Williams and Mary Daly
7. **An International Tale of Two Consumers**, David Ingram

Key Points to Consider

- Why are reliable statistics essential for good economic policy-making?

- What is the underground economy, and why is it a troubling issue for policy-makers?

- How productive are U.S. workers?

- Identify some problems which one encounters when attempting to measure the general levels of prices and unemployment.

 **Links: www.dushkin.com/online/**
These sites are annotated in the World Wide Web pages.

Bureau of Economic Analysis (BEA)
http://www.bea.doc.gov

Bureau of Labor Statistics (BLS)
http://stats.bls.gov

Dr. Ed Yardeni's Economics Network
http://www.yardeni.com

Economic Statistics Briefing Room
http://www.whitehouse.gov/fsbr/esbr.html

Internet Public Library: Business and Economics Reference
http://ipl.org/ref/RR/static/bus0000.html

New York Times Business Connections
http://www.nytimes.com/library/cyber/reference/busconn.html

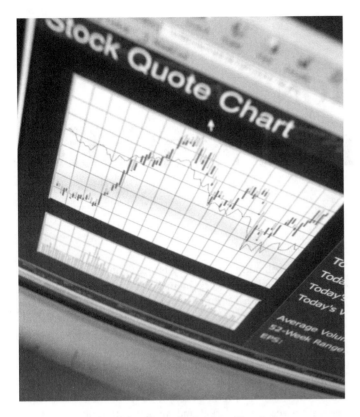

Data! Data! Data! I can't make bricks without clay.

—Sherlock Holmes
The Adventure of the Copper Beeches

Economic decision making involves an assessment of the economy's general health and the informed selection of policies from among many alternatives. Economic analysts, in both the public and private sectors, regularly watch such measures as gross domestic product (GDP), unemployment, and inflation. You are probably familiar with these terms, since they are frequently mentioned in news broadcasts and daily newspapers. However, the popular understanding of economic data is sometimes flawed, partly because the formulation and use of economic statistics is a normative process influenced by value judgments. Arthur Ross summarizes this point quite well:

Let us recognize candidly that statistical truths, like the other truths about man's social life, are created rather than discovered. It may well be different when it comes to measuring the amount of rainfall or the population of redwood trees. These are physical phenomena. It is man who invents and defines these categories. It is man who selects a few dimensions that are capable of measurement and uses them to characterize complex social conditions and relationships. It is man who decides how much effort should be expended in measuring these dimensions or others that might be selected. ("Living with Symbols," *American Statistician,* June 1966)

The articles in this section address a number of important issues involving the measurement and interpretation of macroeconomic data. Policy-makers must be concerned with the relevance and reliability of the statistical truths upon which they base their decisions. This presupposes a knowledge not only of the way in which government statisticians structure their data, but also of the official meaning of these statistics. Beyond this, policy-makers need to develop a sensitivity to at least three issues: that economic data are often subject to wide margins of error (which sometimes cast doubt upon the reliability of such data); that discrepancies between different sets of statistics are common (thereby requiring policy-makers to make choices about the relative importance of one sort of data over another); and finally, that not all economic phenomena can be measured (particularly where such issues as the quality of economic life are concerned). In the end, good policy-making mandates a careful consideration of these issues.

This section begins with a discussion by Robert Eisner of the reliability of economic data. He cites a large number of flaws in official government statistics. Recent federal attempts at cutting costs have seriously impaired the process through which data are collected. As a result, policy-makers often must rely on unreliable information.

Then, Elia Kacapyr explores the "underground economy," where goods and services—some legal, some not—are produced and exchanged but not reported. He contends that, among other things, the existence of this hidden economy may mean that official unemployment and poverty rates may be overestimated.

In "Technology, Productivity, and Public Policy," John Williams and Mary Daly ask: why did U.S. productivity, the nation's economic output per labor hour, suddenly accelerate in 1995 after decades of stagnation? The answer lies in a host of economic, technological, and historical developments.

STATE OF THE UNION:
Black Holes in the Statistics

Robert Eisner

Most of you have probably heard the story of the drunk stumbling around a street lamp. When a policeman asked him what he was doing, he said he was looking for his lost wallet. "Where do you think you lost it?" asked the officer. "I haven't the foggiest idea," was the reply. "Then why are you looking here?" "Because it's light here," the drunk replied.

The moral of the story is, obviously, that restricting our measurement to areas where there is the most light may not be optimal. And although it would be nice to have more light everywhere, we can at least try to cast light—and measure—in areas that economic theory indicates are relevant to resolving critical policy issues. While always striving to be as accurate as possible, we must not shirk from working in relatively dark places. What we find in those dark places should be prominently displayed with whatever caveats are appropriate.

Let me apply this moral to our measures of GDP, public deficits and debt, domestic and foreign investment and saving, productivity, real wages, and the distribution of income and wealth.

Understanding GDP

To many, the single most important measure of the economy is real GDP and its rate of growth. GDP essentially measures the market value of goods and services produced for the market. A huge amount of output—estimated at more than half of conventional GDP—is not produced for the market. This includes almost all of household and government output (Eisner 1989, Tables 1 and 5). The non-market output of households is generally not counted in GDP. Government output in the United States until recently was valued as only the compensation of government employees. That has now been extended to include capital consumption allowances on fixed capital but still lacks any item corresponding to the substantial net profits earned in private production.

The problem is not merely the extent of understatement of total output of the economy; it includes the measurement of rates of growth and major policy issues. Thus, more and more women have gone to work in the market. Home cooking is being replaced with TV dinners and restaurants. Maternal home nurture of children is being replaced with day-care centers, and, conversely, domestic servants and commercial laundries are being replaced with washers and dryers in the basement. We have also moved from movie houses to television and VCRs in the home and from public transportation to private automobiles. These shifts and the privatization of government activity entail moves between non-market and market output and across the conventional line separating final and intermediate product.

Non-market output to households and government is generally harder to measure, without the concrete numbers from market transactions. But we need comprehensive measures of output of all sectors, market and non-market, if we are to get a meaningful picture of what is happening to the economy and what we should be doing to make it better. We may not want to pursue policies that bring increases in market output accompanied by greater decreases in non-market output, and we need measures to inform us.

What Is the Deficit Anyway?

Almost everyone attacks "the deficit," but almost no one knows how it is measured or what it really is. The presumed federal budget deficit in the United States bears little resemblance to any meaningful economic concept. It violates key rules of private accounting in not distinguishing between current and capital outlays. It includes in expenditures the purchase of financial and real assets and counts the sale of assets as negative outlays, akin to receipts. The deficit could be eliminated for many years by selling off federal assets—perhaps in a lease-back arrangement (we could begin with the Capitol, the White House, the entire defense arsenal, and our interstate highway system). And our so-called unified budget—as argued about in Congress—makes no adjustment for inflation. It lumps together the underlying structural or exogenous deficit and the effects of cyclical variations of economic activity.

The U.S. Bureau of Economic Analysis (BEA) does considerably better in its government deficits on national income and product account. Following the internationally formulated and recommended System of National Accounts and the practice of most other countries, it has finally separated investment in physical assets from current expenditures. The BEA also does not count purchases and sales of financial assets. Thus, the savings and loan (S&L) fiasco in the United States did not alternately raise and lower the national income account deficits, as it did the unified budget deficits when the Treasury bought and then sold assets of bankrupt S&Ls. The BEA does not, however, include any of the massive investments by government in education, research, and health. And pressures on its own budget has led the BEA to abandon measures of the high-employment or cyclically adjusted budget, so vital for the measurement and analysis of the impact of the deficit on the economy.

Also largely ignored are measures that offer meaningful evaluation of the deficit in a growing economy with a rising price level. The deficit is meaningful largely because it adds to the financial liabilities of the government and, correspondingly, to the financial assets held outside the government. But surely the major impact of changes in the values of these liabilities and assets must stem from real, not merely nominal, changes. The unified budget deficit in the United States, which was $290 billion in fiscal year 1992, this year is $107 billion (*Economic Indicators,* October 1996, p. 32). But with a federal debt of about $3.7 trillion, even our modest inflation rate of around 2.2 percent implies a reduction in the real value of the debt of $82 billion due to inflation. Counting this "inflation tax" reduces the deficit to about $25 billion—all of one-third of 1 percent of GDP.

A still more comprehensive measure would show the change in the ratio of the federal debt to GDP. Now hovering at about 50 percent, it is actually being reduced. We might thus appropriately report a 1996 *surplus* equal to the amount that the increase in the debt falls short of keeping that ratio constant.

What About National Saving?

Another major concern, in the United States at least, is a purportedly inadequate rate of national saving. But what is national saving? Steve Landefeld notes the vast discrepancy between saving measures in the national income and product accounts and those found in the Federal Reserve Flow of Funds reports (1996). In principle, national saving should correspond to increases in a nation's real wealth. In practice, the two are only barely related.

Our measures of investment, the aggregate of which is equal to saving, include only a very poor and misleading count of net foreign investment, business and non-profit institution acquisition of structures and equipment, business investment in inventories, and government acquisition of structures and equipment— only recently measured in the United States. Omitted are all investment by households in durable goods: If Hertz buys a car, which a household rents, it is counted as investment, while if the household buys a car it is counted as consumption!

Also omitted are all investment in research and development in any sector (other than that already counted in physical capital) and investment in the human capital of education, training, and health. In addition, we ignore most investment in preserving our land, air, and water, as well the capital consumption of these vital assets.

The U.S. Office of Management and Budget estimate of our national wealth at the end of fiscal year 1995, including publicly and privately owned physical assets and education and R&D capital, was $54.1 trillion (1996, p. 27, Tables 2–4). Of that, only $16.5 trillion consisted of structures and equipment included in our measures of investment. The 1995 increase in national wealth in constant 1995 dollars was estimated at $1.2 trillion; net saving (gross saving minus capital consumption allowances) in the national income and product accounts was $316 billion.

And That Net Foreign Investment Figure!

Politicians—and even some economists—often claim that we have become "the world's greatest debtor nation." They base this claim on a misinterpretation of the BEA's bottom line, based on reports of the net international investment position of the United States, as relating to debt rather than total net claims, including equity and direct foreign investment. But it was also based in part on a failure of the BEA, since corrected, to offer some estimates, however imperfect, of the relevant market or replacement-cost values of investment. The net foreign investment in the income and product accounts still includes no adjustments for changes in the value of existing assets, vast as these have been as national economies and their currencies wax and wane.

The direct investment figures themselves are suspect in much of the world, with startling differences between the amounts of the same investment as reported by the investing and receiving countries. Moreover, in a world of multinational companies and substantial migration, are we correctly measuring the nationality of assets? If a wealthy Latin American moves to Miami while maintaining assets in his country of origin, the United States, and Switzerland, should those assets be counted as U.S. assets or foreign claims?

Finally, is it clear that the most recent net negative international investment position of the United States, estimated at $800 billion (Scholl 1996, p. 42, Table 1), is less than 2 percent of the national wealth total of $54 trillion just mentioned? Indeed, if net foreign investment, as officially measured, continues indefinitely at its most recent proportion of negative $140 billion, or 0.3 percent of national wealth, while the national wealth continues to grow even at its modest recent rate of about 5 percent per annum, the ratio of net foreign claims to U.S. national wealth would approach only 6 percent. At a real rate of return of even 4 percent that would mean net payments by the United States to foreigners equal to 0.24 percent of U.S. wealth or, assuming that income–wealth ratios remain about the same, less than 2 percent of GDP.

Measuring Changes in Productivity

I will not try to explain growth in market productivity but would like to suggest one major matter usually overlooked because of our focus on market output. Can we not infer something from the revealed preferences of the millions who have moved from non-market, household production into the labor force? Should we not assume that they moved in large part because the income they could earn in the market, and therefore the output they would be producing in the market, was more than the value of the output they were producing at home? To the extent that they moved into lower-paying and less-productive market jobs than the average for market work, they would be lowering measured *market* output per worker. But if their new, market output exceeded the value of the non-market production they left, total output—market and nonmarket—must have risen.

Measures of real wages are related to measures of productivity. Here again, political rhetoric has at times obscured reality and our statistics-gathering agencies have generally failed to correct popular misconceptions. International comparisons of real wages have been particularly faulty, with many presented on the basis of foreign exchange rates that bear little relation to relative domestic purchasing power and indeed fluctuate greatly from year to year. In the presidential campaign of four years ago we heard repeated assertions that the United States had fallen and was only fourteenth in the world in terms of real wages. The correct statement would certainly be that U.S. real wages, on the basis of purchasing-power parity, were easily the highest among major industrial nations.

The Growing Inequality in the Distribution of Income and Wealth

The growing inequality in the distribution of income and wealth in much of the advanced world and most sharply in the United States may be contributing several factors that are biasing our measures. First, again, we often fail to take into account non-market output. The poor may be increasingly less able to afford a movie, but they can generally watch television at home. Their health services may be inadequate, but the value of what they receive from public hospitals may be more than we measure.

Second, the deterioration of the environment for many of the poor, the loss in security as massive crime invades neighborhoods, and the breakdown of public education in inner cities all suggest that the poor have become even poorer than indicated by our conventional measures.

Third, we have probably underestimated the inequality by failing to take into account the "perks" and nonwage benefits enjoyed by those high on corporate ladders, as well as the free or reimbursed lunches at gatherings like this.

Fourth, our measures of personal income and income distribution exclude the real value of capital gains. The theoretical measures of income, modeled after the Hicksian concept of the amount that we can consume while keeping our real wealth intact, would certainly include these capital gains. But unequal as the income distribution may be by conventional measures, the distribution of wealth is far more skewed. The rich have been getting *much* richer, and much of their new wealth has come from capital gains. Bill Gates, Warren Buffett, Ross Perot, and Donald Trump accumulated their many billions from capital gains, not personal income. My namesake, Michael Eisner, despite his top salaries from the Disney enterprises, must impute most of his enormous wealth to the increases in the value of his assets.

The moral again? Spread the light as far as we can and try to measure what counts, even if it goes beyond areas where precise numbers are easy to come by. Economic theory, which is a vital guide, indicates that God did not limit consumption, investment, and output and income to what is produced by business and can be measured by market transactions. As we recognize this, we realize that the task of statistics gatherers and analysts the world over is that much harder.

So let us tell all our governments to measure their budgets better and to stop squeezing *our* budgets. They should give us more information so that we can determine the status of our economies and where we are really headed.

For Further Reading

Council of Economic Advisers. 1996. *Economic Indicators.* October.

Eisner, Robert. 1989. *The Total Incomes System of Accounts.* Chicago and London: University of Chicago Press.

Kenessey, Zoltan, ed. *Accuracy, Timeliness and Relevance of Economic Statistics.* Materials of a conference of the International Statistical Institute, the Statistical Office of the European Communities, and the Bureau of Economic Analysis of the U.S. Department of Commerce, Washington DC, 1997.

Landefeld, Steven J. 1996. In Kenessey, *Accuracy, Timeliness and Relevance of Economic Statistics.*

Office of Management and Budget. 1996. *Budget of the United States Government, Analytical Perspectives.* Fiscal Year 1997.

Scholl, Russell B. 1996. *Survey of Current Business* (July): 36–44.

ROBERT EISNER is Professor of Economics, Emeritus, at Northwestern University. This article was originally a luncheon address delivered at an international conference in Washington, September 9, 1996. It will also be published in Accuracy, Timeliness and Relevance of Economic Statistics, *ed. Zoltan Kenessey (Washington, 1997).*

Notes from underground:

money that people earn and spend outside the realm of official economic calculations is nonetheless real.

Elia Kacapyr

Money that people earn and spend outside the realm of official economic calculations is nonetheless real.

The Department of Commerce estimates that the U.S. produced $7.6 trillion worth of goods and services in 1996. This is the official assessment of Gross Domestic Product (GDP). Yet, everyone involved with the collection and dissemination of this figure understands that it is a vast underestimate. The Department of Commerce traditionally ignores the wide array of goods and services produced in the *underground* economy.

For instance, illegal gambling and prostitution are not included in the official estimate of GDP. Because of the criminal nature of these activities, it is understandably hard to get a handle on their dollar volume. It's also hard to estimate the value of legal goods and services provided in an illegal fashion, i.e., "off the books." The house painter who insists on being paid in cash to avoid claiming income and paying taxes does not contribute these dollars to the official GDP. Products produced and exchanged through casual or formal barter systems also fly under the department of Commerce's radar.

But by far the largest type of production not included in official accounts is both legal and ethical. It falls under the category of "housework." This includes any goods or services that households provide for themselves. Do-it-yourself auto repairs, cooking and cleaning, vegetable gardening, and much more fall into this classification—virtually everything we do that could be done by someone else if we paid them enough.

The "underground" economy includes all production not accounted for in the official GDP. Estimates of its scope range from 3 percent to 40 percent of the "above-ground" economy. The wide range of estimates is the result of different definitions. For instance, most studies of the underground do not include housework. That is, many researchers, like Edgar Feige, consider the underground to be only illegal and "off-the-books" production. Even so, his estimates suggest that the underground is about 20 percent of the above-board economy. One estimate of the economic value of unpaid housework sits at 31 percent of official 1981 GDP, according to Robert Eisner, in The Total Incomes System of Accounts. Piling other types of underground activity on top of this boosts the size of the underground economy to as much as half of the official total.

Underground money has implications for other economic statistics and economic policy. The official unemployment and poverty rates may be overestimated because of the employment and earnings people make but don't report. The federal government also loses out on at least $100 billion in lost tax revenues. On the other hand, the fact that the money's in consumers' hands means it's flowing somewhere.

If the proportional size of the underground economy remains relatively constant, then economic data expressed in rates, such as the growth rate in GDP, will be accurate despite the fact that they ignore the underground. But such a consistency is unlikely, evidence indicates that when tax rates rise, so does underground activity.

Some statistics that go into the American Demographics Index of Well-Being, such as the employment rate and after-tax income, exclude the underground economy. In their absence, the best we can do is note the inaccuracy. In August 1997, the Well-Being Index stood at 102.47, down about a tenth of a percent from July's revised reading of 102.56. These figures indicate that the typical American has enjoyed an increase in well-being of almost 2.5 percent since April 1990, the base month for the Index.

The decline in August is due to a drop in labor productivity that lowered the productivity and technology component, as well as an increase in the average work week that cut into leisure time. The social and physical environment also gave up ground as a result of increases in crime, divorce, and the number of endangered species. On the upside, income and consumer attitudes improved. The income figures don't account for our under-the-table dealings. But our attitudes might to some extent reflect them.

Technology, Productivity, and Public Policy

This Economic Letter *summarizes papers presented at the conference "Technology, Productivity, and Public Policy" held at the Federal Reserve Bank of San Francisco on November 7-8, 2003.The conference was the inaugural event of the new Center for the Study of Innovation and Productivity (CSIP), which is organized within the Economic Research Department of the Bank.*

The study of productivity growth cuts across many of the fields and approaches in economics—microeconomics, macroeconomics, and international economics; theoretical and empirical analyses—and it is a subject for students of history as well as of current events. The seven papers presented at this conference highlight the breadth of questions and methodologies of recent research on productivity growth.

Three of the conference papers examine productivity growth at the macro economic level. Kahn and Rich propose a method that aims to improve our ability to identify breaks in trend productivity growth of the types that occurred in the 1970s and in the mid-1990s. While such breaks are easy to spot after the fact, they have proven difficult to recognize in real time. In a theoretical paper, Jones asks how production technologies are determined in the first place. He considers how new ideas affect the development of production possibilities in both the short run and the long run. Manuelli and Seshadri consider the link between innovations and the adoption of new production technologies directly. As a

case study of technological diffusion, they examine the long time lag between the invention of the farm tractor and its wide adoption on American farms in the first half of the 20th century.

Two of the papers take a more microeconomic approach. In a theoretical paper, Scotchmer discusses when and why countries engage in intellectual property rights treaties and whether such treaties produce the optimal amount of innovative activity. Lach and Schankerman focus on whether university researchers respond to financial incentives when determining the effort they expend generating inventions. On the basis of these results, they discuss how universities might alter the current compensation system to produce more innovative effort.

The final two papers look at how technology and productivity differentially affect countries and individuals. Considering productivity in an international framework, Hsieh and Klenow examine the extent to which differences in the efficiency of producing investment goods can explain low rates of capital investment in poor countries. Autor, Levy, and Murnane use an array of data and statistical analyses to tie down the relationship between increased computer use in the workplace and the demand for skilled labor. They identify tasks for which computers can substitute for workers and tasks for which computers complement worker skills. They use their results to shed light on the changing relative demand for skilled workers in the U.S. over the last 30 years.

Detecting changes in trend productivity growth

Shifts in trend productivity growth are uncommon and difficult to recognize when they are actually occurring. Kahn and Rich propose and estimate a statistical model in which the rate of trend productivity growth unpredictably switches from a "low-growth" to a "high-growth" regime. Their econometric procedure detects a regime shift from high growth to low growth in the early 1970s, followed by a shift back to high growth in the late 1990s, with the difference between the mean annual growth rates in the two regimes of about 1.5 percentage points. They find that the economy tends to stay in one regime or another for about 20 years on average.

A key assumption of their method is that a common trend underlies long-run movements in real wages, consumption, and productivity. They further assume that this common trend undergoes infrequent shifts between the two growth rate regimes. Because we cannot directly observe which regime the economy is in at any point in time, it must be estimated along with other parameters of their model. They find that estimating a common permanent trend across all three variables does a better job of detecting trend shifts in U.S. data than do methods that are based only on productivity data. They also find that their procedure identifies shifts in regime relatively quickly.

New perspective on production functions

Jones studies how the creation of new "ideas" affects the use of technology and productivity in the economy. In his model, research is directed at finding new ways to produce goods, and the resulting stream of innovations shapes the evolving aggregate production technology that relates inputs of capital and labor to output. At any point in time, producers choose from the available set of production technologies based on the relative costs of inputs. Over time, better ideas are created and the production possibilities frontier shifts out.

This model provides innovation-based microeconomic foundations for a long-run production function of the Cobb-Douglas form that has been widely used in the economics literature and has empirically supported long-run properties. Importantly, Jones's model im-

plies a stable steady state with positive growth, even in the presence of falling relative prices of capital goods, a property that many other production functions fail to possess.

But, the standard Cobb-Douglas function also has some shortcomings at explaining short-and medium run empirical regularities, which the Jones model has the potential to correct. For one, the Cobb-Douglas model implies that the share of income going to labor is constant over time; but, the empirical evidence, especially from European economies, suggests that this may not be the case, and the Jones model does not impose this restriction. Second, the Cobb-Douglas model implies that capital and labor are just as substitutable in the short run as in the long run. In contrast, the evidence suggests that the degree of substitutability of labor and capital is lower in the short run, a feature also consistent with the Jones model.

Technological diffusion

Manuelli and Seshadri look at one important example of innovation, the tractor. They argue that the gradual diffusion of tractor use on U.S. farms from 1900 to 1960 can be explained by technological improvements in tractor design and by the path of real wages during this period. Empirical studies of the diffusion of new technologies have documented that there can be a long time lag between the introduction of a new technology and its wide adoption. Other researchers have argued that there are many impediments to the immediate adoption of new and more productive technologies; in contrast, this paper aims to explain the slow diffusion in the case of tractors without relying on such frictions.

They find that low farm wages through the 1930s reduced the incentive for farmers to switch from horses to tractors during that period. Real farm wages fell by half during the Great Depression, which further slowed the adoption of tractors on American farms. It was not until the 1940s, when wages experienced rapid growth that tractors become widely adopted. In addition, increases in urban wages during this period caused less-skilled farmers to leave the agricultural sector and, as a result, the average skill of the remaining farmers improved over time. This resulted in concentrations of land in favor of larger-sized farms, which also made the adoption of tractors more profitable. Finally, they find that improvement in the quality of tractors over time, especially after the 1940s, played an important role in encouraging the adoption of tractors.

Intellectual property treaties

In 1995 the World Trade Organization passed the Agreement on Trade Related Aspects of Intellectual Property (TRIPS) which set minimum standards for intellectual property rights protections across countries. Scotchmer considers whether the extension of minimum intellectual property rights, like those embodied in TRIPS, produces socially efficient outcomes. Specifically, she asks whether intellectual property agreements improve consumer welfare by enhancing the cross-border exchange of ideas. Scotchmer addresses this question by developing a theoretical model of bilateral intellectual property rights treaties and then investigating the circumstances under which countries enter or do not enter agreements.

She finds that countries may not independently engage in the socially optimal level of intellectual property rights. For example, when countries are not the same size or have different levels of innovativeness, the desire for intellectual property protections may differ, with smaller or less-innovative countries wanting fewer protections. In such cases, harmonization policies, such as TRIPS, can improve social efficiency by increasing protections that fuel innovative activity.

Incentives and inventions in universities

Lach and Schankerman examine whether university researchers respond to financial incentives when determining their innovative effort. Specifically, the authors ask whether academic researchers would create more and/or higher quality inventions if they were allowed to keep a larger share of the revenues generated from licensing the new technologies. The authors set up a simple model of the research effort decision of academic scientists that allows scientists to direct effort toward creating a greater number of inventions or a higher quality of invention.

Taking this model to the data, they find that scientists do respond to financial incentives, but only on the quality component of their effort decision. Scientists who were permitted to keep the largest share of royalties generated the highest quality inventions, all else equal. Financial incentives had no measurable impact on the number of inventions scientists created. Lach and Schankerman also found that the relationship between royalty share and invention quality was strongest at private universities. With this in mind, they support

greater financial remuneration for scientists contributing to the innovative process.

Relative prices and relative prosperity

Hsieh and Klenow examine a well-established relationship between countries' per capita incomes and investment rates in physical capital (equipment, buildings, etc.), evaluated at international prices. The standard story suggests that poor countries have lower purchasing power parity (PPP) investment rates than rich countries because poor countries have low savings rates, due to high tax rates, etc. Hsieh and Klenow argue against this explanation. Using a theoretical model and the predictions from it, they examine an array of nonpolicy alternatives to explain differences in investment across countries.

First, the authors show that investment rates in poor countries only appear low when evaluated at international prices; when valued in the country's own currency, poor countries save and invest at the same rate as rich countries. Second, they argue that the low PPP investment rates in poor countries are not due to low savings rates or to high tax rates or tariffs on investment, but rather owe to low efficiency in poor countries in producing investment goods or exports that can be traded for investment goods.

Skill levels and technological change

Autor, Levy, and Murnane examine the impact of workplace computer use on the demand for different types of workers. They detail what computers are used for and how they substitute for or complement various worker skills. Specifically, they distinguish between routine cognitive or manual tasks that can be performed by following a set of rules and non routine problem-solving and communication tasks that require situational thinking and decision making; computers replace the former and complement the latter. They use their measure of job content and data on increasing computer use over time to explain the rising demand for college-educated workers between 1960 and 1998.

They find a strong relationship between shifts in job tasks and the adoption of computer technology over the period; specifically, increased computerization reduced labor input for routine tasks and increased labor input for non-routine tasks. This pattern occurred both within and across industries and occupations. Based on these calculations, they argue that nearly two-thirds of the relative increase in demand for college-educated workers can be explained by rising workplace computer use. Interestingly, they find that about half of the measured impact of rising workplace computer use owes to increasing requirements within occupations over time; for example, the tasks and requirements for a secretarial job in 1998 involved a much higher level of skills than a secretarial job in 1960, contributing to higher demand for skilled workers in the latter period.

Mary Daly, Research Advisor
John Williams, Senior Research Advisor

Conference Papers

Papers are available in pdf format at `http://www.frbsf.org/economics/conferences/0311/index.html`

References

Author, David, Frank Levy, and Richard Murnane. 2003. "The Skill Content of Recent Technological Change: An Empirical Exploration." Massachusetts Institute of Technology.

Hsieh, Chang-Tai, and Peter Klenow. 2003. "Relative Prices and Relative Prosperity." Stanford University.

Jones, Charles. 2003. "Growth, Capital Shares, and a New Perspective on Production Functions." University of California, Berkeley.

Kahn, James, and Robert Rich. 2003. "Tracking the New Economy: Using Growth Theory to Detect Changes in Trend Productivity." Federal Reserve Bank of New York.

Lach, Saul, and Mark Schankerman. 2003. "Incentives and Invention in Universities." London School of Economics.

Manuelli, Rodolfo, and Ananth Seshadri. 2003. "Frictionless Technology Diffusion: The Case of Tractors." University of Wisconsin, Madison.

Scotchmer, Suzanne. 2003. "The Political Economy of Intellectual Property Treaties." University of California, Berkeley.

An International Tale of Two Consumers

By David Ingram

The difference between the economic performance of the U.S. and Japan is basically a tale of two consumers. It has been the best of times in the United States, where consumers have wallowed in their wealth to the benefit of retailers; and the worst of times in Japan, where consumers remain stubbornly miserly to the detriment of the national economy. The polar-opposite behavior of these two groups reflect fundamental differences in attitudes toward consumption and saving and has presented their respective central banks with opposing policy conundrums.

The fundamental difference between the U.S. and Japanese consumer can be captured by what economists refer to as the personal rate of time preference (RTP). The RTP captures consumers' attitudes toward current versus future consumption. Individuals with high RTP strongly value current consumption over future consumption. That is, they discount future consumption by a large value and tend to borrow in order to consume today. In the opposite case, one where RTP is low, consumption is delayed by investing today in order to purchase and consume more in the future.

Even a casual observer of Japanese and U.S. economic trends can easily identify how the Japanese and American consumers differ. Americans, of course, are world-class spenders—damn the future, we want it all and we want it now! Thus we are willing to borrow against future income in order to augment our current consumption at the expense of future consumption. This trend is augmented by the surge in the stock market during the late 1990s, which makes us feel wealthier. Americans are looking to the stock market to expand their retirement nest egg through the magic of double-digit returns and compound growth. This, in turn, will allow us to, true to our nature and in good conscience, save less out of current income and satisfy our desire to spend more now.

The Japanese, on the other hand, are more future oriented. With a low RTP, they prefer to save their current income in order to augment future consumption possibilities. Part of the reason for this difference is institutional. The Japanese do not have as pervasive a social safety net as Americans do, and are therefore less insouciant about providing for their future. A more immediate reason is the decade-long slump in which the Japanese economy has been mired. With pubic sector debt expected to surpass 130% of GDP this year, many Japanese fear that an undue burden will be placed upon them in the future.

Regardless of the reasons for the different RTPs, one cannot help but wonder if the policy makers at the two countries' central banks would not love to exchange consumers for a while. In the case of the U.S. Federal Reserve, the challenge at hand is to rein in a wealth-effect created consumption binge without pushing the economy into a recession. Their mission is, then, to convince American consumers, who are none too interested in future consumption, to become a little bit more so—or at least act as though they are. Going in the Fed's favor is the fact that they can raise the cost of current consumption by raising interest rates and thus moderate consumer borrowing, even if they cannot change RTPs.

The task facing the Bank of Japan is more daunting. Their modus operandi to date has been to flood the money market with liquidity and reduce the cost of borrowing money to virtually zero, in an effort to entice the Japanese to save less and consume more. Judging from recent statistics that show that retail sales declined for their thirty-eighth consecutive month, department store sales declined for the third consecutive month and chain store sales were off for the eighteenth consecutive month, the Bank of Japan is having little success. To be sure, part of the yen decline in sales is due to deflation in the Japanese economy. But the statistics nevertheless portray a weak consumer sector that is fighting any temptation to reorder preferences.

More importantly still, the Japanese cannot force consumption in the way that the Fed can limit consumption by adding to debt costs and constraining budgets. Therein lies the crucial distinction. By pushing up interest rates, the Fed has made substituting current consumption for future consumption a fiduciary impossibility for many Americans who, absent the tight monetary policy, would be perfectly happy to continue their consumption binge. Alan Greenspan and other members of the

FOMC might not earn congeniality awards, but they are in much better position to achieve their goals. The Bank of Japan knows that even if they were to mail boxes of yen to every household in Japan, there is no way to force their populous to stop their miserly ways and spend the windfall. In other words, no one can convince the Japanese consumer to act more like Americans—that is, raise their RTPs.

This problem is not without precedence. During the Great Depression, the British economist John Maynard Keynes lamented the existence of a so-called liquidity trap by arguing that conducting monetary policy under such circumstances was like "pushing on a string." Unfortunately, until a switch is thrown in the psyche of the Japanese consumer that tells them it is OK to begin consuming again, their on-again/off-again, now on-again, recovery will continue to crawl anemically toward expansion.

UNIT 3

Fiscal Policy and the Federal Budget

Unit Selections

8. **Taxing Terminology: A Primer**, Albert B. Crenshaw
9. **Surplus Mania: A Reality Check**, L. Randall Wray
10. **The Deficit: America's Credibility Gap**, Shawn Tully
11. **The Tax Man Cometh: Consumer Spending and Tax Payments**, Peter S. Yoo
12. **Go Figure**, Jodie Allen
13. **Social Spending and Economic Growth**, Challenge
14. **Social Security Reform Need Not Be Drastic**, Augustine Faucher

Key Points to Consider

- How might an understanding of basic tax concepts help to de-mystify the debate over federal tax cuts?

- How do taxes affect household consumption and saving?

- Were recent cuts in federal taxes a good idea?

- Should the Social Security Program be subjected to major reforms? What about U.S. tax reform?

 **Links: www.dushkin.com/online/**
These sites are annotated in the World Wide Web pages.

Center on Budget and Policy Priorities
http://www.cbpp.org
The Public Debt
http://www.publicdebt.treas.gov/opd/opd.htm
Tax Wire
http://www.taxanalysts.com
U.S. Treasury
http://www.ustreas.gov

Discussion of federal budget policy in the United States has fallen to an abysmally low level. It consists wholly of bumper-sticker slogans, sound bites, and lip reading. It finds public expression in shibboleths like no new taxes, balance the budget, and don't raid Social Security. Prescriptions for dealing with the budget evade the central problem, which is making choices.

Herbert Stein, "Governing the $5 Trillion Economy," *The Brookings Review*

Prior to the 1930s, fiscal policy—changes in taxes and government spending for the purpose of smoothing out the business cycle—was not used explicitly by policy-makers in their pursuit of macroeconomic goals. In fact, the conventional wisdom of the day held that the best fiscal policy was a balanced budget. Most economists (known as "Classicists") maintained that a market economy had enough built-in mechanisms so that any downturns in economic activity would be quickly reversed. According to this line of reasoning, recessions were temporary departures from an economy's normal state of affairs, which was non-inflationary full employment. In the Classical view, since the economy would perform better if the government did not intervene, annually balanced budgets—which served to constrain government—were a good idea.

Classical reasoning was shattered by the events of the Great Depression, a period of prolonged and widespread joblessness, falling incomes, bankruptcies, and political turmoil. In 1936 the British economist John Maynard Keynes attacked the Classical view in his *General Theory of Employment, Interest, and Money*. Keynes demonstrated how market economies could normally produce less than acceptable levels of employment and output. In Keynes's view, a healthy economy (operating at full employment and full production) could only come about if fiscal policy-makers were permitted to administer the right medicine (in the form of carefully unbalanced budgets). As Keynes's ideas gained general acceptance over the next few decades, a national consensus emerged on the need for the federal government to intervene actively in the pursuit of macroeconomic goals. This view was officially sanctioned in the Employment Act of 1946 (which established a federal commitment to policies aimed at achieving "maximum production, employment, and purchasing power").

Although the goals mandated by the 1946 act are relatively clear-cut, actual policy-making experience since World War II demonstrates the difficulties the United States faces in implementing them. It also reflects the limitations of both economic ideology and the political system. Curiously, the early years of the twenty-first century echo with the same question originally raised by Keynes and the Classicists more than a half century ago—are balanced federal budgets a good idea? Should we be concerned over the fact that the federal surpluses of the late 1990s have been replaced by large and growing deficits in the early 2000s? Without surpluses how might we be able to afford such pressing programs as public education and Social Security reform? Were the large income tax cuts of 2002 and 2003 a good idea? The challenge to fiscal policy is that there is no single, generally-accepted answer to such questions.

This unit begins with an article by Albert Crenshaw which discusses terminology used in federal tax policy. Crenshaw says that the debate over federal tax cuts has produced a good deal of ill-informed rhetoric from both sides of the political spectrum, which serves as a reminder of how confusing the working of U.S. tax laws is to ordinary citizens (and even to some government leaders).

Then, in "The Tax Man Cometh," Peter Yoo considers changes in federal tax laws over a forty year period. He provides evidence which shows that tax cuts have generally tended to boost consumer spending, although the response is rather modest.

Most economists would agree that the U.S. tax system is unfair and inefficient, and fails to generate enough revenue to cover government expenditures.

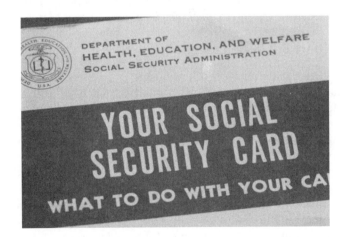

Taxing Terminology: A Primer; Understanding Basics Helps Demystify Debate Over Relief

Abstract:

Now if this single, childless taxpayer's income rises beyond $27,050, the amount by which it exceeds $27,050 is taxed at 28 percent, and the taxpayer is now "in the 28 percent bracket." But the first $27,050 continues to be taxed at 15 percent. Thus, a taxpayer making $30,000 would be said to be in the 28 percent bracket, but the tax would not be $30,000 times 0.28. It would lower. It would be 15 percent of $27,050 plus 28 percent of $2,950 ($30,000 minus $27,050). This amount, as a fraction of the taxpayer's total income, is called the effective tax rate, and it is higher than 15 percent but lower than 28.

Returning to brackets, when a taxpayer earns an additional dollar, the tax rate on that dollar is the earner's marginal tax rate. It would be 28 percent for a single taxpayer earning $30,000 and would continue to be up to an income of $65,550. But this is where the 31 percent bracket begins, so the 65,551st dollar earned would be taxed at 31 percent. The taxpayer would now be in the 31 percent bracket, with a marginal rate of 31 percent.

On the other hand, it's misleading to say, as an opponent did last week, that the [Bush] plan means "earn money as a worker and you are taxed; make money in the stock market and you will be taxed less." That's already true. After the passage of the 1986 Tax Reform Act, capital gains and ordinary income were taxed at the same rate, but in trade-offs during the early '90s between the previous President Bush, President Clinton and Congress, ordinary income rates were ratcheted up and capital gains rates down.

Albert B. Crenshaw

The debate over President Bush's tax proposal has produced a good deal of ill-informed or outright tendentious rhetoric from both sides, which serves as a reminder of how confusing the working of our tax laws is to ordinary citizens and even to some government leaders.

Since this debate is likely to go on for most of the year, it's worth taking a few minutes to review some of the basics, so that when partisans make assertions about the proposal you'll know what they're talking about and whether it makes sense.

We all bandy about tax terms such as brackets and marginal rates and deductions and credits, but how many of us clearly understand what we're talking about when we use them?

Here are a few pointers on what to listen for and how to interpret what you hear.

First, when you listen to the "tax" debate, make sure what tax they are talking about.

Much of Bush's plan centers on the federal income tax. Over the years, low-income people have been largely relieved of this tax, and many low-wage families not only don't pay but get money back under a special program called the earned income tax credit.

But this doesn't mean these workers don't pay tax. They are still subject to Social Security and Medicare taxes, which are known as payroll taxes because they are collected on wages and employers and employees pay matching amounts.

The income tax is progressive, meaning that people with higher incomes pay a higher rate (up to a point). The payroll tax is flat—some would say regressive—because taxpayers pay at the same rates regardless of income.

Then finally there is the estate tax, which opponents call the "death tax," and which Bush proposes to repeal. This tax applies to assets left behind when someone dies. The first $675,000 is not taxed, nor is any amount left to a surviving spouse, but estates that are taxed pay rates that range up to 55 percent.

Next, be sure you understand what is meant by income. Most people think of income as everything they get, so when they see or hear a reference to someone "making"

$37,000 a year, say, they tend to assume that's what is meant.

But in tax talk, not all income is income. Wages, tips, dividends and interest are all income. Alimony is income, but child support is not. You list these on your return.

But then you subtract a number of things, which can include some or all of retirement-plan contributions, certain moving expenses, student-loan interest, health insurance for the self-employed, alimony paid and other items. That produces adjusted gross income, or AGI.

From AGI are subtracted various deductions (itemized or standard), personal exemptions and other reductions to get taxable income. That's the amount to which tax rates are applied.

To make the income tax progressive, lawmakers have set up brackets, which are ranges of income that are taxed at a certain rate. For example, a single taxpayer with no dependents pays a 15 percent tax rate on taxable income from $0 to $27,050. That range is the "15 percent bracket," and such a taxpayer whose income doesn't exceed $27,050 is said to be "in the 15 percent bracket."

Now if this single, childless taxpayer's income rises beyond $27,050, the amount by which it exceeds $27,050 is taxed at 28 percent, and the taxpayer is now "in the 28 percent bracket." But the first $27,050 continues to be taxed at 15 percent. Thus, a taxpayer making $30,000 would be said to be in the 28 percent bracket, but the tax would not be $30,000 times 0.28. It would lower. It would be 15 percent of $27,050 plus 28 percent of $2,950 ($30,000 minus $27,050). This amount, as a fraction of the taxpayer's total income, is called the effective tax rate, and it is higher than 15 percent but lower than 28.

Now, backing up a minute, if you take the total amount of tax you paid and divide that by your total income—that is, the total before subtracting all the adjustments and deductions, you get your average tax rate, the amount of tax you paid on

each dollar of income. This amount is often surprisingly small.

When Bush presented his "tax families" last week, one of them had total income of $36,675 and a taxable income of $15,740 and paid income tax of $1,055 under current law. The family was in the 15 percent bracket, but their effective tax rate was 6.7 percent and their average tax was 2.8 percent.

But this family paid $5,611 in payroll taxes. The Bush plan would reduce their income tax to zero, but their payroll tax would remain the same.

Returning to brackets, when a taxpayer earns an additional dollar, the tax rate on that dollar is the earner's marginal tax rate. It would be 28 percent for a single taxpayer earning $30,000 and would continue to be up to an income of $65,550. But this is where the 31 percent bracket begins, so the 65,551st dollar earned would be taxed at 31 percent. The taxpayer would now be in the 31 percent bracket, with a marginal rate of 31 percent.

This progression continues through the 31 percent bracket to the 36 percent bracket and then to the 39.6 bracket. That's as high as the brackets go, so someone at that level pays 39.6 percent on each additional dollar, ad infinitum.

These brackets, it should be noted, apply to ordinary income, which includes wages, interest, dividends and the like. Short-term capital gains are also taxed at these rates, but there are special rates for long-term capital gains. These are already part of the law and would not be changed by the Bush plan.

Capital gains are profits from the sale of investments, such as stocks, held a year or longer. They are taxed at rates of 10 percent or 20 percent, depending on what bracket the taxpayer is in otherwise. And new lower rates of 8 percent and 18 percent for assets held five years took effect this year, though the holding period must begin this year for higher-income taxpayers, so the 18

percent rate really doesn't kick in for five years.

One function of income-tax progressivity is that it makes deductions more valuable to higher-income taxpayers. If you get to spend a dollar and subtract it from your taxable income, you save 15 cents if you are in the 15 percent bracket, but you save 36 cents if you are in the 36 percent bracket.

To alleviate this effect, tax reductions, including some in the Bush plan, are sometimes done in the form of "credits," which are subtracted dollar for dollar from taxes owed, and thus have the same value for everyone. Some credits are actually "refundable," meaning that if they reduce your tax liability below zero, you get the difference back. The Bush plan doesn't do this, but there is already lobbying to make its per-child credit refundable.

With these items in mind, you can get a better sense of who's saying what in the debate. If nothing else, you can entertain yourself by watching for spin as the talking heads try to show how great or how awful the Bush plan is.

For example, the Bush plan would create a new 10 percent bracket at the bottom of the scale, so that the first $6,000 of taxable income for a single person or $12,000 for a couple would be taxed at 10 percent instead of 15 percent.

This is the most expensive (from the government's point of view) component of the plan, and some plan supporters imply or say outright that this huge cost goes entirely to benefit the lowest-income taxpayers.

But in fact it goes to every taxpayer. Whether it's the CEO or the janitor, the first $6,000 or $12,000 of taxable income would be in the 10 percent bracket. You can argue that the resulting $300 or $600 tax saving is more significant to the janitor, but you can't argue that the CEO doesn't get it.

On the other hand, it's misleading to say, as an opponent did last week, that the Bush plan means "earn money as a worker and you are taxed; make money in the stock market and you will be taxed less." That's already true. After the passage of the 1986 Tax Reform Act, capital gains and ordinary income were taxed at the same rate, but in trade-offs during the early '90s between the previous President Bush, President Clinton and Congress, ordinary income rates were ratcheted up and capital gains rates down.

The Bush plan would leave capital gains rates alone but would cut rates for wage earners.

Another dispute is on what policy wonks call the "distributional effects" of the Bush plan. This refers to how much of the benefit goes to people at different income levels.

Critics charge that the plan gives disproportionate benefits to the rich, often pointing to the large dollar reductions that would occur at higher brackets. Proponents point to percentage reductions of tax liability, which are similar for many groups and in some cases higher for middle-income taxpayers.

Critics also often include the impact of the estate-tax repeal, which certainly benefits wealthy taxpayers. It's proper to consider that when considering the overall plan, but the number for the income-tax cuts alone are different.

But proponents ignore the fact that the plan doesn't do anything about the alternative minimum tax, a long-standing tax designed to prevent the wealthy from using legal breaks to reduce or eliminate their tax liability. The AMT tends to reduce the plan's benefits to upper-income taxpayers, making it seem less weighted toward them. But some critics think Congress is likely to reduce or otherwise change the AMT, in which case the wealthy may do better.

Got all that? No? Well, maybe you can do what they do inside the Beltway: Choose the position that benefits you personally and then adopt the arguments that support it.

Surplus Mania: A Reality Check

A federal government surplus has finally been achieved, and it has been met with pronouncements that it is a great gift for the future and with arguments about what to do with it. However, the surplus will be short-lived, it will depress economic growth, and, in any case, surpluses cannot be "used" for anything.

L. Randall Wray

According to President Clinton's State of the Union address, we are on a course to run federal government budget surpluses for the next 15 to 25 years. He proposes that we set aside most of the surpluses for the future and use 62 percent to rescue Social Security, 15 percent for Medicare, and 12 percent for Universal Savings Accounts. The publicly held debt would be cut by more than two-thirds, dropping the debt-to-GDP ratio from 44 percent today to just over 7 percent by 2014—heralded as "its lowest level since 1917"—and completely eliminating publicly held debt by 2018.

The plan was well received. A number of prominent economists, including six Nobel winners at last count, have been circulating an open letter dubbing the president's plan "good economics" and stating that "Although no one can predict how large the budget surpluses will turn out to be, we can be sure that saving them by reducing outstanding government debt is an excellent way to ease the burden on future workers of supporting an aging population." In "Saving the Surplus Will Protect Retirees" (*Wall Street Journal*, February 18, 1999), Lawrence Summers, deputy secretary of the Treasury, and Janet Yellen, chair of the President's Council of Economic Advisers, assured us that the president's proposal to "lock away" most of the projected budget surpluses in the Social Security Trust Fund is based on "sound accounting" and that it will extend Social Security's solvency through 2055. David Broder's *Washington Post* article (February 7) proclaimed the plan to be "the greatest gift to our children" because it will "help grow the economy" by "raising national savings."

Essentially, the president's plan would use about three-fourths of projected surpluses to retire Treasury debt held by the public, but would then issue new, nonmarketable Treasury debt to be held in the Social Security Trust Fund. Unfortunately, the accounting is not sound, and a policy that would preserve surpluses in an attempt to retire Treasury debt held by the public is anything but a gift to our children.

Reality Check

The federal government has been in debt every year but one since 1776. Far from viewing government debt as a horror to be avoided, at least some of the founding fathers recognized the benefits. Thomas Paine proclaimed that "No nation ought to be without a debt" for "a national debt is a national bond." Alexander Hamilton asserted that "A national debt, if it is not excessive, will be to us a national blessing." Andrew Jackson, however, labeled the public debt a "national curse" and, like President Clinton, set out to retire it. By January 1835, for the first and only time in U.S. history, the public debt was retired, and a budget surplus was maintained for the next two years in order to accumulate what Treasury Secretary Levi Woodbury called "a fund to meet future deficits." In 1837 the economy collapsed into a deep depression that drove the budget into deficit, and the federal government has been in debt ever since.

Since 1776 there have been six periods of substantial budget surpluses and significant reduction of the debt. From 1817 to 1821 the national debt fell by 29 percent; from 1823 to 1836 it was eliminated (Jackson's efforts); from 1852 to 1857 it fell by 59 percent, from 1867 to 1873 by 27 percent, from 1880 to 1893 by more than 50 percent, and from 1920 to 1930 by about a third. The United States has also experienced six periods of depression. The depressions began in 1819, 1837, 1857, 1873, 1893, and 1929. Every significant reduction of the outstanding debt has been followed by a depression, and every depression has been preceded by significant debt reduction. Further, every budget surplus has been followed, sooner or later, by renewed deficits. However, correlation—even where perfect—never proves causation. Is there any reason to suspect that government surpluses are harmful?

At the macroeconomic level, government expenditures generate private sector income; taxes reduce disposable income. When government spending exceeds tax revenue (a budget deficit), there is a net addition to private sector disposable income.

This addition may well have secondary and tertiary and even further effects (for example, households may spend on goods produced domestically or abroad, thereby raising consumption or imports as measured in national GDP accounts). When the Treasury sells bonds, some of that extra disposable income is devoted to saving, accumulated as private sector wealth held in the form of government debt. Even if the Treasury did not sell the bonds, however, the private sector would be wealthier by an amount equal to the government's deficit, but this would be held in the form of non-interest-earning cash (and bank reserves) for the simple reason that the total value of checks issued by the Treasury to finance expenditures would exceed the total value of checks written by the private sector to pay taxes.

When someone in the private sector receives a Treasury check, the check is deposited in a private bank, whose reserve account at the Fed is credited; at the same time the Treasury's deposit at the Fed is debited. When someone in the private sector writes a check to pay taxes, the taxpayer's bank deposit is debited; at the same time the Fed credits the Treasury's deposit and debits the private bank's reserves. When depositors withdraw cash from banks, the banks' reserves are reduced as the Fed issues currency. The sale of Treasury bonds also reduces bank reserves because bond buyers pay with checks drawn on private banks, which leads the Fed to debit bank reserves and credit the Treasury's deposit.

In this way government deficits result in a net increase to bank reserves and cash held by the public. Most of this increase is then drained as the Treasury sells bonds. In other words, government deficits always add disposable income and wealth to the private sector; the income is received first as a Treasury check and then may be transformed into an interest-earning government debt.

Our economy connot continue to grow robustly as the government sucks disposable income and wealth from the private sector by running surpluses. When the economy slows, the surpluses will disappear automatically—and because the private sector will eventually demand that the government stop draining income from the economy.

On the other hand, when tax revenues exceed government spending (a budget surplus), private sector disposable income is reduced. Again, there may be further effects (consumers may cut back spending, for example). Because checks received by the Treasury exceed the value of checks issued by the Treasury whenever there is a surplus, outstanding cash and bank reserves will be reduced. To restore cash and reserves, the private sector sells Treasury bonds. The bonds are purchased by the Fed and the Treasury; the purchase restores reserves and cash. (Sales of bonds between private sector entities cannot add reserves or cash; they simply shift reserves and cash from one "pocket" to another.) Note that if the Treasury refused to buy the bonds (that is, refused to retire outstanding debt), then only the Fed would

be left to buy them. This is why any sustained surpluses *must* be met by Treasury retirement of the debt, for otherwise the Fed would accumulate vast holdings of Treasury debt (on which the Treasury pays interest) while the Treasury would hold huge deposits in its checking account at the Fed. (In practice, the Treasury tries to end each day with a deposit of $5 billion.)

Movements of the budget position are largely automatic. Rapid economic growth, such as that experienced in the United States since 1992 or in Japan previous to 1990, tends to cause tax revenues to rise faster than government spending, resulting in surpluses. Recessions and depressions tend to cause tax revenues to fall as spending rises, resulting in deficits. Many economists focus on the secondary or tertiary effects of government deficits and surpluses. While they might agree that deficits increase disposable income and private sector wealth, they argue that deficits also increase interest rates and thus depress investment or that households reduce consumption on the expectation that tax rates will be increased in the future. They argue that while surpluses might reduce disposable income and private sector wealth, they also lower interest rates and thus spur private capital formation. While I believe these arguments are based on faulty reasoning, it is possible that under some conditions the secondary effects might outweigh the primary effects so that, at least for a while, deficits might depress the private sector and surpluses might stimulate it. However, history suggests that over the longer run, deficits stimulate the economy and surpluses are harmful.

Deficits and Growth; Surpluses and Stagnation

If, as projected, the federal government continues to run surpluses (resulting in Treasury debt retirement), this must as a matter of course remove $4.5 trillion of private sector wealth over the next 15 years. Can an economy withstand such a bloodletting? Our own history suggests not, and we can also look to the recent experience of Japan.

The Great Depression followed persistent surpluses in the 1920s. Real GDP fell from $791 billion (1992$) in 1929 to $577 billion by 1933. What is often not recognized is that real GDP then grew to $832 billion by 1937. In real terms, this is the second-fastest growth in this century, topped only by the World War II boom. However, the rapid growth caused the budget to move from deficit to surplus by 1937, which then caused real GDP to fall to $801 billion in 1938. As growth turned negative, a deficit was restored and GDP began to grow again. At the end of the 1930s and the beginning of the 1940s private demand grew robustly (partly due to wartime demand), which again moved the budget to surplus. This time, however, unprecedented wartime deficits led to the fastest real growth of this century; real GDP grew by 50 percent between 1941 and 1944. After the war, from 1945 to 1947, deficits declined and GDP fell by 12 percent; the drop in 1946 rivaled that of the worst year of the Great Depression.

The economy emerged from World War II in 1945 with a record debt-to-GDP ratio. Since the war we have had the longest depression-free period in the nation's history. We have, however, had nine recessions, each of which was preceded by a

Figure 1 Surpluses and Recessions—the Postwar Evidence

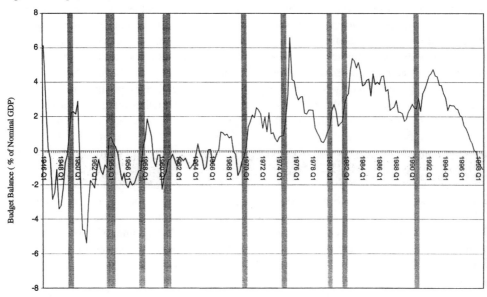

Note: Signs are reversed. A deficit is therefore given a positive value and a surplus is given a negative value. Data are from Haver Analytics Inc. Shaded areas indicate recessions.

reduction of deficits relative to GDP (see Figure 1). The deficit fell rapidly toward the end of the Carter presidency, preceding the deepest recession since the Great Depression. In spite of President Reagan's pledge to balance the budget, he presided over the largest deficits we had seen since World War II. To some extent, the deficits grew because of the economic slow-down; however, tax cuts and spending increases (primarily for defense) caused a discretionary increase of the deficit. The "Reagan boom" lasted from November 1982 to July 1990, the longest expansion in the postwar period (unless it is surpassed by the current expansion). Predictably, this reduced the deficit relative to GDP and preceded the Bush recession. In the early years of the Clinton presidency, the deficit grew again and was projected to continue. However, as a result of the long expansion and budget agreements, the deficit was entirely eliminated last year, and we experienced our first budget surplus in a generation.

Americans know that Japan's growth rate in the 1980s was the envy of the world, but they are generally unaware that the government deficits as a percent of GDP rivaled those in the United States. The enormous growth of the 1980s caused government tax revenue to rise faster than spending so that by 1990 the budget moved to surplus. The Japanese economy moved into a recession-cum-depression from which it has not been able to recover. Government deficits have been restored, but as a result of the sluggish economy, not as a result of discretionary, expansive, fiscal policy. While there have been some small initiatives to cut taxes and increase government spending, Japan has relied on monetary policy. For the second time in a year, Japan is pushing interest rates essentially to zero in an attempt to stimulate the economy. To this point, the most expansive monetary policy the world has seen since World War II still has not succeeded in jump-starting Japan's economy. This might serve as a cautionary tale for those who believe that Chairman Greenspan can keep the U.S. expansion going in spite of budget surpluses that are expected to rise well above 2 percent of GDP early next century.

Can a Surplus Be "Saved"?

Gertrude Stein once said of the city of Oakland, "There is no there there." Those who believe that a surplus can be "saved" for the future or "used" to finance tax cuts or spending increases do not understand the nature of a surplus. There is no "surplus" there for the purpose of "saving" or "use." A surplus is measured as a flow, with tax receipts over the year greater than government spending. The stock or balance sheet implication is that outstanding government debt (whether that be in the form of cash, bank reserves, or interest-earning debt) is reduced. If the government were to retire all the outstanding debt and then continue to run surpluses, these could be accumulated only in the form of claims on the private sector (that is, private sector indebtedness). During any period the government can always choose to spend more (or less), in which case the surplus over the period may be lower (or higher); similarly, it can increase (or decrease) taxes, in which case the surplus may rise (or fall).

Of course, the impact of such fiscal changes on the surplus will depend in a complicated way on the secondary, tertiary, and further impacts discussed above. The conventional thinking that underlies all the projections is that surpluses have positive impacts on private sector saving, investment, and growth. But whether or not that is true, it is irrelevant to the discussions about "what to do with the surplus." The president's plan calls for most of the projected surpluses to be used for debt retirement (as, by definition, they must) with a percentage of this then matched by creation of new Treasury debt to be held by Social

Security. In other words, the projected surpluses have nothing to do with "rescuing" Social Security except to provide a number that can be used to calculate how much new debt should be created so that the government can owe itself. The president could just as easily have proposed that we immediately create a nonmarketable Treasury liability equal to the entire discounted Social Security shortfall and stick that in the Trust Fund today. Or, he could have proposed that we do this in 2020 or whenever Social Security revenues fall short of spending. And there is no reason to "rescue" Social Security only through 2055; if a nonmarketable Treasury IOU can save it, we can save it through 2075 and beyond right now by giving it an IOU worth quadrillions to be cashed in as necessary.

When Social Security runs short and needs to start cashing in its quadrillions, its deficit will add net spending to the rest of the government's budget. Whether that budget is balanced or in deficit or in surplus, there will be some amount of total government spending (including Social Security) and some amount of total tax revenue (including payroll taxes) that will result in a fiscal stance that will generate secondary, tertiary, and so forth effects on the economy. The quadrillions held by Social Security will change none of this in any way. In spite of the claim by Summers and Yellen that "locking away" surpluses to save Social Security is "sound accounting," it is actually nonsense.

Conclusions

It is difficult to take seriously any analysis that begins with the projection that our government will run surpluses for the next 15 or 25 years. Part of our skepticism comes from the inherent difficulty in making projections. Summers and Yellen note, "Today, the U.S. debt held by the public is $1.2 trillion less than was projected in early 1993." A projection made just six years ago missed the mark by more than a trillion dollars. A few trillion here and a few trillion there can really add up to big errors over a couple of decades.

Even more important, our economy cannot continue to grow robustly as the government sucks disposable income and wealth from the private sector by running surpluses. When the economy slows, the surpluses will disappear automatically— and because the private sector will eventually demand that the government stop draining income from the economy. Tax cuts will be rushed through Congress and the president will put forward spending initiatives.

Finally, surpluses, even if realized, cannot be "locked away" for future use by retiring baby boomers. In every period that

government spending falls short of tax revenues, outstanding government debt is retired. Equivalently, the private sector's stock of wealth is reduced (since a budget surplus reduces disposable income, and this shows up as a reduction of government debt in private portfolios). There is simply no "surplus" that can be "spent" or even "saved." Should the government decide to spend more, that simply increases spending relative to taxes and results in a smaller budget surplus. When total federal government revenue falls short of expenditures (including those associated with Social Security), the Treasury will issue new debt to the public to cover the difference. But it must do this whether or not there is a Trust Fund. Neither budget surpluses over the next 15 years nor accounting fictions can change that simple fact. There may be good (noneconomic) reasons for keeping Social Security accounts separately from the rest of the budget, but this should never lead one to believe that a revenue shortfall can be cured by having the government issue IOUs to itself.

Bibliography

Office of the Press Secretary, The White House. "Fact Sheet on Reserving Surpluses for the Future." February 17, 1998.

Tett, Gillian, Naoko Nakamae, and Gerard Baker. "Japan Acts to Cut Long-Term Bond Market Interest Rates." *Financial Times*, February 17, 1999.

Thayer, Frederick C. "Balanced Budgets and Depressions." *American Journal of Economics and Sociology* 55 (April 1996).

——."Do Balanced Budgets Cause Depressions?" *Social Policy* 25 (Summer 1995).

Wray, L. Randall. *Understanding Modern Money: The Key to Full Employment and Price Stability.* Aldershot, U.K.: Elgar, 1999.

Related Publications

For additional Levy Institute research on this subject, see:

David Alan Aschauer, *How Should the Surpluses Be Spent?* Policy Note 1998/2

Dimitri B. Papadimitriou and L. Randall Wray, *What to Do with the Surplus: Fiscal Policy and the Coming Recession,* Policy Note 1998/6

L. Randall Wray, *The Emperor Has No Clothes: President Clinton's Proposed Social Security Reform,* Policy Note 1999/2

L. Randall Wray is a senior scholar at The Jerome Levy Economics Institute and author of *Understanding Modern Money: The Key to Full Employment and Price Stability* (Elgar, 1999). Marc-André Pigeon, of the Levy Institute, provided valuable research assistance.

The Deficit: America's Credibility GAP

Growing deficits. Out-of-control federal spending.
Rising debt. With the budget suddenly an election issue,
it's time for some straight talk.

By Shawn Tully

WHEN ALAN GREENSPAN TESTIFIED BEFORE CONGRESS IN mid-February, the Fed chairman delivered a Valentine's Day garland to the recent performance of the U.S. economy, lauding the "stunning increases in productivity" that have fueled the recovery. But that same testimony included a far darker message: Greenspan reminded Americans that the U.S. economy faces a giant threat in the guise of big budget deficits stretching far into the future. In the past, Greenspan had mainly warned of the looming dangers of deficits in a decade or so, when the baby-boomers start retiring en masse. This time he hinted strongly that raging deficits could derail today's recovery. "Deficits could cause difficulties even in the relatively near term," intoned the chairman in his usual courtly style. In Greenspan-speak, that means the wolf is at the door, and he could start biting in months, not years.

It is astonishing how quickly we've gone from big budget surpluses to massive budget deficits. Between 1998 and 2001, the U.S. generated some $560 billion in surpluses—including a $236 billion surplus in 2000—and it was widely assumed that the era of big deficits was over. Indeed, in 2000 the Clinton administration was giddily predicting that the country would pay off all of the debt held by the public—some $3.4 trillion—by 2010.

But a year later the budget fell into deficit, and it's been spiraling downward ever since. Last year the deficit was $375 billion, and this year it is projected to be a staggering $521 billion. (The government's fiscal year ends in September.) Not surprisingly, the deficit is quickly becoming a hot election-year issue. Which is to say, there's not a lot of straight talk on the subject.

Democrats invoke the need to balance the budget, but they never mention the source of half our fiscal mess, that government spending is now largely out of control. The Bush administration, meanwhile, has projected that the deficit will shrink in half by 2009. But to get to that number, the administration had to make a series of assumptions that are nothing short of laughable, as we shall see. Add to those bogus assumptions the administration's steely determination to not raise taxes, and, well, we've got a big problem.

At every step, this administration has EXACERBATED THE BUDGET DEFICIT with its shocking lack of fiscal restraint.

What's truly scary—what makes this deficit problem different from past deficits—is the trend: huge budget deficits from here to eternity. There is simply no way, with current government spending patterns, that the budget will ever be back in balance—not without tax hikes that would be unacceptably high and ruinous to the economy.

What is also scary, though, is the seeming indifference of this administration to the looming deficit problem. In a widely quoted passage from the new book *The Price of Loyalty*, Bush's former Treasury Secretary, Paul O'Neill—the one real deficit hawk in the administration—quotes Vice President Dick Cheney as telling him, "Reagan proved that deficits don't matter." If that is really what the Bush administration believes—and to be fair, Cheney denies it—then we're in a lot more trouble than we realize.

Deficits matter for three reasons. First, they increase the national debt, which in turn drives government spending even higher by tacking on ever-increasing interest expenses each year. Second, they put our economy at the mercy of foreign governments and investors, whom we have to count on to buy that debt. And third, they represent an unwillingness to come to terms with government spending. The more the government spends as a percentage of GDP—and right now the federal government absorbs 20% of GDP—the greater the drain on resources available for Americans to spend and invest in the private sector. As legendary economist Milton Friedman told Fortune, "What really matters is spending. Whether you finance the increased spending by borrowing or by raising taxes, you're leaving less resources for the private sector."

That is not to say the deficits are always bad. Think of the government like a household: If it borrows to meet an emergency, and if the borrowing is temporary—and creditors know it's temporary—the dollars generated by the debt can prove a boon by sparking economic growth. To put it another way, deficits aren't a problem if they're cyclical—if the creditors believe that as soon as the economy rebounds, the U.S. can bring its revenues back in line with spending.

Right now America is leaning heavily on foreign investors and governments, especially Japan and China, to buy the government debt that funds the deficits. At the moment, those investors are giving us the benefit of the doubt: They're still convinced that we'll get a grip on our deficits. That's the reason they're still buying our 30-year Treasuries for a rock-bottom 5% yield. But if the rest of the world loses confidence in our fiscal management—and that is now a legitimate fear—interest rates will spike. As Greenspan says, America must take action toward "restoring fiscal sanity."

We have, of course, been down this road before. In the late 1970s, deficit spending and, most of all, too much monetary stimulus by the Fed helped push up interest rates to the point where, by the early 1980s, they were wreaking enormous havoc on the economy. Then-Fed chairman Paul Volcker succeeded in squeezing inflation out of the economy, though in the process we had to endure a terrible recession and double-digit unemployment in parts of the country. But deficit spending soared under Ronald Reagan's presidency—and interest rates remained relatively high. Still, even during the Reagan era, the deficit began coming down—in part because Reagan signed a series of tax hikes into law.

In retrospect, the presidencies of George H.W. Bush and Bill Clinton represent something of a golden age of fiscal management. In 1991, displaying the kind of admirable political will that it could use now, Congress passed the hugely important Budget Enforcement Act, which clamped tight caps on discretionary spending, which includes all the money that Congress has to authorize each year—as opposed to mandatory spending, which includes big-ticket entitlement programs like Social Se-

curity and Medicare. The law also forced Congress to pay for the new entitlement spending with cuts in other entitlements, notably Medicare. That same year Bush signed into law his own tax hike—a move that helped doom his presidency, because it went back on his infamous "Read my lips" pledge, but which also helped bring the deficit under control.

The effect of the Budget Enforcement Act was quite stunning: From 1995 to 1998, outlays for nondefense discretionary spending grew by an astoundingly modest 1% a year. By 2000, government outlays had dropped to 18% of GDP, from 22% in 1992. By any measure, that was a heroic accomplishment, though strong growth helped a lot.

"Deficits could cause difficulty even in the short term," says the Fed chairman. IN GREENSPAN-SPEAK, THE WOLF IS AT THE DOOR

The combination of spending restraint and tax hikes helped revenues take off. But there was also some luck involved. First, the peace dividend at the end of the Cold War enabled the U.S. to vastly shrink spending on defense. Between 1990 and 1999, military outlays dropped from $300 billion to $275 billion. Second, in the late 1990s, entitlements still weren't growing as fast as GDP—thanks to a moderation in health-care costs and the slow rate of increase in Social Security beneficiaries. Amazingly, between 1996 and 2000, spending on Social Security, Medicare, and Medicaid actually *fell*, from 8.2% of GDP to 7.6%. And finally there was the effect of the bull market and the Internet bubble. In 2000 and 2001, for instance, receipts from capital gains jumped to more than $100 billion a year after averaging less than $50 billion in the mid-1990s.

Today, of course, the situation is virtually the opposite. Most of the uncontrollable factors that helped create a surplus in the late 1990s pushed us toward a deficit by 2002. Take capital gains. With the market in the doldrums, revenues from capital gains have shrunk from $119 billion in 2000 to $45 billion just three years later. In the wake of 9/11, Bush has understandably ramped up defense spending far above what Clinton planned. Bush's forecasts for future defense spending don't look big until you consider that he's leaving out future appropriations for Iraq, which are estimated at $50 billion next year alone. Homeland security accounts for billions more. Rising health-care charges have driven up the cost of Medicare and Medicaid. By 2010, shifting demographics will cause a steep rise in Social Security payouts. Today those three huge entitlements are up to 8% of GDP and are due to grow to 10% by 2014—and an intolerable 14% by 2030.

But at every step along the way, this administration has exacerbated the deficit problem with its shocking lack of fiscal restraint. One example was the steep tax cuts President Bush first proposed in 2001. The original rationale was that taxpayers should get a portion of the surplus rebated to them. Then the economy started faltering, and the surplus began shrinking. In the face of these changing circumstances, Treasury Secretary O'Neill argued that the tax cuts should be abandoned or at least pared back. But the administration pushed them through anyway, arguing that the weak economy needed the stimulus. By 2003, receipts as a percentage of GDP slumped to 16.5%, a postwar low; this year they're expected to fall even lower.

What's more, although the administration gives lip service to the Republican credo of smaller government, its actions suggest otherwise. Just look at the numbers: From 2001 to 2004, in a mere three years, spending outside defense and homeland security and defense-oriented foreign aid has jumped 23%, or more than 7% annually. In the same period, federal aid to education, for example, rose almost 50%, to $57 billion. Discretionary spending on health care, a category that includes the budgets of the NIH and CDC, rose 44% in those three years. The result? Federal spending is back up to 20% of GDP, and the Brookings Institution estimates that it is on track to reach 22% of GDP by 2014. "Within only a few years," concluded a recent report by the International Monetary Fund, "the hard-won gains of the previous decade have been lost." That same report concluded that about half of the big swing from surplus to deficit was due to the stock market crash and the economy's slowdown. The

other 50% was a product of the Bush tax cuts and the big ramp-up in federal spending.

Perhaps the best single example of lack of spending discipline was the Medicare prescription-drug benefit Congress passed—and the President eagerly signed—in late 2003. By the administration's own (undoubtedly conservative) calculations, the new Medicare drug benefit will cost $60 billion a year by 2009. Without it, Medicare spending was expected to rise around 6% annually. With the drug benefit, Medicare spending is likely to jump over 10% a year. It's a budget breaker if ever there was one.

SO WHAT IS THE BUSH ADMINISTRATION PROPOSING TO GET THE deficit back under control? So far, not much—which is precisely what has to make our creditors nervous. White House budget projections over the next five years call for the deficit to shrink in half—but many of the assumptions upon which that number is based are simply not realistic. For instance, it assumes that the economy will grow at an average rate of 3.5% from 2004 to 2009, which is pretty optimistic. ("Achieving 3.5% would be a record worth crowing over," says Robert Reischauer, former chief of the Congressional Budget Office.) It also assumes that

Bush's Budget Man Tries to Explain His Numbers

Even partisan Republicans have expressed deep skepticism about President Bush's budget's fiscal responsibility—or lack thereof. **Joshua Bolten**, *the director of the Office of Management and Budget, took some time to speak with* FORTUNE *writer Jeremy Kahn about President Bush's budget. For a man in the hot seat, he sounds awfully serene. Here are edited excerpts. (For a longer version, see foriune.com.)*

What parts of the budget demonstrate hard-nosed fiscal responsibility?

There are a number of tough calls to be made. For example, while we are substantially increasing the federal commitment to homeland-security spending, we have shifted our emphasis to high-threat areas. So the bulk of our federal assistance will go to those areas that the Department of Homeland Security operation thinks are most under threat. Now that's a politically difficult thing to do. On its merits it's absolutely the right thing to do.

Can the administration really persuade Congress to hold nondefense discretionary spending growth to 0.5% a year?

There is always pressure in Congress to spend more, but we've heard from some

members in the Republican caucus that they would like to be even slightly more restrained than the President has been. So we think we've hit it about straight down the middle of the fairway as far as what is both sensible and realistic. We'll see what Congress does with it. I think there is a good prospect of achieving an '05 budget that is very close to, if not exactly on, the numbers the President has sent up.

If Congress does not hold spending to those levels, is the President going to start vetoing spending bills?

The President hasn't needed to veto bills in the past because the leadership in Congress has ensured that bills fall within his parameters. Last year is a good example. The President set some limits, and it was agreed to by the Republican leadership [of the House and Senate]. There are plenty of complaints about the priorities chosen by Congress in some of those bills, but in terms of the overall spending restraints, Congress lived within the limits the President asked for. And I am very optimistic that we'll be able to do the same or better this year.

There's criticism that the administration's revenue projections are unrealistic too.

I think the revenue projections in the budget are realistic. If anything they're conservative. We've chosen a conservative growth rate of 4.4% for this year. Blue Chip [an organization that pools the forecasts of Wall Street economists] is now at 4.6% and CBO [the Congressional Budget Office] is now at 4.8%, so the growth rates are conservative.

Some argue that the U.S. has always managed to grow itself out of deficits. Can we simply grow ourselves out of this one?

History tells us that the projections are often wrong, and it could well be that we have underestimated economic growth and therefore the revenues coming in. But I don't think we should count on just growing ourselves out of this deficit. We also need to exercise serious fiscal restraint. I think that is well reflected in the budget that's been presented in '05 and in our assumptions going forward.

nondefense discretionary spending, excluding Homeland Security, will drop in actual dollars, from $454 billion to $430 billion, from 2005 to 2009. This isn't just optimistic, it's implausible; over the past 40 years, discretionary spending has never dropped for a sustained period. What dropped was the rate of increase.

It gets worse. The Bush budget offers $65 billion in refunds to help uninsured Americans purchase health-care coverage—but doesn't include a concomitant $65 billion rise in spending. Why? Because it promises to find $65 billion in offsetting spending cuts. How? It doesn't say.

Or take the alternative minimum tax, a complicated levy that imposes a surcharge on high-earning taxpayers with lots of itemized deductions. In 2001 and 2003, Congress lifted the amount of income excepted from AMT from $45,000 to $58,000 until 2004. But though the administration swears it is dedicated to reforming and reducing the AMT, its budget assumes just the opposite: that the AMT exemption will revert to $45,000 from 2006 to 2009—which would result in 30 million Americans paying the tax by 2009. It's hard to imagine that the administration would allow that to happen—and yet without it, tax revenues will fall by 3% from current White House forecasts.

The Brookings Institution ran numbers using more realistic forecasts for spending increases (higher) and tax receipts (lower) than in the President's highly optimistic budget. Though Brookings is a liberal think tank, its spending numbers are fairly conservative; if anything, they could get far worse. Brookings reckons that even if Congress imposes relatively spartan restraint on discretionary spending, the deficit will still stand at $500 billion in 2009, precisely where it is today.

IT'S NOT JUST THE BROOKINGS INSTITUTION EITHER. MOST TOP Republicans don't believe the White House numbers. "It will be extremely difficult to reduce the deficit below today's dollar levels at all over the next five years," says Bill Hoagland, budget advisor to Senate Majority Leader Bill Frist.

And that's the real problem. It's not so much the current size of the deficit—which at 4.5% of GDP is actually smaller than the Reagan deficits of the mid-1980s—it's the trend. Put simply, using reasonable assumptions, spending is slated to remain far higher than revenues into the blue horizon. That's what has to be reversed—and quickly. Otherwise, America's fiscal credibility is at risk.

So what should we do? For starters, we need to bring back the Budget Enforcement Act, which expired in 2002. What was so important about the BEA is that it forced Congress and the White House to make tough choices: If politicians wanted to up spending in one area, they had to find offsetting cuts in another area.

To its credit, the Bush administration has suggested reviving the BEA. Under its plan, the law would cap increases in all discretionary spending at less than 1% a year, while requiring that all new spending legislation be offset by cuts of equal size in other entitlements. Bush's plan doesn't go far enough, though. It should also include another set of sharp teeth in the original BEA: Any new tax cuts should also trigger equal cuts in spending or tax hikes somewhere else.

Ultimately, the goal should be to keep federal spending right where it is now, at about 20% of GDP, while balancing the budget over, say, a ten-year span. To do so will require more than just controlling spending, important though that is. It will also mean imposing some tax increases—or rolling back recent tax cuts.

Most painful of all, it will require regaining control over entitlements, especially Social Security and Medicare. "They're America's exploding cigar," says Bill Gale, a senior fellow at Brookings. According to the OMB, if entitlements are left alone, federal spending as a share of GDP will grow from 20% to 28% by 2035. Though they remain America's biggest sacred cows, entitlement programs will break us if we remain unwilling to wrestle them to the ground.

Two possible ideas: Social Security benefits are currently indexed to the consumer price index, despite strong evidence that the CPI overstates cost-of-living increases. Greenspan recommends moving to a more accurate index, which would lower the annual benefit increases. Another good idea: Raise the eligibility age to 68, reflecting the greater longevity of Americans nearing retirement.

If the deficits keep running, America's total debt will hit $9.7 trillion by 2014. That's 54% of GDP, the highest number in 50 years and a major red flag for the foreign investors buying our debt. By then we'd be drowning in $500 billion a year in interest payments, three times the current amount.

That's the bad news. The good news is that Americans are starting to pay attention to the growing deficit. It's beginning to feel a little like 1992, when Ross Perot ran for President using his famous charts that illustrated the nation's growing sea of red ink. "I've seen the budget issue swing from big attention to lack of attention," says Hoagland, Senator Frist's budget expert. "I'm a deficit hawk. Now I'm back in vogue." Not a moment too soon.

REPORTER ASSOCIATE: *Christopher Tkaczyk*
FEEDBACK stully@fortunemail.com

The Tax Man Cometh:
Consumer Spending and Tax Payments

Peter S. Yoo

April 15. It causes much anxiety, with last-minute rushing to the post office. Of course tax day also spurs anger, especially in Americans who owe the government money. Surprisingly, people put themselves through this ritual year after year, undoubtedly promising themselves that they will never again wait until the eleventh hour. Paying taxes is after all one of life's certainties.

Unfortunately, the disruptions tax payments cause may go beyond mere annoyance. Early in 1995, the growth of personal spending—as measured by personal consumption expenditures—slowed sharply, increasing a meager 0.1 percent in April. Analysts immediately blamed tax payments for the slowdown in consumer spending. "One of the major reasons for the weakness in consumer spending this spring was the sharp rise in payments among many homeowners and affluent taxpayers to cover their unexpectedly high 1994 income tax obligations.... Many economists have cited the slow pace at which the Internal Revenue Service [IRS] issued tax refunds this year as a chief culprit for weak consumer spending."[1]

Indeed, certain circumstances increased individual tax liabilities in April 1995. High-income taxpayers saw their taxes rise as a result of the Omnibus Budget Reconciliation Act (OBRA) of 1993, which increased their taxes retroactively. The act gave them the option of distributing their increased tax bill over three years. The second installment was due in April 1995. In addition, the IRS was more careful in its review of tax returns, delaying some tax refunds.[2] Both of these factors increased individual tax payments in April, even though the increase attributable to refund delays was temporary. The story for the analysts, therefore, was simple: Tax payments went up, disposable income fell, and so consumer spending fell.

Is the story so simple? Does consumer spending change when tax payments change? To answer this, I present several episodes in which tax payments changed noticeably.

TAXES AND CONSUMER SPENDING

Traditional economic models present consumer spending as a function of disposable personal income. So any change in tax payments directly affects disposable personal income, thereby changing consumer spending. Typically, these models do not include expectations about future income. Because changes in tax payments reduce current disposable personal income dollar for dollar, the models predict that such changes contemporaneously have a large effect on consumer spending.

Recent models of consumer behavior, however, are more ambiguous about the contemporaneous link between tax payments and consumer spending. These models argue that people consider their lifetime resources when making spending decisions. If this indeed is the case, individuals should adjust their savings, thereby spreading the impact of tax liability changes over a longer period. In essence, these models assert that people have other and possibly better alternatives to merely changing their spending dollar for dollar because they can adjust their mix of consumption expenditures and savings.

Another reason to be wary of analyses that attribute changes in consumer spending to changes in tax payments is that changes in personal income also induce dollar-for-dollar changes in disposable personal income. (The two measures of income are related by the following national income accounting identity: disposable personal income = personal income – personal tax and nontax payments.) So there may be periods when changes in consumer spending are in response to changes in personal income and not to changes in tax payments. That is what most likely happened early in 1995. As the growth of personal consumption expenditures fell, personal income growth also fell. Personal income grew 0.5 percent in March 1995 but rose only 0.2 percent in April 1995. It is likely, therefore, that the slowdown in personal income growth accounted for the slowdown in consumer spending.

TABLE 1

Changes in Individual Tax Liabilities

Act/Event	Month Enacted	Effective Date	Description
Revenue Act of 1964	February 1964	March 1964	$11 billion tax cut
Revenue and Expenditure Control Act of 1968	June 1968	April 1968	10 percent surcharge
Tax Reform Act of 1969	December 1969	January 1970	Extended surcharge
Revenue Act of 1978	November 1978	January 1979	$19 billion tax cut
Economic Recovery Act of 1981	August 1981	October 1981	25 percent cut in tax rates
Tax Reform Act of 1986	October 1986	January 1987	Major tax code overhaul
OBRA 1990	October 1990	January 1991	Tax increase on high income
OBRA 1993	August 1993	January 1993	Tax increase on high income
Tax Rebate 1975	March 1975	May 1975	Up to $200 tax rebate
Refund Delays*			

*Delays in tax refunds starting in March 1985, mostly reversed by May 1985.

Any examination of the relationship between changes in tax liabilities and changes in consumer spending, therefore, should consider a wide time frame, changes in personal income, and the possibility that individuals diffuse the impact of such changes by altering their savings. First, in my analysis, I use a 12-month window surrounding the changes in tax payments. This provides a time frame in which to observe the response of consumer spending beyond the period when a change in tax payment occurred.

Second, the analysis asks how much individuals spent out of every dollar of personal income and disposable personal income. Economists call this measure of spending *the average propensity to consume*— merely a ratio of consumer spending to a measure of personal income:

(1) $\quad APC$ out of $PI = \dfrac{PCE}{PI}$

(2) $\quad APC$ out of $DPI = \dfrac{PCE}{DPI(= PI - T)'}$

where *APC* is average propensity to consume, *PI* is personal income, *DPI* is disposable personal income, *PCE* is personal consumption expenditures, and *T* is tax and nontax payments.

Typically, these two measures of *APC* move in tandem, but there are occasions when the relative movements diverge. The divergences occur because any change in tax payments affects *disposable* personal income dollar-for-dollar but has no effect on personal income. Since changes in tax liabilities do not affect personal income, *APC* out of personal income will reflect the response of consumer spending to changes in tax payments. Changes in tax liabilities do affect disposable personal income, however. So, if

consumer spending does not react to a change in tax payments, *APC* out of disposable income will move in the [same] direction of the change in tax liabilities. If consumer spending is not responsive to changes in tax liabilities, the two ratios will thus behave differently.

Finally, in my analysis I track the behavior of personal saving because individuals may use their savings as a buffer against changes in tax liabilities, increasing the amount saved if tax payments fall and reducing the amount saved or borrowed if tax payments increase. I therefore examine the behavior of personal saving rates, ratios of personal savings to personal and disposable personal incomes.

IDENTIFYING CHANGES IN TAX LIABILITIES

To examine the relationship between taxes and consumer spending, I first had to identify periods in which tax payments increased or decreased. The personal income tax rate changed at least eight times from 1959 through 1995 because of the Revenue Act of 1964, Revenue and Expenditure Control Act of 1968, Tax Reform Act of 1969, Revenue Act of 1978, Economic Recovery Act of 1981, Tax Reform Act of 1986, OBRA 1990, and OBRA 1993.[3] Table 1 provides a brief summary of these tax law changes. Pechman (1987), Hakkio et al. (1993) and *Congress and the Nation* provide more comprehensive summaries about the changes in the tax code.

The Department of Commerce publishes seasonally adjusted, monthly estimates of personal tax and nontax payments.[4] These estimates include federal, state, and local taxes, as well as nontax payments. Figure 1 shows the path of monthly personal tax and nontax payments since 1959, and it indicates that some of the changes in federal tax laws had identifiable effects on this series. Figure 1 also shows

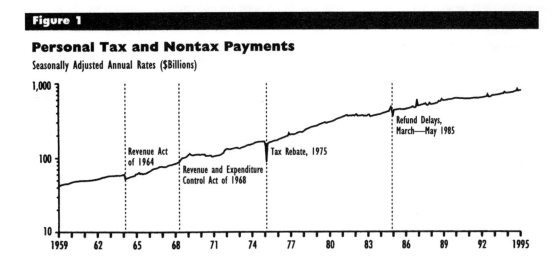

Figure 1

Personal Tax and Nontax Payments

Seasonally Adjusted Annual Rates ($Billions)

few prominent spikes that do not correspond to one of the noted changes in tax law. Personal tax and nontax payments show a sharp drop in 1975. This is attributable to a tax rebate offered in May 1975. The series also behaved oddly in early 1985 because there was a delay in tax refunds. Table 1 briefly describes these two special cases as well.

As you can see in Figure 1, not all tax law changes noted in Table 1 show changes in personal tax payments. This is probably because of changes in economic conditions or because individuals altered their behavior to circumvent the changes in the tax code. This presents a problem with the simple analysis I have proposed. Therefore, I focus on one tax cut (the Revenue Act of 1964) and one tax increase (the Revenue and Expenditure Control Act of 1968). I also examine two other episodes—the tax rebate of 1975 and the refund delays of 1985. Unlike the first two episodes, these two were unexpected or nearly unexpected. An episode's forecastability is important because modern consumption theory states that individuals adjust their behavior to minimize the disruptive nature of predictable future events. It is possible, therefore, that consumer spending did not respond contemporaneously to changes in taxes because consumers had adjusted their behavior well in advance of the changes taking effect. All four episodes show observable changes in personal tax and nontax payments.

WHAT HAPPENED TO CONSUMPTION?

Revenue Act of 1964

Congress passed the Revenue Act of 1964 in February of that year, and the changes took effect that March. The act substantially reduced individual taxes, decreasing personal tax and nontax payments by $8.1 billion between February and March.

So how did consumers react to this tax cut? Consumer expenditures, as illustrated in Figure 2, suggest consumers did not react during the 12 months surrounding the tax cut.

Figure 2

Revenue Act of 1964
Income and Consumption

Seasonally Adjusted Annual Rates ($ Billions)

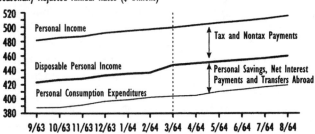

Average Propensitites to Consume

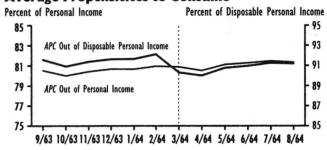

Personal Saving Rates

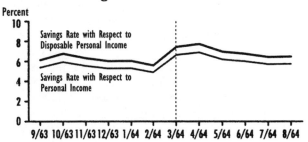

Table 2 summarizes the behavior of tax and nontax payments, personal consumption expenditures, and personal saving near the effective dates of the four episodes.

TABLE 2

Impact of Changes in Tax Liabilities*

	Tax and Nontax Payments	Personal Consumption Expenditures	Personal Saving
Revenue Act of 1964 (February–March)	-8.1	1.6	8.8
Revenue and Expenditure Control Act of 1968 (June–July)	6.0	6.8	-7.1
Tax Rebate of 1975 (April–May)	-60.1	24.2	49.0
Refund Delays of 1985 (February–March) (April–May)	30.1 -66.6	6.2 35.2	-16.2 21.3

*Changes in seasonally adjusted annual rates ($billions).

The path of consumer spending shows little discernable movement between February and March of 1964. The change in personal consumption expenditures between the two months was merely $1.6 billion. It is possible, however, that other factors (like changes in personal income) may be distorting the picture. The top panel of Figure 2 also shows that personal income growth was relatively constant during the sample period. In contrast, disposable personal income rose noticeably when the tax cut took effect.

Disposable income rose, and consumer spending did not change. What happened to the extra money? Most likely, people saved it. Personal saving rose by $8.8 billion between February and March, very close to the reduction in tax payments between the same two months. The difference between disposable personal income and personal consumption expenditures (personal savings, net interest payments, and transfers abroad) rose sharply once the tax cut took effect, corresponding to the increase in personal saving.[5] The sharp increase in personal savings of nearly the same magnitude as the drop in personal tax and nontax payments suggests that the tax cut that took place in 1964 did not affect consumer spending near the time the cut took place, but rather led individuals to save more.

Figure 2 provides another way to see what happened to consumer spending's response to the change in tax liabilities. The middle panel shows the two measures of *APC* out of income. *APC* out of personal income shows little change during the 12 months, but *APC* out of disposable personal income shows a noticeable drop between February and March of 1964. The divergence of the two ratios is consistent with the hypothesis that the tax cut did not coincide with a change in consumer spending in the short run. *APC* out of personal income did not change because neither personal consumption expenditures nor personal income changed, whereas *APC* out of disposable personal income decreased because disposable personal income increased when tax payments fell. People responded by

increasing their saving rates as indicated by the rise in the two personal saving rates between the two months in the third panel of Figure 2.

Revenue and Expenditure Control Act of 1968

The Revenue and Expenditure Control Act of 1968 provides an opportunity to see the response of consumer spending to increased tax payments. The act, established in June 1968, called for a 10 percent income-tax surcharge, retroactive to April 1968. The effect on personal tax and nontax payments began in July of the same year. Personal tax and nontax payments increased by $6 billion between June and July 1968.

How did individuals respond to the increase in tax payments? Personal consumption expenditures increased $6.8 billion between June and July, not at all consistent with the traditional theory that higher taxes reduce consumer spending. Moreover, the relative stability of personal income and personal consumption expenditures occurring at a time of increased tax payments produce the divergence of the two measures of *APC,* as shown in Figure 3. *APC* out of personal incomes shows little change during the 12 months, but *APC* out of disposable personal income shows a noticeable increase between June and July because disposable personal income fell as a result of the tax increase. This is consistent with the hypothesis that the tax increase did not affect personal consumption expenditures. How then did they pay for the additional taxes? Personal saving fell by $7.1 billion between the two months, an amount more than enough to pay for the higher tax payments. This drop in saving accounts for the fall in the two measures of personal saving rates shown in the bottom panel of Figure 3.

Tax Rebate of 1975

As a result of the tax rebate bill enacted in March 1975, the IRS issued rebate checks. This reduced personal tax and

Figure 3

Revenue Act of 1968
Income and Consumption

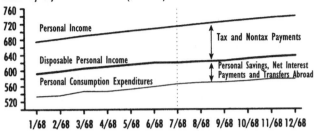

Average Propensities to Consume

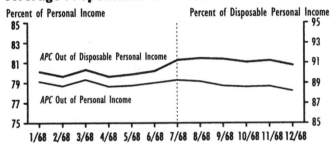

Personal Savings Rates

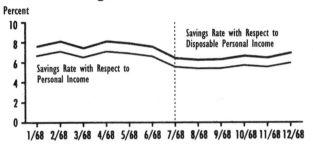

Figure 4

Tax Rebate of 1975
Income and Consumption

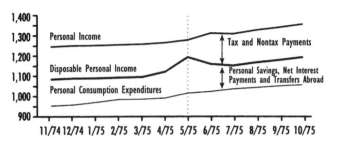

Average Propensities to Consume

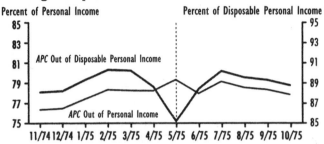

Personal Savings Rates

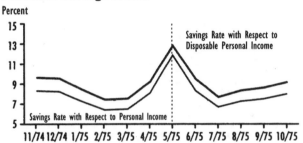

nontax payments by $60.1 billion between April and May 1975. Consumers reacted by increasing personal consumption expenditures by $24.2 billion—a large amount, but less than half the reduction in tax payments.[6] Therefore, the upward tick in *APC* out of personal income reflects an increase in consumption. The sharp drop in *APC* out of disposable income and the increase in *APC* out of personal income is consistent with the hypothesis that people spent some of, but not all, the extra money they received from the rebate. The rebate increased *disposable* personal income but did not affect personal income, as shown in Figure 4.

What was not spend was saved. Personal saving increased $49 billion, which more than accounts for the difference between the drop in tax payments and the increase in spending. The higher saving increased personal saving rates with respect to personal and disposable personal incomes. So unlike the revenue acts discussed earlier, the data indicate that there was some contemporaneous movement of consumer spending to a change in tax liabilities; however, individuals absorbed most of the

Refund Delay of 1985

In 1985 the IRS fell behind in issuing refunds because it was updating its computers. This caused an initial rise in tax payments in March. By May, however, refunds were back on track, depressing tax payments. The initial delay coincided with an increase in personal tax and nontax payments of $30.1 billion between February and March. Once the IRS resolved its problems, tax payments dropped $66.6 billion between April and May.

So what did consumers do when their promised checks were late? Personal consumption expenditures increased $6.2 billion during the delay; a $35.2 billion increase in consumer spending coincided with the reversal. The initial increase is once again contrary to the reaction typically attributed to increases in tax payments. The latter increase accounts for nearly half of the reversal in refund delays. A delay in refunds first increases net tax payments, reducing disposable income, as shown on Figure 5. So if consumer spending does not change, the ratio of consumption to personal income does not move because

Figure 5

Refund Delays of 1985
Income and Consumption

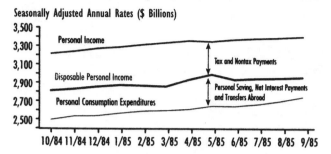

Seasonally Adjusted Annual Rates ($ Billions)

Average Propensitites to Consume

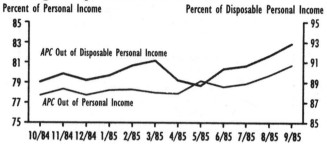

Personal Saving Rates

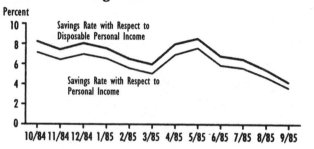

changes in tax payments. As net tax payments increased between February and March, personal saving fell $16.2 billion, then as net tax payments decreased between April and May, personal saving rose $21.3 billion. Although these figures are not as large as the changes in personal tax and nontax payments, they account for a sizable portion of the changes in taxes. Figure 5 indicates that personal saving rates with respect to personal and disposable personal incomes decreased then increased as net tax payments rose and fell.[7] It appears that individuals thus offset the negative impact of refund delays with reduced spending and saving. They then reversed their actions once they received their refunds.

CONSUMERS REACT—SOMEWHAT

My analysis suggests that consumers react only somewhat to changes in tax liabilities. The tax cut of 1964 and the tax hike of 1968 produced very little response in consumer spending. Moreover, accounting for individuals' ability to adjust to predictable events does not significantly change the conclusion about consumer sensitivity. The four cases suggest that consumers are reluctant to change their spending patterns and thus alter their savings to compensate for changes in their tax payments. If any sensitivity exists, it appears to be more in response to unexpected, rather than expected, events—even then the reaction is not large.

NOTES

31. See Johnston (1995).
32. Berry (1995) and Hershey (1995) reported that some economists attributed the slowdown in February's retail sales to the slow refunds.
33. I examined this period because personal consumption expenditure data are available back to January 1959.
34. Nontax payments include passport fees, fines and penalties, donations, and tuitions and fees paid to government-operated schools and hospitals. See Byrnes et al. (1979) for a discussion of the construction of the personal income statistics.
35. Although personal saving is only a part of this sum, it is the largest of the three components. Furthermore, net interest payments and transfers abroad did not change much during the period.
36. Shapiro and Slemrod (1995) used survey data to analyze the impact of the 1992 reduction in withholding. They found that the temporary tax cut affected consumer spending among some individuals, increasing consumer spending 43 cents for every dollar reduction in withholding. Their number shows what happened to an average dollar of additional income. A crude, comparable number is a ratio of the change in personal consumption expenditures to the change in tax payments. That ratio is 40.3 cents.
37. Wilcox (1990) studied the effects of the timing of tax refunds on consumer spending, including the 1985 delay. He found that a dollar of received tax refunds translates into 7.5 cents of additional spending.

movements in tax payments do not affect personal income. In contrast, the ratio of consumption to disposable income rises as disposable income falls. Once refunds arrive, consumers have more disposable income, but if they have not altered their spending, their *APC* out of disposable personal income falls while their *APC* out of personal income remains constant.

Figure 5 indicates that people reacted somewhat to the timing of refunds because of *APC* out of personal income shows a small decrease in March and a large increase in May. This is consistent with an initial drop followed by a rise in consumer spending in response to the timing of the refunds. The behavior of *APC* out of disposable personal income is also consistent with consumers' slight reaction to the timing of refunds. *APC* out of disposable income rose between February and March 1985 and then fell between April and May.

Again, data are consistent with the hypothesis that individuals used their savings to absorb most of the

REFERENCES

Berry, John M. "Retail Sales Fell 0.5% in February," *Washington Post,* March 15, 1995.

Byrnes, James C., et al. "Monthly Estimates of Personal Income, Taxes, and Outlays," *Survey of Current Business* (November 1979), pp. 18–37.

Congressional Quarterly Service, Inc. *Congress and the Nation* (various issues).

Hakkio, Craig, S., Mark Rush, and Timothy J. Schmidt. "The Marginal Income Tax Rate Schedule from 1930 to 1990," Federal Reserve Bank of Kansas City *Research Working Paper 93-12* (October 1993).

Hershey, Robert D., Jr. "February Retail Sales Had Surprising Slide," *New York Times,* March 15, 1995.

Johnston, David Cay. "Weak Consumer Spending is Linked to Tax Bite," *New York Times,* June 2, 1995.

Pechman, Joseph A. *Federal Tax Policy.* The Brookings Institution, 1987.

Shapiro, Matthew D., and Joel Slemrod. "Consumer Response to the Timing of Income: Evidence from a Change in Tax Withholding," *American Economic Review* (March 1995), pp. 274–83.

Wilcox, David W. "Income Tax Refunds and the Timing of Consumption Expenditure," Board of Governors of the Federal Reserve System *Working Paper Series No. 106* (April 1990).

Peter S. Yoo is an economist at the Federal Reserve Bank of St. Louis. Richard D. Taylor provided research assistance.

Reprinted with permission from *Review,* published by the Federal Reserve Bank of St. Louis, January/February 1996, pp. 37–44.

Go Figure

THE GOOD NEWS is that you might be in for a tax cut. The bad news is that you'll only get it if you behave properly. And what is the required behavior? Never fear. Congress and the White House, with the help of the Internal Revenue Service's rule writers, will be glad to detail it for you. It won't take more than a few thousand pages.

Over the past few weeks, Congress has been hard at work marking up tax bills intended to reward key groups of voters, such as married couples and heirs to substantial estates. And, while some of these bills are likely (even designed) to be vetoed, others will ultimately make it into law—if not under this administration then under the next. With projected budget surpluses mounting with every recount, it's a near certainty that Congress will sooner or later return a big chunk of that extra revenue to taxpayers.

There is, of course, some chance that the tax cut we ultimately see will be straightforward: a decrease in income tax rates plus the elimination of some of the anomalies that make the tax code so complex and so often unfair. Some chance—but not much.

The tax code, you see, has become the lawmakers' code of good conduct. Way back during the reigns of FDR, Kennedy, Johnson, and, yes, even Nixon, if the government wanted to support some worthy purpose, it funded a program—along with some (often inadequate) mechanism for administering it and judging its success. But that was before "spending" became a curse and "tax cuts" a blessing. Spending has been deemed woefully inefficient, resulting in large, unresponsive government bureaucracies that consume much of their money in overhead and redundant activity. Tax cuts, by comparison, are simplicity it-

self—the money stays right in your pocket, and you can spend it as you please, with maximum flexibility and efficiency. So these days if politicians want, for instance, to increase the supply of affordable, quality child care, they don't fund and license day care centers. Instead, they give parents a tax credit so that they can make arrangements on their own. True, in a momentary lapse in 1986, Congress dumped a lot of older tax preferences, making the code both simpler and fairer. But that, as it turned out, just cleared the way for a glut of new gimmicks—embedded in some 78 subsequent tax laws—all engineered to reward the right kind of behavior.

Here is a sample of things the current tax code encourages you to do: Get married (if your spouse doesn't hold a job); have kids (or adopt some); educate said kids (or send them to day care); get old; save money (take your choice here of seven different types of IRA accounts, including "Traditional IRA," "Spousal IRA," "SEP IRA," and the euphemistic "Simple IRA"); enjoy capital gains; suffer passive losses; and inherit a family business or farm.

If Al Gore becomes president, look for new or bigger breaks for caring for kids or disabled relatives, running a small business, pursuing "lifelong learning," and saving for retirement. If George W. Bush takes over, he'll push an across-the-board rate cut, as well as special breaks for farmers, ranchers, adopted and foster kids, donors to churches and charities, and families setting aside money for private kindergarten and grade school.

Which would all be well and good—these are, after all, mostly worthy purposes—if tax breaks really were as simple and efficient as today's politicians would have you believe. But they're not. Take

their alleged simplicity. Democrats, in particular, try to ensure that any new tax subsidy is "means-tested"—that is, targeted to low- and middle-bracket taxpayers (or paid directly to those owing no taxes). But that means creating for each new tax benefit what the Urban Institute's Eugene Steuerle dubs a "mini-tax system," with its own rules for determining eligibility and measuring income. When, for example, does a child count as a child for tax purposes? That depends on whether you want to claim a dependent-care credit, a Hope credit, or any of a host of other credits on his or her behalf. Will getting married cut or increase your tax bill? Better check out the 60-plus provisions of the tax code that depend on marital status.

Things don't get any better higher up the income spectrum. The fact that so many tax breaks are phased out as income increases produces a wildly erratic tax-rate schedule. If your family earnings total around $100,000 and you get a modest pay raise, for example, you could end up forking over more of your gain to the feds than if you were earning $1 million. That's because you may face cutbacks in the amount you can now deduct for Hope, child, or adoption credits, for example. With somewhat more income, you'll start losing your itemized deductions and personal exemptions, too. At higher levels of income, however, the phaseouts have all been completed, so Bill Gates can probably keep more of his next dollar than you can. "People have no idea what their marginal rate is," says Stephen Corrick, a tax partner at Arthur Andersen.

And if tax breaks aren't very simple, neither are they very efficient. It has been well-documented that tax preferences mostly subsidize activities—such as saving money, hiring workers, or having kids—that would have occurred anyway. And much of the money doesn't go toward the intended purpose at all. Shocking as it may seem, people cheat. They take advantage of even the most high-minded tax breaks—exaggerating, for example, their contributions to the collection plate each Sunday—if they think they can get away with it. And the more complicated the tax laws, the more people can get away with. Back in 1990, Congress was horrified to discover that some 40 percent of the Earned Income Tax Credit, a refundable payment to low-earning breadwinners, was going to families not entitled to it. (This did not, however, deter Congress from subsequently expanding and further complicating the EITC.) In response, the IRS was forced to step up EITC audits—enforcement being yet another casualty of a complicated tax code. As Representative Amo Houghton, chair of the Ways and Means Oversight Committee, noted at a recent hearing, "A provision we pass may make good sense in terms of fairness and equity but may be absolutely unworkable in the real world."

All this well-meaning complexity doesn't just breed tax evasion; it breeds cynicism. Taxpayers know the system is irrational, and they suspect, often correctly, that they're getting screwed. This is a prime factor—Democrats, take note—in the public's support for replacing the income tax with a far less progressive but presumably simpler "flat" tax.

Congress, of course, is not insensitive to these problems. Only two years ago it added a provision to the tax code requiring the IRS to prepare an annual report pinpointing "sources of complexity in the administration of the Federal tax laws." (Simply handing out mirrors to each of the 535 members was not considered.) Then, having duly noted its concern, Congress returned to the more congenial business of conjuring up new sources of complexity for the IRS to document.

JODIE ALLEN

JODIE ALLEN is a senior writer at *U.S. News & World Report* covering political economy.

Social Spending and Economic Growth

Interview with Peter Lindert

Prevailing opinion holds that big government and high taxes reduce growth. Social programs are claimed to be a matter of social justice, even if they impede economic growth. But Peter Lindert in a new book argues that these claims are fiction. States that spend a lot on social programs grow no more slowly than those that spend little. He discusses his views and the evidence below.

Q **The conventional wisdom, not merely among laymen but among many economists, is that the bigger the government as a proportion of one's economy, the more likely you will grow more slowly. You say there is no serious evidence to support this claim. In that case, why do so many make the claim that big government undermines growth?**

A. The source is ideology and a valid theory that if governments were run badly, they would drag down economic growth.

Q. The valid theory?

A. The valid theory is that if governments did nothing but tax people on the basis of their productivity and give it to other people who were unproductive—encouraging them to be unproductive with those grants—it would make everybody work less, take less risk, and innovate less.

Q **So, Is the theory valid, then? Some economists do present evidence that purports to support that theory. Not least of them is Martin Feldstein, the Harvard professor who is head of the National Bureau of Economic Research, along with some other well-known economists. What kind of empirical evidence do they present?**

A. Most of it is off the mark. Most of it is evidence of what would happen in a fictitious world. When you see a computer simulation or general equilibrium model, or many common economic models with supply-and-demand curves, they are imagining a world, a world of their own creation. They are not actually using data from the real world. Now, there are other studies that suggest costs of larger government are empirically based, but many of them are still inappropriate. For example, some studies using large samples of individuals show that if people had a lower after-tax wage, they might work less. But that is not

a policy experiment, one that changes the whole incentive structure of the economy. It is an isolated case that just shows how different people with different wage rates decide how much to work as individuals. So it is off the mark.

Q **Explain, for the sake of clarity, what you mean when you say it is not a policy experiment.**

A. Typically, studies use a data set in which people all faced one particular government's set of policies. Within that government's set of policies, people who had different wage rates decided to work different amounts. But those are all differences among individuals within one policy regime. That study cannot by its design tell us what happens if you shift the entire regime and shift all the tax rates and incentives.

Q **You were going to give another example.**

A. There are studies that are very close to what we would want ideally. They are also microeconomically based—that is, they are studies of how labor reacts to changed circumstances. These were the famous negative-income-tax experiments in the 1960s and '70s. Those had the virtue of really being a policy experiment for a few months' time, and they did face people with different tax systems. Now, what did those experiments show? Here is the answer: They did not show any huge effect on people's tendency to work. Furthermore, they failed to take into account other aspects of the welfare state, like health care, pensions, and so forth. Within their confines, they showed a modest loss of work if you gave people generous unemployment and welfare benefits. Now, some do not agree with my summary of these experiments. Charles Murray, the conservative author who severely criticized the welfare system, is one of these. But what he did was pick and choose among the results of these negative-income-tax experiments and picked the ones he liked. In particular, the results from Seattle and Denver seemed to show a stronger dampening effect on labor supply. But auditors found that the Seattle and Denver ones that he chose to highlight were marred by the fact that the people receiving the temporary welfare benefits had an incentive to hide some of their earnings. So they were, in fact, working more than was stated.

Q. So the empirical evidence presented, you think, has almost always been seriously flawed or did not show the results that people claimed they showed?

A. That's correct. Now, the last kind of evidence is international pooled studies where researchers compare the experience of many countries over many years. The conclusions of these studies had already begun to move in the direction of my findings that high social spending does not deter growth. While I think I have improved on their tests, Joel Slemrod, William Easterly, and others were already finding this puzzling result before I did. There was no net negative effect on GDP per capita higher government social spending per capita.

Q. When were the original studies done?

A. They are all in the 1990s. Before then, there was not a major result that had tested over many countries and many years. It is not that ideologically there was a shift in the nature of the results. There were no pooled international results before the 1990s because we did not have enough numbers.

Q What improvements did you make?

A. The improvements are technical in nature. I gave more attention to simultaneous feedback, to nonlinearity, and to differences in error variance. Let me explain a bit. On the simultaneity, in any of these studies you have to reckon that the GDP per capita itself is an influence on the policies chosen. The higher the GDP per capita, the more likely there will be higher social spending. So we cannot get the right answer unless we seriously try to take this feedback into account.

Q. So you tried to allow for that?

A. Yes, I did. Most previous studies had not. Now, my results [published in *Growing Public: Social Spending and Economic Growth Since the Eighteenth Century* (2004)] are not radically different from those of Slemrod and others, but I made this extra step.

Q. And you concentrated on social spending as opposed to, say, government spending in general per GDP, or greater growth of government spending in general?

A. Yes. And it is important in considering my study to see that not only did I leave out non-social spending, such as military spending, highways, subsidies to producer groups, and so forth. It is also different because of the way I defined the welfare state.

Q. Please explain.

A. I have realized that I have to explain in my studies what the welfare state is and is not. It is a system that generally gives relatively universal social transfers to much of the population in the form of public health, public education, worker retraining, unemployment compensation, and especially pensions. But it does not include, for the purposes of my analysis, union power, special laws to protect jobs or business groups from competition, or nationalized industries. I do not measure the impact of these because they are really separate, and I would give them some label other than welfare state. Most of them I consider by-products of past class struggles.

Q What about subsidies, like earned income tax credits or tax deductibility of mortgage interest?

A. I pay some theoretical attention to these in the book, but my statistical work did not include them. I did not view earned income tax credits as welfare expenditure. One could argue that I should have done so. I do not think it would have affected the results.

Q. What did your results show, finally?

A. When it came to the effects of larger welfare states on GDP per capita and economic growth, there were two results I need to emphasize. First, I made a hypothetical extrapolation away from what actually happened in history. I took an extreme case where a hypothetical country took 40 percent of GDP from the capitalists alone—it just soaked the rich, and even the middle. If I gave that all back in the form of unemployment compensation—yes, even my statistical patterns say that would be very costly to the level and growth rate of GDP. But then comes the second result, which is that nobody in real life ever did that. It never happened. None of the welfare states did anything as foolish as we constantly describe in our Anglo-American parables that criticize their welfare states.

Q. And those Anglo-American parables are about the danger of the welfare state? So we oversimplify and exaggerate this welfare state, creating a world that is easy to criticize because it does not exist.

A. Right. It does not really exist. These kinds of flights of fiction would be socially useful in a world that might have tried such mistakes, but they never happened and have been seriously overblown.

Q. Then what did your statistical results show?

A. Statistical results showed that the difference, other things equal, between 10 percent of GDP going into social transfers, as in the social programs in the United States or Japan, and 33 percent, as in Sweden, is indistinguishable from zero.

Q. So the conclusion, therefore, is that it has no consequence?

A. It has no consequence for GDP.

Q. For the growth or the level of GDP?

A. Either one.

Q. What period did you examine?

A. So far I have examined periods going way back to the late nineteenth century, but the most important data are between 1960 and 1995. People have asked, what if you extend it beyond 1995? Has not the day of doom suddenly arrived since then for the welfare states? And my answer is no, and you and I might want to go into that.

Q. Yes.

A. Here is what people are saying … and this is really interesting. It is just so interesting to see how social debate works in these areas. People are amazingly selective because they know the story they are after, and in their minds they will find a story that seems to work for them. So here is what happens.

People wanting to comment on welfare state versus low-budget market economies have made this debate into a contrast between Europe and America. In particular, we have seen people say, look at how much worse Germany is doing than the United States since 1995. This is very selective because Germany has special problems going back to costly reunification with East Germany. In that particular time the United States was having its high-tech boom. In such a comparison, the result looks the way one might have thought on conventional grounds—high social spending impedes growth. But we cannot be so selective. There are so many decades and so many countries to study. I can just as easily counter that one. I could say: Compare the growth rates of high-spending Sweden versus low-spending Japan since 1995, or some welfare state like Denmark or Austria versus low-spending Switzerland. In each case, the welfare states are growing faster. So would that prove that the welfare state is tremendously good for growth? Certainly not. You have to study all the experiences. It is amazing how people select what they want to hear. The bad growth in the European Union since 1995 really reflects Germany's experience, while in the raw data the rest of the EU is doing just as well on average as North America.

Q So where is the theory wrong? Why does high government spending not impede economic growth? Before breaking this down into a number of issues, let us get a general answer first.

A. Here is the overall view. Real-world democratic governments, realizing they could be thrown out of office, knew they had to design the system in such a way as to minimize the defects of high spending and taxes and add additional benefits. What defects, what benefits? This is a three-part answer. First, they have designed a mix of taxes that more pro-growth than people have realized. People are very surprised to find that Scandinavians and Europeans do not just soak the rich. To the contrary, they have the kinds of taxes that conventional mainstream North American economists say they wish they had— namely a consumption tax. Second, when it comes to the incentives for people who receive public transfers, they do not get it as wrong in the basic welfare programs as we say they do in our theories.

Q. You mean they do not create disincentives to work?

A. The disincentives to work are not nearly so bad as we have said in our classic imaginations. Third, some kinds of

social transfers really have positive productivity and positive GDP effects. The best example is public health. But that is also true of some worker retraining programs and, of course, education. As a parenthesis, education does not get emphasized much in my new book because it is not controversial an aspect of the welfare state, and educational spending out of public tax money is hardly un-American. America is among the leaders in that.

Q To fill in some of the blanks here, let us get back to the first part—the tax system. When you say it is a tax system that many U.S. mainstream economists would propose, what do you mean by that?

A. When the American economists specializing in public finance and labor have been polled, they say, "We would like to avoid a taxation on capital; we would rather you tax labor a lot." And Anglo-American economists in general have long said that it is better to tax consumption than income, because taxing income invariably means the double taxing of savings. Those are the conventional desires about a good tax system. We would like something like a flat tax, and a tax on special "sin" goods, like gasoline and alcohol. This wish list is better delivered in the welfare states than in the countries spending the least on social programs.

Q. The welfare states have big value-added taxes?

A. Yes.

Q. But they have pretty progressive income taxes?

A. Not much more than we, no. Even in the overall structure, the Swedish system is only slightly, if at all, more progressive than the British or American as of the 1980s. Now, high incomes from labor—think of physicians, in particular—are heavily taxed in Europe. If there is a wealthy group in the welfare states that is much aggrieved by the tax system, it would be top-income professionals, and doctors in particular would have the further complaint that their incomes are constrained by the public health system. Those countries' taxes on earnings made on capital are more forgiving because they did not want capital to flee. But everybody who earns from his or her own labor pays a whopping tax.

Q Now the second point. We keep seeing that the welfare state creates disincentives to work. For example, high unemployment insurance would presumably induce people not to bother to look for a job. That is not as true in the welfare states as we think it is?

A. It is not as true as people usually think it is. Their systems are more universal. They do not cut you off as fast if you get a job or your income rises. Before the mid-1990s it was America and Britain whose systems most told an unemployed single mother, "Do not work. We will tax you heavily," because they had means-tested welfare systems that restrained total spending. So the moment you got any kind of job, you lost your benefits because you moved out of the bottom 1 percent of the income spectrum. That was a defect in America that first crept in and got big in the 1960s under the "Great Society" but was also reinstated by the first Reagan administration. The minute those women got jobs, they lost the benefits. That was a mistake that the European welfare states did not make. They had a more universal sliding system. You can go partway up the scale and still be getting some benefits, so you will keep some of your extra earnings as you work. Now, in the 1990s America made significant reforms, followed by Britain in 2000, to reduce these disincentives, and they are working. One was the expansion of the earned income tax credit (EITC) in 1993; the other was welfare reform in 1996, with its work requirements. I know liberals are proud of the EITC but say welfare reform is not working. But there seems to be some job creation here that has even survived the recent recession.

The main area where we are still getting it wrong is parental leave and public day care. These are handled much better in certain European countries—Sweden is the leader. Why is that good for economic growth? It is because in an economy where everybody's earning really largely depend on their buildup of human capital, their buildup of skills, and knowing how to work within a particular firm, the chance to go back to your jobs and to have high-quality day care in Europe provides the opportunity to maintain your progress and your own skills. If you have to drop out and then come back later and search for a new job, you start at a lower level, and you never do catch up to your previous path. I wish I could tell you how much more of GDP that is worth. I cannot quantify it. But the main clue is when you look at the median wage of women relative to men. You can see that the countries that do not supply these generous programs for day care and parental leave—Britain, America and Japan—have much lower relative women's earnings. Also, in places like America, there is probably a statistical bias against all women because corporations anticipate that some of them will leave the workforce. So they do not promote them, they do not invest in them—at least as much.

Q What lessons should America learn from your studies?

A. We could look at which social areas are ones where America has done the best; and which are ones where America has done the worst and, therefore, might work hardest on changing. America has done the best in higher education. We are by far the best because we got the incentives all right. We actually had subsidies from the taxpayers because the advance of knowledge deserves some

subsidy. But we forced every public institution to compete against other public institutions and the private ones. Berkeley must compete against both UCLA and Stanford in all respects—for government grants, for top faculty, for top students. Even the teachers get evaluated by their students in America, which the other countries have failed to do, to their disadvantage. Now, that is only higher education, but that is specifically the subsector for which there is the most American advantage. The biggest American disadvantage is health, in which we are near the bottom of the Organization for Economic Cooperation and Development countries.

Q. In terms of outcomes?

A. In terms of outcomes and the cost of the outcomes. So the World Health Organization has America ranking thirty-seventh in the world in the quality of its health care. In terms of outcomes, we save fewer lives with our system, and we have a much more bureaucratic and administratively costly system than the government systems that Americans usually think of as the essence of bureaucracy. It is costing us a ton, and we have higher price markups on all these services. When it comes to people saying that Medicare is in crisis—Medicare being our main government program in the health care area—yes, it is in crisis, not because there is something wrong with government health care, but it is in crisis because it has to operate within this environment of price spirals.

Q. Let us get right to the bottom line.

A. Here it is. We are trapped, and it would be good if we could get out of the trap forced on us by a kind of class warfare rhetoric. We have Democrats who will use phrases like "fat cats," and they do not like anything that looks like it is a tax on ordinary people, as opposed to just the rich. And we have Republicans who use phrases like "bloated welfare queen" and the worst one of all, "socialized medicine." This is the trap. Social programs can enhance growth if run well. They can reduce costs and provide funding and useful programs for education, human and social capital, and health. Higher taxes need not impede growth if the tax regime is developed carefully and acknowledges that ordinary people must pay their share as well as the rich. Meantime, however, we in the United States are neglecting health care reforms and the social capital of women, among other important areas. We have created an imaginary welfare state to attack, one that does not exist.

PETER LINDERT is Distinguished Professor of Economics at the University of California at Davis and a research associate of the National Bureau of Economic Research. He is author of Growing Public: Social Spending and Economic Growth Since the Eighteenth Century, 2 vols. *(Cambridge University Press, 2004).*

Social Security Reform Need Not Be Drastic

By Augustine Faucher

The news from the Trustees of the Social Security Trust Fund annual report on Social Security's finances was mostly good (see The 2001 OASDI Trustees Report). The Trust Fund is secure for the next 35 to 40 years, and the report projects a small reduction in the program's deficit over the next 75 years. Nevertheless, the demographics are clear: over the long term, there will be fewer workers supporting each Social Security beneficiary. This is not an insurmountable challenge, however, and with the right changes, some of them politically difficult, Social Security can continue to provide retirement security.

The program's six Trustees (the Secretaries of the Treasury, Health and Human Services, and Labor; the Social Security Commissioner; and two members of the public) develop the demographic and economic assumptions used in these projections. It's difficult to predict what the economy will be doing over the next six months, much less the next 75 years. Some commentators regard the Trustees' assumptions, particularly the economic ones, as conservative, but "prudent" would be a better word, particularly given that the projections are for 75 years. The long-term economic growth numbers look low compared to recent experience, but they are based on labor force growth consistent with demographics and productivity growth consistent with historical experience, including the 1974–1995 slowdown.

The demographic assumptions are actually much more important for the program than the economic ones. The "baby boomers" will start to retire in less than 10 years, life expectancy is increasing, and the new cohorts entering the labor force are relatively small. The result? There are now about 3.4 workers per Social Security beneficiary; that number will fall rapidly to about 2.1 by 2030 (see chart), and will continue to fall, although more slowly, through 2075.

Social Security is largely a "pay-as-you-go" system, with current tax revenues used to fund current benefits. Right now, Social Security is running a surplus, taking in more in taxes than it is paying out in benefits. However, as the number of workers per beneficiary declines, those surpluses will start to fall, and by about 2016, Social Security will be a net drain on the total federal budget. The assets in the Social Security Trust Fund will

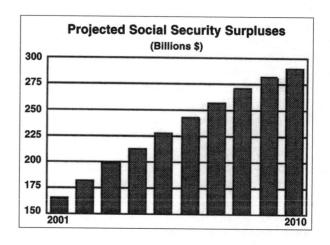

make up the deficits for a while, but eventually the Trust Fund will become exhausted, and the program will not be able to pay full benefits. In 2039, the year the Trust Fund is projected to become exhausted, tax revenues would be enough to fund about three-quarters of benefits promised under current law; in 2075, taxes would be able to fund only about two-thirds of benefits.

The problem cannot be ignored; with current demographic trends, there is a long-term financing problem for Social Security, no matter how strong economic growth is. However, there are modifications that can be made to improve Social Security's financial position while keeping the program's current structure largely in place. One possibility is to further increase the retirement age for full benefits (it is already scheduled to gradually rise from 65 to 67 over the next 25 years), and perhaps link it to life expectancy. Other options include raising the maximum income that workers and employers pay Social Security taxes on ($80,400 in 2001, and tied to average wages in the economy), small reductions in benefits, and small increases in the tax rate. Making changes relatively soon will protect current beneficiaries and give workers more time to adjust.

Nonetheless, the program's finances are not so bad that they call for drastic changes. In particular, it is not necessary to establish personal retirement savings accounts in order to "save"

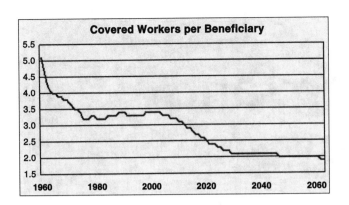

Covered Workers per Beneficiary

Perhaps the best thing that can be done to assure the future of Social Security is to promote strong long-term economic growth. Strong growth by itself will not completely solve the problem, but it will make it easier for both workers and beneficiaries to enjoy rising real incomes. One positive development is that both political parties have agreed to use the current Social Security surpluses to reduce publicly-held debt and thereby increase national saving, a step that should promote strong growth in labor productivity and real wages.

The proposed large tax cut, on the other hand, may do more harm than good. It would reduce future surpluses and could reduce national saving, making the job of fostering long-term growth more difficult. This would be in addition to the projected reduction in national saving from Social Security in about 15 years, as taxes start to fall short of costs. In addition, a large tax cut would reduce surpluses in the non-Social Security portion of the budget, reducing funds available to fund the transition to a system of private retirement accounts.

Social Security. In fact, some proposals would siphon off a portion of tax revenues now used to pay current benefits to private accounts, making the financing problem worse. There are many benefits to personal retirement accounts, and they should be strongly considered in any Social Security reform. However, the current financial imbalance in the Social Security program should not be used to justify them.

UNIT 4

Money, Banking, and Monetary Policy

Unit Selections

15. **What Should Central Banks Do?**, Frederic S. Mishkin
16. **How Does Monetary Policy Affect the U.S. Economy?**, FRBSF Economic Letter (Federal Reserve Bank of San Francisco)
17. **How Does the Fed Decide the Appropriate Setting for the Policy Instrument?**, FRBSF Economic Letter (Federal Reserve Bank of San Francisco)
18. **How Sluggish Is the Fed?**, Glenn D. Rudebusch
19. **The Science (and Art) of Monetary Policy**, Carl E. Walsh
20. **The New World of Banking**, Jim Campen
21. **Banking Consolidation**, Simon Kwan
22. **Why an Old Prohibition Against Linking Loans and Services is Obsolete**, Mara Der Hovanesian
23. **The Cycles of Financial Scandal**, Kevin Phillips

Key Points to Consider

- How is monetary policy used for the purpose of achieving national macroeconomic goals?

- Is monetary policy-making subject to political influences? What might be done about this problem?

- Why is monetary policy-making both a science and an art?

- What are the effects of major recent changes in U.S. banking laws?

 **Links: www.dushkin.com/online/**
These sites are annotated in the World Wide Web pages.

History of Money
http://www.ex.ac.uk/~RDavies/arian/llyfr.html

Mark Bernkopf's Central Banks of the World: Central Banking Resources Center
http://patriot.net/~bernkopf

Money works, but it doesn't work miracles.

Paul Samuelson, 1970
Nobel Laureate in Economics

Compared to fiscal policy, monetary policy—the deliberate control of the money supply for the purpose of achieving macroeconomic goals—receives less attention in political debates and the media. Part of its apparent obscurity may be traced to differences in the manner in which the two policies are conducted: fiscal policy decisions are made by elected representatives in Congress following sometimes lengthy public debates, while monetary policies are determined by a small handful of Federal Reserve (Fed) officials meeting in closed session. In addition, the role of money in an economy is itself a fairly obscure topic for the average person; the effect of changes in the nation's money supply is generally less understood than, say, a tax cut, the effect of which can be felt immediately in a person's pockets. Nevertheless, monetary policy can have a powerful impact on a nation's economy.

The importance of monetary policy as a stabilizing instrument has increased significantly in recent years. The implementation of monetary policy requires the Federal Reserve to adjust what are known as "intermediate targets" (such as the money supply or short-term interest rates). These targets stand intermediate between certain ultimate objectives (such as high employment, low inflation, and so forth) and the instruments of monetary pol-

icy (including open market operations, discount rate policy, and reserve requirement changes). The intermediate targets are of interest not for their own sake, but for the close relationship they may bear to the ultimate goal of stabilizing the economy.

The unit begins with articles which offer insights into the conduct of U.S. monetary policy. The first two are studies by the Federal Reserve Bank of San Francisco which detail ways in which monetary policy affects the economy and the techniques which policy-makers use to determine how the economy is doing. Then, in "The Science (and Art) of Monetary Policy," Carl Walsh shows how good policy-making requires good policy-makers (combining the science of the economist with the art of the practitioner).

This is followed by articles which examine specific issues in the U.S. banking system. Profound changes in banking laws occurred in the 1990s. In the first article Simon Kwan explains why the ever-growing number of bank mergers raises some challenging policy questions. Next, in "Why an Old Prohibition Against Linking Loans and Services Is Obsolete," Mara Der Hovanesian examines the possibility that a standard banking practice may be in violation of U.S. antitrust laws. Finally, Kevin Phillips explains what he calls the "financialization" of the economy. Securities management, corporate reorganization, derivatives trading, and other forms of financial packaging are steadily replacing the act of making, growing, and transporting things. Phillips asks: will an era of reform follow a decade of excess?

What Should Central Banks Do?

This paper was prepared for the Homer Jones Lecture, Federal Reserve Bank of St. Louis, March 30, 2000. Frederic S. Mishkin is a professor at the Graduate School of Business, Columbia University and a scholar at the National Bureau of Economic Research. He thanks Dan Thornton, Bill Poole, Lars Svensson, and the participants in the Macro Lunch at Columbia University for their helpful comments. Any views expressed in this paper are those of the author only and not those of Columbia University or the National Bureau of Economic Research.

Frederic S. Mishkin

INTRODUCTION

In the last twenty years, there has been substantial rethinking about how central banks should do their job. This rethinking has led to major changes in how central banks operate, and we are now in an era in which central banks in many countries throughout the world have had notable success—keeping inflation low, while their economies experience rapid economic growth. In this lecture, I outline what we think we have learned about how central banks should be set up to conduct monetary policy and then apply these lessons to see if there is room for institutional improvement in the way the Federal Reserve operates.

The lecture begins by discussing seven guiding principles for central banks and then uses these principles to outline what the role of central banks should be. This framework is then used to see how the institutional features of the Fed measure up. I will take the view that despite the Fed's extraordinarily successful performance in recent years, we should not be complacent. Changes in the way the Fed is set up to conduct its business may be needed to help ensure that the Fed continues to be as successful in the future.

GUIDING PRINCIPLES FOR CENTRAL BANKS

Recent theorizing in monetary economics suggests seven basic principles that can serve as useful guides for

central banks to help them achieve successful outcomes in their conduct of monetary policy. These are:

- Price stability provides substantial benefits;
- Fiscal policy should be aligned with monetary policy;
- Time inconsistency is a serious problem to be avoided;
- Monetary policy should be forward looking;
- Accountability is a basic principle of democracy;
- Monetary policy should be concerned about output as well as price fluctuations; and
- The most serious economic downturns are associated with financial instability.

We will look at each of these principles in turn.

Price Stability Provides Substantial Benefits to the Economy

In recent years a growing consensus has emerged that price stability—a low and stable inflation rate—provides substantial benefits to the economy. Price stability prevents overinvestment in the financial sector, which in a high-inflation environment expands to profitably act as a middleman to help individuals and businesses escape some of the costs of inflation.[1] Price stability lowers the uncertainty about relative prices and the future price level, making it easier for firms and individuals to make appropriate decisions, thereby increasing economic efficiency.[2]

Price stability also lowers the distortions from the inter-action of the tax system and inflation.[3] Price stability lowers the uncertainty about relative prices and the future price level, making it easier for firms and individuals to make appropriate decisions, thereby increasing economic efficiency.[2] Price stability also lowers the distortions from the interaction of the tax system and inflation.[3]

All of these benefits of price stability suggest that low and stable inflation can increase the level of resources productively employed in the economy, and might even help increase the rate of economic growth. While time-series studies of individual countries and cross-national comparisons of growth rates are not in total agreement, there is a consensus that inflation is detrimental to economic growth, particularly when inflation is at high levels.[4] Therefore, both theory and evidence suggest that monetary policy should focus on promoting price stability.

Align Fiscal Policy with Monetary Policy

One lesson from the "unpleasant monetarist arith-metic" discussed in Sargent and Wallace (1981) and the recent literature on fiscal theories of the price level (Woodford, 1994 and 1995) is that irresponsible fiscal policy may make it more difficult for the monetary authorities to pursue price stability. Large government deficits may put pressure on the monetary authorities to monetize the debt, thereby producing rapid money growth and inflation. Restraining the fiscal authorities from engaging in excessive deficit financing thus aligns fiscal policy with monetary policy and makes it easier for the monetary authorities to keep inflation under control.

Time Inconsistency Is a Serious Problem To Be Avoided

One of the key problems facing monetary policy-makers is the time-inconsistency problem described by Calvo (1978), Kydland and Prescott (1977), and Barro and Gordon (1983). The time-inconsistency problem arises because there are incentives for a policymaker to try to exploit the short-run tradeoff between employment and inflation to pursue short-run employment objectives, even though the result is poor long-run outcomes. Expan-sionary monetary policy will produce higher growth and employment in the short-run. Therefore, policymakers will be tempted to pursue this policy even though it will not produce higher growth and employment in the long-run because economic agents adjust their wage and price expectations upward to reflect the expansionary policy. Unfortunately, however, expansionary monetary policy will lead to higher inflation in the long-run, with its negative consequences for the economy.

McCallum (1995) points out that the time-inconsis-tency problem by itself does not imply that a central bank will pursue expansionary monetary policy that leads to inflation. Simply by recognizing the problem that forward-looking expectations in the wage- and price-

setting process promotes a strategy of pursuing expan-sionary monetary policy, central banks can decide not to play that game. From my first-hand experience as a central banker, I can testify that central bankers are very aware of the time-inconsistency problem and are, indeed, extremely averse to falling into a time-inconsistency trap. However, even if central bankers recognize the problem, there still will be pressures on the central bank to pursue overly expansionary monetary policy and inflation may result, so that the time-inconsistency problem remains. The time-inconsistency problem is just shifted back one step; its source is not in the central bank, but rather, resides in the political process.

The time-inconsistency literature points out both why there will be pressures on central banks to pursue overly expansionary monetary policy and why central banks whose commitment to price stability is in doubt are more likely to experience higher inflation. In order to prevent high inflation and the pursuit of a suboptimal monetary policy, monetary policy institutions need to be designed in order to avoid the time-inconsistency trap.

Monetary Policy Should Be Forward Looking

The existence of long lags from monetary policy actions to their intended effects on output and inflation suggests that monetary policy should be forward looking. If policymakers wait until undesirable outcomes on inflation and output fluctuations actually arise, their policy actions are likely to be counterproductive. For example, by waiting until inflation has already appeared before tightening monetary policy, the monetary author-ities will be too late; inflation expectations will already be embedded into the wage- and price-setting process, creating an inflation momentum that will be hard to contain. Once the inflation process has gotten rolling, the process of stopping it will be slower and costlier. Similarly, by waiting until the economy is already in recession, expansionary policy may kick in well after the economy has recovered, thus promoting unnecessary output fluctuations and possible inflation.

To avoid these problems, monetary authorities must behave in a forward-looking fashion and act preemp-tively. For example, assume that it takes two years for monetary policy to have a significant effect on inflation. Under these circumstances, even if inflation is quiescent currently (with an unchanged stance of monetary policy) and policymakers forecast inflation to rise in two years time, they must act immediately to head off the infla-tionary surge.

Policymakers Should Be Accountable

A basic principle of democracy is that the public should have the right to control the actions of the government: In other and more famous words, "The government should be of the people, by the people and for the people." Thus, the public in a democracy must have the capability to "throw the bums out" or punish incompetent policymakers through other methods in order to control their actions. If policymakers cannot be removed from office or punished in some other way, this basic principle of democracy is violated. In a democracy, government policymakers need to be held accountable to the public.

A second reason why accountability of policymakers is important is that it helps to promote efficiency in government. Making policymakers subject to punishment makes it more likely that incompetent policymakers will be replaced by competent ones and creates better incentives for policymakers to do their jobs well. Knowing that they are subject to punishment when performance is poor, policymakers will strive to get policy right. If policymakers are able to avoid accountability, then their incentives to do a good job drop appreciably, making poor policy outcomes more likely.

Monetary Policy Should Be Concerned with Output as well as Price Fluctuations

Price stability is a means to an end—a healthy economy—and should not be treated as an end in itself. Thus, central bankers should not be obsessed with inflation control and become what Mervyn King (1997) has characterized as "inflation nutters." Clearly, the public cares about output as well as inflation fluctuations, and so the objectives for a central bank in the context of a long-run strategy should not only include minimizing inflation fluctuations, but should also include minimizing output fluctuations. Objective functions with these characteristics have now become standard in the monetary economics literature, which focuses on the conduct of monetary policy (e.g., see the papers in Taylor, 1999).

The Most Serious Economic Downturns Are Associated with Financial Instability

A reading of U.S. monetary history (Friedman and Schwartz, 1963, Bernanke, 1983, and Mishkin, 1991) indicates that the most serious economic contractions in U.S. history, including the Great Depression, have all been associated with financial instability. Indeed, this literature suggests that financial instability is a key reason for the depth of these economic contractions. The recent financial crises and depressions in Mexico and East Asia also support this view (Mishkin, 1996, 1999a and Corsetti, Pesenti, and Roubini, 1998). Preventing financial instability is, therefore, crucial to promoting a healthy economy and reducing output fluctuations, an important objective for central banks, as we have seen above.

IMPLICATIONS FOR THE ROLE OF A CENTRAL BANK

Armed with these seven guiding principles, we can now look at what institutional features a central bank should have in conducting its operations. We derive the following implications/criteria for the role of a central bank:

- Price stability should be the overriding, long-run goal of monetary policy;
- An explicit nominal anchor should be adopted;
- A central bank should be goal dependent;
- A central bank should be instrument independent;
- A central bank should be accountable;
- A central bank should stress transparency and communication;
- A central bank should also have the goal of financial stability.

Price Stability Should Be the Overriding, Long-Run Goal of Monetary Policy

Together, the first three principles for monetary policy outlined above suggest that the overriding, long-run goal of monetary policy should be price stability. A goal of price stability immediately follows from the benefits of low and stable inflation, which promote higher economic output. Furthermore, an institutional commitment to price stability is one way to make time-inconsistency of monetary policy less likely. An institutional commitment to the price stability goal provides a counter to time-inconsistency because it makes it clear that the central bank must focus on the long-run and thus resist the temptation to pursue short-run expansionary policies that are inconsistent with the long-run, price stability goal.

The third principle, that fiscal policy should be aligned with monetary policy, provides another reason why price stability should be the overriding, long-run goal of monetary policy. As McCallum (1990) has pointed out, "unpleasant monetarist arithmetic" only arises if the fiscal authorities are the first mover. In other words, if the fiscal authorities are the dominant player and can move first—thus setting fiscal policy exogenously, knowing that the monetary authorities will be forced to accommodate their policies to maintain the long-run government budget constraint—then fiscal policy will determine the inflation rate. Indeed, this is the essence of the fiscal theory of the price level. On the other hand, as McCallum (1990) points out, if the monetary authorities are the dominant player and move first, then it will be fiscal policy that will accommodate in order to satisfy the long-run government budget constraint and monetary policy will determine the inflation rate. An institutional commitment to price stability as the overriding, long-run goal, is just one way to ensure that monetary policy moves first and dominates, forcing fiscal policy to align with monetary policy.

The sixth guiding principle, that output fluctuations should also be a concern of monetary policy, suggests that a fanatic pursuit of price stability could be problematic because policymakers should see not only price fluctuations, but also output fluctuations as undesirable. This is why the price stability goal should be seen as overriding in the long-run but not in the short-run. As Lars Svensson (1999) states, central banks should pursue what he calls "flexible inflation targeting," in which the speed at which a central bank tries to get to price stability reflects their concerns about output fluctuations. The more heavily a central bank cares about output fluctuations, the more time it should take to return to price stability when it is not already there. However, because a "flexible inflation targeter" always sets a long-term price stability goal for inflation, the fact that a central bank cares about output fluctuations is entirely consistent with price stability as the long-run, overriding goal.

An Explicit Nominal Anchor Should Be Adopted

Although an institutional commitment to price stability helps solve time-inconsistency and fiscal alignment problems, it does not go far enough because price stability is not a clearly defined concept. Typical definitions of price stability have many elements in common with the commonly used legal definition of pornography in the United States—you know it when you see it. Thus, constraints on fiscal policy and discretionary monetary policy to avoid inflation might end up being quite weak because not everyone will agree on what price stability means in practice, providing both monetary policymakers and politicians a loophole to avoid making tough decisions to keep inflation under control. A solution to this problem, which supports the first three guiding principles, is to adopt an explicit nominal anchor that ties down exactly what the commitment to price stability means.

There are several forms that an explicit nominal anchor can take. One is a commitment to a fixed exchange rate. For example, in 1991, Argentina established a currency board that required the central bank to exchange U.S. dollars for new pesos at a fixed exchange rate of one to one. A second nominal anchor is for the central bank to have a money-growth target, as was the case in Germany. A third nominal anchor is for there to be an explicit numerical inflation goal as in inflation-targeting countries such as New Zealand, Canada, the United Kingdom, Australia, and Brazil, among others. All these forms of explicit nominal anchors can help reduce the time-inconsistency problem, as the success of countries using them in lowering and controlling inflation demonstrates (Mishkin, 1999b). These nominal anchors also help restrain fiscal policy and also are seen as an important benefit of inflation targeting in countries such as New Zealand and Canada (Mishkin and Posen, 1997, and Bernanke, Laubach, Mishkin, and Posen, 1999).

One criticism of adopting an explicit nominal anchor, such as an inflation target, is that it will necessarily result in too little emphasis on reducing output fluctuations, which is inconsistent with the guiding principle that monetary policy should be concerned with output as well as price fluctuations. However, this view is mistaken. Inflation targeting, as it has actually been practiced (Mishkin and Posen, 1997, and Bernanke, Laubach, Mishkin, and Posen, 1999), has been quite flexible and has not led to larger output fluctuations. Indeed, adoption of an inflation target can actually make it easier for central banks to deal with negative shocks to the aggregate economy. Because a decline in aggregate demand also leads to lower-than-expected inflation, a central bank is able to respond with a monetary easing, without causing the public to question its anti-inflationary resolve. Furthermore, inflation targeting can make it less likely that deflation, a fall in the price level, would occur. There are particularly valid reasons for fearing deflation in today's world, including the possibility that it might promote financial instability and precipitate a severe economic contraction. Indeed, deflation has been associated with deep recessions or even depressions, as in the 1930s, and the recent deflation in Japan has been one factor that has weakened the financial system and the economy. Targeting inflation rates of above zero, as all inflation targeters have done, makes periods of deflation less likely. The evidence on inflation expectations from surveys and interest rate levels suggest that maintaining a target for inflation above zero (but not too far above) for an extended period does not lead to instability in inflation expectations or to a decline in the central bank's credibility.

Central Banks Should Be Goal Dependent

Although there is a strong rationale for the price stability goal and an explicit nominal anchor, who should make the institutional commitment? Should the central bank independently announce its commitment to the price stability goal or would it be better to have this commitment be mandated by the government?

Here the distinction between goal independence and instrument independence made by Debelle and Fischer (1994) and Fischer (1994) is quite useful. Goal independence is the ability of the central bank to set its own goals for monetary policy, while instrument independence is the ability of the central bank to independently set the instruments of monetary policy to achieve the goals. The fifth guiding principle that the public must be able to exercise control over government actions and that policymakers must be accountable, so basic to democracy, strongly suggests that the goals of monetary policy should be set by the elected government. In other words, a central bank should not be goal independent. The corollary of this view is that the institutional commitment to price stability should come from the government in the form of an explicit, legislated mandate for the central bank to pursue price stability as its overriding, long-run goal.

Not only is the principle of a legislated mandate and goal dependence of the central bank consistent with basic principles of democracy, but it has the further advantage that it is consistent with the second and third guiding principles—it makes time-inconsistency less likely, while making alignment of fiscal policy with monetary policy more likely. As we discussed above, the source of the time-inconsistency problem is more likely to be embedded in the political process than it is in the central bank. Once politicians commit to the price stability goal by passing central bank legislation with a price stability mandate, it becomes harder for them to put pressure on the central bank to pursue short-run expansionary policies that are inconsistent with the price stability goal. Furthermore, a government commitment to price stability also is a commitment to making monetary policy dominant over fiscal policy, ensuring a better alignment of fiscal policy with monetary policy.

An alternative way to solve time-inconsistency problems has been suggested by Rogoff (1985): Grant both goal and instrument independence to a central bank and then appoint conservative central bankers to run it, who put more weight on controlling inflation (relative to output) than does the general public. The result will be low inflation, but at the cost of higher output variability than the public desires.

There are two problems with this solution. First, having "conservative" central bankers impose different preferences from those of the public on the conduct of monetary policy is inherently undemocratic. Basic democratic principles indicate that the preferences of policymaking should be aligned with those of the society at large. Second, in the long run, a central bank cannot operate without the support of the public. If the central bank is seen to be pursuing goals that are not what the public wants, support for central bank independence is likely to erode. Thus appointment of "conservative" central bankers may not be stable in the long run and will not provide a permanent solution to the time-inconsistency problem.

The same principles that suggest that the central bank should be goal dependent, with the commitment to the price stability goal mandated by the government, also suggest that the commitment to an explicit nominal anchor should be made by the government. In the case of an exchange-rate target, the government should set the target, as in Argentina, or in the case of an inflation target, the government should set the numerical inflation goal. The fact that the government sets these targets so that the central bank as goal dependent does not mean that the central bank should be cut out of the decision-making process. Because the central bank has both prestige and expertise in the conduct of monetary policy, governments will almost always be better served by setting these targets in consultation with the central bank.

Although it is clear that the government should set the goal for the explicit nominal anchor in the long-run, it is more controversial whether it should set it in the short-run or intermediate-run. If a government, for example, set a short-run inflation or exchange rate target that was changed every month or every quarter, this could easily lead to time inconsistency in which short-run objectives would dominate. In many countries that target inflation, the Ministry of Finance, as the representative of the government, does set an annual inflation target; however, as documented in Bernanke, Laubach, Mishkin, and Posen (1999), the target rarely is changed once price stability is achieved. Thus, even though (in theory) governments could manipulate an annual inflation target to pursue short-run objectives, the transparency of goal-setting leads to a long-run approach to setting inflation targets even when it is done on an annual basis. The situation for the United States is even more complicated. Because of our congressional system, the Treasury Secretary is not the representative of Congress, in contrast to the Minister of Finance who does represent parliament in a parliamentary system. Instead the Treasury Secretary represents the executive branch. Thus, who represents the American government in setting a short- or interme-diate-term target for monetary policy is not clear cut. This problem is not as severe for setting the long-run goal of monetary policy, which could be done by a congressional commission with representatives from both the executive and legislative branches, as well as from the public and the central bank. However, the difficulties of delegating the setting of shorter run targets for monetary policy in a congressional system may require that the central bank keep this responsibility.[5]

Central Banks Should Be Instrument Independent

Although the arguments above suggest that central banks should be goal dependent, the guiding principles in the previous section provide a strong case that central banks should be instrument independent. Allowing central banks to control the setting of monetary policy instruments provides additional insulation from political pressures to exploit short-run tradeoffs between employment and inflation. Instrument independence means that the central bank is better able to avoid the pursuit of time-inconsistent policies in line with the third guiding principle.

The fourth guiding principle, that monetary policy needs to be forward looking in order to take account of the long lags in the effect of monetary policy on inflation, provides another rationale for instrument independence. Instrument independence insulates the central bank from the myopia that is frequently a feature of the political process arising from politicians' concerns about getting elected in the near future. Thus, instrument indepen-dence makes it more likely that the central bank will be forward looking and adequately allow for the long lags from monetary policy actions to inflation in setting their policy instruments.

Recent evidence seems to support the conjecture that macroeconomic performance is improved when central banks are more independent. When central banks in industrialized countries are ranked from least legally independent to most legally independent, the inflation performance is found to be the best for countries with the most independent central banks (see Alesina and Summers, 1993, Cukierman, 1992, and Fischer, 1994, among others). However, there is some question whether causality runs from central bank independence to low inflation or, rather, whether a third factor is involved, such as the general public's preferences for low inflation that create both central bank independence and low inflation (Posen, 1995).

The bottom line is that basic principles for monetary policy and democracy suggests that central banks should have instrument but not goal independence. This degree of independence for central banks is analogous to the relationship between the U.S. military and the government during the successfully prosecuted Gulf War in 1991. The military had instrument independence. It had complete control over the prosecution of the war with little interference from the government (in contrast to the less successfully waged Vietnam War). On the other hand, the military did not have goal independence. It was the Commander in Chief, George Bush, who made the decisions as to what the objectives and goals of the war would be.

Central Banks Should Be Accountable

The fifth guiding principle, that policymakers should be accountable, indicates that the central bank should be subject to government and public scrutiny. One way of ensuring accountability is to make the independence of the central bank subject to legislative change by allowing the act that created the central bank to be modified by legislation at any time. Another way is to mandate periodic reporting requirements to the government. For example, as was done in the Humphrey-Hawkins legislation which requires the Chairman of the Federal Reserve to testify to Congress twice a year.

The need for central banks to be accountable provides an additional reason why central banks should have an explicit nominal anchor. If there is no explicit nominal anchor, it is far less clear upon what criterion the central bank should be judged, and thus it is harder to hold it accountable. On the other hand, with an explicit nominal anchor, like a target for inflation or the exchange rate, the public and the politicians have a clear cut benchmark to assess the performance of the central bank. Thus, an explicit nominal anchor enhances the accountability of the central bank. Indeed, with an explicit nominal anchor, accountability can be enforced by making the central bank governor subject to dismissal if

he or she breaches the goals set by the government, as is the case in New Zealand.

Central Banks Should Stress Transparency and Communication

Increased transparency of monetary policymaking is another important way to increase central bank accountability in line with the fifth guiding principle. Central banks need to communicate clearly their monetary policy strategy in order to explain their objectives and how they plan to achieve them. Each time they change their policy instruments, such as the interbank interest rate, they also need to clearly state the decision and then explain the rationale for it. Transparency can be further increased by publication of the central bank's forecast and the minutes of the discussion of monetary policy.

In addition, central banks need to pursue many outreach vehicles to communicate with the public. These include the continual making of speeches to all elements of society, more openness with the press and media, and the development of brochures and reports that are accessible to the public. Particularly noteworthy in this regard are the "Inflation Report" type documents initially developed by the Bank of England and now emulated by many other central banks. These documents depart from the usual dull-looking, formal reports of central banks to take on the best elements of textbook writing (fancy graphics, use of boxes) in order to better communicate with the public.

Increasing transparency and accountability not only helps to align central banks with democratic principles, and is thus worthy of its own right, but it also has benefits for the ability of central banks to conduct monetary policy successfully. Transparency reduces the uncertainty about monetary policy, interest rates, and inflation, thus making private-sector planning easier. Transparency and communication also promote a better public understanding of what central banks can do—promote price stability which, as suggested by the first guiding principle, has the potential to enhance economic growth in the long run—and what central banks cannot do—create permanent increases in output and employment through expansionary policy. Better public understanding of what central banks can and cannot do is then likely to help generate more public support for monetary policy, which is focused on price stability, becoming the long-run, overriding goal.

Although central bankers find their life to be a more comfortable one when they are not accountable and can avoid intense public scrutiny, increased transparency and accountability have important benefits for central bankers, helping them to adhere to the first five guiding principles outlined in the previous section. Because transparency and accountability can increase the public support for the price stability goal and longer-term thinking on the part of the central bank, they can reduce political pressures on the central bank to pursue inflationary monetary policy and, thus, limit the time-inconsistency problem, while generating more support for forward-looking policy by the central bank. Also, greater transparency and communication can help the central bank convince the public that fiscal policy needs to be aligned with monetary policy.

In addition, transparency and accountability can increase support for independence of the central bank.[6] An instructive example is provided by the granting of instrument independence to the Bank of England in May 1997. Prior to this date, monetary-policy decisions in the United Kingdom were made by the government (the Chancellor of the Exchequer) rather than by the Bank of England. When, on May 6, 1997, the Chancellor of the Exchequer, Gordon Brown, announced the granting of instrument independence to the Bank of England, giving it the power to set the overnight interest rate, he made it particularly clear at the press conference that, in his view, the action had been made possible by the increased transparency and accountability of policy under the recently adopted inflation-targeting regime.

Central Banks Should also Have a Financial Stability Goal

Because central banks should care about output fluctuations (Principle 6) and the most serious economic contractions arise when there is financial instability (Principle 7), central banks also need to focus on preventing financial instability. The primary way that central banks prevent financial instability is by acting as a lender of last resort, that is, by supplying liquidity to the financial system to keep a financial crisis from spinning out of control. Because acting as a lender of last resort, in effect, provides a safety net for financial institutions to whom the funds will be channeled, it creates a moral hazard problem in which these institutions who are potential borrowers have incentives to take on excessive risk, which can make financial instability more likely. Thus, central banks need to consider the tradeoff between the moral hazard cost of the role as lender of last resort and the benefit of preventing financial crises. Keeping moral hazard from getting out of hand indicates that central banks should not perform the role of lender of last resort unless it is absolutely necessary; and, therefore, this role should occur very infrequently.

Because lender-of-last-resort lending should be directed at providing funds to solvent, but illiquid, financial institutions and not to insolvent institutions, in order to reduce incentives to take on too much risk by these institutions, the central bank needs to have information regarding to whom it might have to extend loans when it performs this role. One way for the central bank to get this information is for it to have a supervisory role over these institutions. This is an argument for giving central banks a role in prudential supervision (see, e.g.,

Mishkin, 1992, and Bernanke, 2000). In addition, a supervisory role for the central bank can help it obtain information about whether a situation really is likely to lead to a financial crisis and, thus, requires a lender-of-last-resort intervention. Without this information, the central bank may either intervene too frequently or fail to do so when it is really needed, thus making financial instability more likely. It is possible that central banks can acquire the information they need from supervisory agencies which are separate from the central bank, but some central bank officials doubt this (see Peek, Rosengren, and Tootell, 2000). Thus, there is an argument for the central bank to have a role in prudential supervision, but it is by no means clear cut. Furthermore, there are arguments against central bank involvement in prudential supervision because it may cause a central bank to lose its focus on the price-stability objective.

A FEDERAL RESERVE SCORECARD

Now that we have outlined what the role of a central bank should be, we can assess how the institutional features of the Federal Reserve measure up. We provide an assessment of whether the way the Fed is set up to conduct its operations is consistent with each of the seven criteria discussed in the previous section.

Price Stability Should Be the Overriding, Long-Run Goal of Monetary Policy

Through their testimony and speeches, high officials in the Federal Reserve System, and especially Alan Greenspan, have made it quite clear that the overriding long-run goal for Fed monetary policy is price stability. However, there is no clear mandate from the U.S. government that price stability should be a long-run, overriding goal. The Humphrey-Hawkins Act passed in 1978, with the revealing title, "Full Employment and Balanced Growth Act," stipulates that monetary policy should have goals of full employment and economic growth, as well as price stability. It is true that the Humphrey-Hawkins Act could be interpreted as allowing for price stability to be the overriding, long-run goal because, as was indicated previously, price stability is a means of promoting high economic growth and full employment in the long-run. However, it is even easier to interpret the legislation as supporting an emphasis on pursuit of full employment and economic growth in the short-run, which is inconsistent with the pursuit of price stability. The lack of a clear mandate for price stability can lead to the time-inconsistency problem in which political pressure is put on the Fed to engage in expansionary policy to pursue short-run goals.

In contrast to the United States, many other countries now have legislation which mandates price stability as the overriding, long-run goal of monetary policy, and this is a growing trend. For example, a mandate for price stability as the overriding, long-run goal for monetary policy was a requirement for entry into the European Monetary Union, and the Maastricht Treaty gives this mandate to the central banking system for the European Monetary Union, which most accurately referred to as the Eurosystem.[7] This trend also has been evident even in emerging market countries, where many central banks have had their mandate revised to focus on price stability.

On the first criterion of the need for an institutional commitment to price stability, as the overriding long-run goal, the United States does not score well.

An Explicit Nominal Anchor Should Be Adopted

Not only has the U.S. government not committed to price stability as the overriding, long-run goal, but also neither it nor the Fed has adopted an explicit nominal anchor. The actions and rhetoric of the Greenspan Fed have made it clear that it will fight to keep inflation from rising from the current level of around 2 percent, and it is fair to characterize the Fed as having an implicit nominal anchor. Nonetheless, the Federal Reserve has not come out and articulated an explicit goal for inflation and has, instead, stated its commitment to price stability. This has been loosely defined by Alan Greenspan as a situation in which changes in the price level are not a major consideration for businesses and households. At the present time, the public (and maybe even members of the FOMC) have no idea of whether the Fed's goal for inflation is 1 percent, 2 percent, or possibly higher. I think it is fair to say that right now the nominal anchor in the United States is Alan Greenspan. The problem is that this leaves some ambiguity as to what the Fed's target is. Even more importantly, the existence of this implicit nominal anchor depends on personalities. Alan Greenspan, despite his recent reappointment, will not be around forever. When he steps down, will the public believe that there is sufficient commitment to a nominal anchor to keep inflation from appearing again?

On the criterion of having an explicit nominal anchor, the institutional set up of the Fed also does not score well.

Central Banks Should Be Instrument Independent

The Federal Reserve has been set up to be far more independent than other government agencies in the United States. Members of the Board of Governors are appointed by the government by 14-year terms, insulating them from political pressure, while Reserve Bank presidents, who also sit on the FOMC, are appointed by the boards of directors at each Reserve Bank and are not subject to Congressional review. Even more important is that the Federal Reserve generates substantial profits, on the order of $20 billion per year, most of which it returns to the U.S. Treasury, so that it has its own revenue base and is not dependent on funds from the government. Indeed, by law the Federal Reserve is

exempt from General Accounting Office (GAO) audits of deliberations, decisions, or actions on monetary policy matters.

Given its insulation from the political process and its financial independence, it should be no surprise that the Fed has complete control over setting its monetary policy instruments. This has the benefits of enabling the Fed to resist political pressure to engage in time-inconsistent expansionary policy and to be forward-looking in the setting of its policy instruments.

On the criteria of instrument independence the Fed scores well.

Central Banks Should Be Goal Dependent

We have already seen that independence can go too far. Instrument independence is desirable but goal independence is problematic. The independence of the Fed—described above—and the lack of a clear mandate from the government allows the Fed to make the decisions on what the goals of its policies should be. Thus the Fed has a high degree of goal independence. In some ways goal independence makes the Fed's job easier because it insulates it from political pressure, but it does have a downside. The substantial goal independence of the Federal reserve creates a fair amount of tension in a democratic society because it allows an elite group to set the goals of monetary policy. Indeed, recent criticism of the Federal Reserve may have been prompted by the impression that the Federal Reserve, and particularly its Chairman, has become too powerful.

The goal independence of the Federal Reserve should not be seen as total, however. Politicians do have the ability to influence the goals of the Fed because the Congress can modify the Federal Reserve Act at any time. Also, the Fed has a great interest in other legislation that affects its operations. A case in point is the recent Gramm-Bliley-Leach Financial Services Modernization Act, passed in 1999, which had major implications for whether the Federal Reserve would continue to have supervisory responsibilities over large banking organizations (which it continued to keep). Furthermore, Congress can criticize the budget of the Fed for items that are unrelated to monetary policy or foreign-exchange operations. As an example, in 1996 Senators Dorgan and Reid called for Congress to exercise budgetary authority over the nonmonetary activities of the Federal Reserve because they were concerned that the Fed was too focused on fighting inflation and not enough on reducing unemployment.

As a comparison, the Eurosystem should be seen in some ways as more goal independent than the Federal Reserve System and in other ways less. The Maastricht Treaty specifies that the overriding, long-run goal of the ECB is price stability, so that the goal for the Eurosystem is more clearly specified than it is for the Federal Reserve System. However, Maastricht did not specify exactly what this price stability means so the Eurosystem has defined the quantitative goal for monetary policy, an inflation rate between 0 and 2 percent. From this perspective, the Federal Reserve System is slightly less goal dependent than the Eurosystem. On the other hand, the Eurosystem's statutes cannot be changed by legislation, but only by alterations to the Maastricht Treaty. From this perspective, the Eurosystem is much less goal dependent than the Federal Reserve System because its statutes are specified in a treaty and thus are far harder to change than statutes that are embedded in legislation.

As the examples above indicate, the Federal Reserve is not goal dependent, but we should not take this view too far. Thus, on the goal dependence criteria, the Fed's score is mixed.

Central Banks Should Be Accountable

Closely related to goal dependence is the accountability of the central bank to meet its goals. There are formal accountability mechanisms for the Fed. For example, the Chairman of the Board of Governors has been required to testify twice a year to Congress about the conduct of monetary policy under the Humphrey-Hawkins legislation. Also, as we have seen, the Fed is subject to punitive actions by the Congress if it so chooses, either by amending the Federal Reserve Act or through passage of other legislation that affects the Fed.

On these grounds the Federal Reserve System is more accountable than the Eurosystem. As we have seen, the Eurosystem's statutes cannot be modified by legislation but, rather, requires amendment to a treaty, a far more difficult process. Moreover, although the President of the European Central Bank is required to testify once a year to the European Parliament, this requirement may not guarantee sufficient oversight of the Eurosystem's policies. Since the European Parliament is currently significantly less powerful than the national parliaments of the countries that make up the Monetary Union, scrutiny by that organization would not influence the Eurosystem's behavior as strongly as would oversight by a more powerful body, such as a consortium of national parliaments or the individual parliaments themselves. It is not clear to whom the Eurosystem would be accountable.

However, the absence of an explicit nominal anchor means that there is no benchmark against which the public or Congress can measure the performance of the Federal Reserve System. In contrast, the Eurosystem has outlined its price-stability goal of inflation between 0 and 2 percent, so there is a predetermined criterion to judge its performance. Thus, despite the requirement that the Fed testify to Congress, the accountability of the Fed is not very strong. The Federal Reserve is able to obscure what its strategy and goals are and has indeed done this in the past. This leaves open the possibility that there could be a political backlash against a "high-handed" Federal Reserve that could have adverse consequences on its independence and ability to successfully conduct monetary policy in the future.

On the accountability criteria, the Fed also does not score very well.

Central Banks Should Stress Transparency and Communication

In recent years, the Fed has come a long way on the transparency and communication front. In the past, the Fed had a reputation for not only being unclear about its goals and strategy, but for keeping markets in the dark about its setting of policy instruments. This has changed dramatically in recent years. Starting in 1994, the Fed began to announce its policy actions after every FOMC meeting. It then moved in 1999 to announcing the bias in the direction of future moves in the federal funds rate, which caused some confusion, and so replaced this announcement at the beginning of this year with one that indicates the balance of risks for the future—whether toward higher inflation or toward a weaker economy. Fed officials also have been more active in articulating the strategy of monetary policy, its need to be preemptive, and the importance of the pursuit of price stability.

Despite improved transparency and communication, the lack of explicit goals has meant that Fed transparency is still much less than at many other central banks. In contrast to central banks that have adopted inflation targeting, the Fed produces nothing like an "Inflation Report" in which it clearly lays out in plain English the strategy for monetary policy and how well the central bank has been doing. One consequence of the weakness of Fed transparency and communication is that the public debate on monetary policy in the United States still has a tendency to focus on short-run considerations, as reflected in politicians' focus on "jobs, jobs, jobs" when discussing monetary policy. This focus on short-run considerations is substantially less in countries where central banks use communication vehicles such as "Inflation Reports" to refocus the public debate on longer-run considerations such as price stability.

It is interesting to contrast the way public debate is conducted with what has occurred in Canada, which has adopted an inflation-targeting regime with high transparency and accountability. In 1996, the president of the Canadian Economic Association made a speech criticizing the Bank of Canada for pursuing monetary policy that (he claimed) was too contractionary. His speech sparked off a widespread public debate. Instead of degenerating into calls for the immediate expansion of monetary policy with little reference to the long-run consequences of such a policy change, the debate was channeled into a substantive discussion over what should be the appropriate target for inflation, with both the Bank and its critics obliged to make explicit their assumptions and estimates of the costs and benefits of different levels of inflation. Indeed, the debate and the Bank of Canada's record and responsiveness led to increased support for the Bank of Canada, with the result that criticism of the Bank and its conduct of monetary policy was not a major issue in the 1997 elections as it had been during the 1993 elections.

On the transparency and communication criteria, the Fed's score is mixed, although it has been improving over time.

Central Banks Should also Have a Financial Stability Goal

Here the Fed's performance has been very strong. The Greenspan Fed has made it very clear that it will act decisively to prevent financial crises and has done so not only with words but with actions. The Fed's actions immediately after the October 19, 1987, stock market crash are a textbook case of how a lender-of-last-resort role can be performed brilliantly.[8] The Fed's action was immediate, with Greenspan announcing right before the market opened on October 20 of the Federal Reserve System's "readiness to serve as a source of liquidity to support the economic and financial system," which operated to decrease uncertainty in the marketplace. Reserves were injected into the system, but once the crisis was over, they were withdrawn. Not only was a crisis averted so that the business cycle expansion continued, but also the inflationary consequences of this exercise of the lender-of-last-resort role were small. The 75 basis point decrease in the federal funds rate in the Fall of 1998 immediately after the Russian financial crisis and the near-failure of Long-Term Capital Management, which roiled U.S. capital markets, also illustrated the Fed's commitment to act decisively to prevent financial instability. The aftermath was an economy that continued to expand, with inflation staying at the 2 percent level.

On the criteria of the commitment to the financial stability goal, the Fed's score is excellent.

CONCLUSION: WHAT SHOULD THE FED DO?

Our scorecard for the Fed indicates that although the institutional set up of the Fed scores well on some criteria, there is room for improvement in others. But, is there a need for the Fed as an institution to change? The Fed's performance in recent years has been extraordinary. It has been able to bring down inflation in the United States to the 2 percent level, which can reasonably be characterized as being consistent with price stability, while the economy has been experiencing the longest business cycle expansion in U.S. history, with very high rates of economic growth. As my son likes to say, "It don't get no better than this." The natural question then arises: If it ain't broke, why fix it?

However, our Fed scorecard suggests that we do need to consider institutional improvements in the way the central bank operates. The absence of an institutional commitment to price stability, along with weak Fed transparency, which stems from the absence of an explicit nominal anchor, leaves the Fed open to political pressure to pursue short-run objectives (i.e., job creation). This might lead to time-inconsistent expansionary policy and would produce inflation. In the past, after a successful period of low inflation, the Federal Reserve has "fallen off the wagon" and reverted to inflationary monetary policy—the 1970s are one example—and, without an explicit nominal anchor, this could certainly happen again in the future.

Indeed, the most serious problem with the Fed's institutional framework and the way it currently operates is the strong dependence on the preferences, skills, and trustworthiness of the individuals in charge of the central bank. Yes, the Fed under Alan Greenspan has been doing a great job, and so the Fed's prestige and creditability with the public have risen accordingly. But the Fed's leadership will eventually change, and there is no guarantee that the new leadership will be committed to the same approach. Nor is there any guarantee that the relatively good working relationship that now exists between the Fed and the executive branch will continue. In a different economic or political environment—and considering the possibility for a backlash against the Fed's lack of accountability—the Fed might face far stronger attacks on its independence and increased pressure to engage in over-expansionary policies, further raising the possibility that inflation will shoot up again.

So what should the Fed do? The answer is that the Fed should continue in the direction that it has already begun to increase its transparency and accountability. First, it should advocate a change in its mandate to put price stability as the overriding, long-run goal of monetary policy. Second, it should advocate that the price-stability goal should be made explicit, with a numerical long-run inflation goal. Government involvement in setting this explicit goal would be highly desirable, making the Fed goal independent, which should help retain public support for the Fed's instrument independence. Third, the Fed should produce an "Inflation Report" type of document that clearly explains its strategy for monetary policy and how well it has been doing in achieving its announced inflation goal.

The outcome of these changes is that the Fed would be moving to an inflation-targeting regime of the type described in our book, which has been recently published by the Princeton University Press (Bernanke, Laubach, Mishkin, and Posen, 1999). Clearly, the U.S. Congress and executive branch need to play an important role in encouraging the Fed to move toward inflation targeting. A detailed outline of a proposal for how this might be done can be found in our book. I leave you to read it on your own. Otherwise, you will be subjected to another full lecture.

References

Alesina, Alberto, and Lawrence H. Summers. "Central Bank Independence and Macroeconomic Performance: Some comparative Evidence," *Journal of Money, Credit, and Banking* (May 1993), pp. 151–62.

Andersen, Palle, and David Gruen. "Macroeconomic Policies and Growth," in *Productivity and Growth*, Palle Andersen, Jacqueline Dwyer, and David Gruen, eds., Reserve Bank of Australia, 1995, pp. 279–319.

Barro, Robert J., and David Gordon. "A Positive Theory of Monetary Policy in a Natural Rate Model," *Journal of Political Economy* (August 1983), pp. 589–610.

Bernanke, Ben S. "Non-Monetary Effects of the Financial Crisis in the Propagation of the Great Depression," *American Economic Review* (March 1983), pp. 257–76.

_____. "Comment on 'The Synergies Between Bank Supervision and Monetary Policy: Implications for the Design of Bank Regulatory Structure'," in *Prudential Supervision: What Works and What Doesn't*, Frederick S. Mishkin, ed., University of Chicago Press, forthcoming.

_____. Thomas Laubach, Frederic S. Mishkin, and Adam S. Posen. *Inflation Targeting: Lessons from the International Experience*, Princeton University Press, 1999.

Blinder, Alan S. *Central Banking in Theory and Practice*, MIT Press, 1998.

Briault, Clive. "The Costs of Inflation," *Bank of England Quarterly Bulletin* (February 1995), pp. 33–45.

Calvo, Guillermo. "On the Time Consistency of Optimal Policy in the Monetary Economy," *Econometrica* (November 1978), pp. 1411–28.

Corsetti, Giorgio, Paolo Pesenti, and Noriel Roubini. "What Caused the Asian Currency and Financial Crisis? Part I and II," NBER Working Papers, nos. 6833 and 6834, 1998.

Cukierman, Alex. *Central Bank Strategy, Credibility, and Independence: Theory and Evidence*, MIT Press, 1992.

Debelle, Guy, and Stanley Fischer. "How Independent Should a Central Bank Be?" in *Goals, Guidelines, and Constraints Facing Monetary Policymakers*, Jeffrey C. Fuhrer, ed., Federal Reserve Bank of Boston, 1994, pp. 195–221.

English, William B. "Inflation and Financial Sector Size," Finance and Economics Discussion Series No. 96-16, Board of Governors of the Federal Reserve System, April 1996.

Feldstein, Martin. "Capital Income Taxes and the Benefits of Price Stabilization," NBER Working Paper 6200, September 1997.

Fischer, Stanley. "Modern Central Banking," in *The Future of Central Banking*, Forrest Capie, Charles A. E. Goodhart, Stanley Fischer, and Norbert Schnadt, eds., Cambridge University Press, 1994, pp. 262–308.

Friedman, Milton, and Anna J. Schwartz. *A Monetary History of the United States, 1867–1960*, Princeton University Press, 1963.

King, Mervyn, "Changes in UK Monetary Policy: Rules and Discretion in Practice," *Journal of Monetary Economics*, (June 1997), pp. 81–97.

Kydland, Finn, and Edward Prescott. "Rules Rather than Discretion: The Inconsistency of Optimal Plans," *Journal of Political Economy* (June 1977), pp. 473–91.

McCallum, Bennett T. "Inflation: Theory and Evidence," in *Handbook of Monetary Economics*, Ben M. Friedman and Frank H. Hahn, eds., Elsevier Press, 1990, pp. 963–1012.

_____. "Two Fallacies Concerning Central-Bank Independence," *American Economic Review* (May 1995), pp. 207–11.

Mishkin, Frederic S. "Asymmetric Information and Financial Crises: A Historical Perspective," in *Financial Markets and Financial Crises*, R. Glenn Hubbard, ed., University of Chicago Press, 1991, pp. 69–108.

_____. "An evaluation of the Treasury Plan for Banking Reform," *Journal of Economic Perspectives* (Winter 1992), pp. 133–53.

_____. "Understanding Financial Crises: A Developing Country Perspective," in *Annual World Bank Conference on Development Economics*, 1996, pp. 29–62.

_____. *The Economics of Money, Banking, and Financial Markets*, 5th ed., Addison-Wesley Publishing Co., 1998.

_____. "Lessons from the Asian Crisis," *Journal of International Money and Finance* (August 1999a), pp. 709–23.

_____. "International Experiences with Different Monetary Policy Regimes," *Journal of Monetary Economics* (June 1999b), pp. 579–605.

_____, and Adam S. Posen. "Inflation Targeting: Lessons from Four Countries," *Economic Policy Review*. Federal Reserve Bank of New York (August 1997), pp. 9–110.

Peek, Joe, Eric Rosengren, and Geoffrey Tootell, "The Synergies Between Bank Supervision and Monetary Policy: Implications for the Design of Bank Regulatory Structure," in *Prudential Supervision: What Works and What Doesn't*, Frederick S. Mishkin, ed., University of Chicago Press, forthcoming.

Posen, Adam S. "Declarations Are Not Enough: Financial Sector Sources of Central Bank Independence," in *NBER Macroeconomics Annual*, Ben S. Bernanke and Julio J. Rotemberg, eds., MIT Press, 1995, pp. 253–74.

Rogoff, Kenneth. "The Optimal Degree of Commitment to an Intermediate Monetary Target," *Quarterly Journal of Economics* (November 1985), pp. 1169–89.

Sargent, Thomas, and Neil Wallace. "Some Unpleasant Monetarist Arithmetic," *Quarterly Review*, Federal Reserve Bank of Minneapolis (Fall 1981), pp. 1–17.

Svensson, Lars. "Inflation Targeting as Monetary Policy Rule," *Journal of Monetary Economics* (June 1999), pp. 607–54.

Taylor, John, ed. *Monetary Policy Rules*, University of Chicago Press, Chicago, 1999.

Woodford, Michael. "Monetary Policy and Price Level Determinacy in a Cash-in-Advance Economy," *Economic Theory*, vol. 4, no. 3 (1994), pp. 345–80.

_____. "Price-Level Determinacy with Control of a Monetary Aggregate." *Carnegie-Rochester Conference Series on Public Policy* (December 1995), pp. 1–46.

Notes

1. E.g., see English (1996).

2. E.g., see Briault (1995).

3. E. G., see Fischer (1994) and Feldstein (1997).

4. See the survey in Andersen and Gruen (1995).

5. For further discussion of who should set an inflation target in the United States, see Bernanke, Laubach, Mishkin, and Posen (1999).

6. Blinder (1998) also makes a strong case for increased transparency and accountability of central banks.

7. The Eurosystem currently is made up of the eleven national central banks of the countries that have joined EMU, with the European Central Bank (ECB) at the center having a role similar to that of the Board of Governors in the Federal Reserve System.

8. Indeed, this example appears in my textbook (Mishkin, 1998).

From *Review*, November/December 2000, Vol. 82, No. 6, pp. 1–13. © 2000 by the Federal Reserve Bank of St. Louis. Reprinted by permission.

How does monetary policy affect the U.S. economy?

This is the third of four consecutive issues devoted to our updated and expanded Q&A on monetary policy: (1) "How is the Federal Reserve structured?" and "What are the tools of U.S. monetary policy?" (2) "What are the goals of U.S. monetary policy?" (3) "How does monetary policy affect the U.S. economy?" and (4) "How does the Fed decide the appropriate setting for the policy instrument?" The revised text will appear in a pamphlet soon.

The point of implementing policy through raising or lowering interest rates is to affect people's and firms' demand for goods and services. This section discusses how policy actions affect real interest rates, which in turn affect demand and ultimately output, employment, and inflation.

What are real interest rates and why do they matter?

For the most part, the demand for goods and services is not related to the market interest rates quoted in the financial pages of newspapers, known as nominal rates. Instead, it is related to *real* interest rates—that is, nominal interest rates minus the expected rate of inflation.

For example, a borrower is likely to feel a lot happier about a car loan at 8% when the inflation rate is close to 10% (as it was in the late 1970s) than when the inflation rate is close to 2% (as it was in the late 1990s). In the first case, the real (or inflation-adjusted) value of the money that the borrower would pay back would actually be lower than the real value of the money when it was borrowed. Borrowers, of course, would love this situation, while lenders would be disinclined to make any loans.

So why doesn't the Fed just set the real interest rate on loans?

Remember, the Fed operates only in the market for bank reserves. Because it is the sole supplier of reserves, it can set the nominal funds rate. The Fed can't set real interest rates directly because it can't set inflation expectations directly, even though expected inflation is closely tied to what the Fed is expected to do in the future. Also, in general, the Fed has stayed out of the business of setting nom-

inal rates for longer-term instruments and instead allows financial markets to determine longer-term interest rates.

How can the Fed influence long-term rates then?

Long-term interest rates reflect, in part, what people in financial markets expect the Fed to do in the future. For instance, if they think the Fed isn't focused on containing inflation, they'll be concerned that inflation might move up over the next few years. So they'll add a risk premium to long-term rates, which will make them higher. In other words, the markets' expectations about monetary policy tomorrow have a substantial impact on long-term interest rates today. Researchers have pointed out that the Fed could inform markets about future values of the funds rate in a number of ways. For example, the Fed could follow a policy of moving gradually once it starts changing interest rates. Or, the Fed could issue statements about what kinds of developments the FOMC is likely to focus on in the foreseeable future; the Fed even could make more explicit statements about the future stance of policy.

How do these policy-induced changes in real interest rates affect the economy?

Changes in real interest rates affect the public's demand for goods and services mainly by altering borrowing costs, the availability of bank loans, the wealth of households, and foreign exchange rates.

For example, a decrease in real interest rates lowers the cost of borrowing; that leads businesses to increase investment spending, and it leads households to buy durable goods, such as autos and new homes.

In addition, lower real rates and a healthy economy may increase banks' willingness to lend to businesses and households. This may increase spending, especially by smaller borrowers who have few sources of credit other than banks.

Lower real rates also make common stocks and other such investments more attractive than bonds and other debt instruments; as a result, common stock prices tend to rise. Households with stocks in their portfolios find that the value of their holdings is higher, and this increase in wealth makes them willing to spend more. Higher stock prices also make it more attractive for businesses to invest in plant and equipment by issuing stock.

In the short run, lower real interest rates in the U.S. also tend to reduce the foreign exchange value of the dollar, which lowers the prices of the U.S.-produced goods we sell abroad and raises the prices we pay for foreign-produced goods. This leads to higher aggregate spending on goods and services produced in the U.S.

The increase in aggregate demand for the economy's output through these different channels leads firms to raise production and employment, which in turn increases business spending on capital goods even further by making greater demands on existing factory capacity. It also boosts consumption further because of the income gains that result from the higher level of economic output.

How does monetary policy affect inflation?

Wages and prices will begin to rise at faster rates if monetary policy stimulates aggregate demand enough to push labor and capital markets beyond their long-run capacities. In fact, a monetary policy that persistently attempts to keep short-term real rates low will lead eventually to higher inflation and higher nominal interest rates, with no permanent increases in the growth of output or decreases in unemployment. As noted earlier, in the long run, output and employment cannot be set by monetary policy. In other words, while there is a trade-off between higher inflation and lower unemployment in the short run, the trade-off disappears in the long run.

Policy also affects inflation directly through people's expectations about future inflation. For example, suppose the Fed eases monetary policy. If consumers and businesspeople figure that will mean higher inflation in the future, they'll ask for bigger increases in wages and prices. That in itself will raise inflation without big changes in employment and output.

Doesn't U.S. inflation depend on worldwide capacity, not just U.S. capacity?

In this era of intense global competition, it might seem parochial to focus on U.S. capacity as a determinant of U.S. inflation, rather than on world capacity. For example, some argue that even if unemployment in the U.S. drops to very low levels, U.S. workers wouldn't be able to push for higher wages because they're competing for jobs with workers abroad, who are willing to accept much lower wages. The implication is that inflation is unlikely to rise even if the Fed adopts an easier monetary policy.

This reasoning doesn't hold up too well, however, for a couple of reasons. First, a large proportion of what we consume in the U.S. isn't affected very much by foreign trade. One example is health care, which isn't traded internationally and which amounts to nearly 15% of U.S. GDP.

More important, perhaps, is the fact that such arguments ignore the role of flexible exchange rates. If the Fed were to adopt an easier policy, it would tend to increase the supply of U.S. dollars in the market. Ultimately, this would tend to drive down the value of the dollar relative to other countries, as U.S. consumers and firms used some of this increased money supply to buy foreign goods and foreigners got rid of the additional U.S. currency they did not want. Thus, the price of foreign goods in terms of U.S. dollars would go up—even though they would not in terms of the foreign currency. The higher prices of imported goods would, in turn, tend to raise the prices of U.S. goods.

How long does it take a policy action to affect the economy and inflation?

It can take a fairly long time for a monetary policy action to affect the economy and inflation. And the lags can vary a lot, too. For example, the major effects on output can take anywhere from three months to two years. And the effects on inflation tend to involve even longer lags, perhaps one to three years, or more.

Why are the lags so hard to predict?

So far, we've described a complex chain of events that links a change in the funds rate with subsequent changes in output and inflation. Developments anywhere along this chain can alter how much a policy action will affect the economy and when.

For example, one link in the chain is long-term interest rates, and they can respond differently to a policy action, depending on the market's expectations about future Fed policy. If markets expect a change in the funds rate to be the beginning of a series of moves in the same direction, they'll factor in those future changes right away, and long-term rates will react by more than if markets had expected the Fed to take no further action. In contrast, if markets had anticipated the policy action, long-term rates may not move much at all because they would have factored it into the rates already. As a result, the same policy move can appear to have different effects on financial markets and, through them, on output and inflation.

Similarly, the effect of a policy action on the economy also depends on what people and firms outside the financial sector think the Fed action means for inflation in the future. If people believe that a tightening of policy means the Fed is determined to keep inflation under control, they'll immediately expect low inflation in the future, so they're likely to ask for smaller wage and price increases, and this will help achieve low inflation. But if people aren't convinced that the Fed is going to contain inflation, they're likely to ask for bigger wage and price increases, and that means that inflation is likely to rise. In this case, the only way to bring inflation down is to tighten so much and for so long that there are significant losses in employment and output.

What problems do lags cause?

The Fed's job would be much easier if monetary policy had swift and sure effects. Policymakers could set policy, see its effects, and then adjust the settings until they eliminated any discrepancy between economic developments and the goals.

But with the long lags associated with monetary policy actions, the Fed must try to anticipate the effects of its policy actions into the distant future.

To see why, suppose the Fed waits to shift its policy stance until it actually sees an increase in inflation. That would mean that inflationary momentum already had developed, so the task of reducing inflation would be that much harder and more costly in terms of job losses. Not surprisingly, anticipating policy effects in the future is one of the more difficult parts of conducting monetary policy, and it's a key issue in the next and final *Economic Letter* in this series, "How does the Fed decide the appropriate setting for the policy instrument?"

Suggested reading

For further discussion of the topics in this article, see the following issues of the *FRBSF Economic Letter*.

93–38 "Real Interest Rates," by Bharat Trehan. `http://www.frbsf.org/publications/economics/letter/1993/el93-38.pdf`

95–35 "What Are the Lags in Monetary Policy?" by Glenn Rudebusch. `http://www.frbsf.org/publications/economics/letter/1995/el1995-05.pdf`

95–23 "Federal Reserve Policy and the Predictability of Interest Rates," by Glenn Rudebusch. `http://www.frbsf.org/publications/economics/letter/1995/el1995-23.pdf`

97–18 "Interest Rates and Monetary Policy," by Glenn Rudebusch `http://www.frbsf.org/econrsrch/wklyltr/el97-18.html`

2002–30 "Setting the Interest Rates," by Milton Marquis. `http://www.frbsf.org/publications/economics/letter/2002/el2002-30.pdf`

How Does the Fed Decide the Appropriate Setting for the Policy Instrument?

This is the last of four issues devoted to our updated and expanded Q&A on monetary policy: (1) "How is the Federal Reserve structured?" and "What are the tools of U.S. monetary policy?" (2) "What are the goals of U.S. monetary policy?" (3) "How does monetary policy affect the U.S. economy?" and (4) "How does the Fed decide the appropriate setting for the policy instrument?" The revised text will appear in a pamphlet soon.

The Fed's job of stabilizing output in the short run and promoting price stability in the long run involves several steps. First, the Fed tries to estimate how the economy is doing now and how it's likely to do in the near term—say, over the next couple of years or so. Then it compares these estimates to its goals for the economy and inflation. If there's a gap between the estimates and the goals, the Fed then has to decide how forcefully and how swiftly to act to close that gap. Of course, the lags in policy complicate this process. But so do a host of other things.

What things complicate the process of determining how the economy is doing?

Even the most up-to-date data on key variables like employment, growth, productivity, and so on, reflect conditions in the past, not conditions today; that's why the process of monetary policymaking has been compared to driving while looking only in the rearview mirror. So, to get a reasonable estimate of current and near-term economic conditions, the Fed first tries to figure out what the most relevant economic developments are; these might be things like the government's taxing and spending policies, economic developments abroad, financial conditions at home and abroad, and the use of new technologies that boost productivity. These developments can then be incorporated into an economic model to see how the economy is likely to evolve over time.

Sounds easy—plug the numbers into the model and get an answer. So what's the problem?

There are lots of problems. One problem is that models are only approximations—they can't capture the full complexity of the economy. Another problem is that, so far, no single model adequately explains the entire economy—at least, you can't get economists to agree on a single model; and no single model outperforms others in predicting future developments in every situation. Another problem is that the forecast can be off base because of unexpected, even unprecedented, developments— the September 11 attacks are a case in point. So in practice, the Fed tries to deal with this uncertainty by using a variety of models and indicators, as well as informal methods, to construct a picture of the economy. These informal methods can include anecdotes and other information collected from all kinds of sources, such as the Directors of the Federal Reserve Banks, the Fed's various advisory bodies, and the press.

So now are we in a position to compare the Fed's estimates with its goals?

Not so fast. Coming up with operational measures of the goals is harder than you might think, especially the goal for the rate of maximum sustainable output growth. Unfortunately, this is not something you can go out and measure. So, once again, the Fed has to turn to some sort of model or indicator to estimate it. And it's hard to be certain about any estimate, in part because it's hard to be certain that the model or indicator the estimate is based on is the right one. There's one more important complication in estimating the rate of maximum sustainable growth— it can shift over time!

What problems does a shift in the rate of maximum sustainable growth cause?

The experience of the late 1990s provides a good example of the policy problems caused by such a shift. During this period, output and productivity surged at the same time that rapid innovation was transforming the information technology industry.

In the early stages, there was no way for the Fed—or anybody else—to tell why output was growing so fast. In other words, the Fed had to determine how much of the surge in output was due to unusually rapid technical progress and whether this implied an increase in the economy's trend growth rate.

This was a crucial issue because policy would respond differently depending on exactly why the economy was growing faster. If it was largely due to the spread of new technologies that enhanced worker and capital productivity, implying that the trend growth rate was higher, then the economy could expand faster without creating inflationary pressures. In that case, monetary policy could stand pat. But if it was just the economy experiencing a more normal business cycle expansion, then inflation could heat up. In that case, monetary policy would need to tighten up.

The Fed's job was complicated by the fact that statistical models did not find sufficient evidence to suggest a change in the trend growth rate. But the Fed looked at a variety of indicators, such as the profit data from firms, as well as at informal evidence, such as anecdotes, to conclude that the majority of the evidence was consistent with an increase in the trend growth rate. On that basis, the Fed refrained from tightening policy as much as it would have otherwise.

Does the trend growth rate ever get slower?

Yes, it does. A good example, with a pretty bad outcome, was what happened in the early 1970s, a period marked by a significant *slowdown* in the trend growth rate. A number of economists have argued that the difficulty in determining that such a slowdown had actually taken place caused the Fed to adopt an easier monetary policy than it might otherwise have, which in turn contributed to the substantial acceleration in inflation observed later in the decade.

What happens when the estimates for growth and inflation are different from the Fed's goals?

Let's take the case where the forecast is that growth will be below the goal. That would suggest a need to ease policy. But that's not all. The Fed also must decide two other things: (1) how strongly to respond to this deviation from the goal and (2) how quickly to try to eliminate the gap. Once again, it can use its models to try to determine the effects of various policy actions. And, once again, the Fed must deal with the problems associated with uncertainty as well as with the measurement problems we have already discussed.

Uncertainty seems to be a problem at every stage. How does the Fed deal with it?

Uncertainty does, indeed, pervade every part of the monetary policymaking process. There is as yet no set of policies and procedures that policymakers can use to deal with all the situations that may arise. Instead, policymakers must decide how to proceed by going case by case.

For instance, when policymakers are more uncertain about their reading of the current state of the economy, they may react more gradually to economic developments than they would otherwise. And because it's hard to come up with unambiguous benchmarks for the economy's performance, the Fed may look at more than one kind of benchmark. For instance, because it's hard to get a precise estimate of the trend growth rate of output, the Fed may look at the labor market to try to figure out where the unemployment rate is relative to some kind of benchmark or "natural rate," that is, the rate that would be consistent with price stability. Alternatively, it might try to determine whether the stance of policy is appropriate by comparing the real funds rate to an estimate of the "equilibrium interest rate," which can be defined as the real rate that would be consistent with maximum sustainable output in the long run.

These issues are far from settled. Indeed the Fed spends a great deal of time and effort in researching various ways to deal with different kinds of uncertainty and in trying to figure out what kind of model or indicator is likely to perform best in a given situation. Since these issues aren't likely to be resolved anytime soon, the Fed is likely to continue to look at everything.

Suggested reading

For further discussion of the topics in this article, see the following issues of the *FRBSF Economic Letter.*

93-01 "An Alternative Strategy for Monetary Policy," by Brian Motley and John Judd. http://www.frbsf.org/publications/economics/letter/1993/el93-01.pdf

93-38 "Real Interest Rates," by Bharat Trehan. http://www.frbsf.org/publications/economics/letter/1993/el93-38.pdf

93-42 "Monetary Policy and Long-Term Real Interest Rates," by Timothy Cogley. http://www.frbsf.org/publications/economics/letter/1993/el93-42.pdf

97-29 "A New Paradigm?" by Bharat Trehan. http://www.frbsf.org/econrsrch/wklyltr/el97-29.html

97-35 "NAIRU: Is It Useful for Monetary Policy?" by John Judd. http://www.frbsf.org/econrsrch/wklyltr/el97-35.html

98-28 "The Natural Rate, NAIRU, and Monetary Policy," by Carl Walsh. http://www.frbsf.org/econrsrch/wklyltr/wklyltr98/el98-28.html

98-38 "Describing Fed Behavior," by John Judd and Glenn Rudebusch. http://www.frbsf.org/econrsrch/wklyltr/wklyltr98/el98-38.html

99-21 "Supply Shocks and the Conduct of Monetary Policy," by Bharat Trehan. http://www.frbsf.org/econrsrch/wklyltr/wklyltr99/el99-21.html

99-33 "Risks in the Economic Outlook" by Robert T. Parry. http://www.frbsf.org/econrsrch/wklyltr/wklyltr99/el99-33.html

2000-21 "Exploring the Causes of the Great Inflation," by Kevin Lansing. http://www.frbsf.org/econrsrch/wklyltr/2000/el2000-21.html

2000-31 "Monetary Policy in a New Environment: The U.S. Experience" by Robert T. Parry. http://www.frbsf.org/econrsrch/wklyltr/2000/el2000-31.html

2001-05 "How Sluggish Is the Fed?" by Glenn Rudebusch. http://www.frbsf.org/publications/economics/letter/2001/el2001-05.html

2001-13 "The Science (and Art) of Monetary Policy" by Carl Walsh. http://www.frbsf.org/publications/economics/letter/2001/el2001-13.html

2003-14 "Minding the Speed Limit" by Carl Walsh. http://www.frbsf.org/publications/economics/letter/2003/el2003-14.html

2003-32 "The Natural Rate of Interest" by John Williams. http://www.frbsf.org/publications/economics/letter/2003/el2003-32.html

2003-34 "Should the Fed React to the Stock Market?" by Kevin Lansing. http://www.frbsf.org/publications/economics/letter/2003/el2003-34.html

How Sluggish Is the Fed?

How quickly does the Fed adjust monetary policy in response to developments in the economy? A common view among economists is that the Fed changes the short-term policy interest rate at a very sluggish pace over several quarters. Under this view, if the Fed wanted to increase the policy rate by a percentage point, it would typically change the rate by only about 25 basis points per quarter for the next few quarters. The evidence supporting this "monetary policy inertia" view is found in the many monetary policy rules or reaction functions estimated in the literature with quarterly data. These estimates appear to imply a very slow speed of adjustment of the policy rate to its fundamental determinants. For example, Clarida, Gali, and Gertler (2000, pp. 157–158) describe their empirical estimates of Fed behavior as " . . .suggesting considerable interest rate inertia: only between 10% and 30% of a change in the [desired interest rate] is reflected in the Funds rate within the quarter of the change." This conventional wisdom is also adopted in Woodford (1999), Levin, Wieland, and Williams (1999), Amato and Laubach (1999), Sack and Wieland (2000), and many other analyses.

This *Economic Letter*, which summarizes Rudebusch (2001), argues that this widespread view is mistaken and that the Fed actually responds quite promptly within the quarter to economic developments. The evidence against the existence of an inertial policy rule is obtained from the behavior of short-term market interest rates. There appears to be very little information generally available in financial markets regarding future interest rate movements beyond the next one or two months. This absence of interest rate predictability cannot be reconciled with a significant degree of interest rate partial adjustment by the Fed; however, an alternative explanation that stresses the persistence of shocks that the Fed faces is consistent with the evidence.

Policy inertia and interest rate predictability

Recently, there have been many attempts to estimate policy rules or reaction functions that explain Fed behavior. These es-

timation equations take a general partial adjustment form, where the level of the policy interest rate in a given quarter is set as a weighted average of the current desired level and last quarter's actual interest rate. Based on quarterly data, estimates of this weighted average put about one-fifth of the weight on the desired rate and about four-fifths on the lagged actual rate. Thus, these empirical rules appear to imply a very slow speed of adjustment of the policy rate—about a 20% adjustment each quarter. This gradual adjustment of the short-term rate over several quarters to its desired level is widely interpreted as evidence of an "interest rate smoothing" or "monetary policy inertia" behavior by central banks.

One implication that has been overlooked in the literature is that a significant amount of policy inertia should imply a lot of predictive information in financial markets about the future path of short-term interest rates. Intuitively, if the funds rate is typically adjusted by only 20% toward its desired target in a given quarter, then the remaining 80% adjustment should be expected to occur in future quarters. (Rudebusch (2001) shows that this link between predictable interest rate variation and monetary inertia ought to hold in a wide variety of settings.)

In a statistical analysis of the data, the sluggish adjustment of interest rates by the Fed means that a regression of actual changes in interest rates on predicted changes should yield a good fit (i.e., a moderately high R^2). In fact, many researchers have estimated such interest rate predictability regressions using postwar data in order to determine how much information financial markets actually have about future interest rate movements (see, for example, Mankiw and Miron 1986 and Rudebusch 1995). These studies typically have found little predictive information. In particular, beyond a horizon of a few months, there appears to be very little ability to forecast changes in short-term interest rates (i.e., a forecast regression R^2 close to zero).

Indeed, the literature on interest rate predictability explicitly rejects any notion of sluggish adjustment by the Fed. Mankiw and Miron (1986, p. 225) note that the postwar data suggest that at a quarterly frequency ". . . while the Fed might change the short rate in response to new information, it always (rationally) expected to maintain the short rate at its current level." Goodfriend (1991, p. 10) provides an identical random-walk characterization of the policy rate and argues that changes in the rate set by the Fed ". . . are essentially unpredictable at forecast horizons longer than a month or two." Similarly, Rudebusch (1995, p. 264) characterizes the Fed's behavior as, ". . . beyond a horizon of about a month, there are no planned movements to react to information already known."

The illusion of monetary policy inertia

Although many policy rule and reaction function estimates appear to provide direct empirical evidence of sluggish adjustment by the Fed, the presence of such quarterly partial adjustment or inertia is contradicted by the lack of interest rate forecastability in financial markets. Thus, the apparent monetary policy inertia is an illusion and must be explained by an alternative interpretation of the Fed's behavior.

As a first step in this explanation, note that there is a large literature that argues that the partial adjustment model widely used to explain the Fed's behavior is very difficult to identify and estimate in the presence of persistent shocks or unobserved omitted variables. In particular, rather than reflecting some form of partial adjustment, the significant lagged funds rate in the estimated policy rule may be evidence of persistent special factors, or shocks, that are not properly accounted for in the rule. Accordingly, it is hard to tell whether the Fed's adjustment was sluggish, or whether the Fed generally followed a rule with no policy inertia but sometimes deviated from this rule for several quarters at a time.

What would cause such persistent deviations from the rule? Recall the original analysis of Taylor (1993), which put forward a description of monetary policy that did not involve partial adjustment. Taylor argued that recent historical monetary policy had followed a rule only as a guide, so occasional deviations from the rule were appropriate responses to special circumstances, not evidence of partial adjustment. This view is illustrated in Figure 1, which displays the historical values of the federal funds rate and the fitted values from an estimated noninertial Taylor rule, which sets this policy interest rate in response to the output gap and inflation. The large persistent shocks, the deviations between the two lines, appear to correspond to several special circumstances (rather than to sluggish adjustment). Most notably, the deviations in 1992 and 1993 are commonly interpreted as responses to a disruption in the flow of credit. As Fed Chairman Alan Greenspan testified to Congress on June 22, 1994:

> Households and businesses became much more reluctant to
> borrow and spend and lenders to extend credit—a phenome-
> non often referred to as the "credit crunch." In an endeavor
> to defuse these financial strains, we moved short-term rates

Figure 1
Historical funds rate and fitted Taylor rule

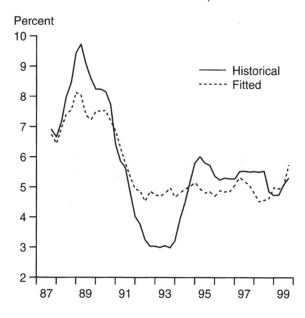

lower in a long series of steps that ended in the late summer of 1992, and we held them at unusually low levels through the end of 1993—both absolutely and, importantly, relative to inflation.

Thus, this episode is better described as a persistent "credit crunch" shock or omitted unobservable variable than as a sluggish partial adjustment to a known desired rate. In terms of the Taylor rule, the disruption of credit supply can be treated as a temporary fall in the equilibrium real rate, which the Fed responds to by lowering the funds rate (relative to readings on output and inflation). Similarly, a worldwide financial crisis appeared to play a large role in lowering rates in 1998 and 1999, and commodity price scares helped push rates up in 1988–1989 and 1994–1995. Alternatively, Lansing (2000) argues that the Fed may have deviated from the rule because of persistent errors in the real-time measurement of the output gap.

While the rule with partial adjustment and the rule with persistent shocks both appear to fit the data, they have very different economic interpretations. In the former rule, persistent deviations from an output and inflation response occur because policymakers are slow to react. In the latter rule, these deviations reflect the policymaker's response to other influences. The two types of rules can be distinguished, however, because only the rule with persistent shocks is consistent with the historical evidence that short-term interest rates are largely uninformative about the future course of the policy rate.

Should the Fed be sluggish?

Some researchers also have argued that monetary policy inertia may be an optimal behavioral response on the part of central banks. For example, one popular argument contends that policy inertia helps the central bank focus the public's expectations on its stabilization goals and thereby achieve a better outcome (e.g., Levin, Wieland, and Williams, 1999, Woodford, 1999, and Sack and Wieland, 2000). However, central bankers tend to be skeptical of such arguments, especially having been accused of moving too slowly during the run-up in inflation in the 1970s and having had some success with a forward-looking "preemptive" policy more recently. Indeed, the absence of partial adjustment does not mean that central banks are not trying to influence expectations of future short-term interest rates as well as long-term interest rates. In order to influence such rates, central banks only must present a clear future path for the policy rate. The partial adjustment rule provides one such path, but it is not the only one. As noted by Goodfriend (1991) and Rudebusch (1995), the expectation of a constant interest rate path, which is approximately what the non-inertial rules deliver, is another obvious choice to communicate policy intentions.

Glenn D. Rudebusch
Senior Research Advisor

References

Amato, Jeffery, and Thomas Laubach. 1999. "The Value of Interest Rate Smoothing: How the Private Sector Helps the Federal Reserve." *Economic Review*, Federal Reserve Bank of Kansas, Third Quarter, pp. 47–64.

Clarida, Richard, Jordi Gali, and Mark Gertler. 2000. "Monetary Policy Rules and Macroeconomic Stability: Evidence and Some Theory." *Quarterly Journal of Economics* 115, pp. 147–180.

Goodfriend, Marvin. 1991. "Interest Rates and the Conduct of Monetary Policy." *Carnegie-Rochester Series on Public Policy* 34, pp. 7–30.

Lansing, Kevin. 2000. "Learning about a Shift in Trend Output: Implications for Monetary Policy and Inflation." FRBSF Working Paper 2000-16. http://www.frbsf.org/econrsrch/workingp/2000/ wp00-16bk.pdf.

Levin, Andrew, Volker Wieland, and John C. Williams. 1999. "*Robustness of Simple Monetary Policy Rules under Model Uncertainty.*" In Monetary Policy Rules, ed. John B. Taylor, pp. 263–299. Chicago: Chicago University Press.

Mankiw, N. Gregory, and Jeffrey A. Miron. 1986. "The Changing Behavior of the Term Structure of Interest Rates." *The Quarterly Journal of Economics* 101, pp. 211–228.

Rudebusch, Glenn D. 1995. "Federal Reserve Interest Rate Targeting, Rational Expectations, and the Term Structure." *Journal of Monetary Economics* 35, pp. 245–274.

Rudebusch, Glenn D. 2001. "Term Structure Evidence on Interest Rate Smoothing and Monetary Policy Inertia." FRBSF Working Paper 2001–02. http://www.frbsf.org/publications/economics/papers/2001/wp01-02bk.pdf.

Sack, Brian, and Volker Wieland. 2000. "Interest Rate Smoothing and Optimal Monetary Policy: A Review of Recent Empirical Evidence." *Journal of Economics and Business* 52, pp. 205–228.

Taylor, John B. 1993. "Discretion versus Policy Rules in Practice." Carnegie- Rochester Conference Series on Public Policy 39, pp. 195–214.

Woodford, Michael. 1999. "Optimal Monetary Policy Inertia." *The Manchester School Supplement*, pp. 1–35.

The Science (and Art) of Monetary Policy

During most of the 1990s, the United States experienced exceptionally good times, and the Federal Reserve received some of the credit for the booming economy and low inflation. Figure 1 shows the marked decline in the civilian unemployment rate from a peak of 7.8% in June 1992 to a low of 3.9% in September 2000. In May 1997, the unemployment rate fell below 5% for the first time since 1973—and it stayed there for the rest of the decade. Although some were concerned that inflation would re-ignite because of tight labor markets, instead it remained in check. In fact, the inflation rate, measured by the Consumer Price Index (CPI), actually *declined* through most of the 1990s. When the more volatile food and energy components of the CPI are removed, the resulting measure of inflation has remained below 3% since 1993.

The last eighteen months, however, have presented the Federal Reserve with particularly difficult policy decisions. In the summer of 1999, concerned that inflation was threatening, the Fed raised its target for the federal funds interest rate. From a level of 4.74% in May 1999, the funds rate rose as a result of Fed policy until it peaked at 6.54% in August 2000. As 2000 drew to a close, increasing signs of economic slowing led the Fed to cut interest rates, lowering its target for the funds rate twice in January, once in March, and once in April.

This swing in interest rates, together with some criticism that the Fed might have raised rates too much in 2000 and not cut them enough in 2001, raises the question of whether there are any guiding principles that the Fed has followed, or could have followed, in making its decisions. Are there rules for designing and implementing good monetary policy that all economists agree on? Or is policymaking inherently a subjective task, one that depends critically on combining both good economics and insightful judgment?

Is monetary policy a science?

A recent article by three leading monetary economists, Rich Clarida, Jordi Gali, and Mark Gertler, is titled "The Science of Monetary Policy." The word "science" in the title suggests that economists now have all the knowledge they need to design and implement good monetary policy. If that were so, the public's focus on Alan Greenspan as the Chairman of the Federal Reserve would be misplaced—monetary policy would not depend on an individual's judgment. Instead, just as sending a rocket to Mars or building a bridge depends critically on the input from scientists and engineers, implementing the science of monetary policy would require only a staff of good economists.

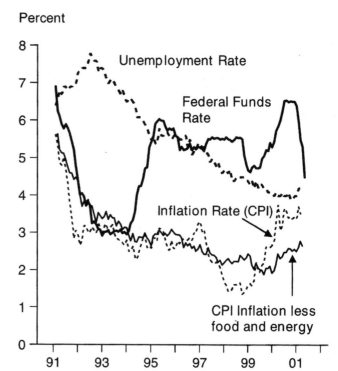

Figure 1 Unemployment, inflation, and the funds rate

Currently, many economists are in agreement with three basic principles that form the core of the "scientific" approach to monetary policy. Each of these principles is designed to guide central bankers.

Principle 1: Focus on the output gap. A huge literature in the 1980s and 1990s showed how excessive inflation can result if a central bank aims for output objectives that are too ambitious. If, for example, the central bank engages in expansionary policies in an attempt to keep output above potential, the net result will only be a higher average rate of inflation. Well-meaning central banks could find themselves generating rates of inflation well above what they had wanted without any gains in long-term output.

Many solutions to this problem have been suggested. The simplest is to have the central bank adopt a realistic output objective. Specifically, the central bank should strive to stabilize output around potential output, sometimes also called full-employment output. This objective is usually expressed by saying the central bank should stabilize the *output gap*, the difference between actual real output and potential. In the words of economist Lars Svensson, "…there is considerable agreement among academics and central bankers that the appropriate [monetary policy objective] both involves stabilizing inflation around an inflation target and stabilizing the real economy, represented by the output gap" (Svensson 1999).

Principle 2: Follow the Taylor Principle. The second principle in the "scientific" approach to monetary policy is to follow the Taylor Principle. This principle states that the central bank's policy interest rate should be increased more than one for one with increases in the inflation rate. Named after Stanford University economist John Taylor, the Taylor Principle ensures that an increase in the inflation rate produces a policy reaction that increases the real rate of interest—the interest rate corrected for inflation. The rise in the real interest rate reduces private spending, slows the economy down, and brings inflation back to the central bank's inflation target. Conversely, if inflation falls below the central bank's target, the Taylor Principle calls for a more than one for one cut in the central bank's policy interest rate. This reduces the real rate of interest, stimulates private spending, and pushes inflation back to its target level.

Policies that violate the Taylor Principle can lead to serious problems. If a rise in inflation is met by a less than one for one increase in the policy rate, then real interest rates actually fall. This fuels further economic expansion, pushing inflation even higher. Rather than acting to bring inflation back down to its target level, such a policy can cause inflation to spiral out of control.

One way to implement the Taylor Principle is to follow a Taylor Rule, also named after John Taylor, which specifies exactly how much to change the federal funds rate in response to changes in inflation and the output gap.

Principle 3: Be forward-looking. Monetary policy actions affect the economy with a lag. An interest rate cut may not have its maximum impact on real output for twelve or even eighteen months, and the effects on inflation may take longer still. Central banks cannot wait to act until inflation has increased or the economy has gone into a recession. These lags mean that central banks must be

forward-looking. For example, when the Fed raised interest rates in 2000, inflation was still quite low, once the volatile food and energy components were removed. The Fed acted because it was concerned that inflation would otherwise begin to rise.

The public clearly believes that implementing monetary policy is not something that can be delegated to unknown government economists in Washington.

One policy framework that satisfies these three principles is *inflation forecast targeting*. Under an inflation forecast targeting procedure, the central bank is concerned with stabilizing inflation at low levels and with stabilizing the output gap. Because of the lags in policy, the emphasis is on responding to the central bank's forecast of future inflation. If the forecast says inflation will rise, the central bank should act to slow the economy down—it doesn't wait until inflation actually has increased. Because inflation forecast targeting is based on the three policy principles, it has gained many adherents among academic and central bank economists.

Economists have significantly advanced their understanding of the principles of good monetary policy in recent years. Yet the public clearly believes that implementing monetary policy is not something that can be delegated to unknown government economists in Washington. The public believes leadership matters, and that it matters that Federal Reserve Chairman Alan Greenspan is in charge of policy. Is there more to achieving good monetary policies than simply following the economist's scientific principles?

Is monetary policy an art?

Perhaps the public believes Alan Greenspan's leadership matters because they believe monetary policy is, in part, an art. It requires the fine touch of a master policymaker, one whose feel for the correct moment to change interest rates cannot be reduced to a few scientific principles. But if making policy isn't a science, what exactly is nonscientific about it? The best way to understand the "art" of policymaking is to revisit our three policy principles.

How can we focus on the output gap when we don't know what it is? It's all very well to tell central banks to focus on the output gap, but how are they supposed to know what the gap is? When major shifts in productivity growth occur—as happened in the 1970s with the productivity slowdown and again in the 1990s with the productivity speedup, measuring the output gap can be difficult. The output gap is the difference between something we can measure (real GDP) and something we can't (the economy's potential output level). Trying to determine how new information technologies would affect productivity growth and whether the growth speedup would be sustained was a major issue confronting policymakers in the 1990s. As the economy grew rapidly during the second half of the decade, economists were uncertain whether real output was rising above potential, in which case interest rate hikes would be called for, or whether both actual and potential output were growing more rapidly, leaving the output gap stable.

A similar problem had beset the Fed during the 1970s. Then, the problem was the productivity slowdown. Some economists have argued that the Fed failed to recognize at the time that potential was growing more slowly than before. As a consequence, the Fed interpreted the slowdown in actual growth as a reflection that output was falling below potential. In fact, both actual and potential declined relative to their previous trends. Because the gap had not fallen, policy was too expansionary in the early 1970s, helping to fuel inflation.

Implementing the Taylor Principle. The Taylor Principle calls for adjusting the policy interest rate more than one for one with changes in inflation. But how much more? If inflation rises by 1 percentage point, should the federal funds rate be increased by 1.5 percentage points? 2 percentage points? Or 1.01 percentage points? The Taylor Principle alone does not offer guidance.

The art of conducting policy lies in the ability to translate the general principles into actual policy decisions.

Responding strongly to changes in inflation will help keep inflation more stable around a low average level, but it also will result in larger fluctuations in output and employment. A weaker response results in greater fluctuations in the inflation rate but more stable output and employment. Hence, there is a trade-off between inflation stability and employment stability. Making the right trade-off requires good judgment.

The art of forecasting. Implementing inflation forecast targeting means the central bank has to be able to forecast future economic conditions. This is not an easy task. Last summer, economic forecasts did not foresee the growth slowdown that began during the third quarter. The Fed had to respond quickly in early 2001 as signs of an economic slowdown developed.

Good forecasts are based on good data, good economic models, *and* good judgment. Mechanical forecasts based on a few key indicators inevitably ignore information that might be relevant. While statistical models provide a baseline for developing economic forecasts, good forecasters always supplement the models' predictions with judgmental adjustment.

Conclusion

Economists have contributed much to making the design of monetary policy more scientific. From the articulation of general principles for good policy to the construction of small models that can be used to simulate the impacts of alternative policies, recent research by academic and central bank economists has contributed to our knowledge about monetary policy. Despite these advances, however, conducting policy is far from routine. General principles are important, but they're not sufficient—policymakers also need quantifiable guidance. They need to know whether the current output gap is +2% or -2%. They need to know whether the funds rate should be increased by 150 basis points or 200 for every 1 percentage point rise in inflation. And they need to know how much inflation will rise or fall over the next six months. This level of guidance is still missing from the science of monetary policy. The art of conducting policy lies in the ability to translate the general principles into actual policy decisions.

There is a long tradition of trying to take discretion out of monetary policy—Milton Friedman's proposal that the Fed should just ensure a constant annual growth rate for the money supply was an example of a policy designed to remove the role of the individual policymaker. While economists have identified broad principles to guide policymakers, making policy is not a science. Good policy will probably always require good policymakers, as it requires combining the science of the economist with the art of the practitioner.

Carl E. Walsh
Professor of Economics, UC Santa Cruz, and Visiting Scholar, FRBSF

References

Clarida, Richard, Jordi Galí, and Mark Gertler. 1999. "The Science of Monetary Policy: A New Keynesian Perspective." *Journal of Economic Literature 37* (December) pp. 1,661–1,707.

Svensson, Lars E. O. 1999. "How Should Monetary Policy Be Conducted in an Era of Price Stability?" In *New Challenges for Monetary Policy*, pp. 195–259. Federal Reserve Bank of Kansas City.

THE NEW WORLD OF BANKING

BY JIM CAMPEN

ART BY JULIE DELTON

Beginning when Jimmy Carter was president in the late 1970s, the halls of Congress echoed almost annually with passionate speeches about the need to modernize the nation's banking laws. These laws, most importantly the Glass-Steagall Act of 1933 and the Bank Holding Company Act of 1956, prohibited banks, insurance companies, and securities firms from entering each other's businesses. For more than two decades, Congress remained gridlocked as different types of financial firms fought over who would gain the most from rewriting the laws.

Last year, however, things were different. On November 12, shortly after Congress approved a compromise acceptable to all three industries, Bill Clinton signed into law the Gramm-Leach-Bliley Financial Service Modernization Act of 1999 (named for the chairmen of the three Congressional committees that shaped the legislation). The key provisions of the act make possible a new kind of corporation—called a *financial holding company*—that allows any number of banks, insurance companies, and securities firms to be brought together under the same corporate umbrella. The result is likely to be another wave of financial megamergers, as the largest firms in each of the three industries begin buying each other.

A preview of what is to come was provided by the 1998 deal that joined Citibank, Travelers Insurance, and the Wall Street firm Solomon Smith Barney into Citigroup, the country's largest financial firm with over $700 billion in assets. This merger, which gained temporary approval under a loophole in the law, is now fully legal; without the change in the law, Citigroup would have had to be broken apart in a few years. In fact, pressure from Citigroup helped ensure that the long-delayed legislation actually passed.

THE "ON-GOING REVOLUTION"

Some observers hailed the new law as the most important financial legislation in over 60 years. They view the repeal of the Glass-Steagall Act as a long-overdue piece of "financial modernization" that allows U.S. financial companies to offer their services more cheaply and conveniently and to better compete in the global economy. They forsee the creation of "financial supermarkets" where customers—both businesses and consumers—can engage in "one-stop" shopping for all of their financial needs.

This view is greatly exaggerated. Rather than being a dramatic break from the past, the Gramm-Leach-Bliley Act is best seen as one symbolically important milestone in what former Federal Reserve Board Chairman Arthur Burns, writing in 1987, described as "the on-going revolution in American banking."

The new law increases financial systems unfairness by its failure to deal effectively with the growing threats to consumer privacy.

During the three decades following World War II, the U.S. financial system, operating under a set of laws and regulations established during the Great Depression of the 1930s, changed very little. These laws compartmentalized the financial system both by type of product and by geography. But for at least the last 25 years, these barriers have steadily eroded as high-paid lawyers found loopholes in the existing laws and regulators relaxed their interpretations of the rules.

Years before last fall's new law, it was possible to buy insurance or invest in mutual funds at many banks, to get checking accounts from investment companies, or to invest in the stock and bond markets through insurance companies. By 1997, the barriers to banks expanding both within and between states had disappeared, and now one bank—BankAmerica—has over 4,500 branches ranging from Alaska to Florida. Even the heart of the Glass-Steagall Act, the wall separating commercial banks—which offer checking accounts and business loans—from investment banks—which help corporations raise money by selling stocks and bonds—was already seriously breached.

Thus, the new law is best regarded as tidying up and consolidating the dramatic set of changes in the financial system that had been going on for many years. Nevertheless, its passage provides a good opportunity to consider the significance and impact of these changes.

ASSESSING "FINANCIAL DEFORM"

As always, it is useful to ask who wins and who loses as a result of a new law. Although the President, Congressional leaders, and bank spokespeople all claimed the new law would benefit consumers, consumer advocates themselves strongly disagreed. Not long before the law passed, 41 national organizations— including consumer, civil rights, labor, affordable housing,

human services, and environmental groups—had sent a joint letter to Congress urging lawmakers to vote against the measure. Consumer advocate Ralph Nader concluded that under the new law consumers would face "fewer choices, higher prices, and greater risks for taxpayers." That the real winners were the country's largest financial corporations could be seen in the upward surge of their stock prices in mid-October when it finally became clear that the new law would go through.

Megabanks lose touch with the details of local economic life needed to actually direct financial resources to their most productive use.

To better assess the impact of the new banking law, we need to consider the relationship between the financial system and the rest of the economy. Banks and other financial companies are not particularly important in themselves. For example, the banking industry employs less than 1.2% of the nation's workers. What does matter is the financial system's crucial effects on what happens in the "real" productive sectors of the economy. Banks and other financial companies channel funds from investors and savers who have more money than they will spend to borrowers who want to spend more than they currently have. Almost every major expenditure—whether by a business building a new factory, a family buying a new home, or a local government upgrading school facilities— involves borrowing money.

To evaluate the functioning of our financial system, we should consider first whether its operation contributes to *stability* in the economy. Lawmakers designed the 1930s system of banking laws and regulations in the well-founded belief that speculation and collapse in financial markets and widespread bank failures played a crucial role in bringing about the Great Depression.

Second, we should consider whether the financial system promotes economic *efficiency* by channeling funds to those who will make the best use of them. Third, we should consider whether the operation of the financial system promotes *fairness* by providing capital, credit, and financial services in a nondiscriminatory and nonexploitative manner that enables all citizens to participate equitably in economic life.

Unfortunately, in important ways the Gramm-Leach-Bliley Act will make things worse according to all three criteria. That's why Hubert Von Tol, of the Wisconsin Rural Development Center, refers to the changes as financial "deform" rather than "reform."

THE BIGGER THEY ARE, THE HARDER THEY FALL

As banking institutions get bigger and bigger, there is growing danger that the failure of a single company could destabilize the entire financial structure and send the real economy into a tailspin. This is exactly the fear of Federal Reserve Board Chairman Alan Greenspan who has warned that the megabanks are becoming "complex entities that create the potential for unusually large systemic risks in the national and international economy should they fail." Senator Paul Wellstone, the Democrat from Minnesota, used more expressive language: "Today's quest for giantism has swept aside the voices of prudence."

The law imposes absolutely no limits on the ability of the various affiliated companies operating under the same corporate umbrella to share all of this information among themselves.

The probability that one of the new financial conglomerates will fail is increased because top managers of the new firms may have neither the expertise nor the attention span to be able to effectively monitor and control all of their broad range of activities. This problem is made worse by the fragmented nature of financial regulation under the new law, which divides oversight responsibility among the Fed, three other bank regulators, the Securities and Exchange Commission, and other agencies, none of which wanted to lose power in the restructuring. Furthermore, even though insurance companies can now affiliate with federally insured banks in the newly authorized financial holding companies, Congress decided to leave regulation of the insurance industry exclusively to the states, where regulatory agencies are generally understaffed, under-funded, and no match for the insurance companies that they are supposed to supervise. As a result there is growing danger that some risky activity will fall between the cracks and not be effectively supervised by any of the regulators.

MONOPOLY POWER AND INEFFICIENCY

One of the basic assumptions of mainstream economics is that producers and customers, each seeking their own advantage in competitive markets, will generally bring about efficient (although nor necessarily just) use of resources. On the other hand, mainstream economic theory also recognizes that unregulated markets don't always work properly and that in these cases of "market failure," the government needs to intervene to bring about efficient outcomes.

As financial companies become ever larger, their growing power increases the likelihood of "market failure." In the marketplace, concentrated economic power becomes monopoly power that enables large financial companies to set prices (such as checking account fees) higher than they could in a competitive market where many banks vie for business. At the same time, the concentrations of economic power contribute to con-

centrations of political power that can be used to block government policies the big banks didn't like.

In addition, as banks get bigger and bigger their decision-making power is concentrated in headquarters located hundreds or even thousands of miles from the communities where their customers live. Megabanks may be able to mass-produce standardized loan products at relatively low cost, but they lose touch with the details of local economic life needed to actually direct financial resources to their most productive use. For example, minority-owned small businesses that are well-adapted to neighborhood conditions may not do well in the new automated "credit-scoring" typically used by the big lenders, and may therefore end up being denied the credit they need to survive and expand.

FADING FAIRNESS

Fairness suffers under the new law not because of what it contains, but because of what it omits. Congress enacted the Community Reinvestment Act (CRA) in 1977 because banks were unfairly neglecting inner city neighborhoods when it came time to lend money. Over the years, and especially in the 1990s, the CRA— which requires banks to loan money in all of the neighborhoods where they do business—has contributed greatly to economic fairness by forcing banks to meet the credit needs of lower-income and minority borrowers and neighborhoods that had previously been underserved.

However, when the Gramm-Leach-Bliley Act "modernized" the financial system by allowing different kinds of financial companies to expand into each other's businesses, it failed to simultaneously "modernize" the CRA, which continues to apply only to banks. The new bank law should have expanded CRA's reach to include the other kinds of financial companies that compete with banks in making loans and by imposing similar obligations on insurance companies and investment firms. As the relative importance of these other financial companies steadily grows, this failure to "modernize" the CRA means that it "will apply to an ever shrinking share of the financial services world," according to Debby Goldberg of the Center for Community Change in Washington, D.C.

Some members of the House Banking Committee, including Reps. Maxine Waters of California, and Mike Capuano of Massachusetts, introduced and fought for amendments that would have extended and expanded the CRA. The amendments also would have increased fairness in other ways, such as requiring companies to offer inexpensive "lifeline" bank accounts to people currently shut out of the mainstream financial system.

In the end, however, it took a determined and united stand by Congressional Democrats, backed up by the consistent threat of a presidential veto, simply to stop Congress from seriously gutting the CRA. The Republican assault on the law was led by Senate Banking Committee Chairman—and former economics professor—Phil Gramm of Texas. The *New York Times* quoted Gramm as saying that the existing CRA rules were "an evil like slavery in the pre-Civil War era."

The new law also increases unfairness in the financial system by its failure to deal effectively with the growing threats to consumer privacy. One of the main motivations behind the wave of bank merges in recent years has been the desire to take advantage of new technology that makes it possible to assemble vast databases of information on customers that can be used to aid marketing and decision–making. The new financial holding companies will continue this trend even further, being able to bring together information about a person's spending (from checking and credit card records), investing (from brokerage and mutual fund records), and even medical conditions (from insurance records).

The law imposes absolutely no limits on the ability of the various affiliated companies operating under the same corporate umbrella to share all of this information among themselves, and only weak limits on sharing the information with outside companies. Even conservative senator Richard Shelby of Alabama, the second-ranking Republican on the Senate Banking Committee, called the privacy protections in the new law "a sham." He joined colleagues from both Houses and both parties in organizing a Congressional Privacy Caucus to push for more meaningful protection of people's confidential financial information.

Advocates of greater privacy rights and of expanding the CRA promise to wage grassroots campaigns that will persuade Congress to redress its failures in the Gramm-Leach-Bliley Act of 1999. Their demands for increased financial fairness offer one more reason to see this law as just one important development in an on-going process of change in the financial system, rather than the end of the story.

D&S Associate Jim Campen teaches economics at the University of Massachusetts-Boston.

Banking Consolidation

Until this year, Citigroup was the only $1 trillion banking organization in the U.S. Now, there are two more—Bank of America has merged with FleetBoston, and J.P. Morgan Chase is about to complete its merger with Bank One. These megamergers are notable not only for their size but also for the geographic scope that the new institutions will serve. Indeed, they may signal the beginning of a process for building a truly national banking franchise. As mergers continue to shape the structure of the banking industry in the U.S., this *Economic Letter* looks at the economic drivers behind them and highlights some important policy implications.

Background on recent consolidation

The Riegle-Neal Act allowed interstate branch banking beginning in 1997, and, since then, the number of large bank mergers has increased significantly. Figure 1 plots this trend along with another noteworthy trend, namely, that most of the large bank mergers in recent years involved institutions headquartered in different states; the latter point suggests that these are market-expansion mergers, where the acquirer and the target have few overlapping operations in their respective banking markets. Although the markets they serve are much bigger, so far none of these three megabanks has come close to having a banking franchise that spans all 50 states, which is now legally possible.

Another noteworthy fact about the recently announced megamergers is that the target banking companies are healthy institutions that are likely to survive as independent organizations. This is in stark contrast both to the late 1980s and early 1990s in the U.S., when many bank mergers involved relatively weak banking companies being acquired by somewhat stronger organizations, as well as to some large bank mergers abroad, most notably in Japan. Today the U.S. banking sector is in good shape, with record profits and relatively low volumes of problem loans. For example, the

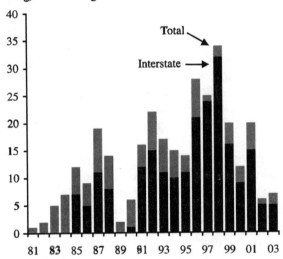

Figure 1

Large bank mergers

Note: Both targets and acquirers have more than $1 billion in total assets.

return on average assets in 2003 for the two merger targets, Bank One and FleetBoston, were 1.27% and 1.34%, respectively, while the top 50 bank holding companies averaged 1.28%. This suggests that the recent megamergers are not motivated by economic weakness but rather by other economic forces.

Economic forces driving megamergers

We can identify four economic forces that may be driving large bank mergers. First is economies of scale—the relationship between the average production cost per unit of output and production volume. A firm that produces a higher volume of output can see its unit cost of production decline because the costs of some of the inputs are fixed, such as administrative and overhead expenses. However, diseconomies of scale also are possible. The average production cost may start to rise when output exceeds a certain volume because it may be more costly to manage a very large firm; these costs may stem from corporate governance issues, difficulties in coordination and execution, and diminished flexibility in responding quickly to changing markets.

While banking researchers generally agree that economies of scale do exist in the industry at low levels of output, there is less agreement about whether diseconomies of scale emerge at high levels of output. Earlier studies found evidence that diseconomies of scale did occur when total banking assets exceeded roughly $10 billion; however, those results were based on banking data prior to the passage of the Riegle-Neal Act, when banking companies operating in multiple states had to maintain separately capitalized, individually chartered bank subsidiaries in those states. The passage of Riegle-Neal allows these banking organizations to consolidate the individual state charters into a single charter, thus greatly streamlining management and operations. On the cost side, it is apparent that the cost structure of running a network of bank branches across multiple states should be more efficient than running a group of individually capitalized bank subsidiaries. On the revenue side, research on megamergers suggests that merged banks experienced higher profit efficiency from increased revenues than did a group of individual banks, because they provided customers with higher value-added products and services (Akhavein, Berger, and Humphrey 1997). Moreover, a banking organization of a certain scale may even earn a "too-big-to-fail" subsidy due to the market's perception of de facto government backing of a megabank in times of crisis. While the combination of all these factors could raise the optimal scale of large banking organizations today, it remains to be seen whether a $1 trillion bank is the "right" size.

The second economic force is economies of scope—a situation where the joint costs of producing two complementary outputs are less than the combined costs of producing the two outputs separately. This may arise when the production processes of both outputs share some common inputs, including both capital (such as the actual building the bank occupies) and labor (such as bank management).The passage of the Gramm-Leach-Bliley Act (GLB) in 1999 changed the scope of permissible financial activities for banking organizations. In the past, banking organizations were not allowed to engage in securities activities except on a limited, case-by-case basis through their so-called Section 20 subsidiaries. Also, general insurance activities were not permitted for banking firms, except in very small towns with fewer than 5,000 residents. GLB al-

lows banking organizations to expand into securities and insurance activities in a much more straightforward way (see Furlong 2000 for more details). Although the two recently announced megamergers mainly involve combining banking activities, the potential of scope economies among banking, securities, and insurance could further increase the optimal size of a large banking organization today compared to pre-GLB days.

The third economic force is the potential for risk diversification. Research suggests that geographic expansion would provide diversification benefits to a banking organization not only by reducing its portfolio risk on the asset side, but also by lowering its funding risk on the liability side, as it spreads funding activities over a larger geographic area (Hughes, Lang, Mester, and Moon 1999). Furthermore, research suggests that product expansion could yield diversification benefits, most notably between banking and securities activities, while less so between banking and insurance (see the survey article by Kwan and Laderman 1999). Thus, a bigger bank is expected to be less vulnerable to economic shocks, and that alone could reduce its cost of capital, further compounding the benefits of scale and scope economies that come only from the production process.

The fourth economic force involves the bank managements' personal incentives. These may include the desire to run a larger firm and the desire to maximize their own personal welfare. Empirical research has shown that managerial compensation and perquisite consumption tend to rise with firm size. Research on stock market reactions to megamerger announcements in the 1990s suggests that, on average, the market did not view mergers of publicly owned banking companies as providing a significant gain to total shareholders' wealth of the combined company (Kwan and Eisenbeis 1999). The muted market response to merger announcements raises questions about the true magnitude of the net economic benefits underlying large bank mergers.

Policy implications

First and foremost, bank mergers have the potential to raise antitrust concerns, which must be resolved satisfactorily before being approved. Because bank mergers can alter banking market structure and because market structure influences banking competition and hence the price of banking services to customers, all bank merger applications are scrutinized by banking regulators. In addition, the Department of Justice has the authority to challenge any mergers that are deemed harmful to competition. Research suggests that the markets for many banking products and services remain local in nature, despite the advances in information technology and electronic commerce (Rhoades 2000). In fact, the recent market-expansion megamergers themselves are testimony to the importance these large banking organizations attach to maintaining a local market presence. Thus, the current regulatory practices of defining banking markets locally in evaluating the effects of proposed mergers on competition seem justified. When a proposed merger is found to result in an unacceptably high level of concentration in local banking markets, divestitures in those markets are often required as a condition for regulatory approval in order to preserve meaningful competition. Looking at western states, Laderman (2003) found that changes in concentration of local banking markets were quite modest despite the large degree of consolidation in banking over the past 20 years.

In addition to concerns about banking concentration effects on local market competition, existing banking legislation also limits banking concentration at the national level. Perhaps motivated by the fear of concentration of banking power, the Riegle-Neal Act prohibits any merger or acquisition that results in a combined banking organization controlling more than 10% of the total amount of deposits of insured depository institutions in the U.S. A banking organization could exceed the deposit cap through internal growth, but it would not be allowed to engage in any more mergers or acquisitions. While the combined Bank of America and FleetBoston organization would control about 9.9% of the national deposit share, it is still not yet close to being a truly national bank. Thus, the drive toward building a truly nationwide franchise could be severely constrained by current law. As banking organizations get closer to the cap, policymakers will face growing pressure to reconsider both the merits of the deposit cap and the best way to accomplish the associated public policy goals.

The creation of megabanks also heightens concerns about systemic risk. When banking activities are concentrated in a few very large banking companies, shocks to these individual companies could have repercussions to the financial system and the real economy. The desire to limit systemic risk may lead policymakers to maintain some kind of cap on banking concentration at the national level.

The increased potential of systemic risk created by megabanks also intensifies concerns about these banks being considered "too-big-to-fail" (TBTF). In the early 1990s, the FDIC Improvement Act (FDICIA) included measures to limit the extension of TBTF to failing banks. Specifically, it mandated that the FDIC use the least cost resolution method to handle bank failures, thus greatly raising uninsured bank creditors' exposure to default risk. It appears to have led market participants to revise their views towards TBTF. This, in conjunction with the National Depositor Preference law (1993), which put depositors ahead of subordinated debt holders, may explain the research findings showing a significant increase in the sensitivity of the default risk premium of bank subordinated debt to banking organizations' underlying risks after FDICIA. However, there is still an exception in FDICIA—which can be invoked only in extraordinary circumstances—that permits the FDIC to pay off a failing bank's uninsured creditors if the use of least cost resolution would have serious adverse effects on economic conditions or financial stability. Megamergers create more such potentially systemically important banks and put a higher premium on credible policies for the orderly resolution of troubled large banking organizations—policies that limit the potential for moral hazard while containing their adverse impacts on financial markets.

Conclusions

There are a number of possible economic drivers for megamergers, from economic efficiency to the self-interest of bank management. Due to the profound changes in banking laws in the 1990s, earlier research on bank mergers may not be applicable to today's environment; therefore, it remains to be seen whether the current bank megamergers result in any measurable efficiency gains. Nevertheless, the ever-growing scale of bank mergers raises challenging policy questions, including banking concentration at the national level and systemic risk concerns, that must be addressed by policymakers in the course of promoting economic efficiency while safeguarding the nation's financial system.

Simon Kwan
Vice President,
Financial Research

References

Akhavein, J.D., A.N. Berger, and D.B. Humphrey. 1997. "The Effects of Megamergers on Efficiency and Prices: Evidence from a Bank Profit Function." *Review of Industrial Organization* 12, pp. 95-139.

Furlong, F. 2000. "The Gramm-Leach-Bliley Act and Financial Integration." *FRBSF Economic Letter* 2000-10.

Hughes, J.P., W. Lang, L.J. Mester, and C.G. Moon. 1999. "The Dollars and Sense of Bank Consolidation." *Journal of Banking and Finance* 23, pp. 291-324.

Kwan, S.H., and R.A. Eisenbeis. 1999. "Mergers of Publicly Traded Banking Organizations Revisited." *Federal Reserve Bank of Atlanta Economic Review* 84(4), pp. 26-37.

Kwan, S.H., and E. Laderman. 1999."On the Portfolio Effects of Financial Convergence: A Review of the Literature." FRBSF *Economic Review* 2, pp. 18-31.

Laderman, E. 2003."Good News on Twelfth District Banking Market Concentration." *FRBSF Economic Letter* 2003-31.

Rhoades, S.A. 2000."Bank Mergers and Banking Structure in the United States, 1980-98." Federal Reserve Staff Study 174.

Commentary:
A Banking Rule for Another Era

Why an old prohibition against linking loans and services is obsolete

By Mara Der Hovanesian

What's so terrible? Big banks give big loans to big companies in return for a promise to do future business deals. The banks make money by selling a bundle of services, while Corporate America gets cheap loans and a bulk discount for one-stop shopping. Yet the whole transaction may be illegal.

That's because a law born of antitrust concerns seven decades ago stayed on the books in 1999 when most other Depression-era restrictions on banks were swept away. The broader reforms allowed banks to do both commercial and investment banking. But banks of all stripes still are banned from making so-called tied loans, or loans granted only on the condition that a borrower agrees to buy other services.

It's time to dump that rule, too. As it stands, the law applies to banks that have a dominant position in the services they provide. But in today's competitive markets, "no one bank has dominance over bank credit," says bank regulator John D. Hawke Jr., Comptroller of the Currency. The notion of widespread abuse "is one of the phoniest issues of all time," he adds. "Are we to believe that big, sophisticated borrowers are going to be coerced?" The Fed agrees. "Cross-marketing and cross-selling, whether suggestive or aggressive, are part of the nature of ordinary business dealings and do not, in and of themselves, represent a violation," it said in an Aug. 25 statement.

Still, the debate rages on. In March, the Association for Financial Professionals, a trade group based in Bethesda, Md., reported that 56% of companies with sales greater than $1 billion say that a commercial bank had denied them credit or changed its terms because they did not award the bank other financial business. "It's naive to think that banks don't hold market power over credit," says James A. Kaitz, AFP's chief.

Investment bankers, no surprise, second that view. The likes of Morgan Stanley and Goldman Sachs Group Inc.—whose market share in either brokerage services or invest-ment banking has been under attack by banks and other new entrants—argue that they are at a competitive disadvantage because they have far less capital and don't want to use it to fund low-margin lending. Says one veteran Wall Street banker: "[Tying] is a form of extortion." But that can cut both ways: Enron Corp. executives may have bullied Wall Street into granting credit in return for receiving investment banking business.

Representative John D. Dingell (D-Mich.) has asked the General Accounting Office to investigate illegal tying—for a second time in five years. There are abuses: In August, the Fed fined German bank WestLB $3 million for requiring that loan clients use it for debt underwriting in 2001. But after studying bank practices from 1990 to 1996, the GAO found "limited evidence" of wrongdoing. Insiders say the new report is unlikely to conclude that tying has resulted in widespread disadvantages to corporate clients.

A bank is entitled to consider its overall relationship with customers before extending them credit. Some banks are doing so quite aggressively: Bank of America has more than halved its loan portfolio in three years, and Bank One Corp. dropped 200 large borrowers because they didn't do enough other business. Chief financial officers are smart enough to raise cash with bonds if they can't get bank loans. They don't need protection from an antique law harking back to the time when it was bank credit, or nothing.

The Cycles of Financial Scandal

Will an era of reform follow a decade of excess?

By Kevin Phillips

GOSHEN, Conn.
America is at a turning point. Corporate scandals, the fall of the stock markets, the sudden mobilizations in Washington of the last few weeks to legislate against some of the more egregious corporate abuses: they all indicate that the nation's attitude toward business is changing. It is potentially a bigger change than many politicians realize. What's unnerving them is that the payback from the market bubble of the late 1990's is becoming apparent to Main Street. The charts of the downside since March 2000 are starting to match the slope of the earlier three-year upside.

Not that it's a new phenomenon. In the Gilded Age of the late 19th century and again in the Roaring Twenties, wealth momentum surged, the rich pulled away from everyone else and financial and technological innovation built a boom. Then it went partially or largely bust in the securities markets. Digging out is never easy. But this time, the deep-rooted nature of "financialization" in the United States that developed in the 1980's and 90's may make it even tougher.

Near the peak of the great booms, old economic cautions are dismissed, financial and managerial operators sidestep increasingly inadequate regulations and ethics surrender to greed. Then, after the collapse, the dirty linen falls out of the closet. Public muttering usually swells into a powerful chorus for reform— deep, systemic changes designed to catch up with a whole new range and capacity for frauds and finagles and bring them under regulatory control.

Even so, correction is difficult, in part because the big wealth momentum booms leave behind a triple corruption: financial, political and philosophic. Besides the swindles and frauds that crest with the great speculative booms, historians have noted a parallel tendency: cash moving into politics also rises with market fevers.

During the Gilded Age, the railroad barons bought legislatures and business leaders bought seats in the United States Senate. In the last years of the 19th century, one senator naïvely proposed a bill to unseat those senators whose offices were found to have been purchased. This prompted a colleague to reply, in all seriousness, "We might lose a quorum here, waiting for the courts to act."

Over the last two decades, the cost of winning a seat in Congress has more than quadrupled. Legislators casting votes on business or financial regulation cannot forget the richest 1 percent of Americans, who make 40 percent of the individual federal campaign donations over $200. Money is buying policy.

Speculative markets and growing wealth momentum also corrupt philosophy and ideology, reshaping them toward familiar justifications of greed and ruthlessness. The 1980's and 1990's have imitated the Gilded Age in intellectual excesses of market worship, laissez-faire and social Darwinism. Notions of commonwealth, civic purpose and fairness have been crowded out of the public debate.

Part of the new clout and behavior of finance is so deep-rooted, however, that it raises questions that go far beyond the excesses of the bubble. In the last few decades, the United States economy has been transformed through what I call financialization. The processes of money movement, securities management, corporate reorganization, securitization of assets, derivatives trading and other forms of financial packaging are steadily replacing the act of making, growing and transporting things.

That transformation has many roots. Finance surged in the 80's partly because deregulation removed old ceilings on interest rates and let financial institutions offer new services. The rising stock market, in turn, drew money from savings accounts into money market funds and mutual funds, turning the securities industry into a huge profit center. Computers underpinned the expansion of everything from A.T.M.'s to scores of new derivative instruments by which traders could gamble with such dice as Treasury note futures or Eurodollar swaps. Meanwhile, the Federal Reserve and Treasury Department proved during the 80's and 90's that nothing too bad could happen in the financial sector, because Washington was always ready with a bailout.

Supported so openly, rescued from the stupid decisions and market forces that pulled down other industries, the finance, insurance and real estate sector of the economy overtook manufacturing, pulling ahead in the G.D.P. and national income charts in 1995. By 2000, this sector also moved out front in profits. It also became the biggest federal elections donor and the biggest spender on Washington lobbying.

The effects have been profoundly inegalitarian—and not just in the loss of manufacturing's blue-collar middle class. In the last two decades, as money shifted from savings accounts into mutual funds, promoting the stock markets and the money culture, corporate executives became preoccupied with stock options, compensation packages and golden parachutes. "More" became the byword.

In the new management handbook as rewritten by finance, the concerns of employees, shareholders and even communities could be jettisoned to raise stock prices. Major companies could make (or fake) larger profits by financial devices: writing futures contracts, investing in stocks, juggling pension funds, moving low-return assets into separate partnerships and substituting stock options for salary expenses. Enron was only the well-publicized tip of a large iceberg.

A century ago, putting a new regulatory framework around abuses of the emergent railroad and industrial sectors became a priority. This effort largely succeeded. Whether another such framework must be put in place around finance in order to safeguard household economic security is a question that at the very least calls for a national debate. Whether the current proposals are the beginnings of that debate or mere window dressing remains to be seen.

Kevin Phillips is the author of "Wealth and Democracy: A Political History of the American Rich."

UNIT 5

Employment, Prices, and the Business Cycle

Unit Selections

24. **Macro Policy Lessons from the Recent Recession**, Christian Weller, Josh Bivens, and Max Sawicky
25. **The New Growth Economics: How to Boost Living Standards Through Technology, Skills, Innovation, and Compensation**, Robert D. Atkinson
26. **The Mystery of Economic Recessions**, Robert J. Shiller
27. **The Cost of Living and Hidden Inflation**, James Devine
28. **A Fight Against Fear As Well As Inflation**, Edmund L. Andrews
29. **Link Between Taxation, Unemployment Is Absent**, Jonathan Weisman
30. **Does Lower Unemployment Reduce Poverty?**, Robert H. Defina
31. **Employment May Be Even Weaker Than You Think**, Francis X. Markey
32. **More Jobs, Worse Work**, Stephen S. Roach
33. **Lighting Labor's Fire**, Barbara Ehrenreich and Thomas Geoghegan

Key Points to Consider

- What is the present outlook for employment, price stability, and economic growth in the U.S. economy?

- How effetive has macroeconomic policy been in countering the recent recession?

- Is there a link between unemployment and inflation? And taxes? And poverty?

- What role might U.S. labor unions play in reducing unemployment?

 **Links: www.dushkin.com/online/**
These sites are annotated in the World Wide Web pages.

U.S. Census Bureau
http://www.census.gov
U.S. Department of Labor
http://www.dol.gov
WorkIndex
http://workindex.com

Beware the economist who forecasted nine of the last five recessions.

Anonymous

Business cycles are a key feature of all market-based, capitalist economies. While no two cycles are identical (either in terms of their intensity or duration), they all share a common characteristic: a wave of expansion (or rising real Gross Domestic Product [GDP]) is always followed by a period of contraction (when real GDP falls)—which ultimately ends and is followed by another expansion. Economists use many terms to characterize these events. The top of the expansion is sometimes called a "boom" or a "peak." If the subsequent contraction lasts for more than six months, it is officially known as a "recession." At the end of the recession there is a "trough," after which the economy expands again (the "recovery"). Whatever the terminology one employs, the "peak-contraction-trough-expansion" pattern is an essential fact of economic life.

Business cycles exert a powerful influence on modern economies. As real output rises, expansions can result in many thousands of new jobs for workers, which then shows up as a drop in the "unemployment rate" (the ratio of the number unemployed to the civilian labor force). New investment opportunities open up, leading to the creation of countless new business ventures. Unfortunately, history also shows that expansions are seldom risk free; if they prove to be too vigorous, shortages of labor and other resources may develop. As the economy's output approaches capacity, pressures on wages and prices can develop, and the rate of inflation accelerates. A quite different scenario might be that, as output expands during the recovery, employment rises, but only slowly (hence the term "jobless recovery.")

One of the more interesting macroeconomic questions is: how much output growth can an economy sustain without overheating? In the 1960s economists developed the notion that there was a close inverse relationship between unemployment and inflation. This theory (represented by what is called a "Phillips curve") holds that when the unemployment rate falls below some critical level, inflation accelerates. The exact nature of this relationship has been the topic of much debate in recent years. At one point it was believed that any drop in unemployment below six percent would trigger inflation. When (in the early 1990s) such a decline did occur—without any acceleration of inflation—some economists revised their estimate of the critical unemployment rate downward, to five-and-a-half, or even five percent. Recent experience provides little evidence in support of the Phillips relationship, however.

This unit begins with an article in which the authors assess macroeconomic policy-making during the recent recession. They conclude that a more coordinated policy could have resulted in an economy that started to recover quickly, would probably have resulted in more job growth, and would not have left America with high future budget deficits.

Economists have yet to be able to pinpoint what ultimately causes recessions. Contrary to what many economists believe, Robert Shiller (in "The Mystery of Economic Recessions") ar-

gues that changes in the level of confidence in the economy, not the Federal Reserve, is what basically determines its ups and downs.

The next article deals with various aspects of inflation. Economists generally maintain that official measures of inflation overstate the nature of price increases to the extent that they do not sufficiently account for the improved quality of products. In "The Cost of Living and Hidden Inflation" James Devine argues that, if we account for all pertinent changes in the quality of life, inflation is understated. Then, Edmund Andrews suggests that inflationary expectations depend heavily on confidence in the Federal Reserve as a guardian of price stability. If that confidence is to remain strong, they may be forced to move at a more "measured pace."

The remaining articles of this unit concern issues of unemployment. Jonathan Weisman contends that the relationship between taxes and unemployment is far more complicated than many people (including politicians) understand. This is followed by an essay in which Robert Defina presents empirical evidence that the link between unemployment and poverty is not as strong as many people believe it is. Stephen Roach then asserts that, even though the U.S. job picture has improved recently, a troubling aspect is that a large share of the new jobs are at the lower end of the economic spectrum.

Macro Policy Lessons from the Recent Recession

It is time to take a look back at how effective the Bush economic policies have been. In one of the most comprehensive analyses of policy to date, these economists present a critical historical analysis of recent policy. They conclude that more coordinated policy could have resulted in an economy that started to recover quickly, would probably have resulted in more job growth, and would not have left America with ongoing sources of instability and high future budget deficits.

Christian Weller, Josh Bivens, and Max Sawicky

Rumors about the death of the business cycle were greatly exaggerated. In March 2001, the United States entered its first recession in more than a decade. Growth recovered by the end of 2001, but two years into the recovery, employment was still lower than at the start of the recovery. Hence the term "job loss" recovery.

A closer look at the macro policies that were pursued during the recession and the recovery teaches us that policymakers, particularly the Bush administration, could have done more to boost economic growth and that a different policy mix would have left the United States more stable in the long-term:

- Monetary policy did not influence investment and only affected consumption by fueling a refinancing boom, which was augmented by rising house prices. Although this was a fortunate occurrence and one that policymakers will be unable to replicate in the future, it still demonstrated the usefulness of aggressively countercyclical monetary policy.

- Fiscal policy has had significant effects on sustaining consumption demand in this recovery. Instead of large, permanent tax cuts, however, well-designed and targeted spending increases could have been more efficient in boosting domestic demand in the short run without creating long-term structural deficits.

- Growth was hampered by a ballooning trade deficit, caused by a high value of the dollar. Policymakers, for instance, could have leaned harder on trading partner countries that manipu-

lated their currencies. This would have helped to stabilize the economy in the long run by reducing its external indebtedness.

As a result of the policy mix during the recession and the recovery, U.S. economic prospects are unstable in the long run. Household debt levels and the trade deficit reached record highs, and long-term federal structural deficits reemerged. Well-designed stimulus plans could have provided much faster growth in the recovery with much less deleterious effects on the long-run balance sheets of the U.S. economy.

Shallow Recession, Sluggish Recovery

Despite initial declines, real gross domestic product (GDP) was slightly higher, 0.2 percent, by the end of the recession than at the start.[1] During all other postwar recessions, the economy declined on average by 1.7 percent, and during the first year after the start of this recession the economy grew modestly by 1.4 percent, compared to its typical decline of 0.6 percent a year after prior recessions. Thus, the output decline in this recession was much less pronounced than in previous ones.

A sluggish recovery followed the shallow recession. During the first year of a recovery, the economy has normally grown by 7.4 percent and by 9.8 percent in the first six quarters. In this recovery, the economy expanded by 2.9 percent in the first year, and by 4.1 percent in the first six quarters. Growth in this recovery was less than half of what it was during prior ones.

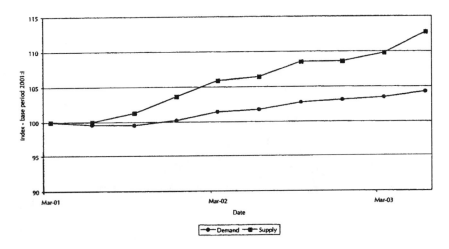

Figure 1. Aggregate Supply and Demand Growth, 2001–2003

The labor market trends reflected the economic growth pattern. The labor market did not decline as much during this recession as it did during the previous ones. The average monthly employment growth in this recession, 0.2 percent, was half of what it was during prior recessions, 0.4 percent. But the labor market fared worse in the latest recovery than in previous ones. While the labor market normally expanded by 4.9 percent in the first year, and by 6.5 percent in the first eighteen months of the expansion, it declined this time by 0.7 percent in the first twelve months and by 1.0 percent in the first eighteen months of the recovery.

These stylized facts suggest that supply grew faster than demand (Figure 1). Because productivity growth remained strong throughout the recession and the recovery, rapid demand growth was needed to avoid a labor market slump. Since this did not happen, the labor market remained in recession even as output grew.

As the following discussion shows, consumption and government spending were strong components of demand, while investment and net exports held back growth. If policymakers had managed to revive net exports (and subsequently investment) and designed fiscal policies more efficiently, demand growth would most likely have been strong enough to avoid the labor market recession. Policymakers had the opportunities to strengthen net exports, which would have helped boost capacity utilization, which in turn would have led to faster investment growth. Also, fiscal policy was inefficiently designed with tax cuts tilted toward those who were least likely to spend the additional money.

Monetary Policy During the Recession and the Recovery

Three macro policy tools are at policymakers' disposal to manage the economy: monetary policy, fiscal policy, and exchange rate policy. Monetary policy refers to the interest rate decisions and accompanying money supply decisions by the Federal Reserve. During a recession and a period of economic recovery, monetary policy tends to be geared toward easing, which means that interest rates are typically lowered. The expectation is that lower interest rates will make it easier for con-

sumers and for businesses to borrow money for consumption and investment. Another effect of lower interest rates should be a depreciation of the foreign exchange rate, which should improve an economy's competitiveness and boost net exports.

Prior to the recession, the Fed began raising interest rates in 1999 to slow what it perceived as an overheating economy. By late 2000, economic growth had markedly declined, and the economy was heading into its first recession in more than a decade. The Fed acted early in 2001 by cutting its main interest rate, the federal funds rate, from a high point of 6.5 percent. By the end of 2001, the Fed had cut interest rates 11 times to 1.75 percent. It continued to cut the federal funds rate in November 2002 to 1.25 percent, and in June 2003 to 1.0 percent in response to a weak recovery.

While the rate cuts during the latest recession were similar to cuts, in prior recessions, they continued longer into the recovery than during other recoveries. The federal funds rate fell by 3.2 percentage points in this recession, compared to an average of 3.0 percentage points in prior ones. However, the federal funds rate was 0.8 percentage points lower eighteen months after the recovery started in this recovery compared to an increase of 0.4 percentage points in prior recoveries. In other words, the Fed used its interest rate tool more aggressively and for longer than in other economic downturns.

Lucky Combination of Factors Boosts Monetary Policy's Impact on Consumption

Households were an important contributing factor to economic growth in the recession and in the recovery. Over the course of the first year after the recession began, real consumption improved by 3.0 percent, compared to 0.8 percent during previous recessions.

Consumption growth was to a large degree funded by a mortgage refinancing boom, which was determined by several factors. For one, the Fed lowered interest rates aggressively in the face of an impending recession starting in early 2001. By June 2003, mortgage rates had fallen to 5.2 percent, their lowest level in more than three decades (Figure 2). Consequently, households

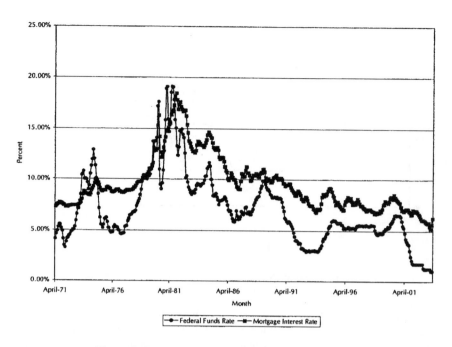

Figure 2. Short-Term and Long-Term Interest Rates

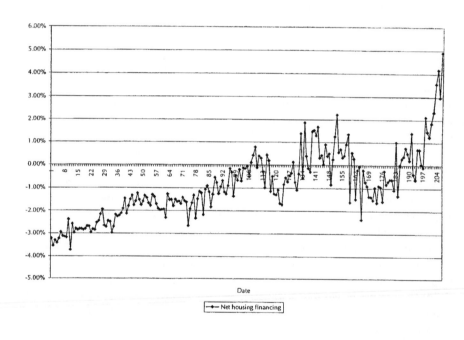

Figure 3. Household Resource Addition from Net Home Financing Change

began borrowing more for their homes, which is reflected in a rising share of mortgage debt relative to home values. By the second quarter of 2003, mortgages amounted to 45.7 percent of homeowners' equity, their highest level since 1952. But house prices also appreciated markedly, providing households with more collateral. From March 2001 through June 2003, house prices increased on average by 1.6 percent per month, compared to overall price increases of just 0.5 percent. Consequently, home equity relative to household disposable income rose from a low point of 92.4 percent in March 2001 to a high of 96.4 percent by the end of 2002, its

highest point in more than twelve years, before receding slightly to 94.6 percent by June 2003. Typically, homeowners' equity declined relative to disposable income by an average of 2.5 percentage points in the first year of prior recessions and 1.7 percentage points after two years.

The resulting refinancing boom was the largest in postwar history. Measured in relationship to households' resource base—disposable income plus other forms of savings—the difference between net new mortgages and additions to the country's residential housing stock gave households on average 3 percent more resources (Figure 3).

The important question for the economy, though, is how households used the additional resources. Households could use them to borrow less elsewhere, to invest more, and to spend more. Compared to the period from the first quarter of 1952 to the first quarter of 2001, the refinancing boom raised the financial resources of households by 3.8 percent. That is, households gained an additional 3 percent from the refinancing boom, and an additional 0.8 percent of households' resources that was used in the past for home expenditures. Instead of reducing credit elsewhere, households actually borrowed slightly more from other sources. Also, households did not use the additional resources to invest more in financial assets. In fact, households spent less of their resources on purchasing new financial assets than they typically did. Instead, households spent about 4.0 percent more of their resources, or the entire amount gained from refinancing, on consumption.

The economic effect was considerable. From the start of the recession to the second quarter of 2003, households received an additional $545 billion in resources from the refinancing boom. Consequently, consumption was about 4.1 percent higher than it otherwise would have been. As a result, real GDP was about $565 billion, or 6.2 percent, greater by the end of the second quarter of 2003 than it would have been without the refinancing boom.[2]

The sheer size of the refinancing boom made it one of the major reasons the recession was shallow. However, the refinancing boom left households with record levels of debt. By the end of the second quarter of 2003, households had accumulated a record 114 percent of their disposable income in debt.

Investment Not Responsive to Monetary Easing Due to Overcapacity

Investment was not responsive to the monetary stimulus, largely because demand growth, outside of consumption, was too slow, leaving firms with too much capacity.

Investment is typically an important force during a recovery. On average, real investment grew by 7.2 percent annually during the first year and by 8.6 percent annually during the first six quarters of prior postwar recoveries. In comparison, investment declined 1.7 percent annually in real terms in the first year since this recovery began and 0.5 percent in the first six quarters of the recovery. As a result, the share of business investment relative to GDP declined from a high point of 13.0 percent at the end of the third quarter of 2000 to 10.4 percent of GDP at the end of the second quarter of 2003. This was only slightly higher than the 10.3 percent recorded at the end of the first quarter of 2003, its lowest level in almost ten years.

The economic effect of investment growth in a recovery is sizable. If investment had merely grown at the average rate that prevailed during the first six quarters of past recoveries (8.6 percent), and if total economic growth had reacted to investment growth in the same way it did in prior recoveries, economic growth in the first six quarters of this latest recovery would have been 3.8 percent instead of the actual 2.7 percent. This probably would have been strong enough to increase the number of jobs since the end of the recession.

The investment decline was especially surprising considering the changing nature of investment goods. The share of investment outlays spent on structures recently fell from 40 percent to about 20 percent (Table 1). By contrast, information technology investments grew to 8 percent of investment in the second quarter of 2003, but these items depreciate more quickly than structures, requiring earlier replacement investments than in the past.

Low capacity utilization appears to be the factor that held back investment growth. For the second quarter of 2003, the average industrial capacity utilization was 74.2 percent—its lowest level in twenty years. Capacity utilization is a consistent determinant of changes in investment relative to GDP (Table 2).

Another traditional cause of slow investment growth is that profit rates are low. However, the profitability of corporations has been increasing in recent years.[3] And after profit rates hit

Table 1

Investment's Role in the Economy and Its Composition (percent)

	Investment as share of GDP	Structures as share of investment	Equipment as share of investment	Information processing equipment as share of investment
1950s	9.4	39.1	60.9	7.6
1960s	9.8	37.8	62.2	11.8
1970s	11.1	35.3	64.7	16.1
1980s	12.1	35.6	64.4	24.2
1990s	11.2	26.6	73.4	31.5
2nd quarter 2003	10.4	23.8	76.9	38.1

Source: Bureau of Economic Analysis, *National Income and Product Accounts* (Washington, DC).

Table 2

Granger Causality Tests for Determinants of Investment

Null Hypothesis	Test statistic	
	3 Lags	4 Lags
Investment causes before-tax profit rate with interest earnings	1.791	1.351
Before-tax profit rate with interest earnings causes investment	7.009***	4.716***
Investment causes before-tax profit rate without interest earnings	3.261**	2.503**
Before-tax profit rate without interest earnings causes investment	5.831***	3.895***
Investment causes after-tax profit rate with interest earnings	0.569	0.791
After-tax profit rate without interest earnings causes investment	8.569***	6.724***
Investment causes after-tax profit rate without interest earnings	1.526	1.280
After-tax profit rate without interest earnings causes investment	6.236***	4.599***
Investment causes capacity utilization	0.984	1.423
Capacity utilization causes investment	8.569***	6.724***

Source: Bureau of Economic Analysis, *National Income and Product Accounts* (Washington, DC), authors' calculations.

Notes: Investment is defined as nonresidential investment relative to GDP. All series, with the exception of capacity utilization, are integrated of order one, and are hence differenced once. The test statistics are F-tests.

  * Significance at 10 percent level.
 ** Significance at 5 percent level.
*** Significance at 1 percent level.

their low point at the start of the recession,[4] they generally tended to be higher in this recovery than during previous recoveries (Table 3).

Since profit rates were improving for at least seven quarters after the first quarter of 2001, investment should also have been growing. But because of recent corporate accounting scandals, corporate managers may feel that they have to generate larger profit rates than in the past to satisfy financial investors. Put differently, shareholders may expect a safety margin in current profit rates. It is possible that the level of profit rates has generally shifted upward over the past two years. In other words, corporate managers will only be able to allocate more resources toward capital expenditures if profit rates are close to what shareholders have come to expect.

Fiscal Policy Ill-Designed and Costly in the Long Term

Fiscal policy can come in the form of tax cuts and spending increases, although the Bush administration has never made a secret out of its preference for the former over the latter. The point of countercyclical fiscal policy, such as tax cuts or spending increases in a recession, is to ensure that stronger growth returns earlier than it would have without policy intervention. Moreover, as growth returns, deficits incurred during the recession should decline, allowing governments to repay their debt. Because fiscal policy measures in the recession and the recovery were ill-designed, growth was slower, and long-term deficits became larger than otherwise would have been the case.

One of the hallmarks of the Bush administration's economic policies is the promotion of tax cuts. The first one was enacted in early 2001, totaling more than $1.3 trillion over ten years (U.S. Congress JCT 2001a). Although not initially intended as economic stimulus, the first tax cuts occurred in late 2001, when the recession was already in full swing. The estimated total for 2001 amounted to $72 billion, with $40 billion for households in the form of so-called rebate checks, and $32 billion for corporations. That is, the year of the recession saw less than 5 percent of the estimated tax cut. As the economy unmistakably entered a recession, further tax cuts followed under the Economic Security and Worker Assistance Act of 20m, totaling an estimated $157 billion over ten years. Although $8 billion was made available for extended unemployment benefits and another $9 billion to help pay for health care for the unemployed and the poor in 2002, the vast majority, $72 billion, of fiscal losses in 2002 came in the form of tax cuts (U.S. Congress JCT 2001b). And when the economic recovery took longer than expected, Congress passed the Jobs and Growth Tax Relief Reconciliation Act of 2003, with an estimated price tag of $350 billion over ten years (U.S. Congress JCT 2003). Almost half of this tax cut resulted from the acceleration of tax cuts already enacted to occur in 2004 instead of later years, and another $148 billion resulted from reduced taxes on corporate dividends, mostly expected to occur between 2005 and 2008. Less than 20 percent of this tax cut was scheduled to go into effect in 2003, the second year of the "job loss" recovery.

As a result of various legislative measures, taxes were reduced substantially during the recession and the recovery. From fiscal years 2001 to 2003, the total cost of the federal tax cuts was ap-

Table 3

Profit Rates 1950–2003

	Before-tax profit rate		After-tax profit rate	
	with net interest earnings	without interest earnings	with net interest earnings	without net interest earnings
During the two years after start of recovery				
1954	16.03	14.20	9.50	7.67
1958	14.91	12.52	9.35	6.97
1961	16.42	13.35	11.06	8.00
1971	16.24	11.33	11.84	6.92
1975	15.15	9.96	11.24	6.04
1983	16.55	8.18	14.07	5.70
1991	17.08	8.92	14.27	6.11
2001	17.31	9.39	14.84	6.92
During decade				
1950s	14.81	12.94	8.72	6.85
1960s	18.16	14.53	12.49	8.86
1970s	15.87	10.53	11.68	6.33
1980s	16.48	8.04	13.72	5.28
1990s	17.61	10.31	14.40	7.10
Q2 2003	18.22	10.27	15.56	7.60

Source: Bureau of Economic Analysis, *National Income and Product Accounts* (Washington, DC).

proximately $264 billion (U.S. Congress JCT 2001b, 2002, 2003). In addition, Eugene Steuerle (2003) estimates an additional $286 billion in stimulus due to revenue losses from reduced taxable income in 2003 alone. Moreover, the ten-year cost of tax cuts could exceed $3.6 trillion if the "sunsets" are removed, as the president has proposed (Gale and Orszag 2003a, 2003b).

Table 4 shows the major components of GDP in non-inflation-adjusted terms, their total change, and their average quarterly and annual growth rates from 2001 to the second quarter of 2003. To account for inflation, we also show changes in price levels. A robust recovery is usually taken to imply growth rates that are above their long-run averages for some time before they settle down subsequently. To determine the long-term average growth rate, we take the real long-run economic growth forecast from the Congressional Budget Office, which lies between 2.7 percent and 3.3 percent (CBO 2002). For ease of presentation, we take the average of 3.0 percent as the real long-term growth rate. We also assume annual inflation of 1.5 percent, which is added to the real long-term growth forecast to arrive at long-run nominal average growth rate of 4.5 percent. So we can gauge the effectiveness of fiscal policy by the extent to which assorted components grow more rapidly than 4.5 percent, in average annual terms. Importantly, public-sector spending grew faster than consumption or investment, at an average growth rate of 7.2 percent. Although the prime force was military spending, nondefense federal spending also grew rapidly, whereas state

and local government spending was disproportionately weak with 3.2 percent annualized growth. The policy relevant questions, though, are whether fiscal policy did contribute to growth, where it occurred, and whether fiscal policy could have boosted growth in any areas, if it had been designed differently.

The spending part of fiscal policy is reflected in increased government expenditures at the federal, state, and local levels. Although the federal government increased its spending above average growth rates, there was more room to raise spending. Importantly, federal nondefense spending growth was only about half of what defense spending was during the period. Important public needs, such as renovations of schools in disrepair, could have been addressed through increased federal spending. Also, lackluster state and local government spending could have been easily augmented by increased federal aid in the form of general assistance (Sawicky 2001). Arguably, spending increases at the federal level would have been a preferred way to boost economic growth, since some federal aid to state and local governments would likely not have been spent but instead deposited into permanent or "rainy day" funds.

Comparing government spending in the most recent recession and recovery with changes during previous recessions illustrates the accidental character of government spending in this recession and highlights the heavier reliance of the federal government on tax cuts rather than spending increases in the most recent recession. Table 5 shows that government spending

Table 4

Nominal Growth of GDP and Its Components, 2001(3Q)–2003(2Q) (percent)

Component of GDP	Total growth	Average quarterly growth	Average annualized growth rate
Total	6.9	1.0	3.9
Consumption	8.8	1.2	4.9
Investment	2.2	0.3	1.3
Nonresidential	−5.7	−0.8	−3.3
Residential	14.5	2.0	8.0
Net exports	−60.6	−7.0	−31.1
Government spending	12.9	1.7	7.2
Federal	29.6	3.8	15.9
National defense	14.9	2.0	8.3
Nondefense	7.0	1.0	4.0
State and local	5.6	0.8	3.2
Implicit price deflator	2.1	0.3	1.2

Source: Bureau of Economic Analysis, *National Income and Product Accounts* (Washington, DC).

Table 5

Government Spending During Recessions and Recoveries, 1948–2003 (percentage point changes)

Recession date	Government spending		Federal government		Federal defense		Federal nondefense		State and local	
	Recession	Recovery	Recession	Recovery	Recession	Recovery	Recession	Recovery	Recession	Recovery
1948:IV–1949:IV	1.76	1.68	0.66	2.32	0.22	3.50	0.47	−1.19	1.11	−0.64
1952:II–1953:II	−1.12	−2.54	−1.99	−2.56	−1.60	−2.32	−0.39	−0.24	0.87	0.05
1957:III–1958:II	1.61	−1.24	0.84	−0.84	0.40	−1.22	0.44	0.38	0.78	−0.40
1960:II–1961:I	1.08	0.15	0.45	0.40	0.44	−0.13	0.01	0.54	0.63	−0.25
1969:IV–1970:IV	0.24	−1.04	−0.62	−0.64	−0.74	−0.82	0.12	0.18	0.86	−0.40
1973:IV–1975:I	1.79	−1.45	0.47	−0.69	0.15	−0.54	0.32	−0.15	1.32	−0.76
1980:I–1982:IV	1.30	−1.07	1.40	−0.30	1.34	−0.07	0.06	−0.23	−0.10	−0.77
1990:III–1991:I	0.64	−0.74	0.36	−0.49	0.30	−0.57	0.06	0.08	0.28	−0.25
2001:I–2001:IV	0.48	0.68	0.26	0.85	0.16	0.74	0.09	0.11	0.23	−0.17
Average all prior recessions	0.91	−0.78	0.20	−0.35	0.06	−0.27	0.14	−0.08	0.72	−0.43

Notes: For recessions, the change is the actual percentage-point change from the peak to the trough relative to GDP. For recoveries, the change is the percentage-point change relative to GDP during the first six quarters after the trough of the business cycle. The average for all prior recessions excludes the data for the most recent recession.
Source: Bureau of Economic Analysis, *National Income and Product Accounts* (Washington, DC).

relative to GDP did not increase as much during this recession as it did in prior recessions. However, it grew faster in this recovery than in previous ones. On average, government spending relative to GDP rose by 0.91 percentage points in all prior recessions, compared to only 0.48 percentage points in the most recent recession.

In comparison, though, government spending rose by 0.68 percentage points relative to GDP in the recent recovery, while it fell by 0.78 percentage points in prior recoveries. Importantly, though, the rise in government spending was almost exclusively attributable to increases in defense spending, which rose relative to GDP for the first time during a recovery since the 1940s.

In comparison to increases in government spending, tax policy is meant to boost personal consumption and household and business investment. It is unclear how housing investment could have been boosted any further with the help of fiscal policy, particularly since household investments in housing already enjoyed substantial tax advantages, for example, income tax deductibility of mortgage interest payments.

With respect to boosting consumption, there is no doubt that tax cuts helped to improve personal consumption during the recovery. But the stimulative effect could have been larger. First, as far as fighting a recession is concerned, tax cuts beyond the period of an employment slump serve no purpose. However, the majority of the enacted tax cuts were expected to take place after the recession and recovery were over. Thus, there is some likelihood of a negative impact on economic growth, as discussed further below.

Second, total consumption increases were comparatively small relative to the size of the tax cuts, largely because they were tilted toward higher-income households. For instance, the centerpiece of the initial tax cuts in 2001 were so-called rebate checks of up to $300 for single filers and up to $600 for joint filers. However, 51 million taxpayers were not eligible for the full rebates since their incomes and hence their income taxes were too low (Citizens for Tax Justice 2001). Ultimately, we estimate that only about 28 percent of the tax cut was spent in the first three months.[5] The fact that this tax cut was largely ineffective in spurring consumption was most likely related to the fact that it excluded many low- and moderate-income earners, who would have been more likely to spend the money than higher-income earners.

The propensity to exhaust one's tax cut in spending is generally expected to diminish with rising income. So a tax cut disproportionately benefiting upper-income persons provides less bang for the federal buck. For 2001–5, 55 percent of the 2001 tax cut had been targeted to the top 20 percent of taxpayers (ITEP 2002). If all the sunsets on cuts were removed, by 2013 the top 20 percent of income earners would realize 69 percent of tax cuts (Gale and Orszag 2003a).[6]

In comparison, the 2003 cuts were targeted directly to investment income—capital gains and dividends. One problem with this strategy is that other factors could easily offset any stimulus due to tax breaks. In particular, businesses must expect increased revenues from sales to permit them to recover their investment costs. Such expectations in a slow economy depend on consumption and employment growth, which remained low, and corresponding capacity utilization. The particular design of the investment-focused cuts on capital gains and dividends in 2003 was problematic because they changed the relative returns of financial assets and therefore encouraged some portfolio adjustment, rather than increased savings. Secondly, the tax cuts rewarded some savings that would have been undertaken in any event. Thus, lower costs of capital did not have the intended effect of spurring business investment.

A second problem is that public borrowing in the wake of tax cuts puts upward pressure on interest rates, possibly impeding business borrowing and investment. A long-standing critique of methodologies used to estimate the revenue losses from tax cuts was the failure to take into account changes in behavior that resulted from the enacted policies. Hence, proposals were advanced for "dynamic scoring" of tax cuts. Advocates of cuts looked forward to estimates that would show reduced revenue losses, due to positive feedback effects. The logic was that tax cuts would stimulate work, saving, and investment, resulting in more taxable income in the future. A larger tax base would generate more tax revenue and at least partially defray the costs of the tax cut. The CBO employed dynamic scoring in 2003, with ambiguous results. Tax cuts were found to have negative and positive effects. Specifically, the negative feedback effects resulted from higher interest rates due to increased government borrowing. In the CBO model—and other similar models—the chief negative impact from tax cuts derives from crowding out of private investment (Gale and Orszag 2003b). Public borrowing prevents some savings from being used for business investment. In other words, tax cuts can reduce the tax rate but increase the rate of interest, with a theoretically ambiguous effect on investment. However; most models estimate a net negative effect (ibid.).

There are reasons to be skeptical about the effectiveness of fiscal policy in the recent recession and recovery. Specifically, the administration used tax cuts as its predominant countercyclical policy tool. However, these tax cuts were "back-loaded," i.e., they scheduled much of the revenue losses in the future, when the economy presumably is no longer in need of a stimulus. Such "back-loading" is highly inefficient and can exert a negative impact on investment and growth. The tax cuts were also biased toward higher-income persons, which reduced the consumption impact of the tax cuts. Furthermore, permanent tax cuts create large future deficits, which add to the pressures on investment in the future.

Trade Deficits Become Bane of the Economy Because of Strong Dollar

To an increasing extent, good macroeconomic policy must focus on trends in the international as well as the domestic economy. Throughout this latest recovery, policymakers pursued measures that propped up an overvalued U.S. dollar, contributing to a large and growing trade deficit. Because of this rising external imbalance, growth in the recovery was hampered, and the long-term stability of the United States was put in danger.

Rapid economic growth in the United States from 1995 to 2000 was accompanied by rising trade deficits. The trade deficit as a share of GDP rose from 1.3 percent in the first quarter of 1995 to 4.0 percent in the last quarter of 2000, due in large part to rapid growth of imports. Exports as a share of GDP grew by 0.5 percentage points, while imports grew by 3.1 percentage points. Underlying the expansion of the trade deficit were three factors: rapid domestic growth, slow growth in our major trading partners, and a rising value of the U.S. dollar. The U.S. boom in the late 1990s was not matched by similarly strong economic growth in many of the United States's major trading partners, especially much of Europe and Japan, but also there was negative growth in countries roiled by financial crises, such as Mexico, Thailand, Korea, and Indonesia, in the mid- to late 1990s. The rapid inflow of imports from trading partner countries was consequently not matched by an equivalent outflow of exports. The rise in the dollar, fueled in part by policy decisions, exacerbated the trade deficit as U.S. exports became increasingly expensive on world markets.

There are a number of reasons to worry about a rising trade deficit. In the short run, a rising trade deficit can impede economic growth, as it constitutes a drag on demand growth. All else equal, a rising trade deficit represents a macroeconomic "leakage" from domestic demand, which reduces domestic income relative to expenditure, which means that domestic demand is satisfied by imports, which do not generate domestic income.

From 1995 to 2000, of course, all else was not equal. The rising trade deficit was accompanied by inflows of foreign capital. These foreign funds increased the supply of liquid capital available to U.S. firms, keeping the cost of capital low even as investment boomed. The investment boom, fueled in part by the inflow of foreign funds, kept the expected drag of the trade deficit on economic growth from occurring. Put differently, a lower trade deficit during the boom of the 1990s would not have translated into higher growth rates, just into a different composition of output and employment.

The rules of national accounting dictate that the shortfall between private income and expenditure must be equal to the government surplus plus the trade deficit. The 1990s boom, given a falling government budget deficit and a rising trade deficit, could only be sustained by rising private indebtedness. In a sense, the rising trade deficit (and accompanying inflows of foreign investment) enabled the boom to be sustained even as U.S. households and firms failed to save enough to finance consumption and investment. While this provided short-term benefits in terms of sustaining rapid economic growth, it was not sustainable, as private debt burdens could not rise indefinitely.

The investment decline in the last half of 2000 triggered the 2001 recession and led to the Fed's cutting interest rates, which had little effect on spurring investment in the initial stages of the recovery. Worse, the trade deficit continued to rise throughout the recession and into the post-recession period. As income growth stagnated, the share of imports in GDP fell from the first quarter of 2001 to the second quarter of 2003 by 0.47 percent, while the export share fell by 1.42 percent. With exports declining, firms had even fewer incentives to invest as their capacity utilization plummeted.

During the boom, inflows of foreign investment that accompanied the rising trade deficit helped fuel domestic investment, keeping the decline in net exports from dragging economic growth. When investment demand fell and did not respond to lower costs of capital, the drag of the rising trade deficit on domestic demand had no counterbalance. In the short run, the trade deficit exerted a powerful pull against a robust economic recovery. Figure 4 shows that the drag of the trade deficit was far stronger than in previous recoveries. Additionally, while trade deficits typically rise during recoveries, the increase during the latest recovery was far larger than previous averages. The trade deficit as a share of GDP rose by a percentage point in the first year of recovery, twice as fast as the average that prevailed in all other recoveries since World War II. It increased by 1.18 percentage points during the first six quarters, also double the rate that prevailed on average in previous recoveries. While extremely rapid growth in consumption, investment, or government spending could theoretically overcome the drag of the trade deficit, this did not occur in this recovery, as was discussed in the previous sections.

At the same time, rising trade deficits have driven large deficits in the wider *current account* and led to an enormous accumulation of foreign debt. The current account is the sum of imports and income earned by U.S. residents on overseas investments minus exports and the income earned by foreign residents on U.S. investments.[7] Its overall value is largely driven

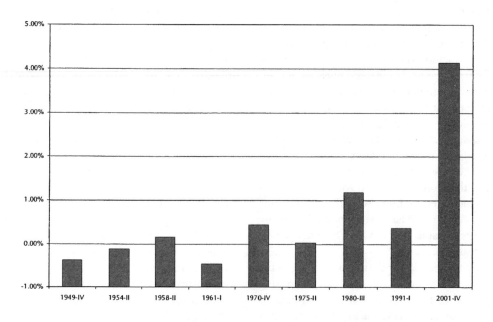

Figure 4. Average Trade Deficit Measured as % of Total GDP: First Seven Quarters After Beginning of Recovery

by the trade deficit, as net foreign investment income has generally hovered around zero for the past decade. This means that income earned on U.S. investments held by foreigners generally balanced with income earned on foreign investments held by U.S. residents. This rough balance may well change in the near future, for reasons sketched out below.

One way to think of the current account is as the difference between a nation's credits (exports and returns on foreign investment) and its debits (imports and returns on domestic investment). Like a household that spends (debits) more than it earns (credits), a nation can only sustain a current account deficit through borrowing. The most common metric measuring the degree of a nation's foreign indebtedness is the *net international investment position* (NIIP). For the United States, this position has deteriorated from –4.7 percent of total GOP in 1995 to –25.0 percent in 2002.

A closer look at the trends of these flows shows that the balance of these income flows, from the position of the United States, will deteriorate sharply in the coming years. International investments can generally be broken into two categories: foreign direct investment (FDI) and financial investment. Figure 5 shows the evolution of the FDI and financial investment positions. Measured in current market prices, the net stock of FDI (FDI owned by U.S. residents abroad minus FDI in the United States owned by foreign residents) declined from 4.8 percent of GOP to zero between 1995 and 2002. The trends in financial investment were even much more dramatic. The net stock of this kind of investment deteriorated from –9.5 percent of GOP in 1995 to –24.8 percent in 2002, indicating that foreigners owned more financial assets in the United States than U.S. residents owned abroad, and that this relationship increased two-and-a-half times over a period of seven years.

These compositional trends are important. The rate of return on FDI is much higher for foreign assets owned by U.S. residents than for domestic assets held by foreigners.[8] This means that income flows from FDI can actually help balance the current-account. In comparison, the spread between foreign and domestic rates of return on financial investments is much smaller. As the net financial position deteriorates, this means that income flows from financial investment are increasingly exacerbating the current account deficit, in addition to the widening trade deficit.

The current trend of the U.S. trade deficit implies that the NIIP will deteriorate to –60 percent of total GDP by 2008.[9] Assuming that FDI and financial investment components continue their current trends, this implies that the debt service obligations of the NIIP (interest payments) will soak up 2.0 percent of total GDP by 2008. To put this number in perspective, this would be equal to half of the *total* federal outlays on nondefense discretionary spending (that is, all federal spending besides social security, Medicare, and the Defense Department) in 2002.

At the height of the 1990s boom, the trade deficit was rising in part because growth in the United States was faster than in its major trading partner. Since the onset of recession in the March 2001, however, the United States has actually grown more slowly than many of its trading partners. One reason for the failure of the U.S. trade deficit to quickly unwind since the onset of recession has to do with the international competitiveness of U.S.-produced products. The income elasticity of demand for imports in the United States is much higher than the foreign income elasticity of demand for U.S. exports. That is, U.S. consumers are more likely to purchase foreign-made products than are foreign consumers to purchase U.S.-made products for a similar percentage point increase in income. So, it would take an extreme divergence in growth rates between the United States and its trading partners to move the trade deficit toward balance.

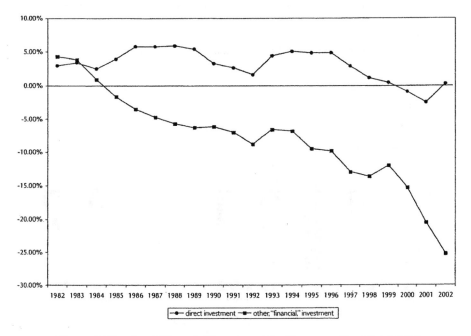

Figure 5. Direct and Financial Investment Positions, as a % of Total GDP

It would take an extreme divergence in growth rates between the United States and its trading partners to move the trade deficit toward balance.

The imbalance between domestic and foreign elasticity of demand for imports and exports, respectively, is probably a parameter that is not malleable over the short run. That is, it represents a deep structural feature of the economy, along the lines of preferences for foreign versus domestic goods or the technological quality of products. These characteristics cannot be changed over a short period of time. Closing the gap between domestic and foreign elasticities of demand (by, say, improving the international competitiveness of U.S. industries) is an important subject, but one that will take time to achieve.

In terms of domestic policy angles, blame for the ballooning trade deficit can be laid pretty squarely at the feet of the appreciating dollar. The real, broad, trade-weighted index compiled by the Federal Reserve shows that the dollar's value appreciated 35.0 percent from the beginning of 1995 to the beginning of

2002. Since its February 2002 peak, this index has lost 9.9 percent by October 2003, less than a third of the increase.

Even as the dollar fell, the trade deficit continued to climb, as long lags in net export response and the unbalanced nature of the dollar's fall have so far hampered adjustment.[10] The bulk of the dollar's fall since its 2002 peak has been against the euro and the Canadian dollar. A bloc of East Asian nations (China, Malaysia, and Taiwan) pegs their currency's values directly to the dollar. These nations account for 29.2 percent of the total trade deficit with the United States, but their currencies have not budged vis-à-vis the dollar. Figure 6 shows a range of nations' currency appreciations and their corresponding share of the total U.S. trade deficit. China, the largest deficit, has seen no appreciation at all, while the EU and Canada have seen large adjustments even as they constitute a smaller share of the total deficit. In short, the adjustment process of the dollar to date has been extremely uneven.

When the dollar's value rises, products produced in the United States become less competitive on world markets, while imports into the United States become cheaper, which encourages greater consumption of foreign-made goods. As a result, changes in the U.S. trade deficit closely mimic movements in the real value of the U.S. dollar, as shown in Figure 7.

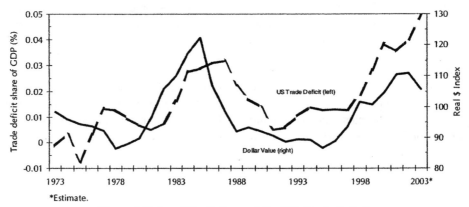

Figure 6. Value of the Dollar and the U.S. Trade Deficit

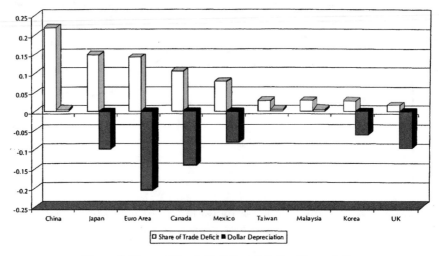

Figure 7. Share of Trade Deficit and Dollar Depreciation

The dollar's value can be influenced by policy. The Bush administration entered office strongly committed to a "strong dollar policy" but has recently implicitly backed a managed decline of the dollar's value. The dollar's appreciation after 1995 was largely a result of economic developments in the late 1990s that helped attract foreign capital inflows (Blecker 1998, 1999).[11] The acceleration of productivity and economic and profit growth after 1995 helped attract investments to the United States and maintain an overvalued currency, especially as U.S. growth rates remained above those of Japan and Europe. After financial crises roiled Asia and Russia in 1997 and 1998, the dollar's role as the world's reserve currency helped attract even more funds to the United States since it was seen as the main safe haven for foreign investors. When the world went into an economic slump and stock prices dropped in 2000, the United States managed to maintain its allure as safe haven, in large part because of anemic growth in the rest of the world. Amid economic and financial market turmoil, the strong dollar seemed to be a safe bet. Consequently, by early 2002, the dollar reached its highest value since January 1986. The Dubai Communiqué in the summer of 2003 obliquely signaled that failure of the dollar to decline in value could lead to some concerted policy action by the G-7 economies.

It is instructive, however, to contrast the actual Dubai Communiqué and follow-up with the Plaza Accord of 1985, which was similarly undertaken to engineer an orderly decline in the value of the U.S. dollar. First, the Plaza Accord (1985) has much stronger wording. It explicitly said that exchange rates were out of line with economic "fundamentals," referring several times to the need to correct U.S. external imbalances and providing for country-specific commitments to allow exchange rates to adjust. In particular, the Japanese representatives committed to allowing the yen to "fully reflect the underlying strength of the Japanese economy."

The Dubai Communiqué (2003), on the other hand, referred only to the desirability of "flexibility" in exchange rates and said that these rates "should" reflect fundamentals. It provided for no country-specific commitments.

The two years following the Plaza Accord saw a significant, though orderly, decline in the value of the dollar against a broad range of its major trading currencies. The dollar started falling in the month after the Plaza Accord was announced and had lost 14.6 percent of its value a year after the accords, then declined by another 9.5 percent in the following year.

While the Dubai Communiqué represented a tacit acknowledgement of the problem of U.S. trade deficits, its response was comparatively weak relative to the Plaza Accord, which was undertaken when the U.S. trade deficit was significantly smaller and when the U.S. economy grew at a faster rate. Much of the current trade deficit of the United States is accounted for by nations that manipulate the value of their currencies. The currencies of China, Malaysia, and Taiwan are all pegged directly to the value of the dollar. The Japanese currency, to a much lesser extent, is managed by the Japanese monetary authorities to

keep' the yen from rising against the dollar. Each of these nations has decided that some measure of exchange rate stability is a worthwhile policy goal. They are unlikely to respond to calls for exchange rate flexibility. Given this, these nations will have to allow a substantial managed revaluation of their currencies vis-à-vis the dollar for the U.S. external accounts to be made sustainable. As an illustration of this problem and the relative weakness of the Dubai Communiqué vis-à-vis the Plaza Accord, three days after the Dubai Communiqué, the Japanese government began buying dollar reserves on world markets to arrest the rise of the yen.

An increase in net export demand offers by far the best hope for sparking a robust recovery in the U.S. economy. Projections in Bivens (2003a) show that the dollar's fall between February 2002 and May 2003 should be expected to add 1–1.5 percent to total GDP before the third quarter of 2004. Further dollar declines should add even more. The greatest impact of the dollar's decline should be felt in trade-sensitive manufacturing industries.[12] These industries especially need the relief, given that they are experiencing employment and capacity utilization rates near historic lows. Low rates of capacity utilization in important industries have dampened the need for U.S. firms to increase investment, which, as pointed previously, has seriously hampered a robust recovery. Serious progress in unwinding the trade deficit would lead to rapid increases in capacity utilization in these industries (Bivens 2003b), helping to provide a spur to investment.

Dollar devaluation is also necessary to ensure the sustainability of the foreign debt position of the United States. Without a broad and deep revaluation of the U.S. dollar, the United States's net external debt situation is likely to worsen for some time. As a result, the United States would have to appropriate a growing share of its income to paying off its international debt.

Conclusion and Policy Implications

A review of macroeconomic policy decisions during the recession and the recovery and their economic effects illustrates a few important lessons. If these lessons are heeded, long-term stability of the U.S. economy could be enhanced, and future "jobless" or even "job-loss" recoveries may be avoided.

The first (and most obvious) lesson from the recent recovery was that all forms of macroeconomic policy matter. Fiscal, monetary, and exchange rate policy all had sizable effects on economic growth. While monetary policy did not have the effects generally predicted, it still helped sustain consumption demand through the recovery. And, while fiscal policy was poorly designed, the present recovery proves that even poorly designed fiscal measures can be a powerful countercyclical tool for policymakers. The adoption of any policy that rules out the use of either fiscal or monetary policy in the future (say, the Federal Reserve adopting inflation targeting rules, or balanced budget amendments in Congress) should be ruled out. Monetary and fiscal policies are too important as recession fighters to give up.

Second, if macroeconomic policies had been coordinated, the effect on growth would likely have been large enough to avoid a "job-loss" recovery. While monetary policy and fiscal policy had a nontrivial positive impact on economic growth, the lack of a coherent policy to address the currency manipulations of major trading partner countries had a substantial negative effect on economic growth. In an environment of accommodating monetary policy, policymakers had sufficient room to maneuver to increase government spending and to lower the value of the dollar. Had all three policies worked in the same direction, less overall effort would likely have been necessary to stimulate economic growth and generate a recovery in the labor market.

Third, growth could have been faster if fiscal policy had been designed better. The accommodative monetary policy stance had little effect on investment due to large overcapacities in businesses. Put differently, businesses needed *more customers* as incentives to increase investment. Consequently, fiscal policy measures that would have boosted aggregate demand more directly than the tax cuts enacted would likely have been more effective in increasing growth. They would have raised capacity utilization faster and boosted investment earlier.

Fourth, a better design of macro policies would have helped avert the rise in macroeconomic imbalances that characterized the U.S. economy two years into the recovery. If exchange rate policy had been targeted toward increasing the value of some trading partner currencies vis-à-vis the dollar instead of maintaining its overvaluation, the trade deficit would have shrunk, or at least stabilized instead of risen, and businesses (especially in the manufacturing sector, hardest hit by job loss in the recovery) would have had an incentive to increase investments. Similarly, fiscal policy consisting of expenditure increases rather than tax cuts could have expanded demand more quickly, leading businesses to increase their investment outlays earlier. As a result, economic growth would have recovered earlier and in greater magnitude, arid with it the labor market.

Quicker improvement in the labor market would have allowed consumption growth to have been fueled by *income* growth, not by an extension of credit. As a result, households, the federal government, and the international accounts of the U.S. economy would have been less indebted two years into the recovery than they are presently. In the coming months, it is likely that employment growth will quicken. This should not be taken as vindication of the policies pursued since the recession's onset. With better policies, we could have had a quicker recovery that left the economy's balance sheets in much better condition.

Notes

1. The recession lasted from March to November 2001.

2. This assumes no feedback effects onto investment, government spending, or net exports.

3. Past sales growth is assumed to be a signal to firms of future sales growth. Also, future profit opportunities are assumed to be the main driving force for firms to invest. Hence, past profit rates may be a proxy for future profit rate expectations, and thus may determine investment. Profit rates tend to be a leading indicator for investment changes during the period prior to the current recession (Table 3). It should be noted that in the Granger causality tests, lags beyond the fourth lag are not statistically significant.

4. Profit rates are corporate profits relative to corporate fixed assets. They can be calculated as before- or after-tax profit rates, and corporate profits can be defined including or excluding interest earnings.

5. As a result of the tax rebates, disposable income grew by an estimated $43.2 billion between July 2001 and September 2001. Although consumption declined in the wake of the terrorist attacks in September 2001, it quickly recovered in the months that followed. From July 2001 through December 2001, however, households spent $31.1 billion less than would have been expected, given the boost to disposable income. December 2001 is chosen as the end date because additional tax cuts took place on January 2002.

6. Many middle-income families in the range of $40,000 to $60,000 received significant gains from the tax cuts as long as they were headed by married couples and had children, which excludes a substantial share of families in this income range (Greenstein 2003).

7. The current account also includes unilateral transfers, but these constitute a trivial share of the wider current account.

8. On the divergence between rates of return to domestic and foreign direct investment, see the 2002 *Economic Report of the President* (pp. 61–62).

9. For this specific forecast, see Godley and Izurieta (2002). A very similar forecast is also offered by Blecker (1999).

10. On the timing and magnitude of the lag in net export response to devaluation, see Marwah and Klein (1996).

11. The low dollar value in the early 1990s was cause for concern and often lamented by the Clinton government since it raised investment costs for U.S. businesses overseas, according to a senior administration official on July 7, 1994, and made financing

of government deficits more expensive (National Archives 1994, 1995). But the strong dollar policy of the Clinton and Bush governments is usually associated with denying that the dollar became overvalued.

12. In particular, the following industries were identified in Bivens (20mb) as standing to benefit the most from the decline in the dollar's value: transportation equipment, computer and electrical products, chemicals, and industrial machinery (except electrical). These industries provide 70 percent and 60 percent of U.S. exports to the euro area and Canada, respectively, and should reap the biggest gains from the falling dollar.

For Further Reading

Bivens, J. 2003a. "The Benefits of the Dollar's Decline." EPI Briefing Paper. Economic Policy Institute, Washington, DC.

———. 2003b. "The Trade Deficit and Capacity in U.S. Manufacturing." Economic Policy Institute, Washington, DC.

Blecker, R. 1998. "International Capital Mobility, Macroeconomic Imbalances, and the Risk of Global Contraction." CEPA working paper no. 5. Center for Economic Policy Analysis, New York.

———. 1999. "The Causes of the U.S. Trade Deficit." Testimony before the U.S. Trade Deficit Review Commission (USTDRC), August 19, Washington, DC.

Citizens for Tax Justice (CTJ). 2001. "51 Million Taxpayers Won't Get Full Rebates from 2001 Tax Bill." Washington, DC.

Congressional Budget Office (CBO). 2002. *The Budget and Economic Outlook, an Update*. Washington, DC (August).

Dubai Communiqué. 2003. Statement of G7 Finance Ministers and Central Bank Governors. Available at `www.g8.utoronto.ca/finance/fm030930.htm`.

Economic Report of the President. 2002. Washington, DC: GPO.

Gale, W., and Orszag, P. 2003a. "Sunsets in the Tax Code." *Tax Notes* (June 9): 1553–61.

———. 2003b. "The Economic Effects of Long-Term Fiscal Discipline." Discussion paper no. 8, April. Brookings Institution, Washington DC.

Godley, Wynne, and Alex Izurieta. 2002. *Strategic Prospects and Policies for the U.S. Economy*. Annandale on Hudson, NY; Levy Institute Strategic Analysis.

Greenstein, R. 2003. "New Treasury Tax Cut Examples Mislead More Than They Inform." Washington, DC: Center on Budget and Policy Priorities.

Institute for Taxation and Economic Policy (ITEP). 2002. "Year-by-Year Analysis of the Bush Tax Cuts Shows Growing Tilt to the Very Rich." Washington, DC.

Marwah, K., and L. Klein. 1996. "Estimation J-Curves: United States and Canada." *Canadian Journal of Economics* 29, no. 3: 523–39.

National Archives. 1994. Clinton Presidential Materials Project, Background Briefing by Senior Administration Official, Aboard Press Plane en Route to Naples, July 7. Available at `http://search2.nara.gov`.

———. 1995. Clinton Presidential Materials Project, Press Conference by the President and Prime Minister Jean Chretien, Reading Room, The Parliament, Ottawa, Canada, February 24. Available at `http://search2.nara.gov`.

Plaza Accord. 1985. Statement by the Ministers of Finance and Central Bank Governors of France, Germany, Japan, the United Kingdom, and the United States. Available at `www.g7.utoronto.ca/finance/fm850922.htm`.

Sawicky, M. 2001. "An Idea Whose Time Has Returned: Anti-Recession Fiscal Assistance for State and Local Governments." EPI briefing paper no. 117. Economic Policy Institute, Washington, DC.

Steuerle, Eugene. 2003. "Do We Really Need More Stimulus?" *Tax Notes* (January 27): 597–98.

U.S. Congress Joint Committee on Taxation (JCT). 200la. *Estimated Budget Effects of the Conference Agreement on H.R.* 1836, lCX-51-01. 107th Congress, 1st sess. Washington: GPO.

———. 200lb. *Estimated Budget Effects of the Revenue Provisions of the "Economic Security and*

Worker Assistance Act of 2002." JCX-92-01. 107th Congress, 1st sess. Washington, DC: GPO.

————. 2002. *Estimated Revenue Effects of the "Job Creation and Worker Assistance Act of 2002."* JCX-13-02. 107th Congress, 2d sess. Washington, DC; GPO.

————. 2003. *Estimated Budget Effects of the Conference Agreement for H.R. 2—The "Jobs and Growth Tax Relief Reconciliation Act of 2003."* 108th Congress, 1st sess. Washington, DC: GPO.

CHRISTIAN WELLER is a senior economist at the Center for American Progress in Washington, DC. JOSH BIVENS and MAX SAWICKY are economists at the Economic Policy Institute in Washington, DC.

The New Growth Economics:

How to boost living standards through technology, skills, innovation, and competition.

by Robert D. Atkinson

John Maynard Keynes once wrote that "practical men, who believe themselves to be quite exempt from any intellectual influences, are usually the slaves of some defunct economist." That's exactly the situation among today's economic policy makers: As the New Economy continues to displace the Industrial Age economy, our policies are still rooted in that earlier age. While the Clinton administration took significant steps to move its policy framework into the new era, much remains to be done. That's why the new administration should jettison the holdover prescriptions of Keynesian and supply-side economics, with their overriding focus on the business cycle. Instead, the White House should embrace growth economics focused on boosting productivity and wage growth through investment in knowledge, support for competition and innovation, and fiscal discipline. By raising national productivity by only one-half to one percent, the new president can help generate significant improvements over time in the living standards of all Americans.

> **"Because supply-side economics was a reaction against the old system, not a development designed to meet the realities of the New Economy, it did not produce the results its advocates promised."**

Legacy Economic Policy Systems

The foundations of our economic policy system were laid in the 1940s, when that period's own "New Economy" was also emerging. Memories of the Great Depression and the fear of another depression following the conversion from a wartime economy, coupled with the insights of Keynes, led to the passage of the Employment Act of 1946. The Act stated that it was the "continuing policy and responsibility of the Federal Government to use all practicable means . . . to promote maximum employment, production, and purchasing power." The goal of

the legislation, and indeed the central organizing principle of U.S. economic policy to this day, has been not to boost long-term growth of the economy, but rather to make sure that recessions don't cause our economic performance to slip below some natural, immutable rate of growth. (In the last two decades the goal of keeping inflation low has been added as well.) When the Act spoke of maximizing production it meant avoiding recessions, running factories at full capacity, and getting to full employment. Government would do this through demand management—controlling the money supply and federal spending and taxing to boost or restrict consumer spending and company investment depending upon the phase of the business cycle.

The Act was silent on productivity—the key to income growth—in part because economists knew little about productivity and even less about how to boost it. It's only in the last decade that mainstream economics, led by Stanford economist Paul Romer, has begun to focus on why income growth occurs, focusing in particular on the key role of knowledge.

The Supply-Side Sidetrack

By the 1970s, conservatives and liberals shared President Richard Nixon's view that "we are all Keynesians now." However, the emergence of high unemployment with high inflation—a phenomenon that was not supposed to be possible under the old Keynesian model—coupled with a dramatic slowdown in productivity growth soon led many to question the prevailing economic doctrine.

In particular, conservatives, inspired by Jude Wanniski's *The Way the World Works*, attacked Keynesian "demand-side" economic policy. The new supply-side doctrine postulated that the real issue was that high taxes reduced incentives for companies and individuals to invest capital and for workers, particularly high earners, to work more hours. As a result, they argued that sizable tax cuts, particularly for upper-income Americans and businesses, combined with regulatory relief, would stimulate investment and job growth.

Because supply-side economics was a reaction against the old system, not a development designed to meet the realities of the New Economy, it did not produce the results its advocates promised. Conservatives argue that the current economic boom actually began during the Reagan Administration. Yet while it's true that jobs grew then, the growth was largely the result of an unprecedented entry into the labor force of baby boom workers and women. The real measure of success—productivity and wage growth—slowed to a 100-year low.

As a doctrine, supply-side economics failed. It failed because supply-siders were looking at old economy factors—capital and labor supply—and not at New Economy factors of capital and labor quality. These are determined by knowledge, technological innovation, and competition, as well as by education and training. Moreover, even if one were to grant that the supply of capital and labor is the key, it was never clear why reductions in personal tax rates, for example, would stimulate companies to develop or adopt technologies leading to higher productivity.

The New Growth Economics

As the Progressive Policy Institute has articulated in its *New Economy Index*, the New Economy is more global, more knowledge-driven, more entrepreneurial and dynamic, and driven by digital technologies. In this New Economy, neither Keynesianism nor supply-side economics provide the right answers because today's economy is fundamentally different than the one of even 15 years ago. The Clinton Administration moved toward a new conception of economic policy. It's time to build upon that and fully embrace growth economics.

"It may seem obvious that productivity growth should be the object of our economic policies, but strikingly, both liberal and conservative economic doctrines want to take a shortcut to growth."

This means placing the focus of economic policy squarely on boosting per-capita incomes, and that means focusing on productivity. As Paul Romer states, "the most important economic policy question facing the advanced countries of the world is how to increase the trend rate of growth of output per capita."

It may seem obvious that productivity growth should be the object of our economic policies, but strikingly, both liberal and conservative economic doctrines want to take a shortcut to growth, focusing not on productivity but on redistribution. Conservatives want to raise after-tax income by cutting taxes—taking from public expenditures to boost private incomes. Liberals want to tax the rich more, dramatically increase the minimum wage, and spend much of the surplus to funnel the proceeds to programs to benefit "working families." Neither approach recognizes that the only long-term answer to improving the economic well-being of Americans is to focus on productivity.

In addition, neither liberals nor conservatives embrace fiscal discipline. Conservatives would see the surplus go to tax cuts, not paying off the debt. Some have even recently begun preaching supply-side Keynesianism, arguing that large tax cuts are needed to spur consumer demand. Many liberals continue to believe that because government spending boosts consumer demand it leads to more jobs and in turn higher wages (but lower profits or higher inflation since higher wages would have to result from increased bargaining power by workers, not higher productivity). As a result, they attacked efforts by the Clinton administration to pay off the debt, calling it Calvin Coolidge economics. Yet, with full employment, cranking up large new spending programs or tax cuts would only produce inflation and efforts by the Federal Reserve to counteract the stimulative effect.

Growth economics also challenges the mistaken notion of natural limits to growth. Until last year, most economists postulated that the economy could not grow faster than 2 percent to 2.5 percent per year without sparking inflation. Growth economics recognizes that the economy can grow much faster without inflation, as long as productivity grows as fast. In fact, the new administration should set a goal to double living standards for American workers within 30 years. This would require maintaining an annual productivity growth rate of 2.5 percent— even less than the 2.7 percent productivity growth rate the country has seen since 1996.

Embracing growth economics does not mean ignoring past economic policy goals, such as job creation and inflation control. While these still matter, they are no longer central. The information technology revolution, as well as a highly competent Federal Reserve policy, has led to the longest expansion in economic history. Because globalization, increased market competition, and the technology revolution have reduced the threat of inflation, the Federal Reserve does not need to induce anti-inflationary recessions as much as it used to. Although as evidenced by its repeated interest rate hikes in the last 18 months, the Federal Reserve Bank may not have fully heeded its own lesson.

The Foundations of Growth Economics

Growth economics has emerged because of the growing recognition that the economic models created in the Industrial Age dominated by commodity goods production no longer adequately explain growth in an economy powered by knowledge and innovation.

While Keynesian and supply-side economics focused in an almost Newtonian way on adjusting the demand or supply of capital and labor to keep the economy in equilibrium, growth economics is focused on a different set of questions related to how the New Economy creates wealth: are entrepreneurs taking risks to start new ventures; are workers getting skilled and are companies organizing production in ways that use those skills; are companies investing in technological breakthroughs and is government supporting the technology base (e.g., funding research, training scientists and engineers); are regional clusters of firms and other institutions fostering innovation; are we avoiding protecting companies against more innovative competitors; are research institutions transferring knowledge to companies; and are policies supporting the ubiquitous widespread adoption of the Internet and other advanced information technologies?

"Because globalization, increased market competition, and the technology revolution have reduced the threat of inflation, the Federal Reserve does not need to induce anti-inflationary recessions as much as it used to."

Under the old economic policy model, it was not clear that there was a role for government in economic policy beyond managing the business cycle and protecting intellectual property rights. Growth economics makes it clear that government policies can boost long-term income growth. It recognizes the conservative insight that free markets, competition, and innovation boost growth. But it also recognizes the liberal insight that government investments, particularly in science, technology, education, and skills, can provide a foundation upon which productivity growth depends. And finally, growth economics recognizes that fiscal discipline underlies all of this. As a result, growth economics leads to three overriding policy prescriptions:

1) Invest in Knowledge. Economists have long agreed that technology is the most important engine for economic growth. But their economic models couldn't really say how technological innovation spurred productivity or even occurred. New economic research not only recognizes the importance of technical advances but also explains how the process occurs and describes the key role of government in the process.

But it's not just technology that's key to productivity, it's the ability of workers to develop and use technology. The New Economy requires higher levels of education, including high-tech skills, and opportunities for lifelong learning to keep up with the constantly evolving demands of the Information Age.

As a result, growth economics focuses on increasing technological innovation, including support for research and development in the public and private sector, and on increasing the education and skills of the workforce and the ability of firms to use these skills.

In 2000, the Progressive Policy Institute's New Economy Task Force proposed a host of new investments in research and training. The new administration should build on these recommendations and significantly support funding for science, technology, education, and skills. For example, the next budget should increase investments in federal civilian research by 10 percent (in real dollars) and continue that increase every year until federal support for research is double today's level. The administration should also increase funding for Department of Defense research. It should not only make permanent the R&D

tax credit but expand it. It should provide incentives to companies to train workers and work with states to jointly fund industry-led training alliances. And it should significantly increase funding for scholarships and fellowships for science, math, and engineering education.

2) Promote Competition and Innovation. Economists have long acknowledged that competition keeps prices down. The New Economy creates another critical reason for competition: It drives innovation and ultimately provides the greatest benefits to consumers. The next administration should focus on fostering economic competition through expanded trade and globalization, economic deregulation, and promotion of e-commerce competition.

Global integration, open markets, and increased trade allow the U.S. economy to specialize more in the higher value-added activities that it does best. They also increase economic competition, keeping prices down and fostering innovation. As a result, global integration is a key component of growth economics.

Domestically, growth economics means that if government is to promote growth it must facilitate, rather than resist, economic competition. This means moving away from regulating monopolistic or oligopolistic industries and instead promoting competition to achieve public interest goals of lower costs, new products, and greater consumer choice. It also means developing a modern understanding and application of antitrust law to prevent anti-competitive practices.

Growth economics also means not giving in to special interests fearful of change or falling sway to special pleading of incumbent firms threatened by competition. These protectionists need to be rebuffed in a host of areas—including their opposition to bioengineered foods that promise dramatic increases in agricultural productivity, their opposition to mergers that promise heightened efficiencies, and their opposition to those seeking government intervention to shelter them from e-commerce competitors.

Finally, it means crafting a legal and regulatory framework that supports the growth of the digital economy, in such areas as taxation, privacy, digital signatures, telecommunications regulation, and industry regulation (in banking, insurance, and securities, for example).

"Historically, key economic policymaking posts have been held by economists grounded in old economy macroeconomic theory. Most economists are not trained in growth economics and do not understand the factors leading to productivity growth."

---

3) Maintain Fiscal Discipline. While the Bush administration should significantly increase investments in science, technology, skills and education, it should also maintain fiscal discipline and continue to expeditiously pay down the debt. Doing so results in lower interest rates enabling a virtuous cycle of more investments, more growth, and greater surpluses to pay off more of the debt. In a global market that disciplines nations for poor fiscal policies, fiscal discipline is increasingly a requirement.

It's Time to Implement Growth Economics

Historically, key economic policymaking posts have been held by economists grounded in old economy macroeconomic theory. Most economists are not trained in growth economics and do not understand the factors leading to productivity growth. Princeton University economics professor Paul Krugman reflects the conventional view when he states: "We [economists] really don't know why productivity growth ground to a near halt [in the '70s and '80s]. That makes it hard to answer the other question: What can we do to speed it up?" Since Krugman (and most conventionally trained economists) don't know the answer to this, he counsels us to "diminish our expectations."

The principal advisers on economic policy to the new administration need to be individuals who know how to speed up productivity and encourage us to expand our expectations. Therefore, the new administration should appoint individuals grounded in growth economics and technological innovation to head the Council of Economic Advisers, the National Economic Council (NEC), the Treasury Department, and other key economic posts (e.g., Department of Labor, Department of Commerce). In addition, the new administration should create a National Economic Policy Council as part of the NEC. The council should be chaired by the vice president and include as members the heads of major business and labor organizations, CEOs, university presidents, and other civic leaders.

> **"The new administration should support policies that increase standards of living, embracing investment, tax, trade, and regulatory policies that advance that goal."**

Finally, the new administration should support policies that increase standards of living, embracing investment, tax, trade, and regulatory policies that advance that goal and rejecting policies that do not. In particular, it should significantly increase investment in research and technology (including the associated mechanisms to utilize that technology)—as well as in the training and education of workers.

But at the same time the new administration needs to level with the American people. We can either hold on to the old framework and possibly preserve some semblance of the old economic security or we can embrace the New Economy and growth economics. If we do, workers will face increased risks and challenges (e.g., increased requirements to take control of their own lifelong learning, higher risks of being displaced from a job), but they will also reap greater rewards (faster income growth, more rewarding work, and more free time). It is time for growth economics to replace business cycle economics as the dominant organizing framework for U.S. economic policy.

Robert D. Atkinson is director of the Technology & New Economy Project at the Progressive Policy Institute.

From *Blueprint,* Winter 2001, pp. 6-13. © 2001 by Blueprint. Reprinted by permission.

The Mystery of
Economic Recessions

By Robert J. Shiller

A great embarrassment for modern macroeconomic theory is that it has never achieved any consensus on the basic questions of what makes the stock market rise or fall and what ultimately causes recessions.

Today, there is great debate over whether a recession is in the offing— and if there is a recession, how long it will last. Already, signs of an economic downturn are all around—a depressed stock market, layoffs in several business sectors. That's why many Americans looked with relief toward Alan Greenspan and the Federal Reserve Board, which last week cut the benchmark interest rate by half a percentage point for the second time in a month. But will the Fed's action prevent a recession? It's difficult to tell.

Economists know what economic indicators correlate with recessions— stock market declines often precede them, for example. And we know that most movements in the stock market haven't made any straightforward sense as a rational response to interest rates or to news about future profits or dividends. But we have not been able to pinpoint what ultimately causes recessions—probably because the causes are psychological and thus intangible.

The renowned British economist A. C. Pigou wrote in 1929 that psychological factors account for about half of fluctuations in industrial production: he spoke of "psychological interdependence," "sympathetic or epidemic excitement" and "mutual suggestion." His judgment seems about as good today as in 1929—and the factors he described are still not easily measured.

Absent any scientific consensus about the ultimate source of economic fluctuations, oversimplified theories abound. Today's example is the popular theory that the Fed controls everything—that the raising or lowering of interest rates alone causes the economy's ups and downs. The record 14 percent one-day increase in the Nasdaq index on Jan. 3, after the Federal Reserve Board made its first half-point cut in interest rates this year, suggests how strongly some investors buy into this theory.

Confidence, not the Fed, determines our ups and downs.

Of course, the Fed's management of interest rates does have an important role in the way recessions play out, but it would appear unlikely that anything the Fed actively chooses to do will actually disrupt the economy. Something else is driving the periodic recessions.

A recession is generally related to a decline in confidence, a decline that makes consumers less willing to spend and businesses less willing to invest and to employ workers. Eventually we see layoffs and rises in unemployment. The recent string of layoffs and the January decline in manufacturing employment are ultimately due to a decline in confidence.

There are some efforts to measure confidence systematically, notably the Consumer Confidence Index published by the Conference Board. It is based on answers to just five survey questions, about respondents' assessments of business and employment conditions, now and in six months, and of the likely family income in six months. Surely many respondents to these surveys are reflecting what they hear on the evening news, rather than probing their inner psyches.

The index, as simple as it is, however, has been shown in a number of studies to contain valuable information for forecasters. A decline in confidence is a useful predictor that consumer spending will drop. And in the past few months, the index has had its greatest decline since the recession in 1990 and 1991. This suggests some trouble ahead.

Part of our confidence in the past few years has been an exaggerated national faith in Alan Greenspan. This faith may have grown up in part because of the success of the interest rate cuts that he undertook to support the stock market just after the Oct. 19, 1987, crash. It may also stem from the 1998 interest-rate cuts after the Long Term Capital Management debacle, in which the failure of a big hedge fund threatened to cause a chain reaction of bankruptcies. Mr. Greenspan has come to symbolize support for the new economy, and he is an essential part of the current story.

But public confidence based on belief in the acumen of one 74-year-old man cannot be secure. Many critics, in fact, are now going far in the other direction, viewing Mr. Greenspan as the principal cause of the current downturn because of the Fed's persistence in raising interest rates until well into 2000.

Solid confidence is ultimately based on knowledge, on an understanding of underlying mechanisms and a mental accounting of the reasons for security. The problem today is that the economy is in such a cock-eyed and unusual situation that it is easy to imagine that confidence could soon erode a great deal.

After 1982, the Nasdaq stock price index moved in a smooth upward arc, rising at a higher and higher clip, until March of last year, and since then it has fallen roughly in half—as classic a bubble-and-burst pattern as there ever was.

Broader stock-price indexes have followed a similar, though less dramatic, ascending arc since 1982, and real estate prices are also inflated. There have been no bursts yet, but these situations, too, look so much like bubbles that it is hard to imagine how confidence could be secure going forward now.

So are we likely to have a recession?

Some factors suggest that we might. Our economic expansion of the past 10 years has been fueled by some trends that may not be sustainable. One is a historic decline in the average rate of personal savings, from more than 8 percent of income saved each year in 1991 to no saving at all in December 2000—in fact, to households' spending more a year

than their income. Another is high borrowing. The debt burden of the average American household (especially mortgage debt) has risen to record levels.

The problem for forecasters is that we are, by these measures, largely out of the range of our historical experience. When we are out of range, past examples cannot be reliable guides to the future.

Lacking an established theory of the ultimate causes of economic fluctuations, forecasters tend to rely on simple extrapolation of trends or on assumptions that past patterns will repeat themselves. But we are in a moment when confidence and market psychology are changing fast. Surprises—perhaps a serious recession—could be in store for us.

Robert J. Shiller is an economics professor at Yale and author of "Irrational Exuberance."

The Cost of Living and Hidden Inflation

Economists generally argue that inflation is overstated by the federal government because it does not sufficiently account for the improved quality of products. This economist believes that if we account for all pertinent changes in the quality of life, inflation is understated.

James Devine

DESPITE low reported inflation rates in recent years and official recalculations of the inflation rate that reduce it even further, these measures underestimate the true increases in the cost of living. Official measures of inflation, such as the Consumer Price Index (CPI) and the Personal Consumption Expenditure (PCE) deflator, are market-oriented, measuring only the decrease in our money's power to purchase products currently available for sale. This article presents a preliminary alternative measure of inflation, the cost-of-living (COL) inflation rate, which brings in nonmarket elements of people's existence, such as the costs arising from pollution. Compared to the government's official measures of consumer prices, these elements raise the amount of money income needed to keep real standards of living from falling.

The COL measure suggests that in terms of the issues that working people care about, inflation continues above the officially measured rate, even using the most conservative measure of the COL: For the period 1951–1998, the annual COL inflation rate averaged 4.1 percent, about 0.4 of a percentage point higher than the inflation rate implied by the PCE deflator and about 0.1 percent higher than the inflation rate implied by the CPI. (Since the PCE deflator's method of calculation is similar to that of the COL, the former comparison is more meaningful.) Worse, the gaps between the COL and official inflation have widened: Between 1980 and 1998, on average the COL rose about 0.7 of a percentage point per year more than the PCE price and 0.3 more than the CPI.

These numbers imply that the gap between officially measured real wages and the real benefit received from wages has widened (at an increasing rate). To understand this assertion, however, we must reexamine the basics.

Measuring Inflation and "Real" Wages

In addition to measuring the inflation rate (the percentage rise in prices), indices such as the CPI are commonly used to find the "value" of nominal magnitudes. Real wages, for example, are measured as follows:

Constant-price wage = (money wage)/CPI

Thus, for example, because the CPI rose so quickly between 1970 and 1979, real average private-sector weekly earnings fell by 2 percent—even though money (nominal) wages rose by almost 90 percent.

During the late 1990s, controversy raged over technical issues concerning the method of calculation of the CPI.[1] Appointed by Congress to suggest recalculation of the CPI, Stanford professor Michael Boskin and his colleagues argued that the CPI should be reformulated to make it a more accurate measure of the "cost of living." For example, the CPI should be adjusted for the quality improvements that they assumed occurred for many products in the consumption basket used to measure the index, the availability of new products, and the rise of low-cost retail outlets like Wal-Mart.

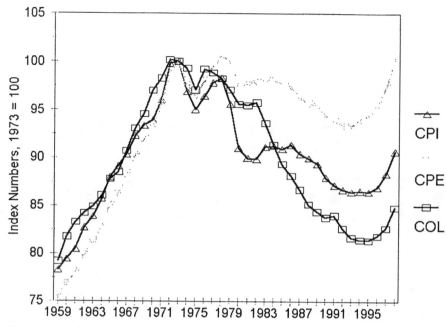

Figure 1. Alternative Real Wages, U.S. Total Private Sector 1959–99

The Bureau of Labor Statistics (BLS) has accepted many or most of the Boskin recommendations, adjusting their estimates of CPI inflation downward. According to *Business Week*, "a significant chunk of the reported downturn in inflation since 1995—perhaps three-quarters of a percentage point—reflects changes in the behavior of statisticians rather than changes in the underlying pace of price hikes" (Koretz 1999). This estimation trend has gone further, with the Federal Reserve recently shifting its emphasis to the PCE deflator for calculating the inflation rate (Cooper and Madigan 2000). This measure generally rises more slowly than even the revamped CPI, because it reflects the rise in prices of the products that consumers actually buy, while ignoring the costs of the way that inflation pushes people to substitute one product for another (chicken for steak, for example).[2]

Other economists argued that the traditional formulation of the CPI was relatively accurate and did not need Boskin-type revisions.[3] They hoped to protect social security beneficiaries and government workers with escalator clauses in their con-tracts from getting automatic raises below that of the actual inflation rate, which they saw as being better measured by the old version of the CPI. These revisions may not be all bad, however, since they delayed or moderated the Federal Reserve's use of economic slowdown or recession as a preemptive strike against inflation.

Often forgotten is that the official CPI is not truly a measure of the "cost of living" that people face, with or without Boskin revisions. As one BLS official notes, "A more complete cost-of-living index would go beyond [the CPI] to take into account the changes in other governmental or environmental factors that affect consumers' well-being" (Gibson 1998, p. 3). Robert Kuttner (1996) argues this point more strenuously: Official price indices leave out even more aspects of the true cost that people face in order to live, such as the cost of crime, lawsuits, pollution, and family breakdown. For example, the cutback in hours at the public library raises the cost of living by pushing people to buy books instead or lowers their quality of life by preventing them from reading. However, this cutback does not raise the measured CPI or PCE.[4] This is why I use the term "hidden inflation."

A calculation in light of Kuttner's criticism implies a gigantic and expensive research project, one that only the government could afford—and seems unlikely to engage in. Rather, I follow another hint from Kuttner: He points to the "Genuine Progress Indicator" (the GPI) calculated by the Redefining Progress think tank as an example of efforts to measure our economic welfare or "true living standards"—an alternative to real gross domestic product (GDP) as a indicator of society's progress. The GPI ... adjusts the official national income and product account measures for real benefits missed, such as contributions from housework, and costs that should be subtracted, such as that of using up nonreproducible natural resources. This article applies this research to calculate estimates of the "cost of living" and the "COL inflation rates" that are implied.

It is beyond this short article's scope to criticize official measures of inflation. However, even if Boskin-type adjustments are needed, if my estimates are anywhere close to being accurate, the costs of increases in pol-

Table 1 Average Annual Additions to Inflation Rates (percentage points).

Dates	Conservative COL	With distributional adjustment	With forward-looking adjustment	With both adjustments
COL Additions to "conservative"				
1951–98	n.a.	0.2	0.8	1.4
1980–98	n.a.	0.6	1.0	2.6
Additions to PCE deflator inflation				
1951–98	0.4	0.6	1.2	1.8
1980–98	0.7	1.3	1.7	3.4
Additions to CPI inflation				
1951–98	0.1	0.2	0.9	1.8
1980–98	0.3	0.9	1.0	2.6

lution, commuting time, labor time, and the like more than cancel out Boskin-type adjustments.[5] As a first guess for calculating inflation rates, we might split the difference, clinging to the official price level as calculated before Boskin-type adjustments. Better, we should use different inflation rates for different purposes (Mitchell 1998). The CPI and the PCE attempt to measure purchasing power of a dollar in the market, while the COL gauges the actual cost of the benefits of everyday life.

The COL is measured by the amount of money spending needed to buy a constant quality of consumption as measured by the GPI calculations. Thus, a new version of the "real wage" can be calculated:

Constant-COL wage = (money wage)/ COL

Figure 1 indicates the impact of this kind of calculation for the total private sector of the United States. During the 1960s, real wages calculated using the COL grew slightly more slowly than those calculated using the CPI or the PCE price. After the late 1970s, real wages calculated using the COL rather than those official price levels fell much more steeply, due to rising hidden inflation. Rises in official real wages since 1995 are also moderated when the COL is used. Similar results can be seen for the manufacturing sector but are not shown here.

Calculating the COL

The basic idea for calculating the COL index is similar to that behind the PCE deflator. The latter is the average price level implied by calculations of real consumption spending. As a first approximation,

PCE deflator = (money spent on consumer goods)/(inflation-corrected sum of those goods)

The denominator is often interpreted as the "real" benefit to consumers of consumer spending.

Based on the Redefining Progress critique of real gross domestic product as a measure of social welfare, my most conservative COL estimate replaces real consumption with a measure of benefit received:

COL = (money spent on consumer goods)/(benefit received from current consumption)

where the denominator is a measure of the those parts of the GPI that contribute to an individual's current enjoyment. Like those of the denominator of the PCE deflator, the components of this number are corrected for inflation. But it changes the official estimates of real consumer purchases by including the impact of extra current benefits and costs usually missed by the National Income and Product Accounts.[6]

Two types of examples explain the idea of COL inflation. Assume that consumption spending in both

money and inflation-corrected terms is constant, so that the PCE price is constant and the official inflation rate using this measure equals zero. Suppose that the current benefits to consumers missed by the official accounts (extra current benefits) decrease. If the amount of unpaid housework, volunteer labor done, leisure time, or the services provided by publicly supplied streets and highways decreases, this means that fewer real benefits are received. Since money spending is constant, there has been a rise in dollars paid on the market per real benefit actually received. As with the public library example, there has been a decline in the benefit received from money spent.

Second, if the current costs missed by the official accounts (extra current costs) rise, that is, if people are suffering from increased pollution while spending the same amount of money buying consumer goods, it represents a decline in their living standard and a decrease in the value of the money spent. Similarly, if individuals suffer from increased costs of commuting (which are necessary to earn income), increased costs of auto accidents and crime, or decreased leisure time or family stability, the money that they spend is providing them with fewer benefits than it used to. Third, spending more money on necessary defensive goods (such as car locks or insurance) does not raise the real benefits received. Rather, it implies that the real benefits one does receive axe more expensive to preserve.

Alternative COL Estimates

My "most conservative" COL estimates are consistent with common-sense notions of inflation and thus do not go as far away from the GDP calculations as the GPI does. First, the COL discussed above ignores distributional issues. As with the CPI, the PCE price, and most conceptions of "inflation," the concept of the cost of living used above is individualistic, referring to an average individual. While widening gaps in the distribution of income encourage the fraying of the social fabric and go against official societal goals, it is hard to assert that changes in distribution directly imply a higher cost of living for any individual. Those results of rising inequality that raise the cost of living, such as increases in street crime, are already measured as part of extra current costs and thus as part of the COL.

Next, forward-looking costs and benefits, which play a major role in the GPI, play no role in the calculation of the COL discussed above. When calculating the CPI or PCE price, aspects of living that refer to future impacts are omitted, since the concern is with current consumption, not with all benefits and costs received by future generations. In other words, the ecologically crucial cost of the destruction of wetlands or the ozone layer has little or no impact on our current cost of living or on the inflation rate as most conceive it. This attitude is very shortsighted, but exactly the same attitude is implicit in official calculations.

Less conservative estimates of COL inflation not only are higher but show an upward trend relative to official measures of the inflation rate. Though these more radical estimates of COL inflation do not fit with the common-sense meaning of the word "inflation" discussed above, these trends are important.

If we drop the individualistic perspective of both the conservative COL and official numbers to include the effects of distributional shifts, my measures of COL inflation rise more in relation to official inflation rates. On average between 1951 and 1998, bringing in distributional issues added 0.2 of a percentage point to the conservative COL inflation rate and 0.6 of a percentage point to the PCE price inflation rate each year (see Table 1). For the period 1980–1998, these additions are 0.6 of a percentage point and 1.3 percentage point, respectively. This results from the well-known widening of the gap between the rich and poor, as indicated by the falling share of total income accruing to the poorest fifth of the population. Alternatively, this says that COL inflation has hit the poorest fifth the hardest.

Another interpretation is that our ability to maintain low COL and CPI inflation rates simply means that the costs of societal problems are being shoved onto the backs of the poor. In terms of the distributional-conflict theory (cf. Rowthorn 1977), inflation can be reduced if one participant in the conflict—here, the poor—is pushed out. In other words, if the widening distributional gap could have been avoided, there would have been higher official inflation rates (or higher unemployment to restrain such inflation). Improving programs such as the minimum wage, unemployment insurance benefits, or "welfare" that help the poorest earn higher wages in order to allow constancy of the income distribution encourages businesses hiring such labor to raise prices. Recent slowing of official inflation rates despite falling unemployment rates is thus linked not only to measurement changes but to the widening distributional gap.

Both the conservative COL and the PCE-based inflation rates are also falling behind COL rates that include future-oriented costs and benefits, such as the cost of global warming and the loss of old-growth forests and the benefits of net invest-ment. For 1951–1998, including such issues added 0.8 of a percentage points to the conservative COL estimate and 1.2 percentage point to the official inflation rate. These additions rise to 1.3 percentage point and 0.9 of a point for the 1980–1998 period. This result indicates that the paying of more and more of the costs of living on earth is being postponed to the future. We are currently enjoying relatively low inflation, as measured by both the conservative COL estimate and the CPI. However, the long-term costs in terms of the environment or slow growth of potential output (due to inadequate investment) will likely have to be paid in the future, in the form of environmental disaster, slow productivity growth, and the like. My measures suggest that if the nation were paying more of the environmental costs now or investing more in the future, both the official and COL inflation rates would be higher (or unemployment would be higher to restrain such inflation).

Policy Issues

Should the Federal Reserve make COL inflation its central concern? Under a literal interpretation of the current Fed goal of attaining zero inflation, it would spark slowdowns more than it has done already. But this is a wrong interpretation, since monetary policy cannot raise the extra current benefits or lower extra current costs as defined here. Since the Fed's main constituency (bondholders and bankers) does not care about negative future effects, distributional changes, current external costs, or uncompensated labor, its policy experts understand this point. The job of fixing the extra costs and promoting the extra benefits belongs to other branches of the government. The problems, of course, arise because these other branches are doing inadequate jobs at dealing with these problems.

Where the COL measure is relevant is in indexing. That is, retirees, workers, and taxpayers should have their income protected (via indexing) from rises in the cost of living, not just those reflected by the official measures. Imposing Boskin-type adjustments on the CPJ and thus on indexed incomes implies real cutbacks in benefits received not only because these modifications may be technically wrong, but also because they ignore the real meaning of the cost of living and thus overlook hidden inflation. Even though the idea of indexing incomes to prevent loss of real purchasing power seems politically utopian at this point, the Boskin "reforms" are nonetheless attacks on people's standards of living.

Notes

13. See the discussions in *Challenge* 40, no. 2 (March/April 1997), *Journal of Economic Perspectives* 12, no. 1 (winter 1998), and Baker (1998a, 1998b).

14. These costs are relevant only when inflation occurs relative to nominal incomes, but it is the race between prices and money incomes that evokes interest in measuring inflation in the first place.

15. See Madrick (1997a, 1997b) and the response by Gordon and Griliches (1997).

16. This example assumes that we do not benefit from tax cuts that match the decrease in public services.

Throughout this paper, I assume that decreases in the tax burden do not cancel out increases in the COL. Given the relative constancy of tax obligations as a percentage of GDP, this is reasonable. But given the increasing regressivity of the tax system over recent decades, it suggests that the COL has risen faster for the bottom half of the income distribution than is indicated by the most conservative COL numbers.

17. This is in comparison to the similarly calculated CPE deflator, which, like the CPI, reflects Boskin-type revisions.

18. This makes the main assumption of the GPI calculation to calculate the benefits received from consumption, i.e., that pleasures received by people can be quantified and added up.

For Further Reading

Baker, Dean. 1998a. *Getting Prices Right: The Debate Over the Consumer Price Index.* Washington, DC: Economic Policy Institute.

———. 1998b. "The Boskin Commission After One Year." *Challenge* 41, no. 2 (March–April): 6–11.

Cooper, James G., and Kathleen Madigan. 2000. Economic Outlook. *Business Week*, May 15, 2000.

Gibson, Sharon. 1998. "Understanding the Consumer Price Index: Answers to Some Questions." stats.bls.gov/cpi1998g.htm.

Gordon, Robert J., and Zvi Griliches. 1997. "Comment on Madrick." *New York Review of Books*, June 26: 64–65.

Koretz, Gene. 1999. "Waving a Statistical Wand," *Business Week*, May 31, p. 34.

Kuttner, Robert. 1996. "An Index That Confuses Apples with Oranges." *Los Angeles Times*, December 6.

Madrick, Jeff. 1997a. "The Cost of Living: A New Myth." *New York Review of Books*, March 6.

———. 1997b. Reply [to Gordon and Griliches]. *New York Review of Books*, June 26: 65–67.

Mitchell, Daniel. 1998. "Calculating the Price of Everything: The CPI." *Challenge* 41, no. 5 (September–October): 99–112.

Rowthorn, Robert E. 1977. "Conflict, Inflation, and Money." *Cambridge Journal of Economics* 1, no. 3 (September): 215–239.

JAMES DEVINE is a professor in the Economics Department of Loyola Marymount University. An earlier version of this article appears as "An Alternative Measure of Cost-of-Living Inflation Using the Genuine Progress Indicator," in *Political Economy and Contemporary Capitalism: Radical Perspectives on Economic Theory and Policy*, ed. Ron Baiman, Heather Boushey, and Dawn Saunders (Armonk, NY: M.E. Sharpe, 2000). The many differences between the two articles reflect the recent reformulation and updating of the GPI by the Redefining Progress think tank.

A Fight Against Fear As Well As Inflation

By EDMUND L. ANDREWS

WASHINGTON—BACK in 1979, when he was battling the scourge of double-digit inflation, Paul A. Volcker often remarked that part of his job was psychological.

"Inflation feeds in part on itself, so part of the job of returning to a more stable and productive economy must be to break the grip of inflationary expectations," said Mr. Volcker, who was chairman of the Federal Reserve from 1979 to 1987. He ultimately did slay the dragon, but only after administering some of the harshest economic medicine—interest rates as high as 18 percent—that Americans have ever seen.

Now, as the central bank gears up to raise interest rates from their lowest levels in decades, the Federal Reserve is again wrestling with inflation expectations.

Alan Greenspan, who was confirmed by the Senate last week for a fifth term as Fed chairman, has gone out of his way to project a dual message.

On the one hand, Mr. Greenspan and other top officials continue to say that inflationary pressures are "not likely to be a serious concern." But they have also gone out of their way to caution that they may be wrong. And if they are, they have promised, the Fed will relinquish its plan to raise rates at a "measured" pace and move more aggressively to cool down the economy.

So which is it? Is the central bank still confident that inflation poses no threat? Or is it acknowledging that there may be a problem after all?

Part of the answer has to do with an important distinction between inflation in its own right and inflation expectations.

Assuming that Mr. Greenspan and other senior officials believe what they say, the Fed still seems to view recent jumps in the prices of gasoline, food and clothing as transitory jolts, rather than part of a longer-term trend. They contend that labor costs, which account for about two-thirds of production costs, are still rising slowly because the number of unemployed workers remains fairly high. And even if the recent surge in new jobs leads to higher wages, which is likely, Fed officials contend that companies can absorb those costs because their profit margins have been unusually high.

But many bond investors are less sanguine. Though it is an imperfect measure of inflation expectations, the premium that investors have been willing to pay for 10-year Treasury inflation-protected securities, or TIPS, has been hovering at about 2.5 percentage points over other Treasury securities. Many analysts predict that inflation will reach 3 percent over the next year.

Consumers, rattled by higher prices for gasoline, food and clothing, have also ratcheted up their expectations. The University of Michigan's survey of consumer confidence in April showed that respondents expect prices to rise 3 percent over the next year. Last year, they expected prices to rise only 2.3 percent.

Fed officials are acutely aware that inflation expectations can themselves contribute to inflation. If people expect car prices to rise sharply over the next year, they will be more inclined to buy earlier, in order to get a cheaper car. But the rush to buy can itself push up prices, which, in turn, feeds inflation anxieties.

"A rise in inflation expectations tends to become self-fulfilling as people seek to protect themselves in the process of setting wages and prices," said Donald L. Kohn, a Fed governor, in a speech two weeks ago.

Consumers have been exposed to a series of price shocks. Gasoline prices, though they have softened in recent days, have soared for much of this year. Clothing prices have climbed and discounting has diminished sharply in many parts of the country. Health care insurance premiums are climbing at double-digit rates, and college tuition costs are rising rapidly.

Andrew Tilton, an economist at Goldman Sachs, noted that perceptions of inflation could be distorted by the mix of prices that are rising or falling at any particular time. Prices for used cars have fallen sharply since 2001. But because most people buy cars only once every few years, they may notice that decline much less than the rising price for the gasoline they buy every few days.

Mr. Tilton, picking apart the Consumer Price Index for May, found that prices for frequent purchases like food and clothing climbed at a torrid annual pace of 11.3 percent in May. By contrast, the overall index climbed at a somewhat slower annual rate of 8 percent and the core measure, excluding energy and food, climbed only 2.5 percent.

Lyle E. Gramley, a former Fed governor and now a senior adviser to Schwab Soundview Capital Markets, said that while the Fed had little direct influence over consumer expectations, it was trying to persuade financial markets that long-term interest rates did not have to rise sharply.

"What's at issue here is whether or not the Fed is right," Mr. Gramley said. "One can make a plausible case that inflationary pressures are not a concern, but it's awfully hard to make a compelling case."

ULTIMATELY, the Fed's loudest signal is interest rates. Adjusted for inflation, the "real" federal funds rate on overnight loans of bank reserves has been below zero for much of the past year. In the context of historical norms, that is the equivalent of begging consumers to borrow money and bid up prices.

For months now, Mr. Greenspan has been slowly changing that tune. But Fed officials are keenly aware that inflation expectations depend heavily on confidence in the Fed as a guardian of price stability. And if that confidence is to remain strong, they may be forced to move at more than a "measured pace."

Link Between Taxation, Unemployment Is Absent

By Jonathan Weisman

When President Bill Clinton raised taxes in 1993, the unemployment rate dropped, from 6.9 to 6.1 percent, and kept falling each of the next seven years. When President Bush cut taxes in 2001, the unemployment rate rose, from 4.7 to 5.8 percent, then drifted to 6 percent last year when taxes were cut again.

It has become conventional wisdom in Washington that rising tax burdens crush labor markets. Bush castigated his political opponents last week for "that old policy of tax and spend" that would be "the enemy of job creation."

Yet an examination of historical tax levels and unemployment rates reveals no obvious correlation.

"The fact of the matter is, we have much higher rates of employment today than we did in 1954, but our level of taxation is considerably higher," said Gary Burtless, a labor economist at the Brookings Institution. "You simply can't look at total taxation to find employment levels."

The issue has become particularly relevant as Congress debates budget resolutions that would extend tax cuts that otherwise would expire over the next five years, and as Bush clashes daily with Sen. John F. Kerry (Mass.), his Democratic rival, over tax policies and job creation. The Senate voted Wednesday night to place new barriers on future tax cuts.

Republican economists—and White House officials—contend that higher marginal tax rates stifle business investment, hiring and the desire to work.

Senior Treasury Department officials said the correlation is "standard macroeconomics" dating to the Kennedy administration. Last year's surge in economic growth can be timed to the week that tax refunds arrived in American mailboxes, they said.

"The bottom line is, cuts in taxes lead to economic growth, which leads to improvements in the labor market to levels that are better than they otherwise would have been," said Mark J. Warshawsky, acting assistant Treasury secretary for economic policy.

But finding the proof in historical data is difficult, conceded Eric M. Engen, a Republican economist at the American Enterprise Institute.

"If you could hold everything else constant, yes," the correlation would be there, he said. "But everything else isn't the same. That's the big problem that economists have always had."

Engen cautioned that total tax takes are affected by economic growth as well as tax levels. A booming economy—driven not just by tax issues but also by interest rates, trade policies, inflation rates and other factors—will pump money into the government's coffers as it pushes unemployment down, he said.

Still, Burtless noted, some prominent conservative economists, including Harvard University's Martin S. Feldstein, predicted wrongly that the Clinton tax cuts would choke off the 1990s recovery and kill jobs, while the millions of new jobs that Bush said his $1.7 trillion in tax cuts would generate have not materialized. The historical disconnect does not stop there.

In 1964, federal taxation as a share of the economy stood at 17.5 percent, while unemployment was at 5.2 percent. That year, income taxes were slashed, lowering the tax rate in 1965 to 17 percent of the economy. Unemployment dropped as well, to 4.5 percent.

But then tax levels rose sharply, to 19.7 percent of the economy in 1969, while unemployment fell steadily, to 3.5 percent.

In 1981, President Ronald Reagan again slashed taxes. Taxation fell from 19.6 percent of the economy that year to 17.4 percent in 1983. The unemployment rate, however, rose over that period, from 7.6 percent to 9.6 percent. By 1989, taxation had drifted upward again, to 18.3 percent of the economy, but unemployment had fallen to 5.3 percent.

Total taxation in Sweden, including local taxes, is equal to 59.2 percent of that country's economy, the highest level in the 27-member Organization for Economic Cooperation and Development. In contrast, the U.S. total tax burden is 30.6 percent, lowest among the OECD members. Yet unemployment for the past two years in Sweden has been considerably lower than U.S. levels.

Burtless suggested that the issue is not tax levels but tax structures. Sweden has high taxation, but its generous social welfare system rewards citizens for the number of years spent working.

The Clinton tax increase was focused on upper-income households, but it included a sizable increase in the earned income credit for low-wage workers, making it more profitable for them to find and keep jobs.

Does Lower Unemployment Reduce Poverty?

Is the link between unemployment and poverty as strong as many people think it is? Possibly not. How strong the link is depends critically on how we measure poverty. And during the past two decades, researchers have identified numerous shortcomings in the government's official procedures for determining the extent of poverty. In this article, Bob DeFina presents empirical evidence that improved measures of poverty are less strongly related to changes in unemployment than the headcount rate.

BY ROBERT H. DEFINA

The record-setting U.S. expansion of the 1990s, especially the torrid growth in the latter half of the decade, helped push the unemployment rate down to its lowest level in 30 years. By October 2000, the jobless rate had hit 3.9 percent, about 3 percentage points below its previous peak. Such a remarkable decline, when sustainable, is to be celebrated for many reasons. In part, an improving labor market signals that the economy's overall prosperity is being more widely shared. These improvements are especially welcome when they help the country's most financially vulnerable population—the poor.

As in most countries, the extent of poverty in the United States is officially gauged using a headcount rate, which is the fraction of the population that is poor. To determine how many people are poor, government statisticians estimate the income needed for a minimally decent life; that number is called a poverty threshold. A person is considered poor if he or she lives in a household with an income less than the poverty threshold. Having counted the number of poor individuals, statisticians then divide that number by the total population, which yields the headcount rate. In 2000, about 31.1 million individuals were classified as poor. With a population of 275.9 million at the time, the headcount rate was 31.1/275.9, or 11.3 percent.

A tightening labor market, indicated by falling unemployment, potentially reduces the headcount rate in several ways. Temporary and longlived changes in unemployment alter job availability, work hours, promotion possibilities, and real wages. These, in turn, influence families' financial positions and their likelihood of falling above or below official poverty thresholds. The impact on the headcount rate need not be immediate or, at times, even strong. Other labor market developments, perhaps specific to population sub-groups, might interfere with the benefits of a generally prosperous economy. Still, analyses of historical data, based on both national and state-level data, indicate that changes in the unemployment rate are related to significant reductions in the fraction of the population that is officially poor, especially once other factors are accounted for.[1] For example, the strong economy of the past decade coincided with a substantial decline in the headcount rate (Figure 1).

While seemingly intuitive and straightforward, the link between unemployment and poverty may not be as strong as it has traditionally been thought to be. Any conclusions about how unemployment affects poverty depend critically on the particular way in which poverty is measured. And during the past two decades, researchers have identified numerous shortcomings in the government's official procedures for determining the headcount rate. They have suggested improvements, both in the way individuals are identified as poor and in the characteristics of the poor population used to measure the extent of poverty.[2]

On the basis of empirical evidence presented in this article, improved measures of poverty are less strongly related to changes in unemployment than the headcount rate. The unemployment rate declines of the 1990s were not related at all to some alternative poverty indicators.

HOW IS POVERTY MEASURED IN THE UNITED STATES?

Poverty in the United States is measured by the Census Bureau, which uses an approach developed in the early 1960s.[3] The procedure begins with a benchmark income threshold meant to gauge the resources an individual needs to purchase a minimally acceptable bundle of goods and services. In 2000, the baseline threshold (for a single, nonelderly adult) was $8959.

The individual baseline threshold is then adjusted to account for different fam-

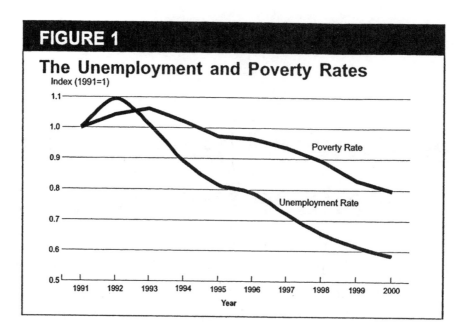

FIGURE 1

The Unemployment and Poverty Rates

Index (1991=1)

ily sizes and for the number of children versus adults. The adjustments recognize that all material needs do not rise proportionately with the number of family members. Whether a family has two or three individuals, it is likely to have, say, only one refrigerator. The less-than-proportional increases in need show up in the official thresholds: for example, moving from a family with one nonelderly adult to a family with two nonelderly adults causes the official 2000 poverty line to rise from $8959 to $11,531, a 29 percent increase. The adjustment factors for different family sizes and types are known as equivalence scales because they are meant to yield an amount of income necessary to leave families of different size or composition with an equivalent standard of living.

The resulting thresholds are increased annually for consumer price inflation nationwide, with the aim of keeping the purchasing power of the poverty level unchanged over time. A lack of data prevents an accounting for differences in the cost of living in different regions of the United States. No adjustment is made for changes in real living standards, such as raising threshold levels in line with increases in the average real income of families.

To identify who is poor, the Census Bureau compares a family's actual pre-tax cash income (including cash payments from the government) with its appropriate poverty threshold. Members of families whose income is below their threshold are deemed poor. The extent of poverty is then gauged by simply summing the number of poor individuals and expressing the result

as a fraction of the population, that is, the headcount rate.

The headcount rate is measured retrospectively once a year. The Census Bureau collects the needed data in its March Current Population Survey, which asks questions about the income that individuals received in the preceding year. The March survey covers about 60,000 households. Thus, the Census Bureau does not literally compare the incomes of every U.S. family to its relevant threshold. Instead, it makes the comparison for a large random sample of U.S. families, then uses the information to statistically estimate the national headcount rate.

PROBLEMS WITH THE OFFICIAL MEASURE

The official poverty measure is not without critics. Indeed, the Census Bureau's approach has widely recognized shortcomings that concern the way individuals are officially *identified* as poor and the way *the extent of poverty* is measured. Because various studies have provided comprehensive discussions of these concerns, only the most important ones are touched on here.[4]

Problems Identifying Who Is Poor...
Numerous researchers have argued that the baseline poverty threshold is too low. As mentioned earlier, the poverty threshold for a family of two adults is $11,531, a fairly meager sum. A more glaring example perhaps is the official threshold for a family of eight adults: $31,704, or less than $4000 a person. The official adjustments to the baseline for different family sizes and

compositions have also come under fire. Critics argue that the adjustments are inconsistent and counterintuitive. Essentially, the changes in thresholds assigned to families as their size and composition change seem somewhat judgmental, with no clear, discernable pattern. These nonsystematic adjustments call into question the extent to which the resulting poverty thresholds represent equivalent standards of living for families of different size or composition.

Poverty analysts and budget experts have prepared alternative thresholds that are 30 percent to 100 percent above the official ones.[5] These suggested increases are based on updated and more complete analyses of budget data and family spending patterns.

The measure of family income that is compared to poverty thresholds is also problematic. Official calculations use a concept called census income, which includes all the money income received by a family before any income taxes are deducted. Money income includes wages and salaries, interest income, government income support payments like unemployment insurance, or even a cash birthday gift.

Researchers have found the concept of census income confusing. On the one hand, it includes the portion of a family's income that may come from some government programs—the cash income support payments from unemployment insurance, Social Security, and the like. On the other hand, it excludes that part of a family's income that may come from other government programs—those providing in-kind payments like food stamps and subsidized housing—even though the in-kind payments represent real purchasing power to families. Census income also ignores the income taxes that families pay, monies obviously not available for spending. A more consistent approach would either (1) ignore all government payments and taxes in order to measure poverty before any government intervention; or (2) recognize them all in order to gauge poverty after the government's actions are taken into account. It would also deduct any work-related expenses, since these decrease a family's spendable income regardless of the government's policy actions.

Addressing these shortcomings in the way poor individuals are identified would alter both the number of individuals officially classified as poor and their demographic mix. Consequently, the relationship between the newly defined poor population and swings in unemployment could be different from that for the old official population. Using higher poverty thresholds, for instance, would mean that the poverty population would include more full-time workers, albeit ones with relatively low wages. The poverty status of such individuals would probably be less sensitive to changes in unemployment, since they would be deemed poor whether or not they work. Correcting the other problems in the official procedure would also change the sensitivity of poverty to unemployment, although the net impact of all the recommended changes is unclear.

...And Problems Determining What the Extent of Poverty Is. The official method for gauging the total degree of poverty has also been criticized, essentially because it neglects characteristics of the poor population other than the number of poor individuals. That is, the official procedure equates the extent of poverty with the headcount rate. But since publication of the landmark work of Nobel Prize-winning economist Amartya Sen, many researchers feel that the official approach is too restrictive. They argue that, at a minimum, any assessment of the degree of poverty should also take into account the *average poverty gap* and *income dispersion among poor individuals*.

The average poverty gap represents the average dollar difference between the income of poor families and their relevant poverty thresholds. In 2000, that gap equaled $6820 per family.[6] Why might the poverty gap be relevant for gauging the extent of poverty? Sen suggests performing

the following mental exercise. Suppose that the number of poor individuals remains unchanged, but each poor family has its income cut in half. Now ask yourself, "Has poverty increased as a result?" Intuitively, many people would answer "yes" because each family now suffers greater financial hardship. Notice that the headcount rate, which is based only on the number of poor individuals, indicates that the extent of poverty has not changed.

Related logic suggests that including income dispersion among poor individuals is important in measuring the degree of poverty. To see why, perform another mental exercise. Suppose that both the number of poor individuals and the average poverty gap remain unchanged. Now, take a dollar from the poor person with the lowest income and give it to the poor person with the highest income. This monetary transfer increases income dispersion among poor individuals, since, other things being equal, poor individuals at the extremes of the income distribution move farther apart. Once again, ask yourself, "Has poverty increased as a result?"

According to Sen, the answer is "yes" because a dollar is worth more to the poorest person than to the least poor person. Essentially, Sen accords greater social weight to the financial situation of the poorest person compared to that of the least poor person. The loss to the poorest person thus outweighs the gain to the least poor person. In this view, greater inequality among the poor, other things equal, suggests a greater degree of poverty. The official headcount rate, by contrast, is unaffected.

Accounting for both the average poverty gap and income dispersion ... when gauging poverty conceivably could alter the perceived benefits of declines in unemployment.

Sen's assessment certainly can be debated. For example, one can reasonably argue that poor individuals are in sufficiently similar circumstances that a dollar in the hands of each should be given equal weight. Still, his framework cannot be dismissed out of hand and, in fact, has been championed by many prominent poverty analysts. During the past two decades, they have developed new poverty indexes that

incorporate and expand upon Sen's original work.

Accounting for both the average poverty gap and income dispersion among the poor when gauging poverty conceivably could alter the perceived benefits of declines in unemployment. It is possible, for instance, that lower unemployment results in a lower average poverty gap without affecting the number of poor individuals. Such an outcome would occur if an unemployed person got a job that paid poverty-level wages. The person would remain officially poor, but the income from the job could reduce his poverty gap. Consequently, lower unemployment would reduce a broader measure of poverty but leave the headcount rate unchanged. Alternatively, lower unemployment might result in fewer poor individuals but leave the average poverty gap unchanged. This would happen, for instance, if the individuals no longer deemed poor had poverty gaps close to the average gap.

In sum, recommended improvements in the way poor individuals are identified and grouped potentially affect the relationship between changes in the unemployment rate and changes in measures of poverty. It is, of course, impossible to know in advance how the suggested changes will actually affect the relationship.

AN EMPIRICAL ANALYSIS OF ALTERNATIVE POVERTY INDICATORS

To explore the practical importance of the suggested improvements, I conducted an empirical analysis of how the unemployment declines of the 1990s were related to the headcount rate and nine alternative poverty indicators.[7] The alternatives incorporate suggested improvements for identifying who is poor and for measuring the extent of poverty. To keep the discussion manageable, I will provide details on the results for only three of the alternatives and simply mention in passing some of the other findings. The results for these three alternatives are, however, representative of the findings for the others.

Three Alternative Indicators. The first alternative indicator is a revised headcount rate, for which poor individuals are identified using higher poverty thresholds, an improved set of equivalence scales, and a pre-tax measure of family income that excludes all government cash and inkind payments and subtracts an estimate of work-related expenses. The new thresh-

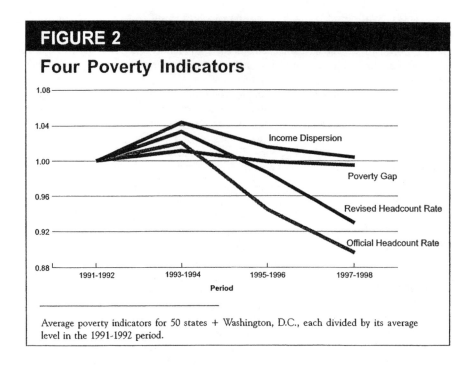

FIGURE 2

Four Poverty Indicators

Average poverty indicators for 50 states + Washington, D.C., each divided by its average level in the 1991-1992 period.

olds and equivalence scales are consistent with the recommendations of the Panel on Poverty and Family Assistance, a group of experts who worked on improving procedures for measuring poverty.[8]

The second alternative indicator is the average poverty gap. To make the gap calculations more meaningful, I express each family's income shortfall as a fraction of its associated poverty threshold. Doing so is a standard procedure. The methods for identifying poor individuals and for measuring income are the same as for the alternative headcount rate.

The third alternative indicator is a gauge of income dispersion among the poor. I use the coefficient of variation, which equals the standard deviation of income among poor individuals divided by the average income of the poor.[9] Once again, the procedures for identifying poor individuals and for measuring income are the same as for the alternative headcount rate.

An Analysis of State-Level Data. My analysis is based on data from all 50 U.S. states (plus Washington, D.C.) covering the years 1991 to 1998. The data come from the Census Bureau's March Current Population Survey, the same information used to calculate the official headcount rate. Using state-level data, as opposed to national data, allows me to increase the number of observations used in the study. It also permits me to control for a variety of demographic influences on the poverty indicators not possible with national data.

These other variables will serve as controls to better isolate the particular relationship with unemployment.

I computed state averages for all of the indicators and other variables in each of the years. Following Census Bureau guidelines for handling statelevel data, I then calculated two-year averages for the years 1991/1992, 1993/1994, 1995/1996, and 1997/1998. Thus, my data set has 204 state-level values for each variable in the study: one for each of the 51 "states" in each of the four time periods.

Average period values for the four poverty indicators are presented in Figure 2. As can be seen, both the official and revised headcount poverty rates initially rose and then fell substantially during the nineties. The decline in the official poverty rate was greater. By contrast the poverty income gap and the dispersion of income among the poor fell much less. Indeed, the level of income dispersion ended the study period higher than where it began. These very different profiles suggest that the relationship of each indicator to unemployment will vary.

It is also useful to examine how closely the different poverty indicators correlate with one another across states and time periods. The degree of correlation suggests whether each poverty indicator provides substantially different information. To measure the degree of correlation, I used a statistic known as a correlation coefficient, where a value of 1 indicates perfect correlation. For the official and alternative

headcount rate, the value of the correlation coefficient is 0.92. That is, despite the different techniques used for identifying poor individuals, the patterns of variation in the alternative headcount rates across states and over time are quite similar. By contrast, the correlation coefficients between the poverty gap and the headcount rates and between income dispersion and the headcount rates are much lower. These range between 0.25 and 0.35. Thus, the poverty gap and income dispersion measures appear to provide a different view of the extent of poverty than the headcount rates. Finally, the poverty gap and income dispersion are themselves quite highly correlated, with a coefficient value of 0.96.

Statistical Models of the Poverty Indicators. What is the relationship between the unemployment rate and each of the indicators? To answer the question, I estimated statistical models in which the movements in each poverty indicator are related to movements in the unemployment rate and the other control variables. The control variables are ones that have been used in other studies. Two of these are meant to account for changes in wages and hours that are not correlated with the unemployment rate: median state real per capita income and the standard deviation in state real per capita income. The others are demographic variables that have been found to vary systematically with poverty indicators: the percent of the population aged 16 years to 19 years, the percent 65 years and older,

FIGURES 3, 4, 5, AND 6

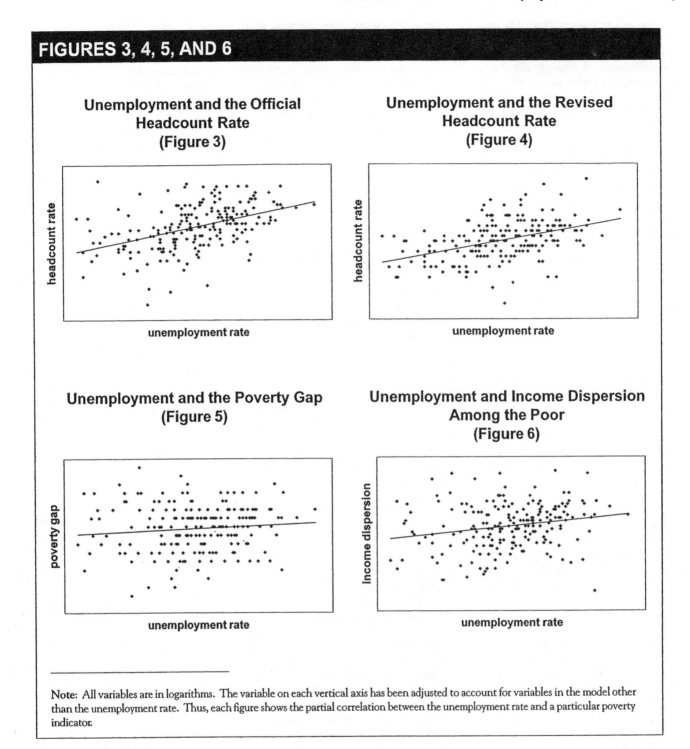

Unemployment and the Official Headcount Rate (Figure 3)

Unemployment and the Revised Headcount Rate (Figure 4)

Unemployment and the Poverty Gap (Figure 5)

Unemployment and Income Dispersion Among the Poor (Figure 6)

Note: All variables are in logarithms. The variable on each vertical axis has been adjusted to account for variables in the model other than the unemployment rate. Thus, each figure shows the partial correlation between the unemployment rate and a particular poverty indicator.

the percent in female-headed families, the percent black, the percent residing in metropolitan areas, the percent with at least a college degree, and the percent not in the labor force.[10] The model also controlled for determinants of poverty that are unique to each state and year but that are not captured by the other variables.[11]

Results of the estimations are represented in Figures 3 through 6. Each figure shows the relationship between the unem-

ployment rate and the particular poverty indicator, after statistically controlling for the influences of all the other variables in the model, based on 51 "states" and 4 two-year periods. As mentioned before, controlling for the other influences allows the link between unemployment and each poverty indicator to be seen more clearly. In statistical terms, the figures show the partial correlation between the unemployment rate and the poverty indicators.

Figure 3 displays the relationship between the unemployment rate and the official headcount rate. The points in the scatterplot indicate a generally positive relationship: As unemployment rates rise, official headcount rates tend to rise as well, even after accounting for all other influences on the headcount rates. The upward-sloping line fitted through the points gives the average relationship: Each 1 percent increase in the unemployment rate is associated with about a 0.12 percent increase in poverty. The estimated magnitude of the response is consistent with that found by other researchers using state-level data. While there is clearly variation in this relationship—not all points lie exactly on the line—the points are clustered closely enough for the relationship to be statistically significant.

Figure 4 presents the results for the revised headcount rate. As is true for the official rate, the revised rate has a clear positive relationship with the unemployment rate, after accounting for the other influences. The points are rather closely clustered around the average response line, and the relationship is statistically significant. The size of the estimated average response is smaller, though, by about half. Further investigation revealed that the smaller response is due mainly to the use of a higher poverty threshold. As noted earlier, the higher thresholds capture more individuals who remain poor whether they work or not.

In contrast to the headcount rates, neither the poverty gap nor income dispersion among the poor is significantly related to unemployment. The relationship between the unemployment rate and the poverty gap is illustrated in Figure 5. The points in Figure 5 suggest a weakly positive relationship. Indeed, the average response line barely slopes upward. Moreover, the points are widely dispersed around the line and are noticeably less clustered than those in Figures 3 and 4. The large amount of dispersion means that both large and small poverty gaps occurred regardless of whether unemployment rates were low or high. Indeed, a formal statistical test confirms the lack of a significant link between the unemployment rate and the poverty gap.

A similar picture emerges for income dispersion among the poor (Figure 6). The average relationship between the unemployment rate and the adjusted income dispersion measure is upward sloping, but less so than that for the headcount rates. And as with the poverty gap, the points in the scatterplot are widely dispersed around the line. A formal test indicates a statistically insignificant link between unemployment and income dispersion.

The results just described appear to hold up under further study. I redid the preceding analysis using a different income definition to compute the three indicators and the conclusions were the same.[12] Namely, the revised headcount rate exhibits a significant link with the unemployment rate, but of a smaller magnitude than does the official headcount rate. Neither the recomputed poverty gap nor re-

computed income dispersion among the poor had a statistically significant relationship with the unemployment rate. I also explored the relationship between the unemployment rate and a comprehensive poverty index, developed by James Foster, Joel Greer and Erik Thorbecke, that simultaneously includes the headcount rate, the average poverty gap, and income dispersion among the poor. No significant link emerged, regardless of the income definition used.

CONCLUSION

Historically, the official headcount rate has generally moved with changes in unemployment, rising as unemployment rose and vice versa. This sympathetic relationship offered one more reason to cheer a strengthening labor market—not only did the average person gain but so did society's most vulnerable.

It is widely recognized, however, that the method by which poverty is officially gauged has a variety of shortcomings. These shortcomings include the methods for identifying who is poor and for measuring the extent of poverty. During the past two decades, researchers have suggested numerous improvements in poverty measurement, including the use of higher poverty thresholds, better equivalence scales, more coherent income definitions, and additional indicators that reflect information beyond simply the number of poor individuals. Should these improvements be implemented, it is quite possible that the measured link between poverty and unemployment could change.

Indeed, my research on the experience of the 1990s reveals that the relationship between unemployment and the revised poverty headcount rate was much weaker than that between the unemployment and the official poverty rate. The revised headcount rate did decline significantly as unemployment fell, but 40 percent less than the official headcount rate did. Moreover, the unemployment rate showed no significant statistical link to either the average poverty gap or income dispersion among the poor. Taken together, the findings caution against overreliance on lower unemployment as an anti-poverty strategy. While helpful in some regards, its impact could well be overstated.

REFERENCES

Asher, Martin A., and Robert H. DeFina. "Has Deunionization Led to Higher Earnings Inequality?" Federal Reserve Bank of Philadelphia *Business Review*, November/ December 1995.

Blank, Rebecca. "Why Were Poverty Rates So High in the 1980s?" in D. Papadimitriou and E. Wolff, eds., *Poverty and Prosperity in the USA in the Late Twentieth Century*. London: Macmillan, 1993.

Blank, Rebecca. "Why Has Economic Growth Been Such an Ineffective Tool Against Poverty in Recent Years?" in J. Neill, ed., *Poverty and Inequality, The Political Economy of Redistribution*. Kalamazoo: W.E. Upjohn Institute, 1996.

Blank, Rebecca. "Fighting Poverty: Lessons From Recent U.S. History," *Journal of Economic Perspectives*, 14, 2000, pp. 3-19.

Blank, Rebecca, and Alan Blinder. "Poverty and the Macroeconomy," in Sheldon Danziger and Daniel Weinberg, eds., *Challenging Poverty: What Works and What Doesn't*. Cambridge, MA: Harvard University Press, 1987.

Blank, Rebecca, and David Card. "Poverty, Income Distribution, and Growth: Are They Still Connected?" *Brookings Papers on Economic Activity*, 2, 1993, pp. 285-339.

Cutler, David, and William Katz. "Macroeconomic Performance and the Disadvantaged," *Brookings Papers on Economic Activity*, 2, 1991, pp. 1-74.

DeFina, Robert. "The Impact of Unemployment on Alternative Poverty Measures," Federal Reserve Bank of Philadelphia Working Paper 02-8, May 2002.

Fisher, Gary. "The Development and History of the Poverty Thresholds," *Social Security Bulletin*, 55, 1992, pp. 3-14.

Foster, J.E., J. Greer, and E. Thorbecke. "A Class of Decomposable Poverty Measures," *Econometrica*, 52, 1984, pp. 761-66.

Haveman, Robert, and John Schwabish. "Has Macroeconomic Performance Regained Its Anti-Poverty Bite?" *Contemporary Economic Policy*, 18, 2000, pp. 415-27.

Orshansky, Mollie. "Counting the Poor: Another Look at Poverty," *Social Security Bulletin*, 28, 1965, pp. 3-29.

Panel on Poverty and Family Assistance. *Measuring Poverty: A New Approach*. Washington, D.C.: National Academy Press, 1995.

Romer, Paul. "Poverty and Macroeconomic Activity," Federal Reserve Bank of Kansas City *Economic Review*, First Quarter 2000, pp. 1-13.

Sen, Amartya. "Poverty: An Ordinal Approach to Measurement," *Econometrica*, 44, 1976, pp. 219-31.

Sen, Amartya. *Poverty and Famines: An Essay on Entitlement and Deprivation.* Oxford: Oxford University Press, 1981.

B. Zheng. "Aggregate Poverty Measures," *Journal of Economic Surveys*, 11, 1997, pp. 123-62.

NOTES

1. Examples can be found in the articles by Rebecca Blank (1996 and 2000) and the articles by Blank and Alan Blinder; David Cutler and William Katz; Blank and David Card; Robert Haveman and John Schwabish; and Paul Romer.

2. There are also variants on the way unemployment is measured. The headline unemployment rate, which measures unemployed workers aged 16 years or older as a percentage of the civilian labor force and which I use in my analysis described below, is one of several measures compiled by the Bureau of Labor Statistics.

3. The procedure is detailed in Mollie Orshansky's article and in the article by Gary Fisher.

4. *Mesuring Poverty: A New Approach*, prepared by the Panel on Poverty and Family assistance, contains a thorough analysis of identification issues. See the article by B. Zheng, for a discussion of aggregation concerns.

5. Many of these alternative budgets are discussed in *Mesuring Poverty: A New Approach*.

6. Official poverty data are published in the Census Bureau's *Current Population Reports*, P-60 series.

7. See my working paper.

8. The new thresholds were set 30 percent higher than the official ones. The new equivalence scales were computed using the poverty threshold of a single adult as the benchmark.

9. This is a standard way of measuring income dispersion, although others, such as the so-called Gini coefficient, are available. See the 1995 *Business Review* article by Martin Asher and me.

10. In theory, the use of the demographic control variables can hinder estimation of the relationship between the unemployment rate and the poverty indicators if the variables are highly correlated with the unemployment rate. This is not an actual concern in teh present study. The correlation coefficients between each of the demographic variables and the unemployment rate are small, the largest being about 0.34.

11. The approach I have used is technically known as a fixed-effects regression. Rebecca Blank and David Card's study also used a fixed-effects regression model to study the relationship between unemployment and poverty. Also, all the non-demographic variables are expressed as natural logarithms. Expressing the variables as natural logs allows the estimated relationship between the unemployment rate and the poverty indicators to be interpreted as an elasticity—the percentage change in the poverty indicator associated with a 1 percent change in the unemployment rate.

12. The other income concept starts with all private-sector income, subtracts all income taxes paid, and adds in all government cash and in-kind payments. It also subtracts an estimate of work expenses.

Bob DeFina is the John A. Murphy Professor of Economics, Villanova University, Villanova, Pennsylvania. When he wrote this article he was a visiting scholar in the Research Department of the Philadelphia Fed.

Employment May Be Even Weaker Than You Think

By Francis X. Markey

With the deceleration of the U.S. economy now beyond question, the only point of debate is exactly how much it has slowed and where growth trends will go from here. Optimists can point to a number of economic indicators for signs of life, including the establishment employment report which, though weak, remains up nearly 1% from one year ago. The employment report could mislead these individuals however, as design flaws in the Bureau of Labor Statistics (BLS) survey may very well be masking greater weakness in U.S. payrolls.

The BLS establishment employment survey is one of the most timely and most watched economic indicators available. Nonetheless, the survey's current methodology has been in place for some time, and the BLS fully acknowledges that the report needs to be revamped to correct the statistical limitations of the current model. Indeed, the federal statistical agency has already begun the gradual introduction of a newly redesigned survey, and the results have already revealed that the BLS may currently be overstating the overall number of jobs.

The current survey uses a quota sample, which is an older method of sample surveying known to be at risk for a number of statistical biases. The survey uses more than 300,000 establishments nationwide to approximate total payroll employment growth from the previous month. The main problem in estimating national employment is accounting for new business births and deaths. That is, firms newly opened or shuttered since the last comprehensive employment count. To adjust the payroll estimates for these firms, a bias adjustment factor is included to the monthly employment totals. Translated, this basically means the BLS adds or subtracts jobs to the report each month in an attempt to account for these firm openings and closures. This bias adjustment factor is constant across the three months making up each quarter.

The problem with the current bias adjustment factors is that they are particularly ineffective in times of rapid acceleration or deceleration in job growth. The adjustment term is derived from historical data and is quite slow to react to changing trends. The current bias adjustment factor is most likely a case in point. The

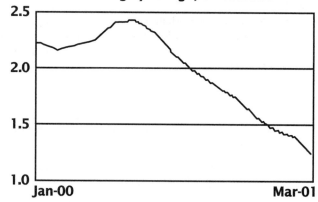

A Clear Picture of Total Employment?
% change year ago, 3–mos. MA

bias used for the first quarter of 2001 is +145,000 jobs. This amounts to nearly 40% of the reported employment gain for the U.S. in the first quarter. Now, clearly the U.S. economy has slowed in the past year, yet the current adjustment factor being used to approximate job gains from new establishments is only slightly below the average of +150,000 jobs used in 1999 during the prime of the recent expansion.

The new survey method is based on a probability sample, which provides a much greater degree of accuracy and promises to be much more flexible in response to current economic conditions. There is still a correction term for business births and deaths; which is unavoidable, as the most recent comprehensive count culled from unemployment insurance (UI) data lags by about nine months. The new adjustment term is much improved, however, by allowing for month-to-month fluctuations in the jobs added or subtracted and incorporating each new month of UI data as the data become available. The end result is that the new establishment employment survey is statistically more accurate and responsive.

The example of the wholesale trade industry illustrates this fact, as well as highlighting the rising probability of an overstatement in current employment totals. The BLS is introducing the new survey in segments. Thus far, the new methodology has only been applied to the wholesale trade industry (it will be used for manufacturing, mining and construction as of the June benchmarks, and the rest will be added in 2002 and 2003). The last benchmark revision for the wholesale trade industry, which is equal to the magnitude of the BLS estimation error, was ten times larger with the old method than with the new, clearly displaying the improved accuracy of the new survey. Even more telling for the payroll report as a whole, the wholesale industry was expanding in line with the all other industries in the first quarter of 2000, but has since decelerated rapidly and is now growing at half the rate of the overall job base.

All of this is not to say that the BLS employment report is no longer a valuable indicator. It remains a timely picture of current economic conditions. In times of rapid acceleration or deceleration in growth, however, it may be wise to take the report with a grain of salt—at least until the new survey is fully expanded into all industries over the next few years.

More Jobs, Worse Work

by Stephen S. Roach

The state of the American labor market remains the defining issue of the current economic debate. Through February, the United States was mired in the depths of the worst jobless recovery of the post-World War II era. Now, there are signs the magic may be back. More than a million jobs have been added to total nonfarm payrolls over the past four months, the sharpest increase since early 2000.

These gains certainly compare favorably with the net loss of 594,000 jobs in the first 27 months of this recovery. But there's little cause for celebration: the increases barely make a dent in the weakest hiring cycle in modern history. From the trough of the last recession in November 2001 through last month, private sector payrolls have risen a paltry 0.2 percent. This stands in contrast to the nearly 7.5 percent increase recorded, on average, over the comparable 31-month interval of the six preceding recoveries.

Nor is there much reason to celebrate the type of jobs that have been created over the past four months. In general, they have been at the lower end of the economic spectrum.

By industry, the leading sources of hiring turn out to be restaurants, temporary hiring agencies and building services. These three categories, which make up only 9.7 percent of total nonfarm payrolls, accounted for 25 percent of the cumulative growth in overall hiring from March to June. Hiring has also accelerated at clothing stores, courier services, hotels, grocery stores, trucking businesses, hospitals, social work agencies, business support companies and providers of personal and laundry services. This group, which makes up 12 percent of the nonfarm work force, accounted for 19 percent of the total growth in business payrolls over the past four months.

That's not to say there hasn't been any improvement at the upper end of the labor market, with the construction industry leading the way. At the same time, there has been increased hiring in several of the higher-end professions: there is more demand for lawyers, architects, engineers, computer scientists and bankers. Manufacturing, however, has continued to lag.

Putting these pieces together, there can be no mistaking the unusual bifurcation of the recent improvement in the American labor market. Lower-end industries, which employ 22 percent of the work force, accounted for 44 percent of new hiring from March to June. Higher-end industries, which make up 24 percent of overall employment, accounted for 29 percent of total job growth over the past four months.

In short, jobs are growing at both ends of the spectrum, but the low-paying jobs are growing much more quickly. The contribution of low-end industries to the recent pick-up in hiring has been almost double the share attributable to high-end industries.

An equally dramatic picture emerges from the survey of American households. According to the Bureau of Labor Statistics, the total count of persons at work part time— both for economic and non-economic reasons—increased by 495,000 from March to June. That amounts to an astonishing 97 percent of the cumulative increase of the total growth in employment measured by the household survey over this period. By this measure, as the hiring dynamic has shifted gears in recent months, the bulk of the benefits have all but escaped America's full-time work force.

Americans want employment that leads somewhere.

Finally, the occupational breakdown of the American labor market, as also sampled by the survey of households, provides yet another facet of the character of the recent hiring upturn. It turns out that fully 81 percent of total job growth over the past year was concentrated in low-end occupations in transportation and material moving, sales and repair and maintenance services. At the upper end of the occupational hierarchy, increases in construction and professional jobs were partly offset by sharp declines in the numbers of production workers, who mainly toil in manufacturing plants.

Consequently, from three different vantage points—employment breakdowns by industry, by occupation and by degree of attachment—the same basic picture emerges: While there has been an increase in job creation over the past four months—an unusually belated and anemic spurt by historical standards—the bulk of the activity has been at the low end of the quality spectrum. The Great American Job Machine is not even close to generating the surge of the high-powered jobs that is typically the driving force behind greater incomes and consumer demand.

This puts households under enormous pressure. Desperate to maintain lifestyles, they have turned to far riskier sources of support. Reliance on tax cuts has led to record budget deficits, and borrowing against homes has led to record household debt. These trends are dangerous and unsustainable, and they pose a serious risk to economic recovery.

We hear repeatedly that the employment disconnect is all about productivity—that America needs to hire fewer workers because the ones already working are more efficient. This may well be true, but there is a more compelling explanation: global labor arbitrage. Under unrelenting pressure to cut costs, American companies are now replacing high-wage workers here with like-quality, low-wage workers abroad. With new information technologies allowing products and now knowledge-based services to flow more easily across borders, global labor arbitrage is likely to be an enduring feature of the economy.

Hiring always moves up and down. But it is evident from the experiences of Europe and Japan that new structural forces can come into play that have a lasting impact on job creation. Such is now the case in America.

It was only a matter of time before the globalization of work affected the United States labor market. The character and quality of American job creation is changing before our very eyes. Which poses the most important question of all: what are we going to do about it?

Stephen S. Roach is chief economist for Morgan Stanley.

LIGHTING LABOR'S FIRE

Barbara Ehrenreich and
Thomas Geoghegan

The collapse of union membership in America, from its peak at 38 percent in the mid-fifties to 9 percent of the private work force today, is the one big reason for our roaring inequality. It's why the poor and middle class are still being cheated of pensions, healthcare and a fair share of the GDP. Yet we have no chance—for now—of reforming the labor laws that make organizing so difficult. There is little hope, for example, of giving the now toothless Wagner Act some bite, in the form of penalties for illegal unionbusting. Not in this Congress. Or the next. Or probably the next. What, then, is left for the American left? To give up on so many of the issues we care about?

The underlying reason for organized labor's decline is that our labor laws do not let people join unions, freely and fairly, without being fired. Yes, as the Service Employees International Union and others have shown, it is possible to do some organizing "outside" the Wagner Act, ducking the National Labor Relations Board and endless court appeals. But this kind of organizing seems to be only enough to keep labor from disappearing. To bring labor back, some change of law has to occur. Yet change of a good kind seems all but utopian. Even under a Democratic President, House and Senate, it was still easy for antilabor senators to stop a striker-replacement ban in 1993, and to do so with a filibuster that didn't even work up a sweat. And without a labor movement, what's left to us but to snicker at Bush and all the Bush clones to come?

No one, not even labor, seems to have a strategy to bring labor back. And without such a strategy, it is hard to see how the American left, such as it is, can "dream responsibly" of, say, national health insurance, or even of a decent defense of Social Security.

What we need is a new approach to rebuilding the unions—and to labor law reform. There is a hint in Nelson Lichtenstein's recent book, *State of the Union*, as to what it might be. Lichten-

stein argues that in many ways, organized labor missed out on the "rights revolution" of the 1960s and '70s, which won individual workers new protections based on gender and race. True, some unions took advantage of the civil rights movement to organize low-wage African-American hospital and other service workers in a number of cities; and grassroots feminism has certainly contributed to the unionization of women.

But the language and, with it, the ethos of individual rights were quickly co-opted by management, with its stress on the "right to work" and the "right" to have a say in how one's dues are spent. Company anti-union propaganda, as at Wal-Mart, for example, claims that a union will deprive the individual of his or her individual access to management. Never mind that management retains its right to fire nonunion workers at will, for infringements as vague as a "bad attitude," or that, for the past two decades, corporations have steadily encroached on workers' privacy and rights through drug testing, personality testing, ever-more sophisticated surveillance and a proliferation of shop-floor rules such as "no talking."

The AFL-CIO has responded only weakly—with a "Voice @ Work" campaign, suggesting that the workers will be empowered individually, as well as collectively, through unionization. But by and large, it has ducked the issue of individual or civil rights other than the right to join a union. As a result, many workers, perhaps especially white males, perceive unions exactly as management would like them to: as overbearing bureaucracies in which the individual is easily lost or even crushed. This is still true even as workers now are angrier and more willing to take on their employers.

To bring a real labor movement back, we may need a more individualist, even libertarian approach, one that finally brings the "rights revolution" to American workers, regardless of gender or race. The ultimate goal is still to change our labor laws and bring back the old union spirit embodied in words like "solidarity" and the use of "brother" and "sister" as affectionate forms of address. But to get there, unions need to engage the individual worker directly, and not only as an atom within a potential bargaining unit. To this end, we propose a number of approaches and initiatives. Some have a libertarian flavor, at least compared with existing union culture. Others are more traditionally "collective." We realize, with humility, that in the field, at the local level, in universities, others may have similar or better ideas than the specific ones we discuss below. What these ideas have in common is that we can start working on them now. To begin with the biggest:

1. Individual Membership

At present the only way for most workers to join a union is to pass through a kind of trial by fire—an arduous, often risky, organizing drive that may last for months. No such ordeal is required of people who would like to join, say, the National Organization for Women or the NAACP, who can simply send in their dues. In many European countries, like Germany, anyone can join a union individually, no matter who they are. Yes, it's true that labor law is different "over there," and labor can often bargain in workplaces that never voted in a union at all. (As a result, labor in Europe can more easily bargain for whole industries.) Still, the Europeans have a point. Why, they ask, do you keep all your "true believers" out? The first step toward the revitalization of American unions should be to create a form of membership accessible to any worker.

Recently in *The Nation* (June 24), Richard Freeman and Joel Rogers took a step in this direction by suggesting that the AFL-CIO try what they called "minority" unions. These would be small groups of pro-union workers, without the collective bargaining rights of old-fashioned majority unions. We're sympathetic to this, of course. But remember, such people would be volunteers for only half a union. And would "half a union" really be half a union, or would it end up being less than zero? Think of a single Starbucks where only three of fifteen people join. They have no contract. The "minority union" members can be picked off and fired (that may be illegal, but there are stiffer penalties for jaywalking). And what can a union staffer do for them? Get them higher wages? No. Cut overtime? Of course not. Indeed, in many a workplace, the business agent, or BA, can't even get in the front door!

Yet Freeman and Rogers are surely right about their big point: Labor has to find a way to let people sign up without necessarily going through an organizing drive. What we have in mind, however, is a very different way of being an "individual" member. There would be no "group," not even a "minority" one. Also, the service being offered would be specific and well defined. Best of all, the AFL-CIO would have to do little more for our project than lend its name.

We're not talking about an AARP-type membership, such as the AFL-CIO tried a few years ago. In that particular case, there was no union-type service that the individuals got.

Nothing but VISA cards, hotel discounts, etc. The idea died of its own silliness.

To make individual memberships work, the member has to get a real union-type service, somehow connected to wages, hours, working conditions. It has to be limited: a fee for a specific service, to be rendered now or even later. And it should offer the one thing that every American, stuck in a job, sooner or later longs to do—take the boss to court!

Or at least, get to talk it over with your lawyer. That's the "service." Two hours a year of free legal services, i.e., a consultation with a real lawyer. About labor law? No, about the maze of special employment laws, civil rights laws, laws from disability to family leave to 401(k)s. What the individual gets, in the name of the AFL-CIO, would be a kind of legal referral off the premises: And if you don't need it this year, you can bank it for later.

As we envision it, this service would not come from the union's own lawyers but from the private bar. It is long overdue for the AFL-CIO to connect with lawyer groups like the National Employment Lawyers Association, a network of progressive lawyers who do civil rights, Title VII, sexual harassment and ERISA (retirement benefits) cases. The unions and NELA would run the program, which would function like an Automobile Club card for your breakdowns at work. Best of all, if we want, we can sign up in secret. But people will feel like they are getting a union-type service and will know just what the service is.

What's the payoff for the AFL-CIO? Millions of new members. Even traveling salesmen may start to join. Then think of all the people labor can mobilize on Election Day!

2. Start Memberships With Other 'Flavors'

We suggest other forms of individual memberships for those who want a connection to the labor movement but do not want or need legal services for themselves. One possibility would be ACLU-type membership. The idea here is to have an ACLU within the existing AFL-CIO, ideally closely tied to the National Workrights Institute in Princeton, New Jersey, which is itself a spinoff of the ACLU. That is, set up an organization, member-based, that is very much like the ACLU, except that its focus would be on civil liberties at work. The issues: cameras in the bathrooms, personnel files, post-9/11 screening, drug testing, undocumented workers, racial profiling, etc. Outsiders can join. Existing union members can check a box that earmarks part of their dues to go to "labor's ACLU."

In addition, we suggest an international-solidarity membership, open to existing members as well as interested outsiders. Dues could help support strikes and organizing drives in other parts of the world. One great thing that a member would receive is a monthly magazine (perhaps by e-mail), with country-by-country reports as to what the labor movement is doing in that country. Some may scoff at a mere magazine, but Seattle showed that there are some people, especially young people, who want some sense of connectedness with labor movements around the world.

3. Do a Few Tammany-Type Things for the Poor

More than just sign up individuals, labor has to raise its profile, especially among the working poor. Long ago the unions thrived among the poor and worked alongside the old big-city Democratic political machines. Now those machines are gone, but the unions could pick up and carry out some of their useful services, albeit updated. We don't just mean that labor should keep reaching out to community groups. They should deliver community services.

For example: the earned-income tax credit. According to a study in 2000 by Katherin Ross Phillips of the Urban Institute, half of those eligible for the EITC fail to get their money. They don't know, or don't submit the tax returns, or are too wary to go to H&R Block, which ends up taking much of the refund. The old urban machines would have put this money in the hands of people. Why not the unions? With help from the rest of us, the unions could scour up foundation money, train people and set up storefront offices to help people fill out the forms. The working poor would come to see the labor movement as a concrete source of help, even in cases where organizing is still only a distant possibility: "The union helped get me my money."

We note, though, as Cesar Chavez often said, that the unions should not give away these services for free. Make people pay a nominal fee and give them individual memberships. Then bring them out on Election Day.

4. Start Ten 'Labor Colleges' in Ten Cities

Here is a sobering thought: What can labor give a twenty-something? In Britain, where it is relatively easy to join a union, the Trades Union Congress has found it difficult to persuade many young people that unions have much to offer. A national health program already exists. And with people switching jobs as often as they do in America, what does a wage increase, even of 2 percent or so, mean in a job you may leave in a few months? So some in British unions propose tying union membership to training: from basic literacy on up.

Imagine if labor, not-for-profits and various schools joined together to create programs in the basic and not-so-basic skills. Imagine if, as part of one's union membership, dues allowed people to invest in themselves. To have such programs in the ten biggest urban areas could mean reaching in effect well over half of the work force. Especially at a time when unions can't raise wages very much, it helps to connect a union membership (in the minds of nonunion America) with a lifetime program of learning—from, say, welding to organizing and public speaking.

All the above ideas are intended to make labor more appealing, to build up our dwindling individual union memberships. But once there are hundreds of thousands of individual members, how should labor use its new political clout?

5. Make California, by Referendum, The Prototype of 'Europe'

We assume for now there is no chance that Congress will enact any law prohibiting striker replacement or the like. But there is a side door to labor law reform: a referendum in California. Go to the people, or at least 25 percent of the nation's people. Seek a state law (which could not be pre-empted by federal law) that changes the state law or common-law rule of employment "at will," requiring instead that no one can be fired, union or nonunion, except for "just cause." Labor has always (unwisely, it seems) resisted such a law, because this kind of protection is supposed to be, at least in America, a benefit of union membership. But in most European countries, this is a right that belongs to everyone, and it is one of the reasons unions remain relatively strong there. It takes away the fear factor. People can put on a union button without fear of being fired.

Such a law, since it extends rights to everyone, is likely to be very popular. Once in place, it need only spread to three or four other big states to become, in effect, the law of the land. Then the entire atmosphere or climate for organizing will change, and people can at least debate joining unions without risking their jobs.

6. Use Soft Money to Organize

The McCain-Feingold campaign-finance reform law has perhaps freed up for organizing some of the soft money that labor customarily gives to the Democratic Party. It is important for labor and progressive candidates everywhere to understand: Money for organizing is a kind of "soft money" contribution. Let's assume that the AFL-CIO statistic is right for white male voters: If they are nonunion, they voted 69 percent for Bush, 35 percent for Gore. If union, the ratio almost flips: 59 percent for Gore, 35 for Bush. Put another way, union organizing "flips" more votes, at least among white males, than any number of television commercials. Progressive politicians should demand such contributions when labor knocks on their door. "If you want my support, organize in my district." Likewise, unions should concentrate their organizing in swing districts and states.

Any organizing, while it lasts, creates a blip, bringing more nonmembers and quasi members into the fold for a while.

7. Push the Mail Ballot

The biggest disaster for labor, and every labor cause (including labor law reform), is that the vast, vast majority of hourly workers, both women and men, simply don't vote at all. This is not just a matter of apathy and alienation: In the new American economy, with working mothers, suburban sprawl and two-hour-a-day commutes, many Americans have a workday that simply does not give them a fair or equal shot at getting to the polls. In a few states, such voters can get an absentee ballot, but that takes foresight and planning that most of us lack.

So if people can't get to the polls, why not bring the polls to the people? By that we mean: Campaign for an Oregon-type mail ballot, sent to the home of every registered voter. When Oregon went to the mail ballot, it already had liberal absentee voting rules and, as a result, already had the highest voting rate in the nation. With the mail ballot, the voting rate shot up by 10–25 percent in some elections. The new voters? Hourly workers, the elderly—in other words, labor's constituency. As we mobilize more of these "quasi" members, this puts pressure on politicians to raise the minimum wage, spend more on childcare, etc., and generally raise working standards. By the way, in the 2002 election, Oregon had a turnout rate of 65 percent, almost equal to Minnesota's and South Dakota's, among the highest in the nation. Now we can turn, finally, to the subject of labor law reform.

8. For God's Sake, Come Up With a Labor Law Reform Americans Can Understand!

Sure, we support a ban on striker replacement. Or repeal of Taft-Hartley's ban on secondary boycotts. (At one time these strikes allowed labor to shut down a whole industry, or an area like an airport.) But reforms like this won't win many hearts and minds. Indeed, how many people even understand what is being discussed? Let's assume there will be no labor law reform for now. At least let's come up with a form of it that ordinary people will understand and be willing, eventually, to fight for: Make the right to join a union a civil right, by adding such a right to those protected by the Civil Rights Act of 1991.

The struggle for such an amendment would finally bring the "rights revolution" of the 1960s and '70s to the labor movement. Part of the appeal would be to American individualism: "We don't care if you join a union or not, but you should be able

to put on a union button without being fired." And if we were to succeed in making the right to join a union a civil right under the act, anyone who is fired could go not just to the National Labor Relations Board, where such cases usually disappear without a trace, but directly to federal court. Just as in Title VII cases, plaintiffs could receive compensatory damages, punitive damages, preliminary injunctions, even temporary restraining orders—and, yes, payment of their legal fees. And with a chance of getting their fees paid, it would be a lot easier for the progressive lawyers of America to join the labor movement on the barricades.

No, it will not pass now, but neither did McCain-Feingold, at first. But it was a bill that, for all its faults, was at least a vehicle for a reform movement. Amending the Civil Rights Act will not solve everything. But at least people would understand it. Women's groups, civil rights groups and others can organize around such a bill as they cannot organize around, say, striker replacement. The point is to frame a reform that in itself helps to build a grassroots movement.

Of course, it may be that even all the new ideas in the world can't bring back the labor movement. But let's suppose the chances are as bleak as one in four. If it were the bottom of the ninth, two out, our side losing, with a .250 hitter coming up, would our side say, "What's the point—the chances of a hit are only one in four"? In the midpoint of the Bush era, we can at least send up a few .250 hitters to the plate.

We would love to see the AFL-CIO take up the reforms we've proposed. But ultimately, the labor movement is too important to be left to the AFL-CIO, however much we may admire John Sweeney and his administration. It's up to all of us, not just to them, to bring the labor movement back.

Barbara Ehrenreich is the author of Nickel and Dimed: On (Not) Getting By in America *(Metropolitan). Thomas Geoghegan, a labor lawyer, is the author of* In America's Court: How a Civil Lawyer Who Likes to Settle Stumbled Into a Criminal Trial *(New Press).*

From *The Nation*, December 23, 2002, p. 111-16. © 2002 by The Nation. Reprinted by permission.

UNIT 6
International Economics

Unit Selections

34. **Foreign Economic Policy for the Next President**, C. Fred Bergsten
35. **Why Do Certain Countries Prosper?**, Virgina Postrel
36. **Perspectives on Global Outsourcing and the Changing Nature of Work**, Christopher B. Clott
37. **The Fall and Rise of the Global Economy**, John G. Fernald and Victoria Greenfield
38. **The "Globalization" Challenge: The U.S. Role in Shaping World Trade and Investment**, Robert E. Litan
39. **Should We Worry About the Large U.S. Current Account Deficit?**, Paul Bergin
40. **Global Shell Games: How the Corporations Operate Tax Free**, Byron Dorgan
41. **Free Trade on Trial—Ten Years of NAFTA**, The Economist
42. **Trade in the Americas: All in the Familia**, The Economist
43. **Latin America's Volatile Financial Markets**, Jonathan Lemco and Scott B. MacDonald
44. **Japan Learns the Sun May Not Come Out Tommorow**, Howard W. French
45. **The Limits to Consumption**, Shawn W. Crispin and Philip Segal
46. **East Asia: Recovery and Restructuring**, Ramon Moreno
47. **China's Economic Power: Enter the Dragon**, The Economist
48. **Changing Today's Consumption Patterns—for Tomorrow's Human Development**, UN Human Development Report

Key Points to Consider

- How should America respond to the challenges of global competition?

- Should we be concerned about the effects of outsourcing on U.S. workers?

- Will efforts at economic integration such as NAFTA and the European Union succeed? Why do certain countries prosper while others don't?

- How do today's consumption patterns affect tomorrow's human development? Why might Malthus' gloomy population forecasts be wrong?

 **Links: www.dushkin.com/online/**
These sites are annotated in the World Wide Web pages.

European Union in the U.S.
http://www.eurunion.org

Institute for International Economics
http://www.iie.com

Inter-American Development Bank (IDB)
http://www.iadb.org

International Monetary Fund (IMF)
http://www.imf.org

Organization for Economic Cooperation and Development (OECD)
http://www.oecd.org

Sustainable Development Organization
http://www.sustainabledevelopment.org

UNCTAD
http://www.unctad.org

World Policy Institute
http://www.worldpolicy.org

World Trade Organization (WTO)
http://www.wto.org

Global free trade by 2010 would enhance the prosperity of all countries by underwriting the ultimate success for competitive liberalization. It would preclude the risk that regional arrangements could develop into hostile blocs. It would terminate any risk of North-South conflict by engaging both sets of countries in a cooperative multilateral enterprise that meets the needs of both. Such a vision should guide this area of international affairs as the world enters the twenty-first century.

—C. Fred Bergsten ("Globalizing Free Trade", Foreign Affairs, May/June 1996.)

Up to this point, the readings in this book have primarily focused on issues involving the U.S. domestic economy. However, many of the world's most pressing economic problems are international in scope, involving the complex web of the trading and financial arrangements that link all countries in a global network. The world economy is in a period of rapid change. Over the last decade we have witnessed a series of unforeseen events: the after- shocks of the 9/11 terrorist attacks; ambitious market reforms in what were formerly centrally-planned economies; an acceleration of the process of economic integration in the Americas, Western Europe, and the Pacific Rim; and increased use of protectionist measures by most major traders. How the United States responds to these challenges may well influence events in the world economy for many years to come.

The U.S. economy is extraordinarily resilient. Historically, it has consistently demonstrated an ability to adjust to change, to adapt new technologies, and to create new jobs. In absolute terms, the United States is presently the world's most important international trader: total U.S. exports and imports each exceed about a trillion dollars annually. In addition, the United States has for many years been able to enjoy the advantages of remaining relatively self-sufficient; whereas Canada and most Western European countries derive roughly a quarter of their national income from trade, the United States obtains just over 10 percent of all income from this source.

However, it is increasingly apparent that an important shift in power has occurred: the United States, once the world's predominant economic power, must now share the spotlight with Western Europe and East Asia. In this new multipolar world, America still appears to be the first among equals. But it no longer has the economic leverage or moral authority to dictate the course of world events. Evidence of the constraints that the United States faces include fierce competition from foreign businesses, continuing trade deficits, and domestic anxieties over the costs which trade liberalization imposes on those Americans who are hurt by it.

We begin with a study by C. Fred Bergsten, who spells out a foreign economic policy for the next U.S. president. He says that while the U.S. may be in a position to undertake unilateral initiatives for the sake of national security, in economic policy unilateralism is simply not an option.

The American economy has done better—and Europe and Japan have done worse—than most people predicted in the 1980s. Virginia Postrel says that, in order to understand this development, we need to know which industries in which countries are more productive and why.

While the global liberalization of trade has reduced barriers to the movement of goods and capital across national boundaries, it has also created a series of problems, including job losses, increasing income inequality, and stagnant or deteriorating real wages. Christopher Clott examines global "outsourcing" and the changing nature of work.

Financial issues are the focus of the next articles. Paul Bergin asks: should we worry about the large U.S. current account deficit? Next, in "Global Shell Games," Byron Dorgan takes a look at how multinational companies operate tax free.

The unit continues with articles that offer perspectives on individual countries and regions. The formation in 1994 of the North American Free Trade Association (NAFTA) was marked by both extravagant promises about its benefits and by bloodcurdling warnings about its costs. Jonathan Lemco and Scott MacDonald note that, despite remarkable growth in the countries of Latin America since the early 1990s, the greatest challenge facing these nations is heavy dependence on international capital markets.

Then, Howard French notes that little more than a decade ago Japan had the gleaming look of one of history's greatest economic successes. But today the desire of Japan's neighbors to follow its model has been replaced by dismay over its decay. This is followed by an article in which Shawn Crispin and Philip Segal trace the sources of economic difficulties currently confronting the countries of Southeast Asia.

The last article deals with a United Nations study which examines implications of the rapid growth of world consumption in the twentieth century for human development in the twenty-first century.

Foreign Economic Policy for the Next President

C. Fred Bergsten

THE DANGERS OF ROLLBACK

AT A TIME when U.S. foreign policy is dominated by war, terrorism, and weapons of mass destruction, economic concerns are often relegated to the back burner. But in reality, economic policy must be an integral component of any successful foreign policy. Some of its elements, such as the suppression of terrorist financing and support for reconstruction efforts in Iraq and Afghanistan, bear directly on the most central national security concerns. The linkage, however, is much broader, because most countries, rich or poor, large or small, depend heavily on the global economy for their prosperity and their stability. Hence, economics ranks at the top of their list of concerns. To continue to be relevant to the rest of the world, the United States must engage effectively on these issues.

As the sole military superpower, the United States may often be able to undertake unilateral initiatives for the sake of national security. But in economic policy, unilateralism is simply not an option. No government, Washington included, can ignore market forces. The European Union's economy is now as large as that of the United States, and the euro has begun to challenge the dollar for global financial leadership. The United States relies on foreign investors—including the monetary authorities of competitor Asian economies—to finance massive external deficits, and it depends on oil imported at prices set by producers in other countries. Cooperation is therefore a necessity in the realm of international economics. Indeed, because of the close connection between economics and other international issues, economic policy often restrains the unilateralist tendencies in U.S. foreign policy as a whole.

Foreign economic policy is also critical to the health of the domestic economy. Over the past generation, the share of trade in U.S. GDP has tripled, to about 30 percent, and over the past decade, the competitive stimulus provided by rapid globalization has helped spur a dramatic increase in productivity, thus contributing to faster growth and job creation as well. On the financial side, foreigners' willingness to invest more than $500 billion a year in the United States funds massive trade deficits and makes up for low domestic savings rates. Overall, the reduction of trade barriers over the past 50 years has raised the annual income of the average family by $2,000.

But for the past decade, U.S. foreign economic policy has been mired in stalemate. For eight years, Congress refused to authorize the president to negotiate new trade agreements. When it finally did so in 2002, it was thanks only to a series of protectionist concessions on the part of the Bush administration. Legislation to replenish the International Monetary Fund (IMF), meanwhile, languished for more than a year at the height of the Asian financial crisis. It was rescued only by the intervention of a farm bloc seeking new funding for sales to major overseas markets.

The main reason for this stalemate is that global economic developments have harmed many individuals in the United States even as they have benefited the economy as a whole. Changes driven by technological advance and globalization have disrupted firms, communities, and workers, and a small but significant number of workers—perhaps 150,000 a year—suffer dislocations and significant earnings losses due to trade. Many others fear that "there but for the grace of God go I." It is now becoming clear that white-collar jobs can be "outsourced" just as blue-collar jobs have been.

U.S. policymakers must decisively overcome the domestic backlash against globalization to create a firm political foundation for a sustainable and constructive foreign economic policy. But the outlook is worrisome, despite the current economic recovery. Overvalued exchange rates and the massive trade deficits they create—characteristics of the current U.S. economy—have historically caused a retreat from openness. The admirable efforts of the Bush administration to revive liberalization have mostly run aground: the Doha Round of World Trade Organization (WTO) negotiations stalled at Cancún in September 2003; the Free Trade Area of the Americas fared similarly poorly at Miami in November 2003; and bilateral free trade agreements are facing stiff congressional resistance and may have to be shelved. Moreover, disputes between Europe and the United States could spark a transatlantic trade war, and a vicious round of China-bashing has erupted over the past year. These developments have put U.S. trade policy, and hence the global trading system, in deep jeopardy and could start to reverse the profound benefits of globalization.

Stopping the advance of globalization would be very dangerous to U.S. foreign policy because globalization—more than terrorism or the end of the Cold War—has been the dominant force for change in international affairs in the past 50 years. And rightly or wrongly, it is equated with Americanization in much of the world. Debates over globalization are often debates over the role of the United States itself. A significant rollback of globalization, or a halt in its continued advance, would therefore represent a major defeat for the United States on the world stage. The next administration must recognize the urgency of the situation and make foreign economic policy a top priority.

A NEW GLOBAL ORDER

More and more, "emerging market economies"—China and India, most notably—are becoming world-class competitors in a range of sectors. This development will require even more rapid improvement in the skills of U.S. workers and the flexibility of U.S.-based companies. It will require more effective safety nets to cushion the inevitable victims of transition. It will necessitate continuing U.S. policy reforms to increase the country's competitiveness and diligent negotiations on trade and other international issues to assure a level playing field.

But new competitors also offer attractive markets for U.S. exports and investment. They are valuable suppliers of high-quality, low-cost goods. And if properly incorporated into the global economy—and paired with effective domestic policies in the United States—they will lead to new gains in global growth, as well as improvements in U.S. productivity that will further magnify the benefits of globalization for the United States.

Washington will have to navigate in very unfamiliar economic waters.

The most difficult challenge facing the next administration stems instead from fundamental changes in the structure of the global economy. Since World War II, the United States has been able to dominate the world economy, even during periods of poor performance and dreadful policy, because it has been the only economic superpower. (U.S. military supremacy may have helped on occasion, but there is, in reality, little day-to-day spillover from security to economic affairs.) Japan has never played a major role in global economic policy, and Eu-rope, even after the creation of the EU, has failed to consolidate its decision-making and speak with a single voice. The notable, and highly instructive, exception has been trade policy: Europe did centralize its policy and so forced Washington to deal with it as an equal.

All of this is now changing rapidly. When it expands to 25 members this year, the EU will have a total output (not to mention a population) greater than that of the United States; it is already the world's largest trading entity, and the euro has become a key currency along with the dollar. Europe has not yet consolidated its decision-making or external representation, but it is sure to do so over time.

Even more dramatic changes could come across the Pacific. China is likely to continue growing rapidly for at least two more decades, becoming an economic super-power in its own right. In addition, East Asia is in the process of creating an economic bloc that could eventually comprise both a regional free trade area and an Asian monetary fund. Such a bloc would claim about one-fifth of the world economy, 20 percent of global trade, and $1.5 trillion in monetary (mostly dollar) reserves—about ten times those of the United States. Such an East Asian group would be a third economic superpower.

This confluence of events could convert the unipolar economic order of the past half-century into a bipolar or tripolar one, forcing Washington to navigate in very unfamiliar waters. U.S. foreign economic policy will have to overcome the challenges of integrating emerging powers into existing global structures and of managing the world economy by committee. It will have to forge new techniques of cooperation among near-equals, as well as compete in increasingly fierce global markets. It will have to draw on its strong ties with both Europe and Asia (which are far stronger than links between the two) to promote its own interests and secure the place of the United States as the pivotal actor in shaping new multilateral regimes.

A reelected President Bush or his successor will have to design and implement new initiatives to address global economic challenges of the highest national and international priority: forging a new domestic consensus in support of globalization; restoring and maintaining a sustainable external financial position; reviving trade liberalization; and freeing the world economy from the manipulation of energy markets by leading producers. He will have to do all of this in a new global economic context, in which a unified Europe, a rising China, and a new Asian bloc are shattering the final vestiges of U.S. economic hegemony.

CREDIT CHECK

THE UNITED STATES is by far the world's largest deficit and debtor nation. Both the U.S. economy and U.S. foreign policy are thus put at serious risk by the prospect of an outbreak of trade protectionism, foreign unwillingness to finance the $4 billion needed every working day to balance U.S. books, or even dumping of large portions of the

$10 trillion in U.S. currency held abroad (driving interest rates up and the U.S. economy down). The continued buildup of debt owed to foreigners, moreover, will steadily erode national income over time. The next administration must work to restore a sustainable current account and international financial position.

The goal should be to cut the external deficit in half, from its present level of $550 billion (or more than 5 percent of GDP). This reduction would have the important effect of stabilizing the ratio of foreign debt (already more than $3 trillion) to GDP. The only lasting way to do so is to sharply increase the savings rate in the U.S. economy, so that massive foreign capital inflows no longer push the dollar to overvalued levels and generate huge trade deficits. There is, unfortunately, no proven policy to increase private saving. Hence the government must convert its own budget deficit into a modest surplus, at least in periods of robust growth as at present.

Unfortunately, budget correction will not likely come soon enough to reduce the vulnerability created by external deficits. More immediate, if less fundamental, remedies are also required. The only feasible option is reducing the value of the dollar by 25 percent from its early 2002 peak. That decline has already begun, in a gradual and orderly manner, and it is probable that markets will also generate the rest of the correction. Because the U.S. economy is performing well relative to other large economies, there is little risk of a "hard landing." U.S. policymakers should thus make sure that market forces are allowed to prevail in lowering the dollar's value, threatening direct intervention if necessary to offset intervention by other countries (especially China and Japan) seeking to block the adjustment.

The problem of U.S. external deficits has been a recurring one over the past 30 years. Therefore, in addition to restoring sustainable trade and current account balances now, U.S. policymakers must recognize the need to revamp the institutional arrangements that govern exchange rates and overall economic relationships between countries. For all the talk of "reforming the international financial architecture" over the past decade, little has been done. The Treasury Department under both Presidents Bill Clinton and Bush—and the group of seven highly industrialized countries (G-7) and the IMF as well—have allowed countries such as China and Japan to violate existing rules while ignoring the need for basic improvements in such rules.

The next administration should negotiate fundamental improvements in the international monetary system, in order both to protect the United States against a return to unsustainable deficit levels and to provide a more stable foundation for the global economy as a whole. The most promising approach would be to implement new mechanisms limiting the deviation of exchange rates from their equilibrium values through close cooperation between economic policymakers in major countries.

NEW PATHS TO OPEN MARKETS

TRADE LIBERALIZATION, an integral aspect of globalization over the past half-century, has dramatically helped the U.S. economy and contributed mightily to Washington's global leadership position. Further efforts in this direction will bring further benefits. Foreign economic policy must therefore remain devoted to the goals pursued by every U.S. administration in the past 70 years: reducing barriers at home and abroad to international exchange, and developing a rules-based trading system built around strong international institutions.

The United States has a strong interest in further opening international markets, moving as close as possible to global free trade, and strengthening the enforcement machinery of the WTO. Its comparative advantage in services and agriculture means that wholesale liberalization of those sectors, through aggressive U.S.-sponsored initiatives, would bring significant benefits. U.S. markets are already quite open, whereas other countries—particularly rapidly growing developing economies—maintain much higher barriers that can be reduced only through new international negotiations. Policymakers should work to eliminate the discrimination inherent in preferential trade deals engineered by Europe and, prospectively, by Asia.

In its first two years, the Bush administration achieved two notable successes in trade policy: the passage of fast-track negotiating authority and the launch of the Doha Round of WTO negotiations. Overall, it has pursued a coherent strategy of "competitive liberalization" in which multilateral, regional, and bilateral agreements reinforce and catalyze one another. These efforts, however, have recently run aground, and potential conflicts with Europe and China darken the picture even more.

The next administration must therefore attach high priority to reviving an effective trade policy. Most urgent is a more forthcoming offer of liberalization by the United States itself, especially in agriculture, to revive the Doha Round that broke down in Cancún. Washington must reverse the subsidy increases of the 2002 farm bill—contingent, of course, on fully reciprocal liberalization by other developed economies (chiefly the EU, Japan, and South Korea) and partial liberalization by the more advanced developing countries (chiefly Brazil and India). The United States should also repeat its offer to eliminate, again on a reciprocal basis, all duties on nonagricultural trade. The breakdown at Cancún proved that developing countries, united in a new G-22, can block multilateral trade progress on their own. Policymakers must recognize this fact and work constructively with the coalition, rather than trying to ignore or dismantle it. A successful Doha Round would then provide a firm foundation for a new "WTO plus" agreement in the western hemisphere.

The next administration must also revise trade policy as it relates to bilateral agreements. The list of bilateral partners chosen to date by the Bush administration (including Australia, Bahrain, Bolivia, Central America, Colombia, Ecuador, Morocco, Peru, the Southern African Customs Union, and Thailand, in addition to existing agreements with Canada, Chile, Israel, Jordan, Mexico, and Singapore) is arbitrary, offering modest benefits and little impetus to "competitive liberalization." Because of their limited benefits, these initiatives attract little support in Congress or the U.S. business community. Some of them have in fact attracted opposition sufficient to make their passage through Congress unlikely (at least in election year 2004). The Bush administration made the same mistake in selecting free trade partners that the Clinton administration made in pursuing fast-track negotiating authority in 1997: attempting to minimize domestic opposition instead of maximizing domestic support.

The next administration should, in close consultation with Congress, spell out four clear criteria for choosing free trade partners, in the following order of priority: net economic gains to the United States, promotion of constructive economic reforms in the partner country, importance for broader U.S. trade policy, and significance for overall U.S. foreign policy objectives. A few of the current candidates for agreements pass this test, but several others not on the list should be top priorities: Brazil (especially if the Free Trade Area of the Americas fails to move forward), South Korea, and, pending necessary internal reforms, Egypt and Indonesia. Washington should also offer a regional free trade agreement to Africa, as it has to Latin America, the Middle East, and Southeast Asia.

A revitalization of the Asia-Pacific Economic Cooperation forum (APEC) should also be part of the U.S. response to any European stalling and to the prospect of a new East Asian bloc. Just as President George H.W. Bush insisted on full U.S. participation when APEC was created in 1989 and President Clinton used APEC to pressure Europe to complete the Uruguay round, the United States should use strengthened transpacific ties as a counterweight to such developments. APEC can once again promote major U.S. foreign policy and economic objectives.

DOMESTIC BACKLASH

THE BIGGEST BARRIER to a constructive and consistent policy on trade and globalization is domestic. The U.S. public is split virtually down the middle on these issues. Congress' rejection of fast track in 1994, 1997, and 1998, and its near-rejection of it in 2002, was an accurate reflection of divided public opinion, not an aberration by deviant legislators.

The country divides along educational lines. Workers with college degrees, or at least some college experience, support globalization because they think they can take advantage of the opportunities it offers. Workers who have not gone beyond high school—half of the U.S. labor force—oppose further globalization because they fear they cannot adjust to it. The only long-term strategy for achieving domestic consensus, therefore, is to improve education and raise the overall skill level of the population. In the short term, effective governmental assistance to workers who are displaced by increased trade flows can help considerably. This assistance should have two components: stronger safety nets to cushion the transitional costs of job displacement, and more effective training and other adjustment programs to help workers qualify for new positions.

Acting on such evidence, Congress insisted that its authorization of new trade negotiations in 2002 be linked to substantial improvement in the Trade Adjustment Assistance program, which has pursued these goals since 1962. The new legislation broadened eligibility for the program, provided more generous levels of aid (especially for job-search and relocation expenditures), and established innovative wage insurance (to cover lost income when workers accept lower-paying jobs) and health insurance improvements. Unfortunately, in its first term the Bush administration (like its predecessors) has failed to implement these programs aggressively. The next administration must do so, in addition to developing other programs to alleviate the negative impacts of liberalization. Coverage should be broadened and benefits increased. There should be more effective support for adjustment, such as lifelong learning programs. Other innovations should include asset-value insurance, full portability of health and pension benefits, and a new "Human Capital Investment Tax Credit" to induce companies to provide more on-the-job training.

The economic gains from globalization to the United States are so large that it can readily afford to set aside a small portion of the proceeds to take care of those who lose out in the process—and basic norms of justice require that it do so. The United States will be unable to build a sustainable political base for a constructive foreign economic policy until it decisively addresses the adverse domestic consequences of globalization.

ENERGY DRAIN

Energy is another area in which the United States is vulnerable, in both economic and foreign policy terms. The lack of an effective energy policy—highlighted once again by the recent failure of Congress to pass adequate legislation after three years of effort—keeps U.S. foreign policy beholden to a few key producers and will probably force the United States to continue to launch periodic military interventions to satisfy its tremendous appetite for energy.

The leaders of the Organization of Petroleum Exporting Countries (OPEC) are allowed to manipulate world energy prices, holding them 50 to 75 percent above market levels in recent years. As a result, the cost of energy as a share of U.S. GDP has tripled since 1997. Since the oil shocks of the 1970s, prices have ranged from 15 to 300 percent of competitive levels, averaging almost double the competitive price. (In addition, as Alan Greenspan noted, the three major U.S. recessions prior to the shallow decline in 2001 "have all been preceded by spikes in the price of oil.") Over this period, inflated energy costs have depressed the U.S. GDP, and those of other oil-importing countries, by 15 to 30 percent. Restoration of market energy prices could alone boost economic growth by one percent a year.

Fortunately, as energy economist Philip Verleger has pointed out, consuming countries now have the capacity to counter the influence of producers. Strategic inventories now exceed 1.2 million barrels, including over 600 million held by the United States alone. These holdings make it possible for consumers to drive prices down until they better reflect the market and to keep them there, by using inventories as price stabilizers rather than thinking of them solely as protection against supply disruptions (which did not occur during either of the wars with Iraq). It is sheer folly for the United States to invest billions of dollars in its petroleum reserves only to sit on them as producers drive up prices.

Disregard for rigged oil prices is a drain on the economy and a gap in the war on terrorism.

Any new campaign to cut world oil prices would inevitably invite charges of being part of a broader anti-Islamic crusade. It would be essential, for political as well as economic reasons, that the initiative be multilateral. The Organization for Economic Cooperation and Development's International Energy Agency (IEA) could manage the effort, with maximum efforts to include China and other oil-importing nations. It should, moreover, be emphasized loudly and repeatedly that large Muslim countries, notably Pakistan and Turkey, would also benefit from lower energy prices.

Oil-consuming countries should offer OPEC a producer-consumer agreement before threatening it with the prospect of sales from strategic stockpiles. The lead producers limit supply and push for higher prices in part because they fear a future loss of market share to Russia, Iraq, and western African countries. The IEA could agree to create mechanisms to provide OPEC countries, particularly those in the Persian Gulf, with a guaranteed market while at the same time offering oil to consumers at prices much lower than what they currently pay. Such an agreement should include larger global oil inventories and a system to share future production cuts, should prices drop too far, among all the major suppliers (rather than just a few cartel members).

The U.S. position would obviously be strengthened greatly if the United States finally took serious steps to limit its own consumption of energy. The most straightfor-

ward way to do so would be to target the most energy-intensive sector, transportation, by raising corporate average fuel economy standards, particularly as they apply to SUVs and light trucks. A sizeable carbon or gasoline tax would help enormously and also reduce the budget deficit.

There is, of course, a direct link between these energy proposals and the war on terrorism. A large portion of terrorist financing comes from Middle Eastern countries that benefit from the institutional arrangements that keep oil prices high. The United States' disregard for rigged oil prices is a gap in the antiterrorism campaign, as well as a major drain on the U.S. economy, and it should be remedied as soon as possible.

INSTITUTING CHANGE

NEW INSTITUTIONS will be needed to conceptualize and implement new policies. At the international level, one key requirement is for the United States and the EU, the world's two economic superpowers (together accounting for well more than half of the global economy), to create a "G-2"—an informal steering committee to manage the world economy and their bilateral relationship.

Although a transatlantic free trade area would be a bad idea, discriminating against the world's poorest countries, close and continuing cooperation between the United States and the EU is necessary for global economic progress. The G-2 would operate informally and would not undermine any other multilateral institutions or associations. Indeed, it would even contribute to a revitalization of such institutions. The G-7 nations, for example, could become the G-3 (the United States, the EU, and Japan) or, eventually, the G-4 (when China is ready to join).

To start, both the United States and the EU should be much more forthcoming with offers to liberalize trade in order to restart the Doha Round. (Their grossly inadequate positions at Cancún led to the current breakdown.) Conflicts over other bilateral issues could also be resolved more easily if they saw themselves as responsible co-leaders of the world economy rather than tit-for-tat antagonists. And cooperation on new economic initiatives would help patch up the political rift opened by the Iraq war. It would serve as a response to a new economic bloc in East Asia, and it could help strengthen the ability of global institutions such as the IMF and the WTO to maintain a multilateral check on new regional steps. The deep economic interpenetration of the United States and Europe—with $500 billion in direct investment in each direction and $400 billion in annual trade—is the main force holding them together. A G-2 initiative would thus have broad benefits for overall foreign policy.

A new institutional approach is needed at home as well. In recent years, foreign economic policy has devolved into a series of uncoordinated, ad hoc decisions, despite the obvious need to coordinate foreign policy with economic policy. Taxes are slashed and vast budget deficits created with little thought for their impact on the U.S. global economic position or international financial vulnerability. The Treasury Department fulminates against bailouts of emerging market economies before meekly complying with White House orders to support the same bailouts for foreign policy reasons (as in Argentina, Brazil, and Turkey). The U.S. Trade Representative is relegated to the sidelines in creating new steel tariffs or shaping the farm bill, despite their centrality to trade policy. Energy legislation is pursued with nary a word about how producer countries rig global prices and levy huge costs on our economy.

The Clinton administration created a National Economic Council to address such issues but never institutionalized the mechanism; it quickly fell into disuse when key personnel changed. A well-managed council, eventually written into law to parallel the National Security Council (NSC), is badly needed now. It would also help if at least one of the two top officials at the State Department and the NSC brought some economic expertise to their positions and were more cognizant of the importance of international economic issues to their broader mandates.

Congress must also get its act together on foreign economic policy. In an earlier era, similar global imperatives, the salience of which is underlined by current events, prompted the creation of the Senate and House intelligence committees to amalgamate foreign policy, national security, and related domestic concerns. The creation of similar committees on globalization could bring together the leadership of the trade committees (Ways and Means in the House, Finance in the Senate), those responsible for international finance, some of the relevant special committees (agriculture and commerce), and the foreign policy committees.

THE PROSPECTS FOR PROGRESS

The United States has great economic strengths. It remains by far the world's largest national economy. Its sharp growth in productivity over the past decade appears likely to continue and perhaps accelerate again,

generating very rapid expansion for a mature industrialized country. Moreover, it is growing much faster than other industrialized economies. The dollar will continue to be the main global currency for some time, and the U.S. model of capitalism and globalization dominates thinking around the world.

Yet the next president will face unprecedented challenges in the conduct of foreign economic policy. The case for globalization will have to be made persuasively, forcefully, and repeatedly. Domestic support could crumble if the president fails to address its internal costs with new safety nets and opportunities for skill enhancement; international support could dissolve if the White House's strategy fails to offer reciprocal benefits to other countries or is conducted without full consideration of their concerns. Such an outcome would be extremely costly. The economy would suffer from trade restrictions and a plummeting dollar in the short term and from reduced productivity growth in the long term. Foreign policy, meanwhile, would be jeopardized if the United States retreated from constructive cooperation with other nations on issues at the top of their agendas.

Most important, foreign economic policy could rescue overall U.S. foreign policy. The United States' biggest problem in the international arena is its tendency to act unilaterally on a range of issues. Such unilateralism is demonstrably ineffective and thus thankfully rare in the economic domain. The international economic initiatives proposed in this essay would convey a new image of U.S. foreign policy while furthering U.S. national interests. They should rank high on the agenda of the next U.S. president.

C. FRED BERGSTEN is Director of the Institute for International Economics. He was Assistant Secretary of the Treasury for International Affairs from 1977 to 1981 and Assistant for Economic Policy to the National Security Council from 1969 to 1971. Copyright © 2004, Institute for International Economics.

ECONOMIC SCENE

Why do certain countries prosper? A new
study looks at productivity and comes up
with some contrarian conclusions.

Virginia Postrel

AN educated work force is not essential for economic growth. Neither is a high saving rate. Manufacturing is not the most influential economic sector.

These contrarian conclusions come from a new book by William W. Lewis, the founding director of the McKinsey Global Institute, a division of the McKinsey & Company consulting firm. Since 1991, the institute's researchers have conducted the most comprehensive international studies available on productivity by industry sector.

In "The Power of Productivity," published by the University of Chicago Press, Mr. Lewis pulls together some results of that decade-long research.

The book helps explain why the American economy has done better—and Europe and Japan have done worse—than most people predicted in the late 1980's. It also offers a simultaneously hopeful and depressing view of economic conditions in poor countries, focusing on Brazil, India and Russia.

"Productivity," Mr. Lewis writes, "is simply the ratio of the value of goods and services provided consumers to the amount of time worked and capital used to produce the goods and services."

What the McKinsey research makes clear is that it's not what you put into the economy that matters, but what you get out of it. Consumption is the goal of production.

To know why some countries prosper while others fall behind, then, we need to know which industries in which countries are more productive and why.

Most studies of the subject, however, concentrate on a narrow slice of the economy: products that are traded in world markets. That's because, thanks to cus-

toms regulations, most countries have excellent data on those goods.

Looking only at traded goods can be highly misleading. International businesses tend to face intense competition. They have to adopt practices that improve productivity. Domestic industries, by contrast, are often protected from competition.

McKinsey's research fills in the picture, providing data and case studies of industries like retailing, food processing and construction.

Poorer countries are hampered mostly by government policies, especially high taxes that drive businesses underground, rather than by the inherent problems of poverty, Mr. Lewis argues. If they could solve their policy problems, they would attract foreign investment. Businesses could train workers on the job, achieving competitive productivity.

"If illiterate Mexican immigrants can reach world-class productivity building apartment houses in Houston," he writes, "there is no reason why illiterate Brazilian agricultural workers cannot achieve the same in São Paulo."

When highly productive multinationals enter previously protected markets, their business practices come with them.

Consider what happened in India after 1983, when Suzuki was allowed to build auto plants as part of a joint venture called Murati. "Suzuki with Indian labor and Indian inputs was able to achieve roughly 50 percent of the productivity of the advanced auto industry in their home country," Mr. Lewis said in an interview. "That's compared to maybe 10 percent for the rest of the Indian industry."

In the 1990's, the Indian government opened the auto business to other foreign investment, with similar results.

The McKinsey Global Institute's first study, published in late 1992, shocked readers then with its conclusion that in most industries, companies in the United States were far more productive than Europeans or Japanese. Back then, notes Mr. Lewis, the conventional wisdom was that the American economy was going down the tubes, and that American workers were duds.

"There were some really pejorative comments about how U.S. workers were lazy and uneducated and unintelligent," he recalls. "Well, it may be that they were lazy, uneducated and unintelligent, but they were still performing in most industries at productivity levels far higher than those in Japan."

Toyota is a world leader in quality and efficiency in manufacturing, for instance, but it's atypical of the Japanese economy, even in manufacturing.

Food processing in Japan, Mr. Lewis writes, "has more employees than the combined total of cars, steel, machine tools and computers," or about 11 percent of all manufacturing workers. While Japan's fiercely competitive auto industry is the most productive in the world, its food-processing industry is only 39 percent as productive as the United States industry, McKinsey found.

As a result, Japanese consumers are paying unnecessarily high prices for food and, Mr. Lewis notes, Japanese workers are "devoting their extraordinary talents to propping up an economic structure with limited future development potential."

Inefficient industries may keep people employed in the short term, but over time their sluggish productivity makes the economy stagnate.

The best predictor of productivity, he argues, is product market competition. That competition takes place not just in manufacturing but with all the services that support a product, before and after it leaves the plant.

Competition in each stage of that process has ripple effects in the others.

Take retailing, arguably the most influential sector in today's advanced economies. Despite some consolidation and the introduction of some big-box retailers, the Japanese food-processing industry remains fragmented and inefficient because

Japanese grocery stores are still mostly tiny mom-and-pop shops protected by strict land use laws.

In the United States, by contrast, a revolution in retailing over the last 25 years has increased productivity not just for stores but for wholesalers and makers of consumer goods as well.

Big retailers, notably Wal-Mart, have bargained down prices and threatened to eliminate wholesalers altogether. In response, manufacturers and wholesalers have found ways to improve their own operations. (So did Wal-Mart's retailing competitors.)

At the same time, retailers have collected better information about what consumers are buying, and what they might

want, and have shared that data with their suppliers. As a result, manufacturers have been able to spend their production dollars more efficiently.

Meanwhile, in a small shop near McKinsey's Tokyo office, a hat has languished unsold on the same shelf for 15 years.

Virginia Postrel is the author of "The Substance of Style: How the Rise of Aesthetic Value Is Remaking Commerce, Culture and Consciousness" (Harper Collins).

Perspectives on Global Outsourcing and the Changing Nature of Work

CHRISTOPHER B. CLOTT

INTRODUCTION

Global outsourcing is a fast-growing aspect of the world economy. Worldwide spending on outsourcing in 2001 was estimated to be $3.7 trillion and is expected to reach $5.1 trillion by the end of 2003 (Corbett, 2002). Researchers estimate that over the next 12 years, 3.3 million jobs accounting for $136 billion in wages will move offshore (McCartney, 2003; Forrester, 2003). Numerous studies portray the strategic benefits of global outsourcing for firms as a means to reduce costs, improve asset efficiency, and increase profits (Quinn, 1997). Criticisms of outsourcing have been almost exclusively in the areas of changing employment patterns, globalization of the labor force, and its effects on individuals and organizations. Outsourcing has been called "one of the greatest organizational and industry structure shifts of the century," with the potential to transform the way businesses operate (Drucker, 1998). Some proponents believe it will turn firms from vertically integrated structures into "virtual organizations" and transform existing fixed structures into variable-cost structures where expenses can move up or down as the business climate dictates (Garr, 2001). For employees, the trend toward outsourcing has been thought to result in a loss of fixed-employment opportunities as a consequence of firms seeking to use cheaper labor overseas. As outsourcing increases within the United States, the portion of the employed workforce made up of part-time, temporary, freelance, or independent contractors is growing (Geiger, 1999; Neikirk, 2002). Continuation of this trend will have a profound effect on the makeup of organizations and the way work is performed.

Global outsourcing is not a new phenomenon, having been performed for centuries as a part of trade between nations and firms seeking to profit from price differences for essential products and services through the use of third-party suppliers. The basic business idea of outsourcing is that if a firm does not specialize in a certain function it will be beneficial to transfer control of the function to a specialist organization that will be able to offer better cost and quality. As worldwide markets have become less closed and more transparent, and with information technology (IT) advances such as the Internet allowing near-instant communication, the ability of firms to procure and source products and services from anywhere in the world has increased dramatically. Commonly outsourced functions include manufacturing, IT, facilities or applications within a firm (such as its communications equipment), and multiple other firm services (also known as business process outsourcing) in areas such as finance and accounting, human resources, marketing and sales, customer support centers, and other industry-specific processes.

Underpinning the move toward outsourcing has been a confluence of structural and theoretical changes in the nature of business and organizations dating back approximately two decades. Numerous theorists have suggested that the changing nature of competition has resulted from two factors: (a) globalization of commerce engendering worldwide competition, and (b) technology developments that have changed basic business processes related to time and distance. Globalization and technology have placed enormous pressure on firms to cut costs and improve efficiency in the interests of self-preservation. Theodore Levitt's seminal article "The Globalization of Markets" (1983) suggests a convergence of developed consumer markets and products and a movement toward global brands. Concurrently, the work of management and strategy theorists such as Michael Porter, Gary Hamel, Peter Drucker, and others indicates the need for organizations to think in terms of core competencies or primary business activities. Areas outside of a business's specialization, or its "noncore" activities, should be moved to external providers. This viewpoint had previously been argued, in slightly different language, by the proponents of total quality management (TQM)—such as Joseph Juran, Philip Crosby, and W. Edwards Deming—as the need for organizations to deliver quality, speed of performance, continuous service improvements, and cost savings to customers.

Shareholder value, as measured by the efficient use of capital invested in the business and the costs of servicing it, gained new acceptance in corporations through the development in the early 1980s of the economic value-added (EVA) formula by the consulting firm of Stern Stewart. Use of EVA put pressure on managers to increase profits and cover the cost of servicing the capital invested in a way that would exceed the minimum rates of return investors would receive by investing in other securities of comparable risk. The logic of EVA use suggests getting as many noncore activities off your balance sheet as possible to increase short-term profitability.

The 1990s brought two additional strategic changes to the way that organizations viewed themselves. Business process reengineering (BPR) was introduced to corporations seeking to reshape and redesign business processes "to achieve dramatic improvements in critical, contemporary measures of performance, such as cost, quality, service and speed" (Hammer and Champy, 1993). To do this, the theorists argued that formerly hierarchal organizations had to become flatter to respond quickly to competition and customer demand. "Reengineering" and "restructuring" the organization to meet new needs was also known as "downsizing," which involved the elimination of numerous positions, primarily in middle management, within areas not deemed as core to the firm. The adoption of supply chain management (SCM) principles incorporated customer information and data with product development, thus decreasing a firm's response time to address customer needs. The advent of new communications technology and demands by customers for lower prices and better products and services spurred the reconfiguration of companies as specialized links along the chain. With fewer permanent employees remaining to perform essential work, companies had little choice but to trust outside vendors with large parts of the business.

THE IMPACT OF GLOBAL OUTSOURCING

Although there is some dispute as to when global outsourcing began, the movement of basic manufacturing from developed nations such as the United States to less economically developed overseas locations to take advantage of lower labor costs has been ongoing since the 1950s. Manufacturers of products as disparate as automobiles, toys, textiles, electronics, and semiconductors have been migrating offshore to remain price competitive. The 1980s and early '90s saw the growth of "contract manufacturing," particularly in the textile and electronics industries, as leading firms found that they could not manufacture to required

price and quality levels in fast-moving consumer markets where product obsolescence could reduce the value of components quickly (Heywood, 2001). Contract equipment manufacturers (CEMs) like Flextronics, Solectron, and Celestica—who could subcontract manufacturing components such as computer chips, capacitors, resistors, liquid crystal displays, electronic equipment, and telecommunications material of all types worldwide—have substantially altered the making and manufacturing of electronics goods by original equipment manufacturers (OEMs). In textiles, Hong Kong-based Li & Fung subcontracts garment manufacturing for major textile brands in the United States and Europe. Contract manufacturers produce branded products in low-wage offshore factories ranging from simple assembly to more sophisticated higher-value activities. Goods are available upon demand, and companies are able to remove low-margin manufacturing and inventory assets from their balance sheets, thus improving their EVA and attractiveness for shareholders.

Global outsourcing has substantially altered the nature of work in companies. While such ancillary services as building security, food service, mail sorting, and janitorial services are considered peripheral functions within firms, the growth of globalized sourcing in formerly core functions (such as final product assembly, customer service, legal and financial services, and design activities) transforms the very nature of organizational culture. Individuals with tenuous links to the underlying business communicate pieces of operations performed allover the world. Jobs with firms become more temporary and force workers to remain adaptable as changing demand alters occupational knowledge and does away with stable career paths (Ansberry 2003a; Skapinker, 2003).

INFORMATION TECHNOLOGY

The industry most closely associated with outsourcing has been information technology. IT functions have been outsourced since the 1970s due to the expensive hardware and software required for state-of-the-art systems (Heywood, 2001). As the corporate world shifted to data storage and retrieval on computers, the need for qualified IT specialists who could implement and monitor these systems outstripped the available supply. Unable to hire skilled specialists, firms turned to contract workers, consulting firms, and specialist companies in Europe and the United States. Eastman Kodak Co. moved the bulk of its IT operations to three outsourcing partners in 1989, triggering a wave of IT outsourcing by other Fortune 500 corporations (Johnson, 1997). These contractor organizations sought experienced IT help from all over the world. The U.S. government raised the number of H-IB visas allowing foreign workers into the United States from 65,000 in 1998 to 115,000 for fiscal years 1999 and 2000. Many of these workers came from India, where the confluence of English language literacy, large numbers of engineering and IT graduates with advanced processing skills, and willingness to work for lower wages fueled the growth of the U.S. IT industry throughout the 1990s.

A governmental shift toward privatization and deregulation of the economy within India was begun in 1984, and spurred investment and modernization of the telecommunications and computer industries. With the election of Prime Minister V. Narasimha Rao in 1991 and the continued strength of the Indian National Congress Party, the country embarked on a path of liberalizing trade, industrial, and foreign investment policies. As a result, India became a very attractive business and investment opportunity for foreign direct investment. Large U.S. firms such as General Electric, American Express, and Hewlett-Packard were the vanguard of a flood of investment into India in the last decade. The "New Silicon Valley" centered in and around the city of Bangalore, which became a major outsourcing provider for IT functions as a result of its lower costs and advanced processing skills. This led to the growth of large Indian outsourcing firms such as Infosys, Tata Consultancy, and Wipro. As of 2003, over 500,000 people were employed in the Indian IT industry (McCartney, 2003). Other countries seeking to replicate India's growth as an IT center for U.S. firms were Ireland, Israel, and the Philippines. All of these countries had similar advantages of large numbers of skilled English-speaking workers willing to work for a fraction of the cost of their U.S. counterparts. The wage scale continues to promote competition as Vietnamese, Chinese, Russian, and former Soviet republics and East European providers vie for cross-border IT services. In response to rising wages in certain Indian cities such as New Delhi and Hyderabad, General Electric has opened a call center in the northern tourist city of Jaipur, where GE staff invoices are scanned and entered by colleagues in Mexico and Florida (Merchant, 2003).

BUSINESS PROCESS OUTSOURCING

At this writing, among the fastest-growing aspects of global outsourcing is business process outsourcing (BPO). BPO began as "back-office" process arrangements to run finance and accounting operations such as payroll, accounts payable and receivable, financial, insurance, and property accounting. Aside from a brief pause after the events of September 11, 2001, these services have expanded into new areas such as call centers, with staff trained to answer and transact basic service-related areas, including order entry and credit card processing. Analysts suggest that there may be as many as 35,000 outsourcing call centers by 2005 in India alone (Moran, 2003). More sophisticated customer service work involving credit collection, benefits administration, pension administration, insurance claims processing, and computer-aided tomography (CAT) scan reading is now being handled by offshore firms for U.S. businesses. Tax accounting and securities research for Wall Street firms is likely to be performed offshore as well (Kirkpatrick, 2003). Recent data suggest that financial services firms spend a greater percentage of their outsourcing dollars with offshore vendors than other industries (Nyberg, 2003).

Facilities and application management have also grown throughout the United States and Europe as a means of transferring the management and day-to-day running of firms' major operational systems, building management, and site maintenance to third-party specialists who can offer basic property management and landscaping as well as maintain the complex hardware systems to run the facility. In addition, global corporations have transferred the transport and storage of goods to third-party or third-party logistics (3PL) providers who offer an array of services, including transportation, warehousing, inventory control, freight forwarding, and customs brokering. Increasingly, these 3PL providers also negotiate contracts with the offshore producers and handle packaging, installation, and subassembly, thus acting as contract manufacturers and supply chain managers for the organizations they work for (Baldiwala, 2001; Hannon, 2002).

GLOBAL OUTSOURCING'S DEFENDERS

Proponents of global outsourcing far outnumber their detractors. Numerous consulting firms, business theorists, corporate champions, economists, and influential opinion leaders have published materials arguing the merits of offshore outsourcing. Arguments in favor of outsourcing can be broken down to five areas: concentration on core business development by firms, cost control, access to state of the art technology, market discipline through greater transparency, and added flexibility to respond to demand changes (Lakenan, Boyd, Frey, 2001).

Concentrations on the core business—Management theorists have argued that firms must focus on those aspects where they are uniquely positioned and have the financial and human resources to excel (Hamel and Prahalad, 1994). For example, brand management firms such as Nike should concentrate on customer understanding whereas firms with a core competence in research and development, such as Intel, ought to focus on product innovation and design. Firms involved in the routine processing of information (such as Citibank, for example) should concentrate on providing quality and uniformity to their offerings (Hagel, 2002).

The core competence argument suggests that specialist firms composed of highly skilled employees interacting with customers will allow for a "demand-pull environment" where the customer pulls product through the supply chain due to aggressive marketing and the entire organization falls into line around the orders as a means of securing performance improvement. Firms will be able to get to market faster with new offerings without the drag of "noncore" aspects that can be better managed and operated by equally skilled specialist firms.

Cost control—A major consideration by firms in global outsourcing is the desire to reduce operating costs (Corbett, 2003). Research suggests that global outsourcing reduces supervisory and administrative expenses, lowers effective wage rates through the use of offshore workers, and eliminates payment for nonproductive time as well as for worker benefits (such as health insurance, liability insurance, and workers' compensation) that must be provided to U.S. employees (Harrison, 1994). Firms that externalize the labor force are better able to determine the timing quantity and skill composition of their workers (Wells, 1996). Contract overseas labor shifts the risks of overcapitalization and unstable demand from the core firm to the overseas contractor, ensuring a competitive labor market while buffering the core firm from market fluctuations and risks (Kusel et al., 2000). This puts firms that are not sourcing globally at a cost disadvantage, because their competitors can more aggressively price their products due to lower production costs generated from globally procured components (Reese-McMahon, 2003).

Although disparities in manufacturing wage rates evolved over decades between developed and less-developed nations, the costs of doing business overseas were usually prohibitive for all but the largest firms. Changing communication technology and global market reform have made formerly remote locations attractive and have permitted small and medium firms, as well as larger businesses, to work with global outsourcing contractors who range far and wide in their quest to locate facilities in areas where the cheapest skilled and unskilled labor is available. Facilities have been relocated, for example, from formerly low-cost areas such as Malaysia, where unskilled labor rates were $2.50 an hour, to China, where it is 60 cents (Wonacott, 2002). A similar strategy could also be seen in service industries during the last decade; for example, call centers with wage rates of $1.50 to $2.00 an hour for recent college graduates in the Philippines and India provide substantial savings over positions that would pay from $10 to $18 an hour in the United States (Kirkpatrick, 2003). Sending IT work to India can reduce labor rates by as much as 65% compared with using a U.S. company (Khirallah, 2002).

Access to state-of-the-art technology—Another benefit believed to result from global outsourcing is the access to a larger and more up-to-date pool of assets held by offshore contractors. Some suppliers in the IT industry, for example, have access to proprietary technology or other intellectual property that the company would otherwise not have access to or that would be beyond the reach of its core competencies. Business organizations lacking the capital to finance new equipment can access new technology without owning it and thus keep operational costs low. Theorists also argue that as work becomes more and more information intensive, it also becomes increasingly placeless. It no longer matters where software is written or a balance sheet is reconciled, or where a toll-free call is answered—as long as essential quality considerations are met. It's irrelevant to the end user whether that activity is taking place down the hall or half a world away. With the investment in state-of-the-art technology so high, companies may evolve into complex enterprises that operate as atomic universes in which core competencies are left in the nucleus and all other functions—from staffing to manufacturing—are performed by flexible part-time workers and specialized satellite suppliers (Corbett, 2003).

Market discipline and transparency—Global outsourcing enables companies to expand choices for their customers by putting standard business functions out to bid. Increased use of EVA modeling forces managers to focus on capital costs, thus quantifying operating performance from a financial perspective and enhancing transparency and accountability of the firm. Innovation and rapid change are promoted through outsourcing as market-based contracts focus on outputs rather than inputs (Baxendale, 2004; Quinn, 1997). This enables firms to reduce overhead and improve shareholder value.

Flexibility—Global outsourcing enables firms to respond to new challenges in volatile markets by redeploying labor where needed. External suppliers can be used as buffers to absorb production fluctuations and provide internal production stability, thus promoting workforce stability (Burt, 2003). Labor headcount can be adjusted quickly in the face of fluctuating demand without the associated costs of employee reduction or increased hiring internally. Legal employee and labor contract negotiations are minimized or negated entirely through use of a global workforce. Firms can also seek to introduce performance-based pay incentives as part of its contracts with suppliers.

GLOBAL OUTSOURCING'S DISSENTERS

Critics of global outsourcing are primarily grouped into two areas: (a) theorists examining the labor and ethical issues of outsourcing on workers, and (b) researchers looking at the effects of strategic outsourcing decisions on organizations. Very few empirical studies exist that examine the effects of global outsourcing on individual firms, perhaps due to the difficulty of procuring such information. More general dissent of global outsourcing has focused on the macroeconomic effects of globalization revealed in increased competition between economies that results in a "race to the bottom" of wage rates and the resultant job insecurity this engenders (Tonelson, 2000; Tomkins, 2001; Thompson, 2001).

LABOR AND ETHICAL ISSUES

Researchers argue that global outsourcing transfers work to countries where labor can be bought much more cheaply (Geewax, 2003). Prevailing wages far below the United States in economically developing countries in areas such as India, the Philippines, and China provide the financial rationale to reduce labor forces in highly developed economies. Research suggests that this depresses wage rates for remaining workers, creates fewer job opportunities in many occupations, reduces job stability, and often results in a loss of benefits, such as health insurance, among workers at affected companies (Ansberry, 2003b and 2003c; Harrison, 1994).

Global outsourcing also falls disproportionately upon older workers who are more highly paid but less mobile in terms of retraining options. Theorists argue that the overall macroeconomic benefits derived from outsourcing are often at the expense of the individual worker (Breslin, 1999). Outsourcing affects organized labor by intimidating the labor force, as the fear of jobs moving overseas may reduce the potential benefits in unionizing (Boudette, 2004; Fevre, 1986). The loss of well-paying positions has a ripple effect on the local economy, resulting in the disappearance of second- and third-tier supplier and service firms that must close or reorganize; this in turn means a loss of competitiveness. This effect has created a "political hot potato" as localities compete with one another through tax incentives to attract new industries as older ones depart. Some recent attempts at global outsourcing by government bodies (such as the attempt by the state of New Jersey to use offshore outsourcing for some basic social services) have resulted in new laws banning the use of foreign workers for essential government services and for those firms that receive government contracts (Hayes and Chabrow, 2003). At this writing, the U.S. Senate and state legislatures in Indiana, North Carolina, and Washington, in addition to New Jersey, are working on bills to restrict or prohibit government contractors from outsourcing work overseas (*Chicago Tribune*, 2004). Global outsourcing has also contributed to the increasing numbers of part-time and contract workers typically earning less pay than permanent workers and without health, life, short- and long-term disability, and retirement benefits (Geiger, 1999).

There is a small body of criticism concerning the ethical implications of the outsourcing movement. These researchers suggest that firms often withhold material information from employees, misrepresent future payoffs of outsourcing agreements, base choices on inaccurate and unfair information, and impose hardships on displaced employees without justification (Reid and Pascalev, 2002). They suggest that a Machiavellian "ends justify the means" model, in which reducing cost as an end is used to justify corporate strategy, violates ethical norms and comes at a high human cost (Breslin, 1999).

STRATEGIC GLOBAL OUTSOURCING

Many researchers call into question the perceived effectiveness of strategic global outsourcing on organizations. Although agreeing with the theory of outsourcing, these critiques are wide-ranging and often prescriptive in their identification of flaws in how outsourcing is performed by firms. They can be grouped into the following areas:

Defining what global outsourcing is and is not—Overlapping definitions of global outsourcing serve to confuse and obfuscate the role it plays in organizations, leading to the mistaken conclusion that global outsourcing is a "cure-all" and will only improve performance and reduce costs. Strategic considerations faced by firms in global make or buy decisions include such factors as technological innovation, customer demand, and financial factors (for example, international taxation policies). The mere offloading of inventory or services to a secondary overseas provider does not negate the risk that an investment may be subject to sudden changes in the industry and world socioeconomic environment. Numerous consulting firms and providers have "sold" global outsourcing as a strategy rather than just one of many means to service delivery (Cant and Jeynes, 1998). Many tactical decisions revolving around cost considerations, changing sales requirements, and product modifications and innovation can create a false sense that firms are no longer responsible for products under their brand names (Heywood, 2001).

Instability of demand—Researchers argue that an underlying problem associated with global outsourcing is the instability of demand, and the failure to recognize and react to it in a timely manner. An outside contractor may not be able to respond quickly to problems and changing consumer needs. Previous commitments of inventory and capacity can create uncertainty about availability and cause a company to become less sensitive to real consumer demand. Agreements between firms and contract suppliers often start from different expectations: The company seeks to move inventory and other costly noncore services off its balance sheet while the contract supplier hopes to gain skills and strategic leverage from contracts and thus enjoy cost advantages with its own suppliers (McCartney, 2003).

Unexpected drops in demand can create buildups of outsourced inventory that rapidly depreciate in value, creating the need for markdowns (Lakenan, Boyd, Frey, 2001). Supply chain software developed to keep up with increasing demand has been less effective in responding to sharp cutbacks by supply chain members.

Offshore supplier problems and loss of control—Organizations involved in global outsourcing depend on others caring as much about the product as they do. If an outside company makes a vital component, the manufacturer can suffer a loss of control over the way the product evolves and form an unhealthy dependency on that third-party provider for key products and services. An outsourcer may attempt to generate additional profits by bringing in less well trained people or subcontracting work elsewhere, a practice known as *double outsourcing* (Burt, 2003). As call centers, help desks, and proprietary information crucial to the underlying business are sent abroad, concern is growing that offshore suppliers may not have effective safeguards in place, leaving the contracting firm, and its unsuspecting customers, in a vulnerable position (Nathan, 2001). The offshore provider may also provide similar outsourced functions for other competing organizations and possibly use key resources from one client firm to support other clients. A larger problem can emerge if outsourcers introduce their own brand at a much better value and begin competing with the brand or service they have contracted with. Strategy theorist Michael Porter has argued that "when you outsource something you tend to make it more generic. You tend to pass a lot of the technology particularly on the manufacturing or service delivery side to your suppliers. That creates strategic vulnerabilities and also tends to commoditize your products. You're sourcing from people who are also your competitors" (qtd. in Byrne, 2001).

Importation and supply costs—Outsourcing decisions made to lower overall costs often do not account for hidden costs, which might include product obsolescence, deterioration, spoilage, taxes, loss to damage or theft, longer delivery times, administrative costs in monitoring the contracted work, and business travel. Contracts can be renegotiated or "benchmarked" to prevailing prices, but in practice this is difficult to do (Nyberg, 2003). Bringing functions back in house, or "insourcing," can be problematic due to the loss of skills and expertise and the need to maintain cost levels commensurate with what was done through outsourcing.

Political and economic risk—Since the terrorist attacks of September 11, 2001, there has been an increased awareness of world instability. Threats of terrorism, religious strife, changing governments, and failing national economies make the general socioeconomic environment hardly risk free. Firms are diversifying their outsourcing into more than one area of the world to reduce risks. Global outsourcing, however, will continue to include difficulties related to geographical differences, cultural diversity, the orientation and social incentives of offshore employees, various interpretations of the English language and differing laws, regulations, and social customs governing the workplace.

CONCLUSION

Any job that is English language based in markets such as the U.S., the U.K., and Australia can be done in India

Scott Bayman, CEO of GE India

Barring a collapse of the world economy, the scope of global outsourcing can be expected to grow for firms seeking to remain competitive in world markets and deliver shareholder value. The impetus toward outsourcing to free up resources that will enable firms to focus on their core specializations is considered to be an inevitable function of growth and development. As companies choose to leave all "service" activities to outside suppliers, they are likely to seek economies of scale and scope within their own core activities, leading to increased mergers and consolidation in a number of business sectors. A veritable avalanche of management theory and economic thinking underpins and buttresses the notion that this is a desired position for

firms and contributes to the "creative destruction" that is the nature of capitalism itself. Firms that are no longer competitive perform inefficiently and ultimately close down, to be replaced by firms that innovate to make better goods and services. Ignored in this movement, however, is the potential for decreasing, rather than increasing, the number of jobs within certain economic sectors due to greater overseas outsourcing. These lost jobs will no longer be merely lower-end manufacturing and service positions; we will see higher-paying skilled labor positions lost as well. As the location of a firm and where its products are made or serviced matters less, and the labor to create the product or perform the service is thus commoditized, developed nations will face increasing wage gaps among workers in highly specific niche-oriented occupations. Occupations such as IT in the United States may be transformed beyond recognition as significant segments of work are performed overseas. Pressure may grow for governmental trade adjustment assistance in various sectors as workforces shrink and displaced workers seek new occupations. The workers remaining within the consolidated industries will be forced to adjust their compensation downward until demand once again rises.

A little over a decade ago, the trend toward globalization of products and services in the United States was looked on as an inevitability that would portend an unequal distribution of wealth and result in a two-tiered society, with the once-solid middle-income tier of American jobs being undermined (Hendricks, 1992). But economic growth in the mid- to late 1990s brought record low unemployment in the United States even as global outsourcing surged. As economic growth has contracted in the current environment, enormous pressure has been placed on firms to justify any increase in permanent employee headcount. We may see the majority of work performed in developed countries through a temporary or contract workforce. This workforce will have less of an affiliation with the locale they are employed in and contribute less to its greater economic well-being. An increasingly migratory and transient workforce will create challenges for public-service planning as growth and decline becomes less predictable. Global companies seeking to constantly lower prices will be caught in a vicious circle as fewer firms will have the profitable means to remain in each type of business. There will be increased calls for federal legislation to introduce new forms of market controls and regulations to slow down, or even halt, rapid changes to the workforce.

To take global outsourcing to its natural progression is to presume at its most optimistic that it will create good jobs in poor countries, shrink the gap between rich and poor nations, and create smaller, more highly innovative firms with resources and skills in their core competencies of, say, marketing and design. We may see a small cadre of specialized professional agents who connect buyers and sellers in the global economy to monitor and manipulate the brand image of firms in specific occupations. Inventory-less virtual firms will put commodities out to bid, and roving subcontractors will perform activities offshore. As new products and services are developed, they will be quickly outsourced to manufacturers and service providers to perform the actual work. A contract workforce of salespeople and delivery workers will interact with the consumer. Economic theory suggests that this is in the best long-term macroeconomic interests of developed nations and the world as a whole; it is, in fact, the very essence of comparative advantage. The problems with this scenario in the near term will be that it will exacerbate structural unemployment in developed nations and create an ever-larger "skills gap" between those fortunate to have skills in short supply and the many who do not.

As we enter this markedly different future, I suggest we will see the development of a far greater degree of protectionism and limits on globalization in the form of exclusive trade treaties, regional trade agreements, tariff and nontariff barriers, and the increased power of "gatekeeping" organizations, such as the International Standards Organization (ISO), to limit global outsourcing partners. Although direct government intervention in all facets of trade by the United States is unlikely at this writing, there will be much pressure to apply selective protection to economic sectors deemed to be in serious decline. Far greater pressure will fall on the European Union (EU) nations and Japan, among other developed nations, to restrict entry to their markets of outsourced products. Emerging nations and country regions that have benefited from previous outsourcing efforts will fight hard to keep business from leaving for even cheaper areas of service and production, and may well institute protections of their own as a means of limiting business movement. Paradoxically, the very success of offshore outsourcing may well prove to be its eventual undoing.

REFERENCES

Ansbeny, C. "A new blue-collar world." *Wall Street Journal*, June 30, 2003a, B1–2.

———. "Laid off factory workers find jobs are drying up for good." *Wall Street Journal*, July 21, 2003b, A1.

———. "Outsourcing abroad draws debate at home." *Wall Street Journal*, July 14, 2003c, A2.

Baldiwala, Q. "Developing a global supply chain." *Logistics Spectrum*. October–December 2001, 25–30.

Banham, R. "Cut to the core." *CFO Magazine*, October 2001, 97–102.

Baxendale, S. "Outsourcing opportunities for small businesses: A quantitative analysis." *Business Horizons*, v. 4, n. 7, January/February 2004, 51–58.

Boudette, N. "As jobs head East in Europe, power shifts away from unions." *Wall Street Journal*, March 11, 2004, A1.

Breslin, D. A. "On the ethics of outsourcing." *PM Magazine*, November–December 1999, 24–26.

Burt, D. N, D.W. Dobler, and S. L. Starling. *World Class Supply Management*. 7th ed. Irwin, NY: McGraw-Hill, 2003.

Cant, M., and L. Jeynes. "What does outsourcing bring you that innovation cannot? How outsourcing is seen—and currently…" *Total Quality Management,* May 1998, 193–202.

Chicago Tribune, "Senate weighs outsourcing curb," January 22, 2004, sec. 3.

Corbett, M. "Outsourcing's future." *Fortune*, June 18, 2003, S1–6.

——"Outsourcing's next wave." *Fortune*, June 14, 2002.

Drucker, P. *Peter Drucker on the Profession of Management.* Cambridge, MA: Harvard Business School Press, 1998.

Ehrbar, A. *EVA: The Real Key to Creating Wealth.* New York: John Wiley & Sons, 1998.

Fevre, R. "Contract work in the recession." In *The Changing Experience of Employment: Restructuring and Recession,* ed. K. Purcell, S. Wood, A. Watson, and S. Allen, 18–34. London: Macmillan, 1986.

Garr, D. "Inside outsourcing." *Fortune Technology Review,* Summer 2001, 85–92.

Gattorna, J. L. and D. W. Walter. *Managing the Supply Chain: A Strategic Perspective.* London: Macmillan Press, 1996.

Geewax, M. "Workers protest export of tech jobs." *Chicago Tribune,* June 29, 2003, S5:5.

Geiger, J. J. "The new emerging temporary workforce." *Proceedings of the Academy of Strategic and Organizational Leadership,* 4: 1, 1999.

Hagel, J. "Leveraged growth: Expanding sales without sacrificing profits." *Harvard Business Review*, October 1, 2002.

Hamel, G. and C. K. Prahalad. *Competing for the Future.* Cambridge, MA: Harvard Business School Press, 1994.

Hammer, M., and J. Champy, J. *Reengineering the Corporation: A Manifesto for Business Revolution.* Cambridge, MA: Harvard Business School Press, 1993.

Hannon, D. "Line blurs between 3PLs and contract manufacturers." *Purchasing,* April 18, 2002, 43–44.

Harrison, B. *Lean and Mean: Changing Landscape of Corporate Power in the Age of Flexibility.* New York: Basic Books, 1994.

Hayes, M. and E. Chabrow. "Foreign policy: Should government pursue offshore outsourcing if it means U.S. jobs?" *InformationWeek,* March 17, 2003, 20–22.

Hayes, M. and P. McDougall. "Gaining ground." *InformationWeek,* March 31, 2003, 34–42.

Hendricks, C. F. *The Rightsizing Remedy: How Managers Can Respond to the Downsizing Dilemma.* Homewood, IL: Society for Human Resource Management, 1992.

Heywood, J. B. *The Outsourcing Dilemma.* London: Pearson Education, 2001.

Hilsenrath, J. E. "Why for many this recovery feels more like a recession." *Wall Street Journal,* May 29, 2003, A1–6.

Jackson, T., K. Iloranta, and S. McKenzie. "Profits or perils? The bottom line on outsourcing." *Strategy + Business,* Fall 2001.

Johnson, M. *Outsourcing in Brief.* Oxford: Butterworth Heinemann, 1997.

Khirallah, D. R. "The politics of outsourcing." *InformationWeek,* September 2, 2002, 74–78.

Kirkpatrick, D. "The net makes it all easier—including exporting U.S. jobs." *Fortune,* May 26, 2003, 146.

Kusel, J., S. Kocher, J. London, L. Buttolph, and E. Schuster. "Effects of displacement and outsourcing on woods workers and their families." *Society and Natural Resources,* 13:2, March 2000.

Lakenan, B., D. Boyd, and E. Frey. "Why Cisco fell: outsourcing and its perils." *Strategy + Business,* Fall 2001.

Legget. K., and P. Wonacott. "Surge in exports from China jolts global industry." *Wall Street Journal,* October 10, 2002. A1–8.

Levitt, T. "The globalization of markets." *Harvard Business Review,* May 1983.

Marsh, P. "A sharp sense of the limits to outsourcing." *Financial Times,* July 31, 2001, 10.

Martin, P. "The limits of outsourcing," *Financial Times.* September 25, 2001, 10.

McCartney, L. "A shore thing?" *CFO-IT Magazine,* Spring 2003, 60–63.

Merchant, K. "GE champions India's world class services." *Financial Times,* June 3, 2003, 11.

Moran, N. "More operations move offshore." *Financial Times,* June 30, 2003, 2.

Nathan, S. J. "Reducing the risk of outsourcing," *Supply Strategy,* May/June 2001, 20.

Neikirk, W. "Future grim for jobless workers," *Chicago Tribune*, December 17, 2002, A1–29.

———. "Futures best bet: technology again." *Chicago Tribune*. December 18, 2002, A1–25.

Nyberg, A. "Will outsourcing still fly?" *CFO Magazine*, February 2003, 57–60.

Porter, M. E., quoted in John A. Byrne, "Caught in the Net," *Business Week*, August 27, 2001.

Quinn. J. B. *Innovation Explosion: Using Intellect and Software to Revolutionize Growth Strategies*. New York: Free Press. 1997.

Reese-McMahon LLC. "The new global sourcing model." *Business-Wise, March 2003, 2.*

Reid. R., and M. Pascalev. "Strategic and ethical issues in outsourcing information technologies." In *Ethical Issues of Information Systems*, ed. A. Salehnia. London: IRM Press, 2002, 232–48.

Ross, C. F. "Can outsourcers really transform IT?" Boston: Forrester Research Inc., June 2003.

Skapinker, M. "Much to question on outsourcing." *Financial Times*, June 30, 2003, 1.

Thompson, J. W. "Globalization: its defenders and dissenters," *Business and Society Review*, Summer 2001, 106:2, 170–79.

Tomkins, R. "Why the protests will go on," *Financial Times*, August 26, 2001, 12.

Tonelson, A. *The Race to the Bottom: Why a Worldwide Worker Surplus and Uncontrolled Free Trade Are Sinking American Living Standards.* Boulder, CO: Westview Press, 2000.

Wells, M. J. *Strawberry Fields: Politics, Class and Work in California Agriculture.* Ithaca, NY: Cornell University Press, 1996.

Wonacott, P. "China's secret weapon: smart, cheap labor for high tech goods." *Wall Street Journal*, March 14, 2002, A1–6.

Christopher B. Clott is associate professor of the Graham School of Management, Saint Xavier University, Chicago.

From *Business and Society Review,* Vol. 109, No. 2, Summer 2004, pp. 153-170. Copyright ©2004 by Blackwell Publishers, Ltd. Reprinted by permission.

The fall and rise of the global economy

Anyone who follows the news, even casually, or reads product labels, is aware that the world economy has become more interdependent in recent decades. Indeed, the worldwide integration of national economies—through goods and services trade, capital flows, and operational linkages among firms—has never before been as broad or as deep.[1]

Nevertheless, the course of globalization has not always been smooth. At the start of the 20th century, the global economy was highly integrated. In some regards, it was nearly as integrated as it is today. Yet two decades later, a noteworthy commentator lamented the apparent end of this economic integration. John Maynard Keynes wrote an eloquent and oft-cited description of the pre–World War I economy.[2]

> What an extraordinary episode in the economic progress of man that age was which came to an end in August, 1914!... life offered, at a low cost and with the least trouble, conveniences, comforts, and amenities beyond the compass of the richest and most powerful monarchs of other ages. The inhabitant of London could order by telephone, sipping his morning tea in bed, the various products of the whole earth... he could at the same moment and by the same means adventure his wealth in the natural resources and new enterprises of any quarter of the world.... But, most important of all, he regarded this state of affairs as normal, certain, and permanent, except in the direction of further improvement, and any deviation from it as aberrant, scandalous, and avoidable.

In the decades that followed, two world wars, the Great Depression, and protectionist policies seemed to bring economic integration to an end. Since then, however, advances in technology and changes in policy have worked to reopen borders. Despite Keynes' characterization of the pre–World War I period as an "extraordinary episode," the economic globalization and buoyancy of that period was not an aberration. Rather, it was the 1913–50 period that stands out for its uncharacteristically weak

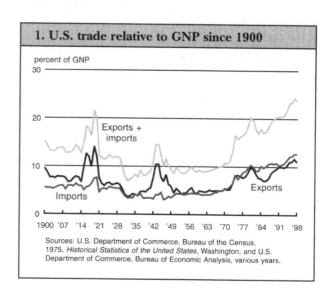

1. U.S. trade relative to GNP since 1900

percent of GNP

Exports + imports

Imports

Exports

1900 '07 '14 '21 '28 '35 '42 '49 '56 '63 '70 '77 '84 '91 '98

Sources: U.S. Department of Commerce, Bureau of the Census, 1975, *Historical Statistics of the United States*, Washington; and U.S. Department of Commerce, Bureau of Economic Analysis, various years.

growth in both output and trade. After 1950, the world economy resumed its trend toward globalization. But it took time to make up the ground lost: In the U.S. and elsewhere, the level of trade relative to output has consistently exceeded early 20th century levels only in the past few decades. Indeed, just a few years ago, academic papers debated whether the world economy in the 1980s and early 1990s was more, or less, integrated than it was in 1900.[3]

This *Chicago Fed Letter* reviews the ebbs and flows of globalization during the past century, and argues that a continuing commitment to open markets is worth pursuing as a way to raise living standards both at home and abroad.

Growing importance of trade and capital flows in the U.S.

Trade and, to a much lesser extent, investment links were well established a century or more ago, but both deteriorated during the interwar period. Today, global economic ties have rebounded and are generally more extensive and intensive than ever before.

Figure 1 illustrates the historical ebb and flow of U.S. trade. Except briefly around the time of each world war, the ratio of trade (exports plus imports) to gross national product (GNP) did not return to turn-of-the-century levels until the 1970s. Recently, however, this ratio has approached 25%, its highest point in at least a century.

During much of the 19th and early 20th centuries, the U.S. participated actively in a generally vibrant world trade.[4] Internationally, there were few nontariff trade barriers. The interwar period that followed, however, was largely one of rising tariff and nontariff barriers—in the U.S. and elsewhere—and global disintegration rather than integration. Since World War II, technological developments and the gradual liberalization of international trade and capital flows have put integration on the upswing.

Some of this rising trade can be attributed to "two-way" intra-industry trade. Anecdotal evidence and recent studies document how production processes have been increasingly divided up and reallocated, either domestically or globally.[5] Tasks, such as research and development, design, assembly, and packaging, are performed by firms in the U.S. and elsewhere, based on countries' relative strengths in completing them. Consider the computer industry. According to a recent report, in 1998 an estimated 43% of domestic producers' total shipments was exported, and an estimated 58% of final and intermediate domestic consumption was imported; some 60%, by value, of the hardware in a typical U.S. personal computer system comes from Asia.[6]

Cross-border capital flows have likewise grown to unprecedented levels, reflecting reduced barriers to capital, an increased desire of investors to diversify their portfolios internationally, and a plethora of new financial instruments and technologies.[7] One survey reports that average daily turnover on world foreign exchange mar-

kets rose from $0.6 trillion in April 1989 to about $1.5 trillion in April 1998.[8]

Official balance of payments data provide a measure of capital flows that, roughly speaking, measure the change in cross-border ownership claims. Figure 2 shows data on inflows of capital to the U.S. by foreigners and outflows of capital sent abroad by U.S. residents. Although U.S. outflows abroad have been rising, foreign inflows have been rising even faster. These cross-border flows typically were no more than 1% of GNP through the 1960s. By contrast, from 1995 through 1998, inflows averaged 7% of GNP.

Role of technology and policy

The forces driving globalization include technology and policy. Technological improvements have reduced the costs of doing business internationally; they have also created opportunities for new kinds of commercial transactions, particularly in financial markets and online. At the same time, policy has worked actively to open markets around the world. Together, technology and policy have helped to lower barriers to trade and investment.

Improved transportation technologies have reduced the cost of moving products. For example, the advent of *containerization* in land- and sea-based shipping has reduced both handling requirements and transit time for deliveries.[9] In addition, air transport has become more economical. Worldwide, the cost of air freight, measured as average revenue per ton-kilometer, dropped by 78% between 1955 and 1996.[10] At the same time, the share of world trade in high-value-to-weight products such as pharmaceuticals has risen. Reflecting the falling cost of air freight as well as the shifting composition of trade, air shipments in 1998 accounted for 28% of the value of U.S. international trade—up from 7% in 1965 and a negligible share in 1950.[11]

Improved communications and information technologies have also facilitated international commerce, particularly trade in services. In 1930, a three-minute phone call from New York to London cost $293, measured in 1998 dollars.[12] By 1998, one widely subscribed discount plan charged only 36 cents for a clearer, more reliable three minute call.[13] Firms' ability to provide customer support by telephone or e-mail at relatively low cost, or to transmit digital products electronically via the Internet, has reduced the importance of market proximity in some industries.

Improved communications and information technologies have also underpinned rapid financial market developments. The range of financial instruments has exploded in recent years, contributing to the massive gross flows of financial capital discussed earlier. For example, advances in computing technology enable traders to implement complex analytical models. This in turn allows financial firms to meet demand for new financial instruments, such

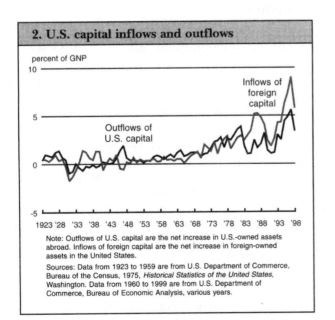

2. U.S. capital inflows and outflows

percent of GNP

Inflows of foreign capital

Outflows of U.S. capital

Note: Outflows of U.S. capital are the net increase in U.S.-owned assets abroad. Inflows of foreign capital are the net increase in foreign-owned assets in the United States.

Sources: Data from 1923 to 1959 are from U.S. Department of Commerce, Bureau of the Census, 1975, *Historical Statistics of the United States*, Washington. Data from 1960 to 1999 are from U.S. Department of Commerce, Bureau of Economic Analysis, various years.

as swaps, options, and futures, which allow market participants to better manage their risk.

Given the economic and technological forces behind globalization, its rise may seem inevitable. Yet governments have taken on a critically important role in opening markets and removing distortions, thereby allowing market forces to play themselves out. In contrast, policy during the interwar period actively promoted protectionism through high tariff and nontariff barriers.[14] Indeed, rising protectionism in a number of countries—including the U.S. through the Tariff Act of 1930 (Smoot-Hawley)—made the Great Depression more severe. Despite U.S. efforts to begin reducing tariffs at home and abroad in 1934, through the Reciprocal Trade Agreements Act, world tariffs remained high on average.

For the past half century, in contrast, policy has worked actively to remove barriers and distortions to the market forces underpinning trade and investment. For example, the General Agreement on Tariffs and Trade and, more recently, the World Trade Organization have championed trade liberalization. Since the 1970s, most industrial countries have removed most controls on international capital movements, and many developing countries have greatly relaxed theirs.

Globalization and living standards

Economists generally argue that openness to the world makes us more prosperous. The freedom of firms to choose from a wider range of inputs, and of consumers to choose from a wider range of products, improves efficiency, promotes innovation, encourages the transfer of technology, and otherwise enhances productivity growth. Through trade, countries can shift resources into those sectors best able to compete internationally, so reaping the benefits of specialization and scale economies. Countries on both sides of a transaction stand to gain.

Some, but not all, of the benefits of market opening are quantifiable. For example, recent studies that evaluate trade liberalizing measures under the Uruguay Round of multilateral negotiations, completed in 1994, tend to focus on the effects of reducing tariffs and export subsidies and eliminating quotas. These studies, which capture only a narrow range of the possible gains, find that annual global income could rise on the order of $200 billion, measured in 1992 dollars.[15]

Opening domestic markets to global capital can also improve living standards. Global capital markets allow investors to allocate their resources where the returns are highest and to diversify their portfolios, thereby reducing their risk. At the same time, countries receiving capital inflows can develop more quickly, since the inflows allow them to increase their productive capital stock without foregoing current consumption. When the capital inflow takes the form of foreign direct investment, the inflow often improves access to international best practices in production, including managerial, technical, and marketing know-how. Therefore, global investment, like trade, benefits both sides of the transaction. These benefits, in turn, can lead to higher real incomes and wages.

Of course, economic globalization is not an end in itself, but rather a means to raise living standards. Like other sources of economic growth, including technological progress, economic integration involves natural tradeoffs. The same processes that bring about economic growth can force costly adjustments for some firms and their workers. Increased trade re-sorts each country's resources, directing them toward their most productive uses, but some industries and their workers may face sharp competition from other countries. Overall, however, economists generally attribute only a small share of worker dislocation in the U.S. to trade, roughly 10% or less.[16] (Such challenges may, of course, be greater in some other countries, particularly those where entrenched cultural and institutional barriers restrict the mobility of workers.) Nevertheless, crafting sound domestic policy to help ease the transition for those affected poses a significant challenge.

The emphasis here on domestic policy is intentional. Even in an increasingly global economy each nation largely controls its own destiny. Sound domestic policy plays an important role in ensuring that the benefits of international economic integration are shared widely, raising living standards within and across the countries that take part. In large measure, active participation in international markets for goods, services, and capital strengthens the case for domestic policies that make sense even without integration. Among these are policies that encourage a flexible and skilled work force, provide an adequate social safety net, reward innovation, and secure the integrity and depth of the financial system.

Conclusion

For centuries, rising prosperity and rising integration of the global economy have gone hand in hand. The U.S. and much of the rest of the world have never before been as affluent as today. Nor has economic globalization—the worldwide integration of national economies through trade, capital flows, and operational linkages among firms—ever before been as broad or as deep. Keynes' description of London at the beginning of the 20th century rings even truer for the United States and many other countries today. This conjuncture of rising wealth and expanding international ties is no coincidence. The U.S. has gained enormously from these linkages. Indeed, future improvements in Americans' living standards depend in part on our continued willingness to embrace international economic integration.

Over the long term, increasing our standard of living in the U.S. requires that Americans embrace change. It is clearly in our interest to forge ahead, both promoting and guiding the process of international economic integration. Yet even as we actively promote and encourage global economic linkages, we must confront the very real challenges that arise from economic globalization. We must find ways to share its benefits as widely as possible. The key lies in maintaining an economy that is sufficiently flexible and vibrant to meet the challenges of reaping those benefits. Ultimately, our prosperity in the global economy depends primarily on our policies at home.

—John G. Fernald
Senior economist
—Victoria Greenfield
Senior economist, RAND

Notes

1. This *Chicago Fed Letter* draws heavily on chapter 6 of Office of the U.S. President, 2000, Economic *Report of the President*, Washington, DC: United States Government Printing Office, February. The authors wish to thank Yu-Chin Chen, John Goldie, and Robert Lawrence for their assistance and insight in preparing the original text.
2. John Maynard Keynes, 1919, *Economic Consequences of the Peace*, London: Macmillan, available on the Internet at www.socsci.mcmaster.ca/.-econ/ugcm/31l3/keynes/peace.htm.
3. See, for example, the discussion and references in Michael Bordo, Barry Eichengreen, and Douglas Irwin, 1999, "Is globalization today really different from globalization a hundred years ago?," *Brookings Trade Forum 1999*, Washington, DC: The Brookings Institution, pp. 1–50.
4. Douglas Irwin, 1985, "The GATT in historical perspective," *American Economic Review*, Vol. 85, No. 2, pp. 323–328, provides an overview of the pre-World War I and interwar periods.
5. See David Hummels, Jun Ishii, and Kei-Mu Yi, 2001, "The nature and growth of vertical specialization in world trade," *Journal of International Economics*, forthcoming; Catherine Mann, 1999, *Is the U.S. Trade Deficit Sustainable?*, Washington, DC: Institute for International Economics, pp. 39–41; Robert Feenstra, 1998, "Integration of trade and disintegration of production in the global economy," *Journal of Economic Perspectives*, Vol. 12, No. 4, pp. 31–50; and others.
6. McGraw-Companies and the U.S. Department of Commerce, International Trade Administration, 1999, U.S. *Industry and Trade Outlook '99*, p. 27–1 and p. 27–5.
7. Maurice Obsfeld and Alan Taylor, 1998, "The Great Depression as a watershed: International capital mobility over the long run," in *The Defining Moment: The Great Depression and the American Economy in the Twentieth Century*, Michael D. Bordo, Claudia Goldin, and Eugene N. White (eds.), Chicago: University of Chicago Press, pp. 353–402, emphasize that *net* capital flows across countries (as measured by current account balances relative to GDP) were larger in the late 19th and early 20th centuries than they are today. By contrast, Bordo, Eichengreen, and Irwin, op cit., emphasize that *gross* capital flows—our focus in this *Fed Letter*—are much larger today than ever before.
8. Bank for International Settlements, 1999, *Central Bank Survey of Foreign Exchange and Derivatives Activity*, available on the Internet at www.bis.org, May.
9. Containerization, as it is called, allows a standard-sized container to be hauled by truck or rail and then, if continuing overseas, loaded by crane directly onto a ship. For more on the transformation of shipping, see, The Economist Newspaper Limited, 1997, "Schools brief, delivering the goods," *The Economist*, available on the Internet at www.economist.com, November 13.
10. *Economic Report of the President*, op cit., p. 209, cites data from David Hummels, 1999, "Have international transportation costs declined?," University of Chicago, unpublished paper, as well as personal correspondence from Hummels.
11. David Hummels, 1999, "Have international transportation costs declined?," University of Chicago, unpublished paper, p. 7, and the U.S. Department of Commerce, various publications.
12. For historical data on the nominal price of a telephone call, see U.S. Department of Commerce, 1975, *Historical Statistics of the United States, Colonial Times to 1970, Part 2*, Washington, DC: U.S. Government Printing Office, p. 791.
13. U.S. Federal Communications Commission, 1999, *Trends in the U.S. International Telecommunications Industry*, Washington, DC, table 16.
14. See Irwin, op cit.
15. These estimates cover only a narrow range of the potential benefits from the Uruguay Round. See Council of Economic Advisers, 1999, "America's interest in the WTO," white paper, p. 22, citing results in Glenn W. Harrison, Thomas Rutherford, and David G. Tarr, 1996, "Quantifying the Uruguay Round," p. 238, and Joseph F. Francois, Bradley McDonald, and Hikan Nordstrom, 1996, "The Uruguay Round: A numerically based quantitative assessment," pp. 282–283, both in *The Uruguay Round and the Developing Countries*, Will Martin and L. Alan Winters (eds.), London: World Bank and Cambridge University Press.
16. Council of Economic Advisers, 1999, "America's interest in the World Trade Organization: An economic assessment," p. 14, citing the *Economic Report of the President*, 1998, pp. 244–245, and other sources.

THE "Globalization" CHALLENGE

The U.S. Role in Shaping World Trade and Investment

BY ROBERT E. LITAN

As the United States enters the 21st century, it stands unchallenged as the world's economic leader, a remarkable turnaround from the 1980s when many Americans had doubts about U.S. "competitiveness." Productivity growth—the engine of improvement in average living standards—has rebounded from a 25-year slump of a little more than 1 percent a year to roughly 2.5 percent since 1995, a gain few had predicted.

Economic engagement with the rest of the world has played a key part in the U.S. economic revival. Our relatively open borders, which permit most foreign goods to come in with a zero or low tariff, have helped keep inflation in check, allowing the Federal Reserve to let the good times roll without hiking up interest rates as quickly as it might otherwise have done. Indeed, the influx of funds from abroad during the Asian financial crisis kept interest rates low and thereby encouraged a continued boom in investment and consumption, which more than offset any decline in American exports to Asia. Even so, during the 1990s, exports accounted for almost a quarter of the growth of output (though just 12 percent of U.S. gross domestic product at the end of the decade).

Yet as the new century dawns, America's increasing economic interdependence with the rest of the world, known loosely as "globalization," has come under attack. Much of the criticism is aimed at two international institutions that the United States helped create and lead: the International Monetary Fund, launched after World War II to provide emergency loans to countries with temporary balance-of-payments problems, and the World Trade Organization, created in 1995 during the last round of world trade negotiations, primarily to help settle trade disputes among countries.

The attacks on both institutions are varied and often inconsistent. But they clearly have taken their toll. For all practical purposes, the IMF is not likely to have its resources augmented any time soon by Congress (and thus by other national governments). Meanwhile, the failure of the WTO meetings in Seattle last December to produce even a roadmap for future trade negotiations—coupled with the protests that soiled the proceedings—has thrown a wrench into plans to reduce remaining barriers to world trade and investment.

For better or worse, it is now up to the United States, as it has been since World War II, to help shape the future of both organizations and arguably the course of the global economy. A broad consensus appears to exist here and elsewhere that governments should strive to improve the stability of the world economy and to advance living standards. But the consensus breaks down over how to do so. As the United States prepares to pick a new president and a new Congress, citizens and policymakers should be asking how best to promote stability and growth in the years ahead.

Unilateralism

A variety of interests and prominent individuals, many of whom otherwise agree on little else, are pushing the United States to adopt a new economic unilateralism, one that at its extremes would abolish the IMF, the WTO, or both.

Some critics of the IMF, for example, argue that because the system of fixed exchange rates that the Fund was created primarily to support has collapsed, so should the Fund. Indeed, some assert that the Fund's role as emergency lender to all countries has encouraged imprudent behavior by governments, borrowers, and lenders. Abolishing the IMF, they argue, would make all parties behave more carefully, with fewer financial crises as a result.

In fact, the supposed "safety net" of IMF lending is far more porous than critics may acknowledge. IMF loans have not bailed out foreign holders of bonds or equities in emerging markets. Furthermore, governments in those countries have had to submit to increasingly onerous conditions (themselves the targets of other criticisms), making it hard to argue that the Fund's continued presence will encourage future recklessness.

The critics do have a point about one thing: IMF funds often find their way, quite legitimately, into troubled banks, which use them to shelter large depositors (often foreign banks) from losses. But abolishing the Fund to address this problem runs enormous risks. During the 1930s the Federal Reserve effectively did not act as a U.S. lender-of-last-resort, allowing a recession to turn into a great depression. World leaders are right to avoid such a risk on a global scale.

U.S. opponents of the WTO claim that subjecting U.S. regulations and standards to an international trade-oriented dispute resolution process risks watering down or even eliminating them. But WTO dispute resolution panels decide whether a country's rules *unfairly discriminate* against foreign goods, not whether the rules are unsound. And even when the WTO finds the rules to be discriminatory, it cannot change them—it can only allow other countries to retaliate (in a proportionate fashion). Nonetheless, since 1995 the process generally has worked as the United States expected: most cases in which our country has been involved have been decided or settled in our favor, expanding access for our exports.

In the end, we cannot avoid the challenge of globalization.

One Worlders

At the other extreme from the unilateralists are the "one worlders," who want to give the WTO and the IMF even more authority and responsibility, primarily in the service of raising environmental and labor standards abroad. Indeed, under recently enacted legislation, the IMF must now report on how well its borrowers are advancing labor and environmental standards. Furthermore, President Clinton suggested during the Seattle meeting that the WTO authorize the use of trade sanctions against countries not conforming to minimum world "core" labor standards (prohibiting child and forced labor, discrimination, and restrictions against unions).

But would such well-intentioned initiatives succeed? The history of developed countries suggests that standards will rise as average incomes grow and citizens demand improved labor and environmental protections. Because trade is a well-documented means for countries to improve their living standards, it would be counterproductive to deny emergency financing or market access to countries that may not adhere to some minimum standards.

But, the one worlders will object, what is wrong with trying to hurry things along with some "sticks," such as sanctions? The answer is that many people and businesses in developing countries already operate outside the law. Passing and enforcing more laws that add first-world protections will slow their economic development—and thus improvements in environmental and labor conditions—by driving more business into the underground economy, where even third-world standards are not enforced.

The Sensible Middle

A middle course between the extremes promises both greater economic stability and advances in living standards. But it will require reform of global institutions, coupled with policies at home to ease anxieties about globalization.

For starters, both the IMF and the WTO need to be more tolerant of dissent. To its credit, the IMF has made its operations much more open since the Asian financial crisis. Now it should reach out to nongovernmental organizations to hear their concerns and explain how its policies are (or are not) consistent with their aims. The WTO, meanwhile, should welcome briefs from nongovernmental parties. If Seattle teaches anything, it is that secrecy breeds mistrust.

Substantively, much more progress has been made toward shoring up the international "financial architecture" than is commonly recognized. It is now widely accepted that countries with weak financial systems should be able to restrict short-term borrowings in foreign currency (such as those that helped lay the foundations for the Asian crisis). It is also generally recognized that countries should not maintain pegged, but adjustable, exchange rates because doing so can invite recurrent speculative attacks on currencies and encourage excessive borrowing by firms that erroneously believe rates to be fixed.

As for the IMF's tendency to encourage too much borrowing and lending—by parties who expect to be bailed out by IMF emergency lending—in the past two years the Fund has refused to lend to both Russia and Ecuador because their policies were not sound. These gutsy decisions have changed market expectations about the automaticity of emergency lending. The central issue that now must be resolved is whether to establish more formal criteria for access to and pricing of IMF loans—to encourage countries to pursue sound policies and to put lenders on notice—or leave the current "constructive ambiguity" in place.

The agenda for the WTO, meanwhile, is simple: pick up the pieces from Seattle and move forward. Otherwise countries will be tempted to strike more regional and, possibly, discriminatory arrangements. At worst, without a strong commitment to multilateral trade liberalization, a future economic downturn could sorely tempt nations to raise import barriers, ignoring the WTO as a toothless tiger.

Getting the WTO back on track will require compromise on all sides. To get U.S. priorities—freer trade in agriculture and services, no barriers to e-commerce—on the agenda, we must entertain creative suggestions from other countries. For example, we could accommodate Europe's political difficulties in committing to a total elimination of farm subsidies by discussing an accelerated phaseout schedule that doesn't yet have zero at the end. Meanwhile, we should work with Europeans and others to allow labeling of goods and services to solve such thorny disputes as EU opposition to the sale of genetically modified foods.

The United States should also offer to modify antidumping policy, which hurts both developing countries and American consumers. One approach would ease antidumping rules unless petitioners at home can demonstrate that foreign exporters are taking advantage of cartels or protected markets in their own countries to sell products cheaper abroad.

With such concessions on the table, the United States would be in a stronger position to ask other countries—separately and outside the WTO process—to help create or strengthen organizations to address labor and environmental standards. The WTO might recognize the legitimacy of multinational environmental agreements, even those that may ban imports of harmful products (as long as harmful domestic goods are given similar treatment). The next WTO round can also advance environmental interests by removing subsidies that promote excessive use of natural resources.

At home U.S. leaders need to do a far better job of helping Americans see the benefits of globalization. One way to do that is to emphasize the consumer gains from trade. The office of the Special Trade Representative, for example, estimates that existing WTO agreements add roughly $3,000 to the purchasing power of the average four-person household every year. Liberalized trade also promotes economic growth and liberty abroad, both in our national interest.

Finally, more must be done to address Americans' continuing anxieties about globalization and, indeed, economic change more broadly. Two possibilities: lifetime loan accounts for workers to use for retraining and wage insurance to compensate for some portion of incomes lost when individuals are laid off. Such measures should be available generally, not just for those who have been displaced because of trade.

In the end, we cannot avoid the challenge of globalization. Meeting it through unilateralism or one worldism is likely both to destabilize the world economy and slow improvements in living standards at home and abroad. Instead we should embrace the opportunities that globalization affords, ease the anxieties it generates, and reform and strengthen the international economic institutions created to promote both global economic stability and growth.

Robert E. Litan is vice president and director of the Brookings Economic Studies program. He also holds the Cabot Family Chair in Economics.

From *The Brookings Review*, Spring 2000, pp. 35-37. © 2000 by the Brookings Institution. Reprinted by permission.

Should We Worry about the Large U.S. Current Account Deficit?

Over the last year the U.S. current account deficit has reached unprecedented levels. Figure 1 illustrates this by charting the falling trajectory of the current account balance, which essentially measures net exports of goods and services plus net income received from foreign investments. One implication of this deficit is that the U.S. overall must borrow from the rest of the world to pay for its excess of imports and to service its external debt.

Is the large current account deficit a problem for the U.S.? Economic theory offers some scenarios in which a current account deficit is a rational response to economic conditions or a response that may even enhance economic welfare. At the same time, recent research suggests that under certain circumstances, a large current account deficit may make the U.S. economy vulnerable to severe disruptions. This *Economic Letter* explores some recent theories and some data to understand how the current account deficit could be either an optimal outcome or a threatening one.

What theory has to say

According to economic theory, the main cost of running a current account deficit is not the cost of actually paying off the accumulated debt but more precisely the cost of servicing the debt. Resources need to be set aside each year to pay the interest on the debt, and diverting economic resources away from alternative uses, like consumption, can lower a country's standard of living.

Standard economic theory suggests at least two circumstances in which this cost may be worthwhile. First, if a country's output is temporarily low, perhaps due to a recession, borrowing from abroad may be justified because buying imports softens the impact on consumption levels. Second, if a country has a sudden abundance of good investment opportunities, it may make sense to borrow from abroad when these opportunities cannot be financed out of domestic saving. After all, these investment projects may generate enhanced income in the future that can be used to finance the associated debt.

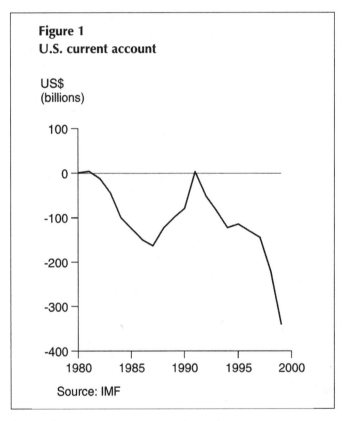

Figure 1
U.S. current account

US$
(billions)

Source: IMF

Theories of this type were developed in models that assumed optimizing economic agents trying to maximize their own welfare in a perfectly frictionless economic setting, that is, where there are no costs to transactions. One implication of these theories is that any current account deficit that arises exclusively from the actions of private agents in this context must be optimal in the sense that it is improving the welfare of people in the economy. So by definition, such a current account deficit is not something the government should worry about.

Recent developments in this theoretical literature have indicated that optimal current account deficits may be more elusive than the standard theory suggests. For example, Obstfeld and Rogoff (2000a) relax the assumption of a frictionless economic setting and augment the standard theoretical model by adding the costs of international trade, representing transportation costs or tariff barriers. They find that the presence of even modest trading frictions can strongly alter the model's predictions; for example, small costs of importing goods can easily discourage optimizing private agents from purchasing imports. This finding suggests that it generally may not be optimal to run a current account deficit as a means to smooth consumption during recessions. In support of their model, the authors note that their prediction is consistent with the fact that national consumption levels tend to have a lower correlation across countries than do national output levels. After all, if countries tended to borrow from each other to smooth their consumption levels over periods of output fluctuations, their consumption levels should tend to move more closely together.

Similarly, the augmented model shows that transaction costs may make it expensive to import goods from abroad to undertake investment projects. As a result, optimizing agents in this environment tend to finance investment mainly out of domestic saving. The authors note that this prediction is consistent with the fact that the levels of saving and investment are highly correlated within most countries.

If the findings of Obstfeld and Rogoff are correct, then the costs of importing goods generally outweigh the potential benefits of running a current account deficit, whether it is to smooth consumption or to finance extra investment. These results, then, certainly make it more difficult to justify a large current account deficit as an optimal, welfare-improving phenomenon.

What data have to say

The empirical literature so far has not fully clarified how well these various theories apply to the real world. One strand of the literature tests these theories using a method called "present value tests." These tests focus on the prediction that the optimal current account is a function of expected future changes in output net of investment. The empirical methodology then infers information about people's expectations for future output using data on the current account itself.

These tests tend to reject the theoretical models quite strongly for most countries. The standard theory usually can explain *why* the current account goes into deficit when it does, typically in response to shocks to the level of output, but it usually *cannot* explain how big the current account deficit is. In other words, most countries tend to run larger current account deficits than can be justified in terms of optimizing behavior.

A recent contribution to this literature, Bergin and Sheffrin (2000), explores the possibility that shocks other than changes in output are driving the current account. In particular, the paper demonstrates with an extended present value test that large fluctuations in the current account in several countries can more easily be explained in terms of shocks to the interest rate or exchange rate. The idea is that fluctuations

in such variables can induce households to "un-smooth" their consumption levels even if output levels are constant.

This finding also raises questions about considering a current account deficit an optimal outcome. The problem is that shocks to the interest rate or exchange rate may well arise from government action. If government action rather than purely private behavior is the underlying cause of the current account deficit, the argument stated previously for not worrying would no longer apply. For example, optimizing agents may generate a current account deficit simply as a way to make the best of a bad government policy. It is possible that corrective government action could improve welfare in this context. The implication is that, depending on the particular economic shock at work, there may be reason for governments to worry about a resulting current account deficit.

Applying the analysis to the U.S.

The theories also have mixed success when applied to the specific case of the U.S. By definition, the current account consists of saving (private saving plus government saving) minus investment. Figure 2 plots the U.S. current account and these components as shares of GNP. The last time the U.S. experienced a large current account deficit was in the mid-1980s. It seems that a major portion of the current account deficit at that time was low government saving, reflecting the large government budget deficit of the time. This relationship is often referred to as the "twin deficits" phenomenon. It is very hard to justify this current account deficit as an optimal response to the need to smooth consumption or to investment opportunities.

The current account deficit experienced in recent years seems to be different, however. Given that the government budget deficit has been resolved, clearly this is not a case of twin deficits. Instead, the figure suggests that the cause lies in a dramatic fall in private saving and a rise in investment. This explanation could be consistent with a theory of optimal current account deficits. For example, one feature of the recent economy has been the widespread implementation of new information technologies. If these represent profitable new investment opportunities, one might argue that it is optimal to run a current account deficit to finance them. Extending the argument further, these technologies and investments may have led consumers to anticipate a higher level of productivity and output in the future. One could argue this has helped spur the fall in private saving, as people try to smooth their consumption relative to the higher levels they anticipate for the future. One channel for these expectations to affect saving would be if the expected future productivity has spurred stock market gains and hence the wealth of consumers.

This argument merely points out that today's large current account deficit could be explained as a rational and optimizing response to economic conditions. At a minimum, the present episode of current account deficits fits this type of explanation far better than the previous episode experienced in the 1980s.

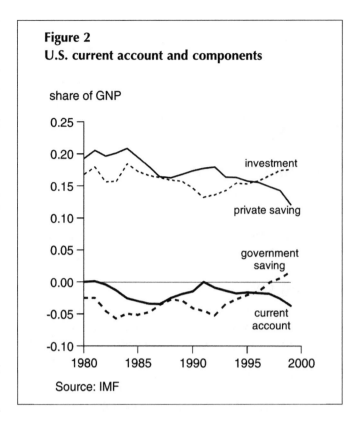

Figure 2
U.S. current account and components

share of GNP

Source: IMF

Taking an alternative perspective

Even if a large current account deficit can be justified from the perspective of macroeconomic theory, recent work by Obstfeld and Rogoff (2000b) offers a different reason for worry. They note that the debt accumulated by the U.S. to finance its deficits over the last decade has grown to about 20% of GDP. The authors acknowledge that this is smaller than has been accumulated by some other developed countries during the decade, and technically, it is possible to sustain and service a debt of this size. But it is unprecedented for such a large country to run a large deficit and debt of this type. The authors consider what might happen if the U.S. were forced to balance its current account suddenly because international investors decided to park their funds elsewhere. Such an event could result from a variety of unforeseen shocks, such as a slowdown in the U.S.

growth rate relative to other countries or a sudden fall in the U.S. stock market.

Obstfeld and Rogoff argue that the effects of such a current account reversal would be especially potent for the U.S. economy, since the U.S. is less integrated into international markets than are other developed countries (perhaps because of the trading frictions the authors considered in the research discussed above). The result is that a modest shift in the quantity of the current account implies a large impact on the international relative price of U.S. goods and the real exchange rate. Using a simple model embodying their theoretical assumptions, the authors compute that a rapid reversal of the current account would generate a real exchange rate depreciation greater than 20% in magnitude.

The authors stop short of arguing that this real exchange rate depreciation would have large effects on the U.S. level of output or welfare. But it clearly has the potential to be severely disruptive. This suggests that even if a current account deficit may be justified as a reasonable response to shocks to output or investment opportunities, it nevertheless is also true that a large current account deficit creates a particular vulnerability to a variety of other shocks that might hit the economy down the road. This offers a warning that while the large U.S. current account deficit may well be rational and perhaps even welfare-improving, it nevertheless cannot be regarded cavalierly.

Paul Bergin
FRBSF Visiting Scholar
Assistant Professor of Economics, UC Davis

References

Bergin, Paul R., and Steven M. Sheffrin. 2000. "Interest Rates, Exchange Rates and Present Value Models of the Current Account." *The Economic Journal* 110, pp. 535–558.

Obstfeld, Maurice, and Kenneth Rogoff. 2000a. "The Six Major Puzzles in International Macroeconomics: Is There a Common Cause?" NBER Working Paper 7777.

Obstfeld, Maurice, and Kenneth Rogoff. 2000b. "Perspective on OECD Economic Integration: Implications for U.S. Current Account Adjustment." Mimeo. Harvard University.

Reprinted with permission from the Federal Reserve Bank of San Francisco *Economic Letter*, December 22, 2000, pp. 1–4. The opinions expressed in this article do not necessarily reflect the views of the management of the FRBSF, or of the Board of Governors of the Federal Reserve System.

Global Shell Games

How the corporations operate tax free

By Sen. Byron Dorgan

Remember the Pentagon's $600 toilet seats and $426 hammers? Now there's a new list to think about: Ball point pens purchased from Trinidad for $8,500. Disposable plastic gloves from Japan at $46.22 a piece. Wrist watch batteries from China at $8,252 each. Apple juice from Israel at $2,052 a liter.

It's a shopping spree a defense contractor might love. But this time the Pentagon is not involved; nor any other part of the government, for that matter. Instead the strange prices are the work of multinational corporations, and one of the biggest tax avoidance scams this country has ever seen. The ideological Right makes a big deal over what it calls "Tax Freedom Day"— the day on which Americans supposedly have fulfilled their tax burden for the year. They neglect to mention that every day is tax freedom day for these multinationals. More than two-thirds of foreign-based multinationals doing business here—and only a slightly smaller fraction of U.S.-based multinational firms— pay no federal income tax at all. Many of the rest are paying a relative pittance. As a result, U.S. taxpayers are losing over $40 billion a year by one estimate, which is enough to pay for a prescription drug benefit in Medicare. Considering that corporate profits have soared in recent years something here does not compute. The manipulation of prices at the border is a big part of this screwy equation.

It points to one of the great contradictions in the push for globalization. From its proponents we hear no end of rhapsodizing over the new "world without borders" that is going to bring peace and prosperity without end. Yet when the discussion turns to the rules of trade, as opposed to the theology of it, then the advocates often sing a different tune. They suddenly become dogged defenders of the very same national borders they deride as obsolete. They want to wipe out national boundaries when it means lowering standards for such things as workplace safety, the integrity of the food supply, and the like. But they want to maintain a balkanized world when national boundaries serve to protect them against higher standards. Tax policy is an example. It is not a coincidence that as global trade has expanded, the tax burden has shifted increasingly onto working people. In the U.S., corporations are contributing a paltry 10 percent of the federal income tax burden, about one-half the level they paid in the 1960s, with further declines projected in coming years. It is a symptom of a set of ground rules that let corporations reap the greatest benefits of trade and make workers bear the primary burdens. It is what happens when the trade debate wafts off into the slogans of the global economy and doesn't attend to the de-

tails—details that may leave ordinary Americans with the short end of the stick.

Moving Out

If there is one provision in the U.S. tax laws that demonstrates the hypocrisy of some free-traders, it is the subsidy for corporations that move their plants abroad. Globalization is supposed to give us a market free of preferences and subsidies, in which nations compete according to their "natural advantage." Yet the same people who preach about this idealized world market support a tax system that violates it in the most fundamental way. The U.S. tax code actually rewards companies that move their factories, know-how, or financial operations abroad. Close shop in the U.S., shift your assets to Singapore, China, or Bermuda, and the U.S. Treasury rewards you for your trouble. Under a practice called "deferral," runaway plants pay no tax at all on their earnings abroad until they bring that income back into the U.S., which may be never.

This may strain belief. Corporations already have no shortage of enticements to abandon the U.S. in favor of such locales—sweat-shop wages, weak environmental standards, sometimes even slave labor. The last thing the federal government should do is create a tax bribe on top of all that—or so one would think. Yet that's exactly what Congress has done. This reward system for runaway plants, and other assets, costs federal taxpayers some $3.4 billion a year and rising. It is part of why the U.S. has lost well over 3 million well-paying manufacturing jobs since 1979.

Why does such a thing exist? Deferral illustrates a basic principle of tax boondoggles: "Once in, never out." There is no provision in the tax code called "deferral." It is the result of other provisions drafted for other purposes. It was tolerable in the beginning because multinationals were not that large a part of commerce. In the aftermath of World War II, when Europe was devastated and America had productive capacity to spare, it seemed justifiable. As Europe and Asia became commercial rivals, however, deferral became an indiscriminate subsidy the U.S. could not afford. But by this time it had a big corporate constituency that had latched onto deferral as a way to multiply the benefits of tax havens around the world. Try to change it, and you will be accused of trying to dismantle the free enterprise system, and of turning America into the next Haiti. I speak from experience on this.

Nowadays the subsidy lobby argues that deferral is necessary for U.S. companies to compete in foreign markets. But I cannot understand why the U.S. government should be so solicitous of U.S.-based firms if they aren't going to invest in the U.S in the first place. Why should American taxpayers pay for the services of a military defense that benefits these companies—including trade negotiations and defense—while they scramble around the globe looking for ways to avoid their fair share of the bill?

Lobbyists also say that the deferral bonus is only temporary, until the earnings come back into the U.S. Yet in practice those profits tend to pile up abroad where they can be used for currency speculation or new overseas investment. "There are huge sums out there—trillions of dollars," says Michael McIntyre, a law professor at Wayne State University. Moreover, tax lawyers have created a minor industry out of devising ways to bring those profits back into the U.S. without the tax collectors noticing. The 1986 tax reform act tightened up this area somewhat. But where there's a tax lawyer, there's a way. "I suspect there are people who do it regularly and are hoping not to be audited," says McIntyre, who used to devise such strategies himself. But let's give them the benefit of the doubt. Let's grant, for the sake of argument, that corporations need deferral to compete in foreign markets. That still doesn't explain why they need it when they move plants abroad and then sell the products back into the U.S. In that case, the provision is a direct subsidy for putting U.S. factory workers out of work. It is a slap in the face to the company that strives to keep its jobs here at home.

The answer to the deferral problem is simple. I have been proposing it in Congress for several years. At the very least we ought to eliminate this practice when U.S. firms set up factories in foreign tax havens and then sell those products back into the U.S. This would provide a measure of justice for the company struggling to keep its workforce in the U.S., and it would move us a step closer to a global marketplace that functions the way its advocates say it should.

Shady Transfers

Moving plants and other assets abroad is one way multinationals avoid their fair share of the tax burden. Another is the use of accounting shell games to shift their income to outside the United States. This second scam is called "transfer pricing." Multinationals can take advantage of transfer pricing because the face they present to tax administrators and other legal authorities is very different from the face they present to the public. To the public, Sony Corporation—to take a random example—is simply Sony. Whether people are shopping in New York or Topeka, Oslo or Gdansk, the company appears the same. And as a general rule when the company reports its earnings to shareholders, it does so as a unified world-wide business. To tax agencies, however, the multinational presents itself as a complicated network of affiliates legally organized hither and yon. There might be a Sony U.S., a Sony Brazil, a Sony in tax havens such as Singapore and Bermuda, ad infinitum. Sometimes there are valid reasons for such arrangements. But in practice, corporations can use their complex intra-corporate webs to play all sorts of games, and taxes are high on the list.

This is where the $8,252 wrist-watch batteries come in. The prices seem ridiculous, but only if you don't understand the game. The multinational doesn't really spend that money because it charges the inflated price to itself. It takes the money out of one pocket—its operations in the U.S.—and puts it into another, which is its operations abroad. The effect is to shift profits out of the U.S. and therefore beyond the shelter of the Internal Revenue Code. You can't make money buying ball-point pens for $8,500 and selling them for $3.98 and that's what transfer pricing is all about.

Transfer pricing is probably the single most important reason that so many major corporations pay little or no federal income tax. "The bottom line is that the American public is being robbed," says Finance Professor Simon Pak of Florida International University who has studied this question closely.

Professor Pak and his colleague, Professor John Zdanowicz, have estimated that this scam cost U.S. taxpayers some $43 billion last year, or more than $117 million a day. They reached this estimate by examining customs receipts, which declare the purchase or sale prices of products passing across the U.S. border. They tallied both the extraordinarily high prices for products coming into the country, and the extraordinarily low prices for products going out. (Low nominal export prices are another way to shift income out of the U.S.) Then they used a sophisticated computer model to make a conservative estimate of the revenue implications.

The results make the Pentagon procurement office seem a model of probity. I've already mentioned some of the super-high prices for imports. The export prices were just as absurd: There were missile launchers sold to Venezuela for $59.50; automatic teller machines to the Dominican Republic for $45.25; venetian blinds to Germany for 12 cents; tractors to Canada for $448.41. I know a lot of farmers in North Dakota who would like to get a deal like that. A revenue loss of over $40 billion is not a small amount of change. But money is not the only issue. It undermines the legitimacy of the whole federal tax system when the large and powerful can avoid their share of the burden through strategies like these. One would think the Treasury would be concerned, and it is in a sense. Yet the way it tries to address the problem is so out of touch with reality that it seems lifted from an episode of the Keystone Kops.

Basically, the Treasury accepts at face value the lawyer's fiction that a multinational corporation is composed of truly independent entities, incorporated in different nations and seeking their own maximum advantage in the market. It pretends that Sony Bermuda, say, really is totally separate from Sony U.S., Sony Japan, and the rest. IRS agents literally comb through the transactions between a U.S. subsidiary and its affiliates abroad, and try to adjust them to "arms length prices"—i.e., what the price would have been if the entities really had been independent of one another.

This is like trying to disentangle a vat of spaghetti with a toothpick. Conceptually, the approach is totally out to lunch. The subsidiaries of a multinational corporation aren't independent. They are like organs of the same body. One reason a multinational exists is to overcome the limitations of arms-length dealing. "The very existence of integrated multinational corporations is evidence that the arms-length system does not reflect economic reality," says Reuven S. Avi-Yonah, assistant professor of law at Harvard University Law School.

In other words, the quest for an arms-length price for transactions within a multinational group is a quest for something that does not generally exist. Stanley I. Langbein, a professor at the University of Miami law school who served in the Treasury's Office of International Tax Counsel, agrees that the arms-length method "does not work and cannot be made to work."

The result is a hapless, bureaucratic undertaking that is an enormous drain on resources. The audit hours are endless, as is the resulting litigation. The General Accounting Office has called these cases "burdensome, time consuming, and expensive" for all concerned. In 1992, a survey found that some $32 billion in disputed revenue was tied up in pending Tax Court proceedings over transfer pricing issues, twice the amount of three years earlier. (The Tax Court has not made such a tally since.) In one such case, the defendant, Mobil Oil, submitted 1.3 million pages of unlabeled documents as evidence. One suspects that judges do not look forward to cases of this kind. But that Mobil Oil is willing to go to all that trouble suggests how much they stand to lose—or gain.

The sad part is, there's a better way. The states have had to deal with the basic problem—corporations operating across jurisdictional borders—much longer than the federal government has. And from necessity, the states devised a method that is relatively simple. It started with the railroads, which tried to tell the states that their property in a given jurisdiction was worth just the salvage value of the tracks and ties. "Wait a minute," the states replied. Those tracks were part of sprawling corporate enterprises, and you couldn't reckon the value of the part without taking into account the value of the whole.

So the states developed the "unit rule," which regards the railroad as what it is—a unitary business, though operating in different states and perhaps through various corporate entities. Accordingly, for purposes of property-tax assessment, the states apportioned the value of the whole over the various parts. Later, when the states enacted income taxes they applied this same basic method. They took the income of the entire enterprise and apportioned it among the different states according to a formula. If a tenth of the property, payroll, and sales were in a particular state, then a tenth of the income got reported there as well, regardless of the accounting gymnastics that a company might contrive. The formula determines only how much a company reports, not how much tax it pays. If the state wants to have low rates, or no tax at all, that's its own business. The formula method isn't perfect of course. No method is. But compared to the Treasury's approach it is a big step forward. It renders moot much of the sophisticated tax lawyering and accounting shell games that corporations employ. If every nation employed a formula approach then tax administration would be simpler and

companies could focus on their business rather than on tax avoidance, which would be good for all concerned.

Some states actually have applied the formula approach to multinationals, which was a natural extension. Is there that much difference—especially after NAFTA—between the border that runs between North Dakota and Montana and the one between those states and Canada? Yet most multinationals went ballistic, and the battle against the "unitary" method quickly became a cash cow on K Street—one of those contentious Washington issues that drags on for years beneath the radar of mainstream media. Eventually, pressure from multinational corporations became too great, and California—the leader in the simplification movement—had to relent. Other states followed suit. Today about half a dozen states permit multinationals to file as unitary businesses but don't require it. Once again, corporations can choose globalization when it suits them but can hide behind national borders when it doesn't.

The truly weird part is that Treasury has seen the futility of its archaic methods. It is moving slowly toward the formula approach—but in an obscure, case-by-case way. The latest chapter in this administrative fiasco is something called Advanced Pricing Agreements or APAs. Basically the corporations sit down with the IRS behind closed doors and negotiate their transfer prices. In effect, they negotiate their own tax bills; and as though that weren't bad enough, Congress, in its infinite solicitude, has made these agreements secret except for publication in vague general terms. To put this another way, there are two income-tax systems in America today. Working people pay what they have to, while the largest corporations pay pretty much what they want to. The IRS actually has shifted audit resources in recent years so that it comes down harder on small taxpayers and easier on the bigger ones. The rampant corporate avoidance is taking us down the path of countries such as Italy, where people think that only suckers pay. Speaking of the secret APAs, Professor Avi-Yonah writes, "This is hardly the type of practice one wishes to encourage in a tax system based on both voluntary compliance and the impression that wealthy taxpayers are subject to the same standards as everyone else."

The practice also confirms what many Americans suspect about the global economy generally—that if you are a real person you bear the burdens, and if you are a large corporation then you enjoy the gains. The burdens should be shared so that the gains can be shared too.

As with deferral, the answer here is not hard. We need to develop consistent formulas to apportion the income of multinational firms. Such an approach would not be perfect. But it would be an improvement and it would demonstrate to people that the actual rules of trade are in synch with the rhetoric of globalization. People are getting taken; and unless we start looking at the details—unless we debate the rules of trade in concrete terms rather than as theologians—things are going to get worse.

Byron Dorgan is a Democratic Senator from North Dakota.

Free Trade on Trial—
Ten Years of NAFTA

The North American Free-Trade Agreement is ten years old this week.
It has proved a success, though not in the way its advocates promised.

FROM the start, the North American Free-Trade Agreement was bitterly controversial in all three of the countries taking part—the United States, Canada and Mexico. Its terms, which went into effect on January 1st 1994, were argued over line by line: despite its name, the agreement fell far short of scrapping all trade restrictions, and the fine print of the various exemptions and exclusions gave rise to heated argument. More than this, the agreement was attacked as bad in principle. Everybody recognised that NAFTA was an extraordinarily bold attempt to accelerate economic integration—or, as critics put it, an experiment in reckless globalisation. As such, they said, it would destroy jobs, make the poor worse off and start an environmental race to the bottom.

Equally, advocates of the agreement made some bold claims about the good it would bring. Far from destroying jobs, it would create lots of new and better ones; incomes would rise and the poor would benefit proportionately; growth would accelerate and, to the extent that this posed environmental challenges, extra resources would be available to meet them.

Unsurprisingly, a mere ten years' experience has settled few of these quarrels. Today, most trade economists read the evidence as saying that NAFTA has worked: intra-area trade and foreign investment have expanded greatly. Trade sceptics and anti-globalists look at the same history and feel no less vindicated. Look at Mexico's growth since 1994, they say—dismal for much of the period. Look at the contraction of manufacturing employment in the United States. As for the environment, go to the places south of the border where the *maquiladoras* cluster, and take a deep breath.

Politically, the sceptics, ten years on, can fairly claim victory. NAFTA is unpopular in all three countries. In Mexico, which stood to gain most from freer trade (since its barriers were so much higher at the outset) and which has indeed benefited greatly according to most economic appraisals, the agreement is widely regarded as having been useless or worse. In a poll conducted at the end of 2002 by Ipsos-Reid for the Woodrow Wilson Centre in Washington, only 29% of Mexicans interviewed said that NAFTA has benefited Mexico; 33% thought that it had hurt the country and 33% said that it had made no difference. In all three countries, the perceived results of NAFTA seem to have eroded support for further trade liberalisation.

NAFTA's champions are partly to blame for this: they oversold their case. It was never plausible, for instance, to expect that NAFTA would be a net creator of jobs. Trade policy is not a driver of overall employment; it affects the pattern of jobs, rather than the total number. To the extent that NAFTA succeeds in stimulating trade and cross-border flows of investment, jobs in each member country are created in some industries and destroyed in others. This was bound to be a painful process for some, even if it succeeded in making the member countries' economies more efficient overall, and hence in raising average incomes. Here was another instance of false advertising: NAFTA was never going to be, as some enthusiasts claimed, a win-win proposition for all of North America's citizens, even if all three countries could hope to gain in the aggregate.

Yes, it worked

So far as its economic effects are concerned, the right question to ask of NAFTA is simply whether it indeed succeeded in stimulating trade and investment. The answer is clear: it did. In 1990 the United States' exports to, and imports from, Canada and Mexico accounted for about a quarter of its trade; now they account for about a third. That is a dramatic switch, especially when one notes that the United States' non-NAFTA trade has itself grown strongly over the period. There is plenty of economic evidence to suggest that expanded trade, as a rule, raises incomes and future rates of growth. So it is pretty clear that NAFTA achieved as much as one could sensibly have expected it to achieve.

Why then is the agreement so widely regarded by non-economists as a failure? The answer lies partly in the interplay of politics and economics, and accordingly is different in each of the member countries. But one theme is common to all three: a tendency to blame NAFTA in particular, and international integration in general, for every economic disappointment of the past ten years, however tenuous the connection may be.

Debate in the United States has been preoccupied by fears over loss of jobs—by the "giant sucking sound" of work moving south, in Ross Perot's phrase from the early 1990s. A variety of estimates of NAFTA's direct effect on American labour have been made—with job losses running as high, according to one disputed study, as 110,000 a year between 1994 and 2000.

But, as already noted, direct losses do not tell the whole story: changing the pattern of employment is after all one of the reasons for promoting trade. So long as lost jobs are balanced by new ones, the overall effect on employment will be small. As Gary Hufbauer and Jeffrey Schott of the Institute for International Economics point out, between 1994 and 2000 the United States economy created more than 2m new jobs a year. Manufacturing employment has dwindled (with NAFTA as one relatively minor cause among many); jobs in other industries have more than made up the losses. And since the mid-1990s, at any rate, the great majority of new jobs created have paid above-median wages.

Against this background, even NAFTA's highest estimated direct losses can hardly be regarded as crippling. America's evident disenchantment with liberal trade has less to do with the economic depredations of the 1990s—when the economy boomed, in fact—than with a political failure to make the case for free trade against its increasingly vocal and well-organised opponents.

In Canada, initial concerns were less to do with the flight of low-skilled manufacturing jobs, because trade with Mexico seemed a less pressing issue than it was for the United States, and more to do with other sorts of international competition. As it turned out, Canadian unemployment fell markedly during the 1990s (from 11% of the labour force in 1993 to 7% in 2000). The main fear, instead, was that closer integration with the American economy would threaten Canada's European-style social-welfare model, either by leading certain practices and policies (such as the generous minimum wage) to be regarded as directly uncompetitive, or else by pressing down on the country's base of corporate and personal taxes, thereby starving public-spending programmes of resources.

Canadian public spending was indeed squeezed somewhat during the 1990s—not because NAFTA eroded the tax base, but because public borrowing had reached an unsustainable level of 8% of GDP in the early 1990s. The problem was successfully addressed: Canada has lately run a budget surplus. Despite the fiscal retrenchment, and despite NAFTA, its social-welfare model stands intact, and in sharp contrast with that of the United States. The fact is, most Canadians are willing to pay the higher taxes that are required to finance generous public services (including universal health care). As long as this remains true, NAFTA poses no threat to the Canadian way of life.

Down south

What about Mexico? The very point of NAFTA, to listen to some of its advocates, was to destroy the Mexican way of life—and replace it with something better. The overall verdict on NAFTA rests heavily on whether the pact proved a success for the country it was bound to affect most. NAFTA was never going to have much impact on the huge economy of the United States. But as recently as the mid-1980s Mexico was still an almost completely closed economy. For Mexico, NAFTA promised to be revolutionary.

Unfortunately, soon after NAFTA came into effect, the country was overwhelmed by a largely unrelated economic shock, the Tequila crisis of 1994-95. Huge capital inflows into the country in the early 1990s were followed by rapid outflows towards the end of 1994, causing the peso to plunge. The authorities were forced to float the currency on December 20th of that year, and before long it had lost nearly half of its value against the dollar.

The financial system collapsed, with many banks going under as years of bad loans were exposed. In the end, at huge cost, the government had to bail out the banks. The repercussions of the Tequila crisis for Mexico were immense. The banks, for instance, have still not fully recovered, and the subsequent lack of credit and financial services does much to explain the anaemic performance of Mexico's domestic economy over the past decade. All this makes judging the effects of NAFTA very difficult.

Take real wages. Although Mexican workers have managed impressive gains in productivity over the past ten years to compete with America and Canada, real wages have not kept pace. This allows NAFTA's critics to argue that the typical Mexican has not benefited from the treaty as he should have done, and that big business has creamed off most of the profits.

The truth is different. The Tequila crisis led to an immediate fall of about 20% in Mexican wages (more in dollar terms), while productivity kept going up. So although real wages have been rising ever since the country began to recover in 1996, they are only just reaching their levels of before the crisis. The lasting influence of higher productivity on wages may not be clear for another decade, when the effects of the Tequila crisis have fully faded away. That said, the country recovered much more quickly from the Tequila crisis than from its previous financial crises in 1982 and 1986—and this was indeed mainly due to NAFTA. Speedily arranged help from Bill Clinton's administration spurred the strong recovery. That aid sprang from America's desire not to let its new partner go under.

The closeness of the link to America, the destination of almost 90% of Mexican exports, is of course a disadvantage when America goes into recession, as it did in 2001. Mexico lost thousands of export jobs in that downswing. On the other hand, NAFTA has insulated Mexico against the financial instability that swept through Argentina, Brazil and other parts of South America in the first years of the new century. It has given Mexico an investment-grade credit rating, and allowed it to issue—almost uniquely in Latin America—very long-term local-currency bonds and mortgage-backed securities. Investors now think of Mexico more as a North American than a Latin American country.

Former President Carlos Salinas de Gortari embraced NAFTA mostly to attract more foreign investment and to boost the *maquiladora* manufacturers (set up in 1965 to allow tariff-free import of materials for assembly and re-export to the United States). Mexico's trade has surged, especially with the United States. In 2002 it totalled $250 billion, and the country's traditional deficit with its northern neighbour has been converted into a surplus in every year of NAFTA membership.

After 1994 foreign direct investment also shot up. NAFTA was designed to make investors feel more legally secure, and foreign companies duly poured in to take advantage of Mexico's closeness to the world's wealthiest market. The rise in export manufacturing also greatly reduced the country's dependence on the volatile price of oil. Moreover, NAFTA jobs in export businesses have usually been good ones, paying on average substantially more than jobs in the rest of the economy.

It hardly needs saying, however, that Mexico has no shortage of problems that NAFTA has so far failed to solve. One is the challenge of providing decently paid work for all those who need it. The chief symptom of the failure to do that, of course, is the continuing outflow of migrants.

The biggest pressure on emigration, in turn, is the crisis in the countryside. The traditional Mexican farmer had about eight hectares of his own land and some communal land for livestock. This made his family self-sufficient in everything from maize and beans to meat and milk. Even before NAFTA this traditional rural economy was disappearing, as demographic pressure caused the land to be subdivided, and many *campesinos* now eke out a living year by year, ever on the edge of disaster. "If the weather does not help us, we are completely lost," says Dionisio Garcia, who farms a smallholding in the southern state of Tlaxcala.

Most of Mr Garcia's colleagues have simply given up. He estimates that up to 90% of the heads of families in his area now spend at least six months of the year working in Canada or the United States. "What they earn there in four months, we don't earn here in a year," he says. They are part of an estimated 1.3m people who have left the land since 1994. The young, besides, are no longer much interested in making a living from the land; they are going off to drive taxis in the city, or to sell air-conditioners.

Mr Garcia says that he can no longer sell his surplus maize to Mexican wholesalers because he has been undercut by cheaper and better American imports. For him, NAFTA and free trade have been "totally bad". And yet trade in Mexico's two staples, maize and beans, is still not free; the last tariffs will remain until 2008.

The flood of corn from America's mid-west is the most hated aspect of NAFTA for Mexicans. The government argues that it has to import so much because Mexico's small farmers cannot feed all Mexicans, let alone turn a profit. But critics allege that Americans are selling so cheap that they are, in effect, dumping the stuff. Besides, they receive vast subsidies from their government. NAFTA explicitly pledges to eliminate these, but it has not done so yet.

Some Mexican farmers have shown that they can make a good living under NAFTA. Export earnings from horticulture have tripled since 1994, to over $3.5 billion; exports of fresh vegetables have risen by 80% and fresh fruit by 90%. If farmers can exploit local conditions and invest in a crop that can be exported during American or European winters, they can make money. The star performer is the Hass avocado from the state of Michoacán, in the west of Mexico, where the climate is mild and the soil fertile. Before NAFTA, the United States banned it because of infestation by insects. After a clean-up and monitoring operation, supervised under NAFTA rules, avocados from Michoacán were accepted into most states of America in 1997. Exports have increased from 6,000 tonnes to 30,000 tonnes a year.

Overall, though, Mexico continues to rely on low-cost assembly, and the advantage of preferential entry into the American market. Increasingly, other countries offer cheaper labour. With China's accession to the World Trade Organisation, Mexico has already lost much of the advantage that NAFTA gave it. Many Mexicans still think that a reviving American economy, by itself, can buoy their own. But in the next upswing, as America deepens its trade links with other states, this may prove untrue.

NAFTA alone has not been enough to modernise the country or guarantee prosperity. It was never reasonable to suppose that it would be—though that did not stop many of its advocates saying so. NAFTA has spurred trade for all its members. That is a good thing. But trade can do only so much. Sadly, successive Mexican governments have failed to deal with the problems—corruption, poor education, red tape, crumbling infrastructure, lack of credit and a puny tax base—that have prevented Mexicans and foreign investors alike from exploiting the openings which freer trade afforded. Don't blame NAFTA for that.

TRADE IN THE AMERICAS:
All in the familia

This weekend's summit in Quebec will concentrate on the creation of a Free-Trade Area of the Americas. The Bush administration is all for it; South America's biggest economy, Brazil, is not so sure

Sao Paulo and Washington, DC

AT THEIR meeting last month to prepare for the 34-country summit of the Americas this weekend, President George Bush kept a promise to look a sceptical President Fernando Henrique Cardoso of Brazil in the eye and swear that the United States really wants free trade. Brazil, by far South America's largest economy, has so far shown little enthusiasm for talking about a Free-Trade Area of the Americas (FTAA). It is doubtful, not least, because it does not believe Mr Bush can overcome free trade's opponents in the United States; and because a watered-down or hobbled FTAA might be worse than no agreement at all.

Mr Bush shows every sign of being keen as mustard on free trade. His trade representative, Robert Zoellick, is even keener. Mr Bush wants to pursue free trade on three levels: bilateral deals with single trading partners, regional pacts such as the FTAA, and global negotiations in the World Trade Organisation (WTO). This makes for a lot of irons in the fire. Getting his wish, however, will depend on exactly the things Brazil is worried about: his capacity to stand up to domestic industries begging for protection, and his ability to get fast-track authority—now renamed Trade Promotion Authority, or TPA—from Congress. Getting that will depend on how persuasively he can sell his policies to Americans at large.

Mr Zoellick, who litters his speeches with quotes from his boss as though he were Chairman Mao, sees the FTAA as the key to regaining momentum for trade policy. He thinks Bill Clinton lost it by failing to obtain the renewal of fast-track power and by presiding over the meltdown in the global trade talks in Seattle in 1999. The FTAA is as good a place as any to get trade policy moving forward again—if, that is, the neighbours can be made to agree.

The draft agreement for the FTAA already exists; it was prepared at a meeting of trade ministers in Buenos Aires earlier this month, though it will not be made public until the summit is over. A framework similar to that of the North American Free-Trade Agreement (NAFTA) between the United States, Canada and Mexico would be extended southwards, with negotiations to finish by January 2005 and implementation to follow by the end of that year. The FTAA would open a free-trade umbrella over nearly 800m people who accounted for more than $11 trillion in GDP last year. If its effects proved to be anything like NAFTA's, the whole continent would be in for a trade boom.

It will be quite a challenge, however, to reach an agreement acceptable to all 34 countries. (Cuba is excluded at the United States' insistence and French Guiana, since it is officially part of France, is not taking part.) Historically, the continent's more far-flung countries have not made much effort to trade with each other, tending instead to do business with their former colonial masters in Europe. (The banana war, the most contentious result of that policy, was resolved last week. In the 1990s, economic liberalisation and the formation of regional trade blocks such as NAFTA and Mercosur (Brazil, Argentina, Uruguay and Paraguay) meant that trade within the continent grew faster than GDP and faster than world trade in general (see chart) but South America's markets are still less open than those of the Asian tigers.

Suspicions in Brazil

Until recently, Brazil was trying to get its South American neighbours to join it in foot-dragging over the FTAA, or at least to

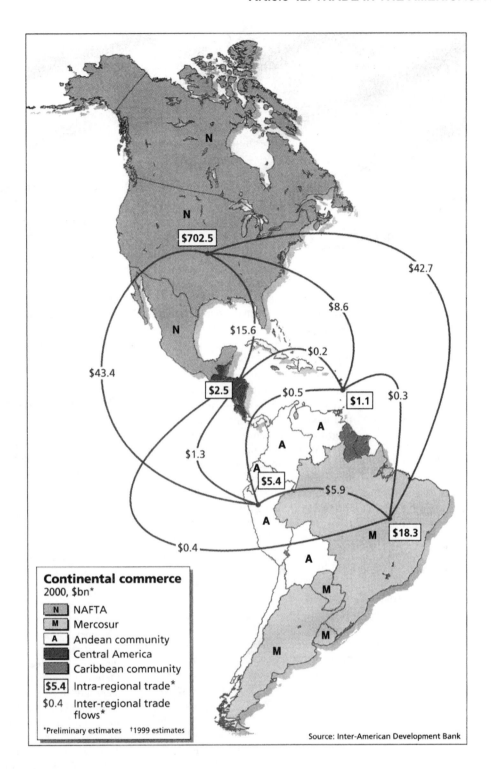

Continental commerce
2000, $bn*

N	NAFTA
M	Mercosur
A	Andean community
■	Central America
■	Caribbean community
$5.4	Intra-regional trade*
$0.4	Inter-regional trade flows*

*Preliminary estimates   †1999 estimates

Source: Inter-American Development Bank

form a united front to take a tough line with the United States. But its strategy has flopped as its neighbours have become ever more enticed by the idea of improved access to the world's biggest consumer market. The United States has been dangling this prospect skilfully in front of the other countries. Chile's president, Ricardo Lagos, was invited to the White House this week to hear from Mr Bush that a bilateral trade deal between them could be signed as

early as this year. Argentina and Uruguay have taken the bait, and have made it clear that any blockage in the FTAA talks would not stop them from doing some other sort of deal with the United States.

As a result, Brazil has come round to the view that, since everyone else wants the talks to go ahead, it might as well join in and seek the best deal it can. One of the most important signs of its change of attitude was the sacking, this month, of Sam-

uel Pinheiro Guimaraes, the head of the foreign ministry's think-tank and a fierce critic of the FTAA. This week, Celso Lafer, the foreign minister, attacked the "ostrich mentality" of those in Brazil, such as his former subordinate, who oppose its participation in the talks. And he admitted, more frankly than any senior Brazilian figure has so far, that his country risks losing much of its existing trade if the rest of the Americas rushes to sign a deal without it.

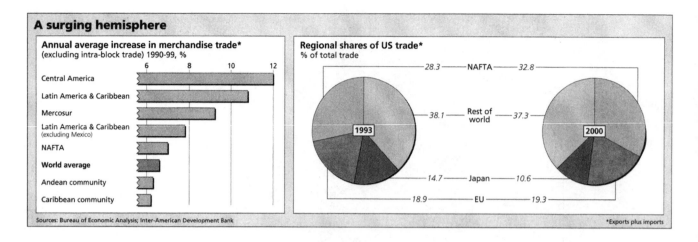

A surging hemisphere

Annual average increase in merchandise trade*
(excluding intra-block trade) 1990-99, %

- Central America
- Latin America & Caribbean
- Mercosur
- Latin America & Caribbean (excluding Mexico)
- NAFTA
- World average
- Andean community
- Caribbean community

Regional shares of US trade*
% of total trade

1993 / 2000

- NAFTA — 28.3 / 32.8
- Rest of world — 38.1 / 37.3
- Japan — 14.7 / 10.6
- EU — 18.9 / 19.3

Sources: Bureau of Economic Analysis; Inter-American Development Bank

*Exports plus imports

Brazil's businesses have suddenly realised that the FTAA is now more than a remote hypothesis and that they ought to be preparing for it. The country's National Confederation of Industry (CNI) has just completed, though not yet published, its first studies of the impact Americas-wide free trade could have on Brazilian industry. Sandra Rios, an economist at the CNI, says there is not yet a consensus that the FTAA would be good for Brazil overall. But whereas, until recently, only those who feared freer trade were making their voices heard, industries that stand to gain are now speaking up in favour of the talks.

One such is the textile industry, which believes its exports of T-shirts and towels to the United States would be far greater if America lifted its import quotas. The Brazilian Textile Industry Association is so keen on the FTAA that it is calling for it to start sooner than 2006—much to the irritation of the Brazilian government, which successfully fought in Buenos Aires this month to stop the United States from bringing forward the date. Other areas where Brazil is highly competitive, and would thus benefit from freer trade, are agriculture, especially beef and soyabeans, steel-making and ceramics.

Some Brazilian industries that fear being wiped out by North American competitors, such as chemicals and paper-making, have mostly themselves to blame. They have failed to merge and restructure to reach world-class competitiveness. They claim they cannot find affordable finance to do so, but Brazilian companies would find it much easier to attract investors if they undid their complicated holding structures and generally treated minority shareholders better. There is plenty of time to do all this by the FTAA's proposed starting date; just as there is plenty of time for

the government to boost the export prospects of all Brazil's industries by pushing reforms of the country's burdensome tax system.

Those industries with most to fear from free trade, such as machinery and electronic goods, are precisely those that successive Brazilian governments have coddled with protectionist tariffs, arguing that this would give them breathing-space to grow big enough to take on foreign rivals. As a result, they have been under little pressure to seek world-class productivity, technology and marketing, and have not bothered. The failure of this strategy is a riposte to the arguments of Mr Guimaraes (the sacked diplomat) and the left-wing Workers' Party, who say that joining the FTAA would mean forgoing independent trade and industrial policies and thus being unable to build competitive industries.

Brazil's neighbours have become increasingly sceptical of such arguments. Argentina is abandoning Mercosur's common tariffs pact and abolishing import duties on machinery because it believes these have served only to prop up inefficient Brazilian firms while preventing Argentine industry from introducing new technology. Francisco Panizza, a Uruguayan political scientist, argues that pleas from Brazilian industries for "time to adjust" are absurd, given that many such industries have been in existence for half a century or more.

Besides, says Heinz-Peter Elstrodt of McKinsey, a management consultancy, many of the Brazilian industries that are, overall, lagging behind include some firms that are close to world-class productivity, and others that are so far behind they may never catch up. The best firms should survive, even with new competition. The

worst, unless they adapt, will die out. Brazil's car industry is an example of this, with its newer, more efficient plants expected to drive out older, unproductive ones. But this process is beneficial, and is happening anyway. The FTAA would simply speed it up.

Protective instincts

Brazil's greatest fear is that the United States is plotting to stop it from becoming a big exporter of high-value manufactured goods and to make it return to its historic role of churning out low-value commodities. This is not entirely paranoia. The United States currently applies a whole range of duties, quotas, price restraints and other measures to processed items from Brazil. Some of these will be politically difficult for Mr Bush to negotiate away.

In fact, of course, Mr Bush's America is something less than a bastion of free trade. It gives subsidies to farmers (though these are generally much reduced from their levels of a decade ago) and has imposed "anti-dumping" measures to protect steel-makers. Only last month, the debilitated American steel industry begged for extra protection from foreign competition while it restructures and updates itself. Last week's merger of NKK and Kawasaki Steel, two Japanese giants, will only enhance congressional pressure to enact emergency tariffs.

Even within NAFTA, American protectionism is by no means dead. With the expiration on March 31st of a five-year agreement on trade in softwood lumber between the United States and Canada, which amounts to roughly $10 billion a year, American producers have filed for anti-dumping measures against Canada's government-supported exporters. Disputes on dairy products and sugar could also flare up if import volumes rise. To make matters worse, Canada is embroiled in a lawsuit, brought by its postal workers' union and an anti-globalisation group, that threatens to invalidate NAFTA on the basis that it infringes Canada's sovereignty.

The toughest obstacle to true free trade is public opinion, both in the United States and in its trading partners in the Americas. Radical opposition to globalisation at grassroots level continues to grab headlines; 20,000 demonstrators are expected in Quebec city this weekend. Non-governmental organisations in the United States still shriek about jobs lost to NAFTA, even though unemployment fell to its lowest levels in decades—well below the supposedly "natural" rate—during the life of the agreement. The gap in understanding has not narrowed noticeably since the protests in Seattle.

It is in this climate that Mr Bush and Mr Zoellick must try to extract TPA from Congress. This power would allow Mr Zoellick and his team (when he has finally got it in place) to negotiate trade deals in full and then present them to Congress for a vote. He has pointed enviously to similar powers vested in the European Union's trade commissioner. The EU has signed 20 substantial pacts since 1990, and has 15 more on the way; over the same period the United States has ratified only two, with four more in the works. Although the United States has never shown a predilection for European-style agreements based on customs unions, the contrast is a stark one.

The fight for TPA, though, is likely to be long. Congress wants to attach provisions requiring Mr Zoellick to seek labour and environmental standards as part of trade agreements. These have featured in previous fast-track authorisations, but Mr Bush is dead-set against them. Developing countries also object to these standards, which they say could open avenues to protection against their exports. Cal Dooley, a Democrat in the House of Representatives who worked closely with Mr Zoellick's predecessor, Charlene Barshefsky, thinks that TPA could become a reality in the next 18 months. But he also says that the current Congress is not ready to take any dramatic decisions to promote freer trade.

This week, Mr Zoellick began meeting business and non-governmental interest groups in an effort to start persuading American dissenters. He has promised to use the Internet to spread his message of free trade. The black and Latino media, representing groups who are traditionally wary of losing jobs to cheap foreign labour, are also likely to get visits from Mr Zoellick. Lastly, he promises that the president will address the country about the importance of trade in due time. As Mr Clinton found during the arguments over NAFTA in the early 1990s, it is not a particularly easy pitch to make.

Given these difficulties on the American side, Brazil still talks of the FTAA as merely one of several options. It argues that Mercosur's parallel talks on a free-trade deal with the European Union have at least as much potential to boost Brazil's trade. This is true, but the talks with the EU are at least as likely as the FTAA ones to founder on the issue of farm protection. As for its other option, a deepened and widened Mercosur, this seems a receding prospect: if the FTAA talks were to fail, the main priority for Brazil's current Mercosur part-

ners, as well as potential members such as Chile and the Andean countries, would be to seek the best possible deal with the United States. The alternative would be to fortify a southern trade block that most feel, rightly or wrongly, has brought more benefits to Brazil than to them in the ten years it has been in existence.

The United States, too, has other options. Abandoning the warm and conciliatory (if often empty) rhetoric of the post-Seattle Clinton era, the new administration has adopted a cocky, take-it-or-leave-it attitude towards its trading partners. Messrs Bush and Zoellick hold the keys to the biggest market in the world, and they know it.

Mr Zoellick has repeatedly stated that the United States is interested in working with fast-moving traders, but will leave laggards by the side of the road. With respect to the FTAA, he says, "We will reward good performers, and while we want to bring on others in the region, we won't wait for ever."

The administration's multi-pronged trade policy fits well with this reluctance to curry favour with other countries. Its strategy might be as follows: if WTO negotiations are going too slowly, then concentrate on the FTAA; if the FTAA bogs down, sign bilateral deals with enthusiastic parties such as Chile. Mr Bush's trade policy echoes his overall approach to foreign affairs. Friendly neighbours are welcome; sceptics need not even knock. Brazil, the third-biggest economy in what Mr Bush likes to call "the hemispheric *familia*", will get some sort of trade deal with the United States; but full free trade can wait until Brazil really wants it.

Latin America's Volatile Financial Markets

"As Latin America enters an era marked by the globalization of communications and markets, two factors dominate its economic development: the region's relatively moderate importance to the world economy, and its continued dependence on international capital markets to fuel local growth."

Jonathan Lemco and Scott B. MacDonald

The major economies of Latin America have made remarkable progress since the early 1990s. Strong growth has been accompanied by sharply curtailed inflation rates and impressive debt management. Foreign investment regimes have been overhauled and considerable attention has been given to attracting outside capital. The region has made an amazing shift: no longer considered a home to bad debtors hostile to foreign capital, it is now one of the more attractive destinations for international financial markets. Nowhere in the world, perhaps, has such an impressive turnaround occurred.

Yet substantial regional problems remain. Although Latin America's economies exhibited surprising resilience in the aftermath of the 1997 Asian financial crisis, concern remains high about local governments' ability to maintain the course of structural reforms and strong economic growth. This concern most recently resurfaced when Argentina's lagging commodity exports and concomitant foreign-debt-repayment pressures ultimately forced it to turn in December to the International Monetary Fund and private banks for nearly $40 billion in assistance.

DEBT DEPENDENCY

As Latin America enters an era marked by the globalization of communications and markets, two factors dominate its economic development: the region's relatively moderate importance to the world economy, and its continued dependence on international capital markets to fuel local growth. Latin America, however, is not an un-derdeveloped region without a dynamic of its own: the region has come a considerable distance in the second half of the twentieth century in terms of economic restructuring, the upgrading of infrastructure, and the creation of a better environment for trade. It has even produced its own crop of international businesses, such as television and media giant Grupo Televisa, cement producer Cemex, and PDVSA, Venezuela's state-owned oil company. Although some of these corporations are active in the United States and Europe, employing thousands, they are the exceptions; Latin America's economy makes up a relatively small part of the global economy. With a GDP of $1.9 trillion (about half that of Japan's), Latin America accounts for only slightly more than 6 percent of the world's economy. Its population of 410 million is but 7 percent of the world's total. In the great scheme of global markets, Latin America is ahead of Africa but behind Asia, the Middle East, and Europe.

The greatest challenge facing the nations of Latin America is dependence on international capital markets. The United States is by far the region's largest investor, although Japan and the European countries are becoming more active. Tapping these markets, Latin American countries raised $65.9 billion in 1998 and another $61.4 billion in 1999 in bonds, equities, and loans. Most investment (over 60 percent), not surprisingly, goes to the three largest economies in the region: Mexico, Brazil, and Argentina. This international source of capital is important, since these three countries incurred current-account deficits (that is, deficits in merchandise and services trade) in 1998 and 1999, with Argentina and Brazil posting deficits in excess of 4 percent of GDP.

Since the late twentieth century, the United States has been a major creditor for Latin America. The root cause of this relationship is Latin America's long tradition of low domestic savings rates, which has made it highly dependent on foreign capital. The fortunes of Argentina, Brazil, Chile, and the region's other nations are thus tied to United States investors' and consumers' appetites for Latin American goods and services. Most or all of the region's nations look to the wealthy American market as a primary target for their exports.

Another point of linkage with the American economy is through the dollar. Some nations, such as Argentina (through a currency board) and the Bahamas, have fixed their currencies to the United States dollar and have little control over interest and inflation rates in their nations. The incentive to follow such a path is the ability to provide greater monetary stability by linking with one of the world's strongest currencies. Dollarization—the adoption of the United States dollar in place of a local currency as legal tender—has also been implemented in El Salvador, Ecuador, and Panama, and is being considered in Mexico. Even in Brazil and Venezuela, the dollar plays a major role in trade and investment patterns. This means that, with the probable exception of Cuba, all the Latin American nations closely follow every pronouncement made by Federal Reserve Chairman Alan Greenspan; his decisions about United States interest rates have immediate consequences for all United States trading and investment partners.

In short, the countries of Latin America are extremely dependent on the United States for their export-driven growth. From an investor's perspective, the close relationship with the United States economy means that the countries offer less diversification from United States assets (stocks and bonds). Investors note other concerns as well. Virtually every nation in the region has common economic problems: relatively low savings rates, current-account deficits, and a reliance on high commodity prices (especially for oil). These are precisely the conditions that will keep foreign investors away.

WEATHERING THE ASIAN STORM

Before becoming too gloomy about Latin America's prospects, it should be acknowledged that its recent track record has been surprisingly strong. When the Asian financial crisis emerged in 1997—the collapse of foreign exchange reserves in Thailand that soon spread to Indonesia and South Asia, eventually resulting in IMF bailouts in all three cases—Latin America seemed relatively insulated at first. Although investors withdrew large sums of cash from Asia during the crisis, Latin American nations registered net inflows from the United States during that period of $17 billion.

Part of Latin America's ability to ride through the worst of the Asian storm without a return to the past of debt defaults was the result of the region's active financial restructuring throughout the late 1980s and into the 1990s. The "tequila crisis," which caused considerable chaos in Mexico in 1994–1995 when the incoming Zedillo administration botched a currency devaluation, forced a number of countries, in particular Argentina and Brazil, to strengthen their own financial sectors, which were hit hard by the overlap of the crisis. Between 1995 and 1997, economic reforms were deepened throughout the region. Consequently, when Asia imploded, Latin America was not severely affected by the crisis.

Although Latin America did not suffer any major defaults during the initial round of the Asian crisis and the default by Russia on its debt obligations in August 1998, the contagion did result in a recession. The economies of the region slowed and several weeks of foreign exchange volatility occurred, with Brazil forced to devalue its currency, the real. Ecuador was also forced to devalue the sucre and ultimately adopted the United States dollar as its currency in 2000. Ecuador also defaulted on part of its Brady bond obligations in 1999.[1] Ecuador's total foreign debt, however, was only $16.5 billion, and most international investors had already walked away from this economic train wreck. (By 2000, Ecuador had suffered two years of economic contraction, created in part by a sharp drop in oil prices.) It would have been a different matter altogether if Brazil had decided to halt payments on part of its $239-billion external debt.

COULD A FINANCIAL CRISIS REEMERGE?

With the direction of the global economy uncertain and economic growth in the United States expected to cool, the chances of another financial or economic crisis in Latin America have increased. Although Latin America enjoyed relatively strong economic growth in 2000, with Chile leading the way with a nearly 6 percent increase in GDP, prospects for 2001 have dimmed, and some have suggested that the region could suffer a major crash. Our suspicion is that it will not, although we expect continued uncertainty leading to volatility. For example, Argentina holds considerable foreign debt, perhaps as much as $123.7 billion. Although the IMF has guaranteed that nation financial support until the third quarter of 2001 through a $40-billion rescue package, at some point the moribund Argentine economy will have to grow rapidly (at a rate of 8 percent or more) to overcome this severe debt problem. The deal between the IMF and Argentina includes a broad series of reforms aimed at putting the country's accounts into the black by 2005. In particular, Argentina agreed to freeze spending for five years, pass a tough 2001 budget, and undertake comprehensive social security and pension system reforms. But it is difficult to be optimistic, especially in light of the weak political support for the program.

Much of Latin America also remains dependent on commodity exports, despite efforts in the past decade to significantly diversify. Venezuela and Ecuador rely almost entirely on their oil wealth for export income. Chile's future still hinges on copper prices, and Brazil and Argentina depend on a variety of low-tech and basic agricultural exports. Most important, Latin America remains in desperate need of more diverse sources of foreign direct investment. Brazil, Mexico, and Argentina have made tremendous efforts in the past five years to restructure their banking sectors and privatize much of their national industrial capacity. Special attempt has been made to open the state-owned utilities, telecommunications, and mining sectors to private investment. But far more must be done to correct the region's still-pervasive problems of slow growth and tremendous economic inequality. Latin America, according to IMF/World Bank data, has one of the most skewed income inequalities in the world, with a small percentage of the population holding an overwhelming amount of national wealth.

A return to the crisis years, however, appears unlikely. The most senior Central Bank and Finance Ministry officials in Brazil, Argentina, Mexico, and Chile have publicly confirmed their commitment to international standards of accounting and transparency. They visit world financial capitals regularly to brief investors and to hear investor concerns. Indeed, much of the arrogance of the past is gone, replaced by a recognition that investor interests must be adhered to or existing and future investment will disappear in the time it takes to strike a computer key.

The leading international credit rating agencies, especially Moody's, Standard and Poor's, and Fitch, carry enormous weight with investors worldwide. Their assignment of a credit rating sends an immediate signal to investors whether a nation is creditworthy. The difference between an investment-grade rating, which Mexico, Chile, Uruguay, and Trinidad and Tobago currently enjoy, and a noninvestment-grade rating, with which Brazil, Argentina, Venezuela, and other Latin American nations are saddled, translates into higher interest rates on the bonds (debts) issued by the latter countries. Hence, the less creditworthy must issue extremely attractive interest rates to entice international investors to buy their bonds; this, however, requires their citizens to pay higher taxes or receive limited public services so that their governments can meet their debt obligations in a timely manner.

Most of the governments of Latin America are intensely aware of this situation; they recognize the fickleness of the international investment community. They have made great strides to enhance their credit ratings by more prudently managing their debt obligation, by privatizing state industries, by restructuring their banking systems, by improving their accounting procedures, and by democratizing. Where there are exceptions—Venezuela, for example—the investment community has punished them severely by selling off their bonds.

As noted earlier, developing economies throughout the world that have substantial trading and investment ties with the United States are extremely vulnerable to the United States government's fiscal policies. When United States interest rate yields rise, investors worldwide reduce their international holdings to buy United States debt. As long as the American economy is recognized as the world's safest and strongest, and as long as the American dollar inspires the world's confidence, the emerging economies will remain vulnerable to changes in United States interest rate policy. Indeed, senior finance officials in Argentina, Brazil, Mexico, and Chile acknowledge freely that despite improving economic fundamentals in their nations, a recession in the United States would be disastrous for them.

Virtually all the Latin American economies are highly vulnerable to adverse shifts in the terms of trade, to slowdowns in global demand for their exports, to changes in investors' appetite for risk, and to crowding out by more creditworthy borrowers. Some are also exposed to exchange rate shocks. These nations need to minimize their vulnerabilities and maximize their adaptability, tasks that are easy to prescribe, but difficult to carry out. Nevertheless, many Latin American governments have been working diligently to mitigate these risks.

LATIN AMERICA'S CAPITAL MARKETS

In the last 10 years, a number of Latin American nations have sought to develop their own domestic bond and equity capital markets to reduce their dependence on foreign capital. Private pension plans and mutual funds have transformed Latin America's capital markets. In Argentina, for example, private pension fund managers and mutual fund industry professionals together manage assets worth $28 billion, up from almost nothing a decade ago. Mexico's private pension funds have more than $15 billion under management. Brazilian mutual funds have assets in excess of $150 billion under management. Chile, which launched its private pension fund system in 1981 and has been considered a model by other Latin American countries, has $35 billion in assets and another $10 billion held by insurance companies.

At first glance, these numbers seem impressive. But in most cases Latin American money managers invest mainly in government bonds, which are safe but offer relatively low returns. Equities are regarded as not just risky, but speculative: small investors in Argentina and Brazil who put money into equities have witnessed their savings disappear during market crises.

This deep-seated regional suspicion of the various financial systems is a serious obstacle to further development of Latin America's capital markets. Indeed, in Argentina and Chile, individuals are required by law to invest in retirement funds. Savers in these countries often see their investments as a form of taxation. It follows that evasion is a serious problem. In Argentina, for example, many people have preferred to move their savings offshore. They currently hold as much as $100 billion outside the country, a large part of it believed to be in bank accounts in neighboring Uruguay, Europe, or the Caribbean.

A similar suspicion can be found in Mexico, despite the considerable progress it has made in modernizing its capital markets. Mexico City's stock market is among the most efficient in the developing world. But after five years of steady growth, Mexican investors continue to exhibit widespread reluctance to invest in domestic equities. In fact, although Mexico has some of the finest companies in Latin America, they raise capital in the United States. Indeed, a large proportion of the Latin American investment community is risk averse. Even when they ship their wealth overseas, Latin American investors usually choose the safest investments: real estate and bank deposits. Miami and southern Florida, which have become major investment havens, have received a windfall from Latin Americans, perhaps exceeding $5 billion in 2000. Because so many Latin American investors choose to place their investments overseas, the issue of credibility remains at the forefront for international investors. Do these domestic investors know something that international investors do not? Is it worth the risk?

A MEASURED ASSESSMENT

Latin America has come a long way from the bad old days of default and near default in the 1980s. The 1990s saw considerable economic restructuring as well as sea change in ideas about the role of the private sector and foreign investment. From the rescheduling of debt and the privatization of large state assets to the liberalization of trading regimes and the advancement of more democratic governments, the nations of Latin America have gained a degree of credibility as prudent managers of their respective economies and as deserving destinations for foreign capital. The process of becoming more fully integrated into global capital markets was difficult, but the

benefit of this policy change was better access to badly needed credit. As a result, greater investor acceptance of Latin America's investment potential now exists in international financial markets.

Yet that acceptance is measured. Doubt remains about Latin America's commitment to market-oriented economic policies. Concerns continue about the vulnerability of a country like Argentina to changes in United States interest rates and its ability to access international capital markets. Political tensions in Colombia, Ecuador, Peru, and Venezuela create investor unease. And substantial socioeconomic disparities and poor educational systems temper optimism about the ability of many Latin American countries to adopt the new information technology that is driving global development.

Latin America must also deal with the nature of the investor it seeks to woo. Many of the participants in international financial markets can be fickle, driven more by herd instincts than by prudent and reasoned decisions. As Roger Lowenstein noted in *When Genius Failed: The Rise and Fall of Long-Term Capital Management* "No matter what the models say, traders are not machines guided by silicon chips; they are impressionable and imitative; they run in flocks and retreat in hordes." Clearly, an element of this can be seen in the case of Argentina in 2000. In could happen again in 2001.

NOTE

1. Brady bonds, named after United States Treasury Secretary Nicholas Brady, are commercial bank loans that have been converted into long-term bonds at a discount from their initial value. Part of the Brady bonds are also supported by United States Treasury zero coupon bonds and part are unsecured. Ecuador defaulted on the unsecured bonds.

JONATHAN LEMCO *is a director at KWR International in New York City.* SCOTT B. MACDONALD *is director of research at Aladdin Capital LLC in Stamford, Connecticut.*

From *Current History* magazine, February 2001, pp. 86-89. © 2001 by Current History, Inc. Reprinted by permission.

Japan Learns the Sun May Not Come Out Tomorrow

Abstract:

"When we remember that Japan runs a large surplus in almost every tradable manufactured product, Japanese manufacturers pay some of the highest wages in the world, and nations with lower wage costs like the United States are rapidly increasing their trade deficits with Japan in high-tech goods, it is surely obvious that the Japanese economy is one of the strongest in the world, particularly judged by the yardsticks that matter to Japanese policy makers," wrote Eamonn Fingleton in a recent book about the global economy, "In Praise of Hard Industries" (Houghton Mifflin, 1999). "Japan's very different economy should be judged by Japanese objectives, and not Western ones."

BY HOWARD W. FRENCH

Japan runs growing trade deficits with China, and now imports more from Asia than it does from North America and Europe combined. What is worse, other Asians are increasingly producing—more cheaply and sometimes more quickly—the kinds of sophisticated goods that made Japan rich. While those countries eat away at Japanese manufacturing from below, this country, at least since the advent of the personal computer, has had difficulty moving up the industrial food chain through the invention or perfection of new products. More often than not nowadays, it finds America's high-tech companies blocking its way.

"Japan is already not a considered source for manufacturing when it comes to new product development for the New Economy," said Zachary Pessin, an associate with CTR Ventures, an investment firm that focuses on start-up companies here. "It may be a producer of systems which can be used to service the New Economy, but wholesaling machinery is one step lower on the value chain than doing the actual production of new revolutionary products which create new markets and enjoy large margins."

LITTLE more than a decade ago, Japan still had the gleaming look of one of history's greatest economic success stories.

Its economy, fully recovered from World War II, was propelling Asia so strongly that Japanese confidently described the region as a flock of geese following in its wake. For many people here, the question wasn't whether Japan would overtake the United States as the world's largest economy, but when.

Rarely have the assumptions about a major nation's trajectory changed so drastically. Now, after 11 years of unrelenting decline, the desire by Japan's neighbors to follow its model have been replaced by dismay over its decay.

Most tellingly, instead of talking about overtaking the United States, the Japanese now look over their shoulders in growing horror, wondering not if, but when their country will be eclipsed by China.

It is worth recalling amid all of the gloom here that conventional wisdom about Japan has often been dead wrong. In the late 1950's, no less an authority than Edwin O. Reischauer, America's pre-eminent postwar expert on Japan, is said to have worried that the country would never manage to export enough to develop its economy.

Even now, many of Japan's economic assets remain surprisingly strong. Not the least of them are manufacturing skills that still lead the world in old industries, like cars, and in newer ones, from industrial robots to esoteric lasers. Then there is the country's sheer financial wealth. Japan alone accounts for about one-third of the world's savings, according to some estimates.

"When we remember that Japan runs a large surplus in almost every tradable manufactured product, Japanese manufacturers pay some of the highest wages in the world, and nations with lower wage costs like the United States are rapidly increasing their trade deficits with Japan in high-tech goods, it is surely obvious that the Japanese economy is one of the strongest in the world, particularly judged by the yardsticks that matter to Japanese policy makers," wrote Eamonn Fingleton in a recent book about the global economy, "In Praise of Hard Industries" (Houghton Mifflin, 1999). "Japan's very different economy should be judged by Japanese objectives, and not Western ones."

Nowadays, though, such arguments run into serious objections from the Japanese themselves. Writing about this century in an essay in the newspaper Asahi Shimbun, Yukichi Amano, a prominent commentator, recently said, "For good or ill, it will be a century in which what we built up with great pains in the 20th century will crumble away."

"The best measure of wealth is money and time," he added. "Measured this way, today's Japanese are rich but too busy to have good time. But the 21st century will make them a poor people with plenty of free time."

If it seems rash to write Japan off altogether as a global economic leader, the trends that underpin such deep pessimism are unmistakably stark. For one, the most basic raw ingredient in economic power—people themselves—is probably Japan's biggest vulnerability.

Its population is both aging and shrinking. The average household size in Tokyo is about to sink below two people, according to a recent report by the municipal government. The number of Japanese of working age peaked at 87 million in 1995, and is, according to official projections, set to decline to 55 million by 2050—a 37 percent drop.

Add to that the strong rise of new and revived competitors almost everywhere the Japanese look, and it becomes easy to understand why many Japanese feel gloomy. The landscape runs from Asia's so-called tigers to India and especially China next door, and on to the United States, whose companies are making huge inroads in Japan's franchise in consumer electronics.

JAPAN runs growing trade deficits with China, and now imports more from Asia than it does from North America and Europe combined. What is worse, other Asians are increasingly producing—more cheaply and sometimes more quickly—the kinds of sophisticated goods that made Japan rich. While those countries eat away at Japanese manufacturing from below, this country, at least since the advent of the personal computer, has had difficulty moving up the industrial food chain through the invention or perfection of new products. More often than not nowadays, it finds America's high-tech companies blocking its way.

"Japan is already not a considered source for manufacturing when it comes to new product development for the New Economy," said Zachary Pessin, an associate with CTR Ventures, an investment firm that focuses on start-up companies here. "It may be a producer of systems which can be used to service the New Economy, but wholesaling machinery is one step lower on the value chain than doing the actual production of new revolutionary products which create new markets and enjoy large margins."

As Japan prepares to choose its eighth prime minister since 1990, many people

are concluding that the country's economic problems are at heart more political than the traditional hand-wringing over slow growth and low productivity suggest.

A study of global trends released by the Central Intelligence Agency in December described Japan as a virtually rudderless nation that "will have difficulty maintaining its current position" in the world.

In fact, many experts in Japanese affairs are increasingly invoking a lack of democratic debate and alternatives as the country's principal source of weakness. The situation is best captured by the fact that the Liberal Democratic Party has been in power almost without interruption since 1955.

"EVEN now, with a prime minister whose popularity rating is at a historic low, and with the Liberal Democrats attracting only about 20 percent voter support, few Japanese are clamoring for change and strong rivals for the Liberal Democrats have yet to emerge.

Japan is a virtual one-party state, and it is the only industrialized economy that you can say that about," said Richard Katz, an economist and author of "Japan, the System that Soured" (M. E. Sharpe, 1998). "People are always expecting the very people who wrecked the economy to fix it. Rather than the fluid change that comes with alternation, problems build up for a long time until there is a wholesale change. It works, but it works differently."

The Limits to Consumption

If Asian governments think expanded domestic consumption is a recipe for sustained economic growth, they should think again. Easy credit is already fuelling personal bankruptcies and threatening the health of the financial system

By Shawn W. Crispin and Philip Segal

THINK THE ASIAN consumer will pull the region's economy along if exports to the United States and Japan should slow this year? If so, a brief look at the most booming consumer economy in Asia—Thailand—may change your mind.

Chet Pattrakornkul, for one, is banking heavily on the Thai consumer. As managing director of Kiatnakin Finance, Chet makes consumer loans to middle- and lower-income Thais to purchase used cars. Business is booming: Kiatnakin's loan portfolio grew by about 27% last year, and as Thailand's consumption boom gathers pace, his company bosses and shareholders are pushing him to boost that growth to 40% in 2003.

So what's the problem? Chet remembers acutely the excesses of the 1990s, when Thai finance companies lent willy-nilly to cash-hungry property developers. Most of those loans went bad, and finally brought on both Kiatnakin's and Thailand's financial collapse in 1997. Relatively less exposed than its competitors, Kiatnakin survived. Now, five years later, Chet is starting to grow wary about how many more low-end consumer credits he should be pushing through the door.

"Many people are buying cars who are not financially ready to have them," says Chet. "But with all the competition to lend, we cannot afford to slow down."

Kiatnakin's bet is one many Asian governments are making these days: that the credit-charged consumer can become the region's new engine for economic growth. In particular, South Korea and Thailand turned in impressive economic growth

records last year, fuelled mainly by economic policies that promote consumption. Across Asia, many other governments—from the Philippines to Malaysia—are starting to follow that lead by implementing their own pro-consumption policies.

Hard Times

Consumer demand in Asia is unlikely to replace exports as the principal engine of regional economic growth because:

- Reforms to spur growth—and thus expectations of rising incomes—are scant
- Financial systems are already stretched
- Real incomes are low compared to those in the West
- Devaluations have weakened spending power

There are plenty of arguments for more consumption-led growth in Asia. Historically high savings rates and—since the end of the Asian Crisis—hearty current-account surpluses have accumulated deep pools of untapped liquidity in many regional economies: If before 1997 Asia imported more capital than it exported in goods and services, the reverse is largely true today. Meanwhile, the lean years following the regional financial crisis have made for plenty of pent-up consumer demand.

And with many corporations still over-leveraged and overbuilt, the consumer has become as a good a bet as any for many of

Asia's banks, finance companies and policymakers. From a banker's perspective, in a region with often rudimentary bankruptcy systems, it can be easier to seize a house or a car someone can't finance than to sue a rich tycoon or Korean conglomerate to recover big money.

It all looks good on paper, but we're not there yet. "2001 was a bad year for exports, but Asia seems to have managed, and consumption was one contributing factor," says Ifzal Ali, chief economist at the Asian Development Bank in Manila. But frequently, the economic impact and importance of Asian consumers has been exaggerated. "Domestic consumption is not a substitute for exports," he says.

The rise of the Asian consumer as an idea is "all well and fine and will happen over a 10-year period," says Bill Belchere, head of Asian economics and policy research at JP Morgan Chase in Hong Kong. But Asia will get there in fits and starts: In Korea, "you're having to re-regulate the market and are probably looking at a slowdown on the consumer side at least for a while," he says.

For example, the rate of South Korean credit-card delinquencies rose to a record high in November as a result of tougher rules which make it harder to issue cards to the riskiest customers. Regulators have also introduced reduced limits on cash advances and tougher lending rules, which make it harder for some cardholders to roll over existing loans. "Private-sector consumption is likely to slow in 2003 in the aftermath of government steps to curb housing prices and household debts," says

Storing Up Trouble at the Banks

Unfinished financial modernization looms over any scenario of a consumer-led economy in Asia. Foreigners financed Asia's expansion until 1997, when the fled as a pack and much of the region crashed. Now, if exports are going to play second fiddle to consumption, foreigners will once again need to be willing to finance the party. That model works well in the United States, which attracts foreign capital thanks to a sound legal system and because it's home of the world's favourite reserve currency.

For Asia to duplicate that will be difficult. While Asian finances look better than they did in 1997, even the rudiments of a truly modern financial system are missing in some countries, and that makes Asia a riskier place to put your money than the U.S. Thailand still lacks a well-functioning centralized credit bureau, for instance. Try sustaining a really big credit card system without one.

Most Thai finance companies and banks insist their delinquency rates are still low, hovering between 2%–6%. But some economists believe banks and finance companies are storing up bigger bad-loan problems than they realize. "Many people are borrowing to buy depreciating assets at huge expense," says Sompop Manarangsan, and economist at Chulalongkorn University in Bangkok. "This will lead to big problems in the future."

JPMorgan chase estimates that nonperforming loans, or NPLs, in Thailand already amount to more than 29% of GDP, the highest among eight Asian economies excluding well-regulated Hong Kong and Singapore. In second place is Asia's other star consumer story, Malaysia, with what JPMorgan says are underestimated NPLs worth more than a quarter of GDP.

In South Korea, where banks are now under pressure to provide more money against potentially bad household debt, underestimated NPLs amount to just 7.6% of GDP. If the Korean government has slammed on the brakes on its credit revolution, shouldn't the rest of Asia be taking heed?

Shawn W. Crispin and Philip Segal

the Korea Development Institute in a recent report.

What ought to give the rest of Asia pause is that the reform that allowed South Korea to get as far as it did in promoting consumerism is still very much the regional anomaly. Compared to other crisis-hit countries Seoul has taken a relative tough tack towards economic restructuring. Companies were closed, banks were consolidated. And real economic efficiency improved as a result. With those gains, Korea is now climbing up the technological ladder and is challenging Japan's long-time dominance over many high-value-added industries, particularly consumer electronics. Real efficiency gains and improved human capital have economically justified greater consumer spending in Korea.

Elsewhere, though, stronger consumption is being driven more by regulatory laxity and fiscal generosity than real improvements in economic efficiency and higher real incomes. Since winning office on a nationalistic ticket in 2001, Prime Minister Thaksin Shinawatra has placed the Thai consumer at the centre of his populist economic policies, pulling out all the demand-side stops to spark a consumer-spending spree in 2002. Regulations restricting consumer-based lending, including minimum salary requirements, have been eased; tax incentives and consumer-friendly lending from state banks have breathed new life into the country's long moribund property market.

Thaksin's policies, so far, have had the desired effect. New car sales were up nearly 30% according to latest statistics for

2002, and there are no signs of a slowdown as sales jumped 50% year on year in November. Mobile-telephone subscriptions have exploded as net additions exceeded 7 million last year, nearly tripling the size of the Thai mobile market. Led by such spending, the Thai economy grew 5.8% in the third quarter, marking the fastest growth for over two years.

But is this sustainable? Thailand has lagged badly in cleaning up its corporate and financial sectors. Industrial capacity utilization is still mired at around 60%, meaning new private investment in plant is still years away. "Consumption is good as a short-term fix, but by itself cannot lead growth over the medium term," says Chalongphob Susangkarn, president of the Thailand Development Research Institute, a Bangkok-based independent think-tank. "Faster growth now only means slower growth later," as consumers repay their debts.

In short, Asia's consumers still aren't powerful enough to replace a slowdown in foreign demand for the region's exports

---

Meanwhile, real spending power in many crisis-hit countries has fallen by almost half since 1997 due to devaluations of their currencies. In fact, the great consumer pullback may already have begun. An ACNielsen consumer-confidence survey released in late December found that

the majority of Asia-Pacific consumers believe that recovery from the global recession is at least another 12-18 months away. "With the exception of Australia and New Zealand, consumers across the region are holding onto their purse strings," it says.

The outlook for Asia gets gloomier still, because the region's old staple—exports—looks to be in some trouble in the year ahead. In the U.S. in November, 13 out of 19 major industry groups had zero or negative growth. While housing prices continue to boom and zero-financing on cars helps the U.S. tick along, it isn't what you would call a healthy economy. Capacity utilization in the U.S. is still at an anaemic 75.6%, up just a tenth of a percentage point from October.

As for hopes that China's headline growth number of 8% will absorb lots of exports from the rest of the region, remember that China feeds into the developed world as a processing and assembly centre, not as a market on its own. "No doubt, China will eventually emerge as a powerful, independent source of demand for exports from the rest of Asia," says Goldman Sachs in a recent report. "But this will materialize over the medium to long term only rather than in this cycle or next."

In the meantime, Asia's dependence on the U.S. has continued to grow. The U.S. took in 22.9% of Asia's exports compared with 20.5% in 1990. In short, Asia's consumers still aren't powerful enough to replace a slowdown in foreign demand for exports. "The relative size of non-Japan Asia's domestic demand is small in the global context, at roughly 24% of the U.S. and 26% of the European Union," says

Goldman Sachs. "Combining Japan, whose domestic demand is about 50% larger than non-Japan Asia's, pan-Asian domestic demand is only around 70% of the EU's."

Most people in Asia typically earn a fraction of what employees in the U.S., Europe or Japan earn, so manufacturing for domestic consumption cannot currently hope to deliver the economic growth rates returned by manufacturing for export. According to ABN Amro, less than 3% of the Thai population, or 2 million Thais, earn more than $300 a month—which is an eighth of what an average American makes.

Thus, from Asia's perspective, in the words of strategist Markus Rosgen at ING Barings, "the U.S. has been getting more—rather than less—important."

Tom Holland contributed to this story

East Asia: Recovery and Restructuring

More than three years have passed since the collapse of the Thai baht triggered a wave of currency and financial crises in East Asia. After experiencing sharp economic contraction in 1998, East Asian economies have rebounded strongly, buttressed by rapid growth in their exports to the United States. While the early recovery is laudable, questions still remain about whether it will last and, in particular, whether a number of these economies will be able to weather external shocks, such as a slowdown in high-tech exports to the U.S. market. One factor that will influence the resilience of these economies is the progress made in financial sector restructuring following the crises of 1997. To shed light on this question, this *Economic Letter* briefly describes the features of East Asia's recovery and its financial restructuring.

Crisis and recovery

The 1997 crises in East Asia were followed by recessions of unprecedented severity. Output declined sharply in several economies in 1998, ranging from 7% in Korea to 13% in Indonesia. However, output growth rebounded in 1999 and, according to recent *Asia Pacific Consensus Forecasts,* is expected to average over 7% in 2000, typical of pre-crisis growth rates.

The rapid recovery of East Asian economies is in some ways a surprise. The disruptions to the financial sector effectively wiped out the capital of many borrowers and their bank lenders. As a result, there was a severe credit crunch in which even borrowers with good projects could not get financing. Given the shortage of credit, it seemed that restoring growth and spending would require a lengthy process of repairing the financial sector by improving the balance sheets of lenders and borrowers. Instead, growth was restored relatively quickly, even before all the problems in East Asian financial sectors had been addressed.

Two explanations may be offered for the region's rapid recovery. First, and most important, robust global demand, notably in the United States, contributed to strong export growth and the replenishment of foreign reserves. For example, in Korea, exports in U.S. dollars fell over 5% in 1998 (Q4/Q4), but then grew nearly 17% in 1999 and accelerated to 22% in the second quarter of 2000, compared to a year earlier. Foreign reserves rose from $20.4 billion at the end of 1997, when the Korean won collapsed, to $92.5 billion in September 2000.

The second stimulus to growth has been expansionary fiscal policies. In an effort to repair the financial sector and attenuate the social impact of the crises, budget balances have switched from surpluses to very large deficits, leading to dramatic increases in the public debt. For example, between 1997 and 2000, the government budget in Thailand switched from near balance to a projected deficit of 7% of GDP, while the ratio of public sector debt to GDP rose from 27% to 66% (of which 21% is foreign). The estimated increase in public debt has been even higher in Indonesia, from less than 25% in 1996, to over 90% in 2000 (World Bank, 2000).

Although the recent performance of many East Asian economies has been impressive, concerns remain about how a slowdown in external demand would affect the region's economic performance. This will depend in part on how policy responses adopted since the crises affect the operation of the financial sector. One question is the extent to which balance sheets of lenders and borrowers that were disrupted by financial crises have been put on a sounder footing, thus restoring the normal flow of credit. In particular, has the overhang of nonperforming loans been reduced? The second question is the extent to which certain institutional practices have been reformed so as to discourage risk-taking while encouraging market adjustment and competition. The answers to these questions will influence the durability of the ongoing recovery and the resilience of East Asian economies to future economic shocks.

Repairing balance sheets

The good news is that East Asian governments have made progress in cleaning up balance sheets. Nonperforming loans have been taken off the books of banks, thus strengthening their financial position in an effort to encourage them to resume lending. These nonperforming loans have either been absorbed by the government or sold to private investors. A recent report by the World Bank (2000) provides data on the adjustment process.

Governments also have encouraged lenders and borrowers to enter negotiations to restructure existing debts or to adopt measures that facilitate foreclosure. For example, in Korea at the end of March 2000 there were 76 firms under workout programs, managing debt amounts equivalent to 9% of Korean GDP (43 trillion won). A system of prepackaged bankruptcies has been introduced, so that companies undergoing workout programs may be forced into receivership if half of the creditors agree or if creditors reach no consensus within a certain time.

Private investors also have acquired or injected capital in banks or weak borrowers. In Thailand, 314 billion baht (over US$7 billion at recent exchange rates) of private (tier 1) capital had flowed into banks by 2000. Some of the mergers or acquisitions have been particularly noteworthy, such as the takeover of a major South Korean bank by a foreign investor.

However, the adjustment process is not complete. According to the World Bank (2000), the share of nonperforming loans still held by the banking sector in Indonesia earlier this year was about 40% of total loans, compared to 9% when the crisis broke out. Another 20% of the bad loans have been absorbed by the government. In Thailand, bad loans were at 32% of total loans or higher, while in Korea they were estimated at 12%, about double what they were around the time the Korean won collapsed in 1997. Some banks in the region also face capital constraints, which reduces their ability to lend.

Financial systems in the region also remain vulnerable to poor performance and liquidity problems of heavily indebted borrowers. In Indonesia, the restructuring of corporate debt only took off this year, and borrowers are still heavily exposed to the debt denominated in foreign currency that was a major factor in the Indonesian crisis. In Korea, corporate debt-to-equity ratios have fallen significantly, but there is evidence of continued financial sector vulnerability.

Reforming institutional practices

It can be argued that while East Asia's financial arrangements in the past contributed to rapid growth, they also provided a safety net to lenders and borrowers that reduced incentives for risk management. Risky investments in domestic property markets in Thailand, exposure to currency risk by the Indonesian corporate sector, and a highly leveraged corporate sector in Korea are examples of behavior that contributed to the widespread bankruptcies and the financial crises that beset the region in 1997 and 1998.

Ongoing efforts to improve the quality of bank supervision and regulation through institutional reforms (such as the creation of independent financial supervision entities with stronger enforcement powers and the training of regulators) are important steps in enhancing risk management. However, significant obstacles remain because traditional arrangements at times protect borrowers from the consequences of poor investment decisions.

One difficulty is that policymakers face an ongoing dilemma in dealing with firms that experience financial difficulties. The traditional response in East Asia is for the government to step in to support such institutions, for example, by encouraging lenders to roll over financing. While such measures may support economic activity in the short run, they effectively reduce the penalties for risk-taking. Indeed, the East Asian crisis revealed that the resulting imbalances may prove too large for the economic system to manage.

Another difficulty is that borrowers defaulting on their obligations have significant advantages over their creditors. A tradition of forbearance implies that creditors are expected to be patient in attempting to secure payment from borrowers. In line with this, there is a perception in a number of countries in the region that bringing bankruptcy petitions to court is not desirable or cost-effective. Through December 1999, only 37 bankruptcy liquidation or rehabilitation petitions had been filed in Thai courts out of 400,000 nonperforming debtors. In part this reflects difficulties in ensuring debtor accountability; before bankruptcy reform was enacted, defaulting debtors could avoid judgment in Thai courts simply by not showing up. Even in those cases when bankruptcy petitions have been brought to court, until recently, success by creditors in some legal jurisdictions has been limited.

There are also obstacles to full market adjustment in the process of taking over weak firms or consolidation. While some major domestic firms have been taken over, in a number of widely publicized instances serious investors have withdrawn their bids after studying the books of the takeover candidate more carefully. This suggests both a lack of transparency in the information initially made available and sale prices that are too high. In some cases, firms experiencing financial difficulties are reluctant to relinquish control or to dilute ownership and are nevertheless able to survive because of institutional arrangements that allow them to do so. They may also have ample say about the terms under which they will divest assets. In other cases, governments are holding these assets, and they appear to be reluctant to allow investors—particularly foreign ones—to acquire them at what are perceived as bargain prices. The temptation to hold on to nonperforming assets or to delay adjustment has been particularly strong in the recent past, because improved economic growth creates expectations that asset prices will eventually recover.

One consequence of this gradual adjustment is that weak firms and their creditors remain vulnerable to sudden collapse. For example, the failure of the Korean conglomerate Daewoo in 1999 forced the Korean government to intervene to preserve the stability of the Korean bond market and of investment companies that held large amounts of Daewoo debt. More recently, liquidity problems experienced by other conglomerates in Korea (such as affiliates of Hyundai, and Ssangyong) have led to fund withdrawals from investment trust companies with exposure to these firms. The large increases in public debt in some East Asian economies partly reflect the costs of delayed adjustment.

These experiences illustrate the difficulties of transition. In East Asia, requiring financial institutions or large business groups to take corrective measures involves a major reassessment of the relationship between government and business, and achieving political consensus for such drastic change is difficult. As in many instances of financial reform throughout the world, change has taken place only as awareness of the rising costs of the status quo has increased.

matic recovery. Although adjustment is not complete, there has been significant progress made in repairing balance sheets disrupted by recent financial crises. Steps also have been taken to improve supervision and regulation. However, the biggest challenge facing East Asian policymakers is to decide how much of certain traditional institutional practices to keep, and how much to discard in favor of the systems in place in advanced market economies. This traditional system was associated with decades of rapid growth, but it also contained implicit or explicit guarantees that led to risky lending and excessive leveraging. Meeting this challenge successfully will significantly enhance the durability of the region's ongoing recovery.

Ramon Moreno
Senior Economist

Conclusions

Since July 1997, when the Thai baht collapsed, East Asia has experienced an unprecedented economic contraction and dra-

Reference

The World Bank. 2000. *East Asia Brief* (September).

CHINA'S ECONOMIC POWER:
Enter the dragon

BEIJING

ASK what has been the most stunning economic event of the past century, and many people might cite the case of China in the two decades since it opened up. In that time the economy has grown more than fivefold, incomes have quadrupled, and 270m Chinese have been lifted out of absolute poverty. Yet with a couple more decades' hindsight, that achievement might be superseded—by what may now be about to happen in the world's most populous country.

Much of China's growth up to now has been merely of a catch-up kind, as animal spirits were unleashed after agricultural communes were disbanded and restrictions on travel and informal enterprise were lifted. The government, in other words, did not have to do much except stand back. And for all the growth in the country's exports as China became a manufacturing colossus, only in 1993 did China's share of world trade reach its pre-1939 peak. Today, average income is a mere $950 a head, and the disparities in wealth are huge. China is still a poor country, in places abjectly so.

The coming two decades, on the other hand, offer the possibility of an even more extraordinary pace of economic change. These could be the decades when China truly joins the world, and when the crushing legacy of a socialist economy is swept away. China certainly has the potential, over this period, to become the second-largest economy in the world. Of course, that would not mean that all Chinese would grow rich. But China no doubt has the means to attain "middle income" status—putting the prosperity of its people, currently 1.3 billion souls, not far from South

Korea or Portugal today. That would be an extraordinary feat for so large a population in so short a time. The geopolitical effects would also be immense.

A new taste for reform

This is the moment to contemplate such a future, because over the past year or so (and after seven years of falling growth) China's rulers have shown a determination to tackle the thorniest issues in the economy that they have never shown before. The most obvious symbols of that determination are the promises that were made, and the steps now being taken, to ensure that China is brought into the world trading system. Nearly all the agreements are in place for China to join the World Trade Organisation (WTO) this year, after 15 years of trying. Over the next five years the country will slash tariff and non-tariff barriers, as well as open up sectors of the economy that have long been off-limits to foreigners, such as banking, telecoms and distribution. China promises to protect foreign intellectual property, and get rid of a raft of local-content requirements that have hobbled foreign manufacturers.

But WTO membership is just the first of the reform initiatives. The central government has declared war on most parts of the socialist economy, all the time insisting it is sticking to "the socialist road". It is bent on separating business from government, by getting rid of many smaller state enterprises and corporatising others. It wants to develop financial markets that bypass a decrepit state banking system and award capital to the deserving. It is building a national infrastructure of roads, railways and fibre-optic lines that promise for the first time in history to tie up the dispar-

ate parts of the Chinese empire, creating something like a unified economy.

The government is also encouraging new sources of domestic demand by privatising socialist housing (in the biggest cities, two-fifths of residents now own their own homes). It is trying to develop a clear and effective tax system, using information technology, it hopes, to monitor and crack down on local-government corruption. And it is attempting to patch together a set of social-welfare initiatives to catch the 5m-odd people being thrown out of work each year by state enterprises, as well as to provide pensions for an ageing population. Most of these ventures are politically fraught, and not for the faint-hearted. In his annual report to the National People's Congress this week, the prime minister, Zhu Rongji, promised more, not less, pain as reforms are redoubled: shutting down more loss-making enterprises, for instance, and selling others.

If the government makes good on all its promises, what assumptions can one make about future growth? First, note that assumptions are rosier if the government's own figures are used. Official growth statistics have long been exaggerated, for a number of reasons. For one, local officials cook the books to make their region look good. For another, China still produces goods that pile up as inventories and are never sold. Yet their production gets added to GDP, when it should be subtracted. The problem is that no one knows by quite how much official GDP is overstated. Last year's announced growth of 8% was perhaps one or two percentage points too high. At least the trend in GDP is fairly reliable, and at least the government is trying hard to improve the quality of its data.

Over time, the figures should get more believable, not less.

Andy Xie, an economist at Morgan Stanley in Hong Kong, reckons that if China sticks to its WTO commitments and, in effect, moves to a market-based economy by 2005, it will grow at 7% a year till 2005, then at 9% during 2006–15, as it reaps the benefits of restructuring, before slowing a bit thereafter. If so, by 2020, China's economy would have grown to $10 trillion in 2000 dollars, making it the size of America's economy today. Income per head will be $6,700. If China were to conform to global norms more quickly than the WTO framework demands—perhaps as a result of foreign pressure and trade tensions, or of domestic pressure to speed change along—then it would grow by 10% a year between 2006 and 2015, passing the $10 trillion mark by 2015. And if China's reforms run into the sand? More of that later.

A giant sucking sound

One of the immediate consequences of impending WTO membership is a swift increase in commitments of foreign direct investment (FDI): last year, committed FDI rose by over a third. Already, though, China's stock of FDI, at $350 billion, and growing by over $40 billion a year, is massive. It is the world's third-largest, behind America ($1.1 trillion) and Britain ($394 billion), and way ahead of countries like Brazil and Mexico that opened their markets much earlier than China. The mainland now accounts for about one-third of emerging markets' total stock of FDI, according to Nicholas Lardy of the Brookings Institution in Washington. Nearly four-fifths of all FDI going to South-East and East Asia, not counting Japan, is sucked up by China—and to its neighbours' growing alarm.

Traditionally, the bulk of FDI to China has gone into its export industries. Foreign trade has grown from almost nothing in the late 1970s to $475 billion last year, far faster than the growth in world trade as a whole (see chart). And foreign-invested firms have grown to account for half of all exports from China. Foreign investment has helped make China a formidable export machine. The country will no doubt continue to be one, thanks to a near-limitless pool of extraordinarily cheap labour, including a large and growing supply of educated graduates. Mainland computer engineers earn about one-tenth as much as

their Taiwanese counterparts, and they are almost as good.

China's manufacturing is getting more sophisticated and employing more capital. Mr Xie argues that even as it moves up the manufacturing chain (eg, to semiconductors and to information-technology hardware, of which it is the world's third-biggest producer), China will not lose its advantages in cheap, labour-intensive areas such as toys, textiles and shoes. Without China's cost structures—that is, its economies of scale and its low standard of living—other exporters in the region, from Indonesia to South Korea, will have trouble staying in business: China can just about out-export them all.

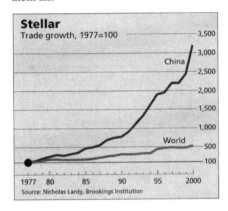

Stellar
Trade growth, 1977=100

China

World

1977 80 85 90 95 2000

Source: Nicholas Lardy, Brookings Institution

This realisation comes as a profound shock to China's neighbours, most of whom have built a development strategy over the past few decades around export-led growth. It will soon come as a shock outside the region: to exporters in India, for instance, and Mexico, who thought themselves far removed from the Chinese threat. Indeed, Mexico has been very reluctant to sign up to China's entry to the WTO, and has been the final country to do so.

On the face of it, China's seems to be an export-driven economy, too. After all, annual exports are equivalent to at least 23% of GDP, making China the world's ninth-largest exporter. Even so, the brute figures conceal how imperfectly China's export sector is tied to its hinterland. Firms wholly or partly owned by foreigners account for about one-half of China's imports as well as its exports. Much export manufacturing, in other words, consists of processing industries that ship in components, bolt them together and ship them out again, often through Hong Kong. The foreign-dominated export sector, especially in China's handful of "special economic zones", should be thought of as an enclave, a giant version of the *maquiladoras* on the Mexican border with the United States.

China, says Mr Lardy, is only shallowly integrated with the world economy.

Segregration carries costs. The technology and the management skills that foreign investment typically brings with it are not easily adopted by domestic firms. Meanwhile, economic growth is stifled within China by the dominance, in many sectors, of the state, by barriers to trade and local protectionism, and by the absence of proper capital markets. For Zhu Rongji and other reformers, WTO entry is important for its domestic consequences. Certainly, with its ability to export, China is a clear net beneficiary of the globalisation of trade. More important, though, is the fact that WTO membership will spur competition at home, acting as a rod to beat back the baneful influence of the state.

Goodbye, hermit China

The "price" that China pays for this is to allow foreigners in. It is the potential scale of China's domestic market, after its entry to the WTO, that most appeals to foreign multinationals. After decades, or rather centuries, of foreigners' dashed dreams about the money to be made from adding an inch to every Chinaman's shirt-tail, the promise that China has long held out may be about to be matched by reality.

Already, in unprotected sectors of the mainland economy, multinationals are a dominant force. Between them, McDonald's and Kentucky Fried Chicken have almost 700 branches. Kodak has half of the market for film and photographic paper, with Fuji holding most of the rest. Procter & Gamble is the biggest seller of shampoo, while foreign manufacturers, led by Motorola, Ericsson and Nokia, have 95% of the market for mobile phones, the world's biggest market in terms of handset sales. Coca-Cola says that China is about to become its biggest Asian market. Some estimates put foreign involvement at about one-tenth of the whole economy. With WTO membership, the proportion could easily double.

Yet China is not yet integrated into the world trading system, and it is no better integrated domestically. Think of China's potential not so much as an international trading economy, but as a vast "continental" one: a proto-America, as it were. Just as America's growth in the 19th century took off with the building of the railways and of a national financial system, so China hopes to unify its hitherto fragmented, disjointed economy. Until recently, it took less time to ship a container from Shanghai to Seattle than from Shanghai to the inland city of Chongqing, 1,000 or so miles up the Yangzi river.

Just a dozen years ago, China had no highway system linking its provinces; now it has over 12,000km (7,500 miles) of such highways. The number of passenger flights has trebled in the past decade. There were 36m new subscribers for fixed-line telephones in 2000 alone, and 42m new mobile subscribers: fixed-line penetration, at 17% of households, grew 30-fold during the 1990s. Internet use, though still tiny, is more than doubling every year. China is integrating fast, and information technology is helping.

Financial integration also holds great promise. Until recently, the big four banks were captive lenders to state-owned enterprises. The state's share of the economy has fallen—to below half, according to some calculations—yet state-owned industries still control more than 70% of all fixed assets and 80% of all working capital in manufacturing, according to Mr Lardy of the Brookings Institution. The corollary is that private enterprise is stifled.

The government has bold plans to develop equity markets and to clean up the state banks. Already, debt-equity swaps have taken some 1.4 trillion yuan ($150 billion) of dud loans off the books of the banks, which have been ordered to lend in future only on merit. Equity markets have assumed a growing role in providing finance: 620 billion yuan last year, compared with 440 billion in 1999. The foreign portion of that grew nearly sevenfold, to 180 billion yuan. Shareholder discipline, at least in theory, should shape up management. Certainly, the flotations of some of the biggest Chinese companies that have recently come to market—Petrochina, China Mobile—were preceded by giant restructurings to make the companies look more like western ones.

Is the regime serious?

This raft of bold reforms has still to reach the other shore. Hopes in China have foundered before. This time, there will be proper ways to measure progress. China must successfully join the WTO, and stand by its commitments within it. It must continue to separate business from government, which eventually means getting the Communist Party out of both. The next

step in this process is developing capital markets which reward good management and punish bad. A great deal more privatisation will be needed. Some analysts are sceptical about the chances of success. Stockmarket regulators, for instance, have announced sweeping initiatives, such as delisting money-losing companies, demanding more financial disclosure and setting up a second stockmarket for entrepreneurial companies. "But the rhetoric," says Mr Lardy, "is far in excess of the action."

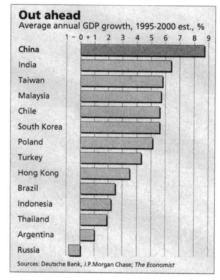

Out ahead
Average annual GDP growth, 1995-2000 est., %

China	
India	
Taiwan	
Malaysia	
Chile	
South Korea	
Poland	
Turkey	
Hong Kong	
Brazil	
Indonesia	
Thailand	
Argentina	
Russia	

Sources: Deutsche Bank, J.P.Morgan Chase; *The Economist*

Yet the regime is deadly serious about reform. It rests its legitimacy upon the goal of getting reform-driven growth, banishing Communist Party corruption along the way, and providing a safety net to catch the victims of wrenching change. Conservative ideologues have largely been beaten. When the current batch of Communist leaders steps down late next year, the new generation that will take its place should be much more cosmopolitan and reform-minded. If it is not, there is cause for worry. For the final measure of progress will be whether the leaders consider reform to the Communist Party's monopoly on power.

What are the economic implications abroad of a China resurgent? In the near term, China's growth promises to be a comfort for the region during a difficult time. Asia's exporters are concerned that America may be on the edge of a recession from which they would suffer grievously: after the Asian crisis of 1997–98, Asian economies counted upon strong American

demand for their exports to pull them back from trouble.

China, on the other hand, will scarcely be affected. Jun Ma, an economist at Deutsche Bank in Hong Kong, estimates that even if China's net exports declined by a quarter this year (after growth of the same last year), a mere half-percentage point would be knocked off the country's growth. This reinforces the point that China's is a continental economy, driven by domestic demand.

It is possibly reassuring for China's neighbours to know that the giant would scarcely stir if the world economy turned down. Chinese imports grew by a staggering $55 billion last year, suggesting that the country is even becoming a regional engine of growth. But China's export threat to neighbouring economies underscores their predicament: in order to compete, they need to undertake much-postponed structural reforms themselves.

Longer-term, some groups in America will also see a resurgent Chinese economy as a threat. China's $60 billion trade surplus with the United States is already a bone of contention, while labour interests, among others, resent China joining the world. Many of the resentful ignore the fact that ties between the American and Chinese economies are already close, and multifaceted. Sales by American companies in China are now almost as large as American exports to China, while investment flows are every bit as important as trade flows. Shutting China out of the world would harm a lot of American interests. Moreover, as Mr Xie of Morgan Stanley emphasises, there is the prospect of some $40 trillion of new wealth over the next 15–20 years to be created by Chinese reforms, and foreigners are being offered a big share—perhaps one-fifth—of it.

These are the economic ties that increasingly bind China to its reforms and to the rest of the world. There are other, less formal ones. Some 50,000 Chinese study in American universities each year, for instance, and there are now even more American-educated Chinese than Soviet-educated ones. The ties are certainly more complex than they have ever been. They require a great deal more effort to manage. But they are surely safer for all that than few ties at all.

OVERVIEW

Changing today's consumption patterns—for tomorrow's human development

World consumption has expanded at an unprecedented pace over the 20th century, with private and public consumption expenditures reaching $24 trillion in 1998, twice the level of 1975 and six times that of 1950. In 1900 real consumption expenditure was barely $1.5 trillion.

The benefits of this consumption have spread far and wide. More people are better fed and housed than ever before. Living standards have risen to enable hundreds of millions to enjoy housing with hot water and cold, warmth and electricity, transport to and from work—with time for leisure and sports, vacations and other activities beyond anything imagined at the start of this century.

How do these achievements relate to human development? Consumption is clearly an essential means, but the links are not automatic. Consumption clearly contributes to human development when it enlarges the capabilities and enriches the lives of people without adversely affecting the well-being of others. It clearly contributes when it is as fair to future generations as it is to the present ones. And it clearly contributes when it encourages lively, creative individuals and communities.

But the links are often broken, and when they are, consumption patterns and trends are inimical to human development. Today's consumption is undermining the environmental resource base. It is exacerbating inequalities. And the dynamics of the consumption-poverty-inequality-environment nexus are accelerating. If the trends continue without change—not redistributing from high-income to low-income consumers, not shifting from polluting to cleaner goods and production technologies, not promoting goods that empower poor producers, not shifting priority from consumption for conspicuous display to meeting basic needs—today's problems of consumption and human development will worsen.

But trend is not destiny, and none of these outcomes is inevitable. Change is needed and change is possible.

In short, consumption must be shared, strengthening, socially responsible and sustainable.

• *Shared.* Ensuring basic needs for all.
• *Strengthening.* Building human capabilities.
• *Socially responsible.* So the consumption of some does not compromise the well-being of others.
• *Sustainable.* Without mortgaging the choices of future generations.

Trend is not destiny— change is possible

Human life is ultimately nourished and sustained by consumption. Abundance of consumption is no crime. It has, in fact, been the life blood of much human advance. The real issue is not consumption itself but its patterns and effects. Consumption patterns today must be changed to advance human development tomorrow. Consumer choices must be turned into a reality for all. Human development paradigms, which aim at enlarging all human choices, must aim at extending and improving consumer choices too, but in ways that promote human life. This is the theme of this report.

The 20th century's growth in consumption, unprecedented in its scale and diversity, has been badly distributed, leaving a backlog of shortfalls and gaping inequalities.

Rapid consumption growth for some, stagnation for others, inequality for all—with mounting environmental costs

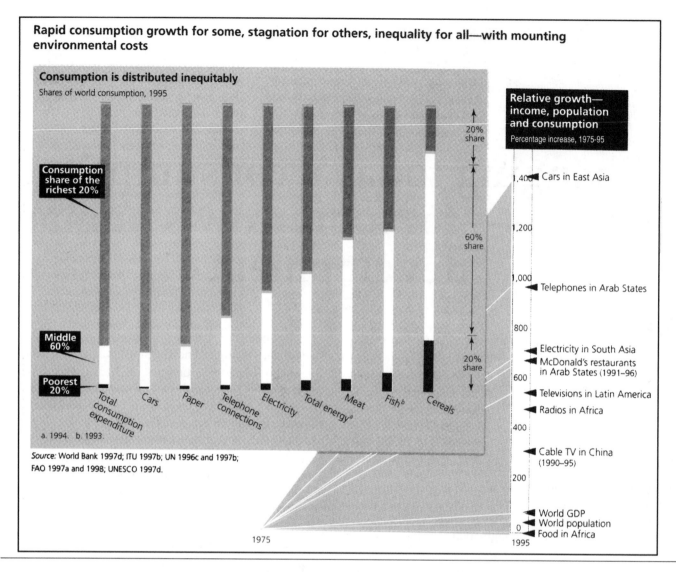

Consumption is distributed inequitably
Shares of world consumption, 1995

Consumption share of the richest 20%

Middle 60%

Poorest 20%

Total consumption expenditure
Cars
Paper
Telephone connections
Electricity
Total energy a
Meat
Fish b
Cereals

a. 1994.   b. 1993.

Source: World Bank 1997d; ITU 1997b; UN 1996c and 1997b;
FAO 1997a and 1998; UNESCO 1997d.

20% share
60% share
20% share

Relative growth—income, population and consumption
Percentage increase, 1975-95

1,400 ◄ Cars in East Asia

1,200

1,000 ◄ Telephones in Arab States

800

◄ Electricity in South Asia
◄ McDonald's restaurants in Arab States (1991–96)
600
◄ Televisions in Latin America
◄ Radios in Africa

400

◄ Cable TV in China (1990–95)

200

◄ World GDP
0 ◄ World population
◄ Food in Africa

1975   1995

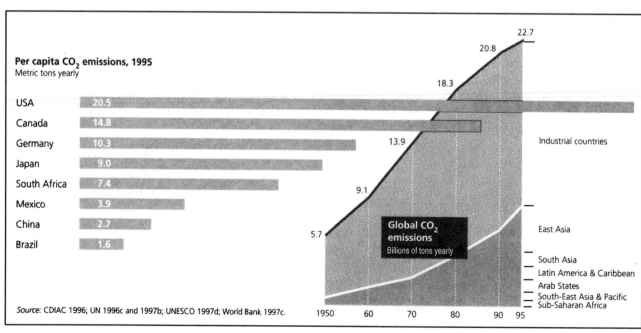

Per capita CO$_2$ emissions, 1995
Metric tons yearly

USA	20.5
Canada	14.8
Germany	10.3
Japan	9.0
South Africa	7.4
Mexico	3.9
China	2.7
Brazil	1.6

Industrial countries

22.7
20.8
18.3
13.9
9.1
5.7

Global CO$_2$ emissions
Billions of tons yearly

East Asia
South Asia
Latin America & Caribbean
Arab States
South-East Asia & Pacific
Sub-Saharan Africa

1950   60   70   80   90   95

Source: CDIAC 1996; UN 1996c and 1997b; UNESCO 1997d; World Bank 1997c.

Consumption per capita has increased steadily in industrial countries (about 2.3% annually) over the past 25 years, spectacularly in East Asia (6.1%) and at a rising rate in South Asia (2.0%). Yet these developing regions are far from catching up to levels of industrial countries, and consumption growth has been slow or stagnant in others. The average African household today consumes 20% less than it did 25 years ago.

The poorest 20% of the world's people and more have been left out of the consumption explosion. Well over a billion people are deprived of basic consumption needs. Of the 4.4 billion people in developing countries, nearly three-fifths lack basic sanitation. Almost a third have no access to clean water. A quarter do not have adequate housing. A fifth have no access to modern health services. A fifth of children do not attend school to grade 5. About a fifth do not have enough dietary energy and protein. Micronutrient deficiencies are even more widespread. Worldwide, 2 billion people are anaemic, including 55 million in industrial countries. In developing countries only a privileged minority has motorized transport, telecommunications and modern energy.

The new human poverty index (HPI-2) shows that some 7-17% of the population in industrial countries is poor

Inequalities in consumption are stark. Globally, the 20% of the world's people in the highest-income countries account for 86% of total private consumption expenditures—the poorest 20% a minuscule 1.3%. More specifically, the richest fifth:

- Consume 45% of all meat and fish, the poorest fifth 5%.
- Consume 58% of total energy, the poorest fifth less than 4%.
- Have 74% of all telephone lines, the poorest fifth 1.5%.
- Consume 84% of all paper, the poorest fifth 1.1%.
- Own 87% of the world's vehicle fleet, the poorest fifth less than 1%.

How rewarding is today's pattern of consumption in terms of human satisfaction? The percentage of Americans calling themselves happy peaked in 1957—even though consumption has more than doubled in the meantime.

Despite high consumption, poverty and deprivation are found in all industrial countries and in some they are growing. This year's Report presents a new index of poverty in industrial countries—multidimensional measure of human deprivation, on the same lines as the human poverty index presented in *Human Development Report 1997* for developing countries but more appropriate to the social and economic conditions of the industrial countries.

The new human poverty index (HPI-2) shows that some 7–17% of the population in industrial countries is poor. These levels of deprivation have little to do with the average income of the country. Sweden has the least poverty (7%), though ranked only thirteenth in average income. The United States, with the highest average income of the countries ranked, has the highest population share experiencing human poverty. And countries with similar per capita incomes have very different levels of human poverty. The Netherlands and the United Kingdom, for example, have HPI-2 values of 8% and 15%, despite similar income levels.

HPI-2 shows conclusively that underconsumption and human deprivation are not just the lot of poor people in the developing world. More than 100 million people in rich nations suffer a similar fate. Nearly 200 million people are not expected to survive to age 60. More than 100 million are homeless. And at least 37 million are without jobs, often experiencing a state of social exclusion. Many conclusions about deprivation apply to them with equal force.

Ever-expanding consumption puts strains on the environment—emissions and wastes that pollute the earth and destroy ecosystems, and growing depletion and degradation of renewable resources that undermine livelihoods.

Runaway growth in consumption in the past 50 years is putting strains on the environment never before seen.

- The burning of fossil fuels has almost quintupled since 1950.
- The consumption of fresh water has almost doubled since 1960.
- The marine catch has increased fourfold.
- Wood consumption, both for industry and for household fuel, is now 40% higher than it was 25 years ago.

Yet growth in the use of material resources has slowed considerably in recent years, and much-publicized fears that the world would run out of such non-renewable resources as oil and minerals have proved false. New reserves have been discovered. The growth of demand has slowed. Consumption has shifted in favour of less material-intensive products and services. Energy efficiency has improved. And technological advance and recycling of raw materials have boosted efficiency in material use, now growing more slowly than economies. Call this dematerialization. The per capita use of basic materials such as steel, timber and copper has stabilized in most OECD countries—and even declined in some countries for some products.

So, non-renewables are not the urgent problem. It is two other crises that are nudging humanity towards the "outer limits" of what earth can stand.

First are the pollution and waste that exceed the planet's sink capacities to absorb and convert them. Reserves of fossil fuels are not running out, but use of these fuels is emitting gases that change the ecosystem—annual carbon dioxide (CO_2) emissions quadrupled over the past 50 years. Global warming is a serious problem, threatening to play havoc with harvests, permanently flood large areas, increase the frequency of storms and droughts, accelerate the extinction of some species, spread infectious diseases—and possibly cause sudden and savage flips in the world's climates. And although material resources may not be running out, waste is mounting, both toxic and non-toxic. In industrial countries per capita waste generation has increased almost threefold in the past 20 years.

Second is the growing deterioration of renewables—water, soil, forests, fish, biodiversity.

• Twenty countries already suffer from water stress, having less than 1,000 cubic metres per capita a year, and water's global availability has dropped from 17,000 cubic metres per capita in 1950 to 7,000 today.
• A sixth of the world's land area—nearly 2 billion hectares—is now degraded as a result of overgrazing and poor farming practices.
• The world's forests—which bind soil and prevent erosion, regulate water supplies and help govern the climate—are shrinking. Since 1970 the wooded area per 1,000 inhabitants has fallen from 11.4 square kilometres to 7.3.
• Fish stocks are declining, with about a quarter currently depleted or in danger of depletion and another 44% being fished at their biological limit.
• Wild species are becoming extinct 50–100 times faster than they would naturally, threatening to tear great holes in the web of life.

The world's dominant consumers are overwhelmingly concentrated among the well-off—but the environmental damage from the world's consumption falls most severely on the poor.

The better-off benefit from the cornucopia of consumption. But poor people and poor countries bear many of its costs. The severest human deprivations arising from environmental damage are concentrated in the poorest regions and affect the poorest people, unable to protect themselves.

• A child born in the industrial world adds more to consumption and pollution over his or her lifetime than do 30–50 children born in developing countries.

• Since 1950 industrial countries, because of their high incomes and consumption levels, have accounted for well over half the increase in resource use.
• The fifth of the world's people in the highest-income countries account for 53% of carbon dioxide emissions, the poorest fifth for 3%. Brazil, China, India, Indonesia and Mexico are among the developing countries with the highest emissions. But with huge populations, their per capita emissions are still tiny—3.9 metric tons a year in Mexico and 2.7 in China, compared with 20.5 metric tons in the United States and 10.2 in Germany. The human consequences of the global warming from carbon dioxide will be devastating for many poor countries—with a rise in sea levels, Bangladesh could see its land area shrink by 17%.
• Almost a billion people in 40 developing countries risk losing access to their primary source of protein, as overfishing driven by export demand for animal feed and oils puts pressure on fish stocks.
• The 132 million people in water-stressed areas are predominantly in Africa and parts of the Arab states—and if present trends continue, their numbers could rise to 1–2.5 billion by 2050.
• Deforestation is concentrated in developing countries. Over the last two decades, Latin America and the Caribbean lost 7 million hectares of tropical forest, Asia and Sub-Saharan Africa 4 million hectares each. Most of it has taken place to meet the demand for wood and paper, which has doubled and quintupled respectively since 1950. But over half the wood and nearly three-quarters of the paper is used in industrial countries.

Poor people and poor countries bear many costs of unequal consumption

The poor are most exposed to fumes and polluted rivers and least able to protect themselves. Of the estimated 2.7 million deaths each year from air pollution, 2.2 million are from indoor pollution, and 80% of the victims are rural poor in developing countries. Smoke from fuelwood and dung is more dangerous to health than tobacco smoke, but every day women have to spend hours cooking over smoky fires.

Leaded petrol, used more in developing and transition economies than in industrial countries, is crippling human health, permanently impairing the development of children's brains. In Bangkok up to 70,000 children are reported to be at risk of losing four or more IQ points because of high lead emissions. In Latin America around 15 million children under two years of age are at similar risk.

These environmental challenges stem not only from affluence but also from growing poverty. As a result of increasing impoverishment and the absence of other alternatives, a swelling number of poor and landless people are putting unprecedented pressures on the natural resource base as they struggle to survive.

Poverty and the environment are caught in a downward spiral. Past resource degradation deepens today's poverty, while today's poverty makes it very hard to care for or restore the agricultural resource base, to find alternatives to deforestation, to prevent desertification, to control erosion and to replenish soil nutrients. Poor people are forced to deplete resources to survive; this degradation of the environment further impoverishes them.

When this reinforcing downward spiral becomes extreme, poor people are forced to move in increasing numbers to ecologically fragile lands. Almost half the world's poorest people—more than 500 million—live on marginal lands.

The poverty–environmental damage nexus in developing countries must be seen in the context of population growth. In the developing world pressures on the environment intensify every day as the population grows. The global population is projected to be 9.5 billion in 2050, with more than 8 billion in developing countries. To feed this population adequately will require three times the basic calories consumed today, the equivalent of about 10 billion tons of grain a year. Population growth will also contribute to overgrazing, overcutting and overfarming.

How people interact with their environment is complex. It is by no means simply a matter of whether they are poor or rich. Ownership of natural resources, access to common properties, the strength of communities and local institutions, the issue of entitlements and rights, risk and uncertainty are important determinants of people's environmental behaviour. Gender inequalities, government policies and incentive systems are also crucial factors.

In recent times environmental awareness has been increasing in both rich and poor countries. The rich countries, with greater resources, have been spending more on environmental protection and clean-up. The developing countries, though they have fewer resources, have also been adopting cleaner technologies and reducing pollution, as in China.

The world community has also been active on environmental problems that directly affect poor people. Such areas include desertification, biodiversity loss and exports of hazardous waste. For example, the Convention on Biological Diversity has near-universal signature, with over 170 parties. The Convention to Combat Desertification has been ratified by more than 100 countries. But the deterioration of arid lands, a major threat to the livelihoods of poor people, continues unabated.

And there are other immediate environmental concerns for poor people, such as water contamination and indoor pollution, that have yet to receive serious international attention. Global forums discuss global warming. But the 2.2 million deaths yearly from indoor air pollution are scarcely mentioned.

Competitive spending and conspicuous consumption turn the affluence of some into the social exclusion of many

Rising pressures for conspicuous consumption can turn destructive, reinforcing exclusion, poverty and inequality.

Pressures of competitive spending and conspicuous consumption turn the affluence of some into the social exclusion of many. When there is heavy social pressure to maintain high consumption standards and society encourages competitive spending for conspicuous displays of wealth, inequalities in consumption deepen poverty and social exclusion.

Some disturbing trends:

• Studies of US households found that the income needed to fulfil consumption aspirations doubled between 1986 and 1994.

• The definition of what constitutes a "necessity" is changing, and the distinctions between luxuries and necessities are blurring. In the 1980s Brazil, Chile, Malaysia, Mexico and South Africa had two to three times as many cars as Austria, France and Germany did when they were at the same income level 30 years earlier.

• Household debt, especially consumer credit, is growing and household savings are falling in many industrial and developing countries. In the United States households save only 3.5% of their incomes, half as much as 15 years ago. In Brazil consumer debt, concentrated among lower-income households, now exceeds $6 billion.

Many voice concerns about the impact of these trends on society's values—and on human lives. Do they further deepen poverty as households compete to meet rising consumption standards—crowding out spending on food, education and health? Do these patterns motivate people to spend more hours working—leaving less time for family, friends and community?

Globalization is creating new inequalities and new challenges for protecting consumer rights

And is globalization accelerating these trends in competitive spending and rising standards?

Globalization is integrating consumer markets around the world and opening opportunities. But it is also creating new inequalities and new challenges for protecting consumer rights.

Globalization is integrating not just trade, investment and financial markets. It is also integrating consumer markets. This has two effects—economic and social. Economic integration has accelerated the opening of consumer markets with a constant flow of new products. There is fierce competition to sell to consumers worldwide, with increasingly aggressive advertising.

On the social side local and national boundaries are breaking down in the setting of social standards and aspirations in consumption. Market research identifies "global elites" and "global middle classes" who follow the same consumption styles, showing preferences for "global brands". There are the "global teens"—some 270 million 15- to 18-year-olds in 40 countries—inhabiting a "global space", a single pop-culture world, soaking up the same videos and music and providing a huge market for designer running shoes, t-shirts and jeans.

What are the consequences? First, a host of consumption options have been opened for many consumers—but many are left out in the cold through lack of income. And pressures for competitive spending mount. Keeping up with the Joneses has shifted from striving to match the consumption of a next-door neighbour to pursuing the life styles of the rich and famous depicted in movies and television shows.

Developing countries today can leapfrog to growth patterns that are pro-environment and pro-poor

Second, protecting consumer rights to product safety and product information has become complex. Increasingly, new products with higher chemical content, such as foods and medicines, are coming on the market. When information is not adequate, or safety standards are not strictly enforced, consumers can suffer—from pesticides that are poisonous, from milk powder that is contaminated.

At the same time the consumer receives a flood of information through commercial advertising. An average American, it is estimated, sees 150,000 advertisements on television in his or her lifetime. And advertising is increasing worldwide, faster than population or incomes. Global advertising spending, by the most conservative reckoning, is now $435 billion. Its growth has been particularly rapid in developing countries—in the Republic of Korea it increased nearly threefold in 1986–96, in the Philippines by 39% a year in 1987–92. In 1986 there were only three developing countries among the 20 biggest spenders in advertising. A decade later there were nine. And in spending relative to income, Colombia ranks first with $1.4 billion, 2.6% of its GDP.

Poor countries need to accelerate their consumption growth—but they need not follow the path taken by the rich and high-growth economies over the past half century.

Not only have consumption levels been too low to meet basic needs for more than a billion people, their growth has often been slow and interrupted by setbacks. In 70 countries with nearly a billion people consumption today is lower than it was 25 years ago. It cannot be raised without accelerating economic growth—but growth has been failing many poor people and poor countries. Despite the spectacular growth of incomes for many people in Asia, only 21 developing countries worldwide achieved growth in GDP per capita of at least 3% each year between 1995 and 1997—the rate needed to set a frame for reducing poverty.

Some suggest that developing countries should restrain their consumption in order to limit environmental damage. But this would mean prolonging the already scandalously deep and extensive deprivation for future generations.

Developing countries today face a strategic choice. They can repeat the industrialization and growth processes of the past half century, and go through a development phase that is inequitable, and creates an enormous legacy of environmental pollution. Or they can leapfrog to growth patterns that are:

•Pro-environment, preserving natural resources and creating less pollution and waste.
•Pro-poor, creating jobs for poor people and households and expanding their access to basic social services.

If poor countries can leapfrog in both consumption patterns and production technologies, they can accelerate consumption growth and human development without the huge costs of environmental damage. They can incorporate many of the available technologies that are not only less environmentally damaging but clean—solar energy, less energy-intensive crop production, cleaner paper production technologies.

Leapfrogging technologies will enhance the prospects for development by saving the huge costs of environmental clean-up that many countries are now incurring. The cost savings will go beyond the direct costs of cleaning up old toxic sites, scrubbing coal power plants and so on. Health care costs linked to environmental damage can also be saved. And leapfrogging will bypass the lock-in that can result from inappropriate infrastructure development.

Some argue that the scope for cheap, effective and politically less contentious antipollution policies is very limited in poor countries. This is a myth. Many actions have already been taken. And further options exist:

•Higher yields can be achieved through more intensive agricultural methods rather than more fertilizers and pesticides.
•Phasing out lead in petrol costs only 1–2 cents per litre for the refinery, as Mexico and Thailand have shown.
•Solar power and compact fluorescent lightbulbs can increase efficiency fourfold and reduce the need for rural electricity grids.
•Clean four-stroke engines can be made compulsory for motorcycles and three-wheelers, as Thailand has done.

These show what is possible. But to realize the potential, more needs to be done to develop and apply innovations.

Affluent societies in industrial countries also face strategic choices. They can continue the trends in consumption of the past decade. Or they can shift to consumption that is pro-people and pro-environment.

Continuing past trends would increase industrial countries' consumption by four- to fivefold over the next half century. Some argue that growth must be slowed and consumption downsized. But the real issue is not growth of consumption but its impacts on people, the environment and society. If societies adopt technologies that diminish the environmental impact of consumption, if patterns shift from consuming material goods to consuming services, growth can help, not hinder, moves to sustainability. The strategic choices of rich countries as the world's dominant consumers, will be critical in determining the future.

AGENDA FOR ACTION

Five goals are central:
•Raise the consumption levels of more than a billion poor people—more than a quarter of humanity—who have

been left out of the global expansion of consumption and are unable to meet their basic needs.
•Move to more sustainable consumption patterns that reduce environmental damage, improve efficiency in resource use and regenerate renewable resources—such as water, wood, soils and fish.
•Protect and promote the rights of consumers to information, product safety and access to products that they need.
•Discourage patterns of consumption that have a negative impact on society and that reinforce inequalities and poverty.
•Achieve more equitable international burden-sharing in reducing and preventing global environmental damage and in reducing global poverty.

The key is to create an enabling environment for sustainable consumption—where both consumers and producers have the incentives and options to move towards consumption patterns that are less environmentally damaging and less socially harmful. People care about the impact of consumption on their own health and safety—and the broader impact on the environment and society. But they are caught up in a system of limited choices and opportunities and perverse incentives. Here's a seven-point agenda for action.

1. Ensure minimum consumption requirements for all—as an explicit policy objective in all countries.

"Everyone has the right to a standard of living adequate for the health and well-being of himself and his family, including food, clothing, housing and medical care and necessary social services.... Everyone has the right to education" (Universal Declaration of Human Rights). These principles of universalism and human rights acknowledge the equal rights of everyone—women, men and children—without discrimination. They demand governance that ensures that all have enough to eat, that no child goes without education, that no human being is denied access to health care, safe water and basic sanitation and that all people can develop their potential capabilities to the full extent.

Strong public action is needed to meet these goals. This means a mix of public provisioning in basic social services and an enabling environment and incentive system for private and voluntary action. It means:

•Strong public policies to promote food security—ranging from conducive monetary, fiscal, commercial and pricing policies to institutions and incentives to promote local production and distribution.
•Priority public expenditures for basic social services—education, health, safe water, basic sanitation. Not only should services be expanded, but access should be made more equitable. Studies in many countries show that

access favours the better-off rather than the poor, and urban rather than rural populations.

•Infrastructure for transport and energy to provide affordable and efficient services for people, not just economic growth. This means, for example, public transport, paths for bicycles and pedestrians and energy from renewable sources in rural areas.

•Incentives to develop "poor people's goods"—low-cost housing materials, energy-saving equipment and food storage systems.

•Institutions and legal frameworks that secure people's rights to housing, to common property, to credit.

John Kenneth Galbraith wrote 40 years ago about private affluence amid public squalor. Far from narrowing, the contrasts have grown, and to them are added private and environmental squalor.

2. Develop and apply technologies and methods that are environmentally sustainable for both poor and affluent consumers.

Human development can be sustained with purposeful action. The challenge is not to stop growth. It is to change the patterns of consumption and production, using new technologies to achieve greater efficiency and to reduce waste and pollution. Many such technologies are already in production or on the drawing board.

Sustainable growth of consumption and production depends on major advances in cleaner, material-saving, resource-saving and low-cost technologies. Also needed are consumption options that are environmentally friendly and low cost and affordable for the poor. But many do not yet exist—these need to be invented. And those that exist need to be better marketed—goods that use less energy and fewer renewables (water and wood), that create less waste and pollution and that are low in cost. Such options may be available in some countries— the zero-emission car, for example—but not worldwide, or they may be only at the experimental stage. Public expenditure on research and development in energy has declined by a third in real terms since the early 1980s. Moreover, less than 10% goes to energy efficiency improvements. The rest goes largely to fossil fuel and nuclear energy development. The case is strong for firms and governments to support more technological development and application.

Rather than attempting to pick and promote winning technologies, governments can help create a dynamic marketplace to perform that task more effectively. The state can require all energy providers—public and private—to supply a fixed minimum share of energy from renewable sources—either by generating it themselves or by purchasing it from other providers. This approach both ensures the introduction of renewable energy sources in the market and stimulates innovation of more efficient and lower-cost technologies.

The benefits of cleaner technologies have been well demonstrated, as with the reduction of material use in OECD countries. Many technological solutions already exist for environmentally friendly goods, but current pricing structures undervalue environmental costs and benefits—and thus reduce market incentives. Increased public support for further research and development could accelerate the pace of technological progress.

There is a particular need for technologies to meet the requirements of the poor. About 2 billion people in developing countries lack access to electricity. Meeting this need through clean, renewable sources of energy can reduce poverty and indoor air pollution. The sun and wind are available at no cost to villages that have little hope of being connected to electricity grids. Windpower, now the world's fastest-growing source of energy, meets only 1% of global demand. India aims by 2012 to provide 10% of its electricity from renewables, which could provide half the world's energy by the middle of the next century.

Perhaps most important among technologies for the poor are those for agricultural production in ecologically marginal environments. Improvements in food production in much of Asia and Latin America would not have been possible without the green revolution—the scientific breakthroughs that provided high-yielding varieties of rice, wheat and maize. The world average yield of these crops has more than doubled over the past 20 years. But this did not happen in areas of lower rainfall and in the more fragile ecological zones, where people subsist on millet and sorghum—and on cattle, sheep and goats. The world average yield of millet and sorghum increased by only 15% over the past two decades.

A second green revolution is needed for these people, among the world's poorest. But this should not just repeat the first revolution—it needs to aim both at increasing yields and incomes and at preserving and developing the environmental base.

The private sector has a critical role too—not just to meet the challenges of social responsibility but to produce environmentally friendly, poverty-reducing goods. The market for environmental goods alone is estimated at $500 billion. But for the private sector to act, it needs the right signals from prices and incentives in the market.

3. Remove perverse subsidies and restructure taxes to shift incentives from consumption that damages the environment to consumption that promotes human development.

Many developing countries use subsidies—on staple foods and basic energy supplies, for example—to help poor people survive and reduce poverty. Yet at the same time, most countries tax employment and subsidize pollution and environmental damage directly and indirectly. Such "perverse" subsidies are particularly common in the sectors of energy, water, road transport and agriculture. Total subsidies worldwide in these four sectors are estimated at $700–900 billion a year. They are also often distributionally regressive, benefiting mostly the wealthy—often political interest groups—while draining the public budget.

The absolute amount of subsidies is about twice as large in the OECD countries as in the rest of the world. In the OECD countries agriculture is most heavily subsidized (more than $330 billion), followed by road transport ($85–200 billion). In developing and transition economies the largest subsidies go to energy ($150–200 billion) and water ($42–47 billion). In the words of the Earth Council, "the world is spending hundreds of billions of dollars annually to subsidize its own destruction."

Environmental taxes—charging for pollution, congestion and depletion—have proved highly effective in both industrial and developing countries. They have been widely used in Western Europe and are the well-accepted core of green tax reforms—the Swedish air pollution tax and the Dutch water pollution tax, for example. But not just in Europe. Malaysia's effluent charges and Singapore's automobile taxes are well established and effective.

In Europe the social costs of environmental damage, unaccounted and unpaid, are estimated to average more than 4% of GDP. Estimates for the United States range from 2% to 12%. Users are encouraged to make excessive and wasteful use of road transport, with private cars most underpriced and most environmentally damaging.

Removing perverse subsidies that encourage environmental damage, lower economic efficiency and benefit the wealthy—and imposing environmental taxes instead—can be a catalyst for reducing inequalities and poverty and improving the prospects for equitable growth. Environmental taxes raise revenues that can be used to spend on environmental protection, to reduce taxes on labour, capital and savings or to improve access to social services for poor people.

The policy instruments described above present a win-win opportunity for changing consumption patterns to reverse environmental damage and increase the consumption of the poor. Removing water subsidies, for example, would reduce water use by 20–30%—and in parts of Asia by as much as 50%. That would make it possible, without large, environmentally destructive water development projects, to supply safe drinking water to most of the 1.3 billion people now lacking it.

Another example: congestion charges can finance improvements in public transport and expand transport options. They can ease congestion, save time, lower the costs of public transport and, usually, improve the distribution of income. Road transport subsidies in developing countries amount to $15 billion. The increased involvement of the private sector in financing, building and operating public transport systems in the 1990s is creating pressure to reduce road subsidies and increase

user fees. Argentina cut subsidies to suburban rail systems by $25 million between 1993 and 1995 when it privatized the operation of urban transport.

The benefits of a shift from taxing employment to taxing pollution and other environmental damage could be considerable. An OECD study on Norway suggests that a revenue-neutral shift would reduce unemployment while encouraging recycling and reducing environmental damage.

More and more countries are realizing that old policies and subsidies have adverse consequences. Thus energy subsidies in developing countries have fallen from more than $300 billion in the early 1990s to about $150–200 billion today. Environmental taxes are multiplying. But perverse subsidies are still huge, and environmental taxes have reached nowhere near their potential. Even in the Nordic countries, where some of the most interesting experiments are being carried out, pollution taxes and congestion charges raise only about 7% of government revenues.

4. Strengthen public action for consumer education and information and environmental protection.

The expansion of consumer choice has little significance if choices are based on wrong or misleading information. Strong public action to protect consumer rights is needed to offset vastly unbalanced information flows dominated by commercial advertisements.

Consumer rights must be defended through:

• Strict standards for consumer health and safety.
• Product labelling about the content and proper use of products and their environmental and social impact.
• Information and awareness campaigns about potential health hazards, such as smoking tobacco and the improper use of feeding formula for infants.

Advertising can serve positive purposes, but controls are needed, especially on television advertising targeting young children. Sweden bans television advertising directed at children under 12.

Where price incentives are inadequate, environmental laws and regulations are needed. Skilfully devised, controls can be enabling for the consumer, not restricting. But implementation is as important as legislation. Strong institutions, free from corruption, are needed to enforce regulations in such areas as rights to land, security of tenure in housing and accurate information on consumer goods to protect the interests of poor people.

Regulation and market interventions can be mutually reinforcing. Sometimes regulation is needed to initiate action that can later be taken further with price incentives. At other times price incentives can be used to make a start—with regulation later to ensure wider compliance, especially after fostering social acceptance.

A new approach that has gained considerable interest and momentum in recent years is self-regulation through publicizing information on industrial polluters. This encourages the production of information about pollution generation, both as a source of incentive for behavioural change and as a benchmark for subsequent regulation. A well-known example is the US Toxic Release Inventory, which requires businesses to report the amounts of toxic materials that they put into the environment. Many companies respond by reducing pollution to preserve their reputations.

5. Strengthen international mechanisms to manage consumption's global impacts.

Environmental damage crosses borders. So do shifts in consumption patterns and habits. Poverty and inequality are issues of global magnitude and thus cannot be tackled by nations singly. They require international action.

International responsibilities for ensuring the sustainability of natural resource use have been debated in numerous forums. The Kuala Lumpur Meeting of the Parties to the Basel Convention on the Ban on Hazardous Waste agreed to ban the export of such waste to poor countries. Both the Convention on Biological Diversity and the Convention on International Trade in Endangered Species of Wild Flora and Fauna have been quite successful.

Although some of these agreements sometimes fall short of expectations and ideals, they are steps in the right direction. The recent Kyoto Meeting on the United Nations Framework Convention on Climate Change has set industrial country targets for emissions of carbon dioxide and proposed a Clean Development Mechanism to assist developing countries. Both the financing and the institutional arrangement for this mechanism must be dealt with by the global community. Another problem that needs to be addressed: the continuing decline of official development assistance and the mounting unsustainable debt of poor countries.

Many global instruments to tackle environmental and poverty issues are under-developed—such as environmental trading permits, debt swaps and fair trade schemes. These instruments tend to be double-edged swords, however, and need to be carefully negotiated so that they do not penalize poor nations and make them even poorer. Trading environmental permits should not mean permanently giving away the rights of developing countries. A coordinating global institution in the form of the proposed international bank for environmental settlements is needed to develop and manage these instruments equitably.

6. Build stronger alliances among the movements for consumer rights, environmental protection, poverty eradication, gender equality and children's rights.

Consumer groups have been a powerful force for protecting consumer rights worldwide. They have helped remove unsafe products from the market and promote proper labelling and the supply of safe and low-cost goods.

Now consumers increasingly are using the power of their purses to push the interests of communities even halfway around the globe. Studies in Europe show that consumers are willing to pay price premiums of 5–10% for products that are more environmentally sound (in production, operation and disposal).

Businesses are responding to consumer demand for cleaner, safer products. Evidence from Eastern Europe shows that firms exporting to the European Union tend to have cleaner production processes than firms that produce for the domestic markets, which are less environmentally demanding.

Conventional wisdom assumes that environmental damage is a necessary consequence of economic growth. This is wrong. Environmental damage is a drain on economic growth, and it is possible to pursue a path to growth that does not damage the environment.

Poverty eradication, environmental sustainability, consumer rights protection—all these build on one another. Eradicating poverty does not require growth that ignores consumer rights or destroys the environment. Quite the opposite. Protecting consumer rights and protecting the environment are necessary for eradicating poverty and reducing inequalities.

There is great potential for building closer alliances among the environmental movement, the women's movement, the movement for children, consumer groups and pressure groups against poverty. Already their central concerns show great convergence. Stronger alliances are needed—and possible—if each movement emphasizes the common need for human development. United and mobilized together, these groups can achieve much more.

7. Think globally, act locally. Build on the burgeoning initiatives of people in communities everywhere and foster synergies in the actions of civil society, the private sector and government.

The growing number and strength of consumer and environmental movements around the world—including the 2,000 town and city Agenda 21s that have been prepared—reflect the commitment of people to taking collective action. Many opinion surveys show that people place a higher value on community and family life than on acquiring material possessions. And many people are asking how they can give more emphasis to human concerns.

Some 100 countries have prepared national human development reports, assessing their present situations and drawing conclusions on actions to achieve more human patterns of development. Most of these plans have analysed needs in the critical areas of education, health and employment, often linking them with opportunities for generating resources from reduced military spending.

These initiatives in many cases are the outcomes of successful alliances of the government, institutions of civil society and international organizations.

Progress has also been made in the area of sustainable consumption and a cleaner environment as a result of civil pressure, public action and private sector responses. The instruments: eco-taxes and subsidy removal, stiff environmental regulations backed by penalties, community efforts for better management of common resources (erosion control, reforestation) and more equitable provisioning of public infrastructure and services.

This shows what is possible. It also shows that support exists for a cleaner environment, a more equitable society and the eradication of poverty. Individuals, households, civil society groups, governments and private businesses—all have a role, and together their complementary efforts can build even more energy and synergy for action.

In the poorer countries many priorities in consumption still need to be addressed. Increases in consumption should be planned and encouraged—but with attention to nurturing the links, to making sure that the increases contribute to human development and to avoiding extremes of inequality. Forward-looking perspectives are also needed—to avoid infrastructure and institutions that may lock a country into unsustainable or socially dysfunctional consumption.

In the better-off countries—most of the industrial countries and some of the richer developing countries—the challenge is different. The priority to eradicate poverty and ensure the basic needs of all remains. Indeed, the failure of the richest countries to do that is a scandal. But as general living standards rise and the proportion in poverty falls, the balance of attention in economic and social policy needs to shift. Increasingly, the policy focus needs to move towards enlarging the options for patterns of consumption in which human creativity can be lived out and carried forward with diversity and fulfilment, with most of the population at comfortable levels of consumption, well above the margins of subsistence. These policies need to be combined with those of the environment and human development.

Recent experiences give considerable hope, with more evidence showing that changes in consumption patterns towards sustainable poverty reduction are possible.

Hope brings challenge. The high levels of consumption and production in the world today, the power and potential of technology and information, present great opportunities. After a century of vast material expansion, will leaders and people have the vision to seek and achieve more equitable and more human advance in the 21st century?

Test Your Knowledge Form

We encourage you to photocopy and use this page as a tool to assess how the articles in *Annual Editions* expand on the information in your textbook. By reflecting on the articles you will gain enhanced text information. You can also access this useful form on a product's book support Web site at *http://www.dushkin.com/online/*.

NAME:

DATE:

TITLE AND NUMBER OF ARTICLE:

BRIEFLY STATE THE MAIN IDEA OF THIS ARTICLE:

LIST THREE IMPORTANT FACTS THAT THE AUTHOR USES TO SUPPORT THE MAIN IDEA:

WHAT INFORMATION OR IDEAS DISCUSSED IN THIS ARTICLE ARE ALSO DISCUSSED IN YOUR TEXTBOOK OR OTHER READINGS THAT YOU HAVE DONE? LIST THE TEXTBOOK CHAPTERS AND PAGE NUMBERS:

LIST ANY EXAMPLES OF BIAS OR FAULTY REASONING THAT YOU FOUND IN THE ARTICLE:

LIST ANY NEW TERMS/CONCEPTS THAT WERE DISCUSSED IN THE ARTICLE, AND WRITE A SHORT DEFINITION: